LAURENCE OLIPHANT
1829–1888

ANNE TAYLOR

LAURENCE OLIPHANT
1829–1888

Oxford New York Toronto Melbourne
OXFORD UNIVERSITY PRESS
1982

Oxford University Press, Walton Street, Oxford OX2 6DP
London Glasgow New York Toronto
Delhi Bombay Calcutta Madras Karachi
Kuala Lumpur Singapore Hong Kong Tokyo
Nairobi Dar es Salaam Cape Town
Melbourne Wellington
and associate companies in
Beirut Berlin Ibadan Mexico City

© Anne Taylor 1982

All rights reserved. No part of this publication may be reproduced,
stored in a retrieval system, or transmitted, in any form or by any means,
electronic, mechanical, photocopying, recording, or otherwise, without
the prior permission of Oxford University Press

British Library Cataloguing in Publication Data
Taylor, Anne
Laurence Oliphant, 1829–1888.
1. Oliphant, Laurence
I. Title
941.081'092'4 DA565.o/
ISBN 0-19-812676-X

Library of Congress Cataloging in Publication Data
Taylor, Anne
Laurence Oliphant, 1829–1888.
Bibliography: p.
Includes index.
1. Oliphant, Laurence, 1829–1888–Biography.
2. Authors, English–19th century–Biography.
3. Travelers–Biography. 4. Mystics–Biography.
I. Title.
PR5112.O8T3 828'.809 [B] 81-18726
ISBN 0-19-812676-X AACR2

Set by Western Printing Services Ltd
Printed in Great Britain
at the University Press, Oxford
by Eric Buckley
Printer to the University

TO DESMOND

ACKNOWLEDGEMENTS

WHEREVER I went in search of Laurence Oliphant I was met with great kindness. I am grateful to many people for advice and permission to see or quote from unpublished sources.

Material from the Royal Archives is used by gracious permission of Her Majesty the Queen. Extracts from the correspondence of Lord and Lady Mount Temple, and from the Palmerston papers, appear by permission of the Trustees of the Broadlands Archives; material from the Blackwood Archive by permission of the Trustees of the National Library of Scotland; and from the Guy Le Strange Bequest by permission of the Syndics of the Fitzwilliam Museum, Cambridge. I am grateful to the Trustees of the Le Strange Settled Estates and Mr Neal Wood for information concerning Alice Le Strange. I have to thank Mr Godfrey Oliphant most warmly for his help and hospitality. Mrs Barbara Halpern kindly allowed me to see letters concerning Laurence Oliphant among the papers of her great grandmother, Hannah Pearsall Smith.

I have specially to thank Mr Gordon Phillips, Archivist of *The Times*, for his generous and amiable help, and I am grateful to Times Newspapers Limited for permission to quote from material in their possession. Mrs Christine Kelly, Archivist of the Royal Geographical Society, gave me most valuable advice. Material from the Sutherland Papers is used by permission of the Staffordshire County Record Office. Extracts from *The Amberley Papers* appear by permission of the directors of George Allen & Unwin. Extracts from the Hughenden Papers appear by permission of the National Trust. Crown copyright material in the Public Record Office is published by permission of the Controller of Her Majesty's Stationery Office. I spent two rewarding days in the Records Department of the General Post Office at St Martin's-le-Grand.

The Harris/Oliphant papers in the United States are in the possession of the Rare Book and Manuscript Library of Columbia University in the City of New York, and I must thank the Librarian, Mr Kenneth A. Lohf, and his staff most warmly for their help. I am very grateful to the Keeper of the Markham Archive in the Horrmann Library, Wagner College, Staten Island, New York, for permission to quote material about the Brotherhood of the New Life from the papers of the poet, Edwin Markham. I have been given much help by Mrs Aline Cook, Librarian of the Workingmen's Institute of New Harmony, Indiana. I am most grateful to Mr Kenneth Dale Owen for permission to reproduce photographs in his possession, and to Mrs Josephine Elliot for her assistance with them. I have to thank Mr Paul T. Heffron of the Department of Manuscripts, Library of Congress, Washington, D.C. for a most welcome gift of photocopies of Harris papers. I received much help from the staff of the New York Public Library.

I am also very grateful to the following: Mr David Attenborough; Mr J. Beckford of the University of Durham; Dr R. J. Bingle of the India Office Library and Records; Sir Charles Buchanan, Bart.; Mr David Doughan of the Fawcett Society; Professor J. Gerson of the University of Toronto; Mrs Gita Johnson of the Institute of Contemporary History and Wiener Library; Mrs Trude Levi of the Mocatta Library, University College, London, Keeper of the Gaster Papers; Mr Arthur McCombie of Aberdeen; Dr John McMaster; Mr D. H. Simpson of the Royal Commonwealth Society; the late Dr Francis Steer.

The staff of the London Library were, as always, most helpful, as were those of the Historical Manuscripts Commission, the British Library, the Newspaper Library at Colindale, the National Library of Scotland and the County Record Offices of Clywd, East Sussex, Hampshire and Staffordshire. I was given much useful information about Thomas Glover by the staff of the Libraries Department of the City of Aberdeen. I would also like to thank the staff of the library of the University of Nottingham, and of Cambridge University Library.

Finally, I owe the greatest debt of gratitude to Mr Peter Sutcliffe of the Oxford University Press who, over a long period of time was infinitely generous with help, encouragement, and patience. He not only made the writing of this book possible but very enjoyable.

CONTENTS

ACKNOWLEDGEMENTS	vii
LIST OF ILLUSTRATIONS	xi
1. Sentenced to Life	1
2. 'This restless, sagacious traveller'	24
3. Mission to China	46
4. Private Diplomacy	65
5. Secret Agent	91
6. The Brotherhood of the New Life	113
7. War Correspondent	146
8. Alice	168
9. Palestine	187
10. Haifa	215
11. Counterparts	231
Aftermath	248
NOTES	261
BIBLIOGRAPHY	287
INDEX	293

LIST OF ILLUSTRATIONS

Laurence Oliphant in 1854, aged 25   *facing page* 84
   Mr Godfrey Oliphant

Laurence Oliphant on the Quarter Deck of HMS *Furious*, 1858
Photographed by the Captain, Sherard Osborn   85
   British Library

Laurence Oliphant as Lord Frank Vanecourt. From the drawing
by Richard Doyle for *Piccadilly*, (1870 edition)   85

Thomas Lake Harris in his study at Vinecliff, before 1875   116
   Harris/Oliphant Papers. Rare Book and Manuscript Library,
   Columbia University, New York

Miss Jane Lee Waring in her late fifties   116
   Harris/Oliphant Papers. Rare Book and Manuscript Library,
   Columbia University, New York

William and Georgiana Cowper-Temple   117
   Reproduced by kind permission of the Broadlands Archives Trust

Laurence Oliphant in 1870   180
   Harris/Oliphant Papers. Rare Book and Manuscript Library,
   Columbia University, New York

Portrait of Alice Le Strange by Madame de Rechten   181
   Trustees of the Le Strange Settled Estates and Mr Neal Wood

Hunstanton Hall, King's Lynn, Norfolk. Photograph taken c.1910   181
   Trustees of the Le Strange Settled Estates and Mr Neal Wood

Laurence and Alice Oliphant in Palestine   212

Rosamond Dale Owen in her thirties   213
   The Robert Owen Memorial Museum, Newtown, Wales

James Murray Templeton   213
   Mr Kenneth Dale Owen

CHAPTER I

SENTENCED TO LIFE

To his contemporaries Laurence Oliphant was one of the most fascinating men of his generation. They knew that his experience of life was exotic, that he had observed at close quarters many of the significant events of the time – European wars and revolutions, the imposition of Western influence upon China and Japan, the collapse of Turkey, the return of Jews to Palestine, the rise of Pan-Islam. All these, and more, formed the content of his vivid and perceptive books. What they did not know, though some suspected, was the extent to which he was active in these affairs, that he was, for example, a player in the great game with Russia, an agent of the British government for a large part of his career. Something of this can be learned from papers scattered in many libraries, but the whole story will never be known for a great deal has been lost or deliberately destroyed. Much more remains of the course of events in the central tragedy of his life which caused him to abandon the opportunity many people believed to lie within his grasp, of attaining to the highest political office in the land. This failure was concerned with his spiritual being and the seeds of the disaster were present at the beginning, in the circumstances of his birth and upbringing.

When he was born at the Cape of Good Hope in 1829, his mother, Maria, was just eighteen and his father, Antony Oliphant, thirty-eight. Though such a difference in age was not unusual at the time, Laurence's parents never came to terms with it. In particular Maria, who was not endowed with perception or tact, harped upon the contrast between what she saw as her lasting youth and her husband's fast approaching age. As for Laurence, at first she treated him in the manner of an elder sister; as a baby he was her plaything. When he grew up his role became more complicated and demanding. Maria exacted constant attention from him and, when she should have relinquished her claims on him, fought to keep him at her side.

Her father was Colonel Campbell, commander of the 72nd

Regiment stationed at the Cape. Though the colony was formally handed over by the Dutch in 1814, British troops had been stationed there throughout the Napoleonic wars to keep its fine harbour out of the hands of the French. It was then that Campbell married a daughter of the Cloete family which occupied a prominent position among the settlers of Dutch descent. Antony Oliphant who married Maria Campbell in 1828, had come to the Cape in the late 1820s at a time when the recently introduced policy of Anglicizing the administration and the way of life of the Boer population was arousing great hostility. In the year of his marriage a new Governor, Sir Lowry Cole, arrived who became fast friends with the Attorney-General and his young wife. He consented to become the new baby's godfather, so Laurence was always called Lowry after him by his nearest relations. Antony Oliphant's family was ancient and distinguished in Scotland but not rich. As a second son he had chosen to make his fortune in the law. Another brother was a Member of Parliament, a third, James Oliphant, Laurence's favourite uncle, became a Director of the East India Company and, eventually, its Chairman.

Both Maria and Antony Oliphant were strict Evangelicals and that was the second of the Wicked Fairy's gifts to Laurence. Evangelicalism was a prison into which the Oliphants and countless numbers of their generation freely locked themselves. That would hardly have mattered except for the fact that they took their children with them, depriving them of light and space in which to grow. As soon as he was old enough to understand, Laurence was subjected to a daily discipline of self-examination, the results of which had to be submitted to his parents. They cross-questioned him as to the smallest departure from the standard of conduct and thought they imposed. According to Mrs Margaret Oliphant (no relation), the celebrated authoress, whose biography of Laurence drew upon papers concerning his childhood that have since been lost, this standard was the strictest possible and required the little boy to renounce the gaieties of the world. This was the more difficult since Antony Oliphant's position in the colony regularly exposed him and his family to such abominations as parties, dancing, and picnics.

In the early 1830s official life at the Cape was friendly and relaxed. Sir Lowry Cole had seven children and an amiable wife who played a large part in the small and somewhat restricted English society. The colony was very poor and sparsely populated, there were hardly any roads through the mountains; if the ladies did not try to amuse themselves there was little to do but note the rare days of rain in their journals. But a bright little boy with a pony and numerous cousins found plenty to occupy him and led his nervous parents a lively dance. In particular his father found the task of guiding and controlling Lowry difficult from the start. In the Victorian *paterfamilias* the Puritan spirit from which Evangelicalism took its descent traditionally manifested itself as high self-confidence and an overweening self-regard. This attitude, though it might inflict hardship on the children in the name of conformity, was at least reassuring in the certainty it proclaimed. But Antony Oliphant lacked this necessary quality; as a father he could not help his son; having identified the moral danger as acute and mapped out a course to be followed, he could offer no hope of rescue. But neither did he bully Laurence in the name of his belief.

The boy's capacity for affection, which was large, always found a response in both parents and, however severe in spiritual matters they might be, in practice they indulged him, which made for confusion in his mind. The essential clue to the elder Oliphant's attitude, as also to the reason for the tragic failure of his son's political career, was the fact that Antony Oliphant, having started life as a young man of normal disposition and unexceptionable habits, had at some time in the 1820s while he was still in England become a convert to the curious doctrines of Edward Irving, a Scottish divine of dynamic presence and dictatorial manner. His sermons, which spoke of the imminent Second Coming of Christ and the fulfilment of other prophecies, evidently met a great need, for a large and enthusiastic congregation flocked to his church in London. Irving represented one of the earliest and most remarkable manifestations of the revival of religious emotion that was to sweep England and America in the next decade, spreading Evangelicalism as it went and colouring the lives of the children of Laurence's generation. Irving was entirely genuine; he believed most sincerely in his mission and made not the slightest attempt to use his power to his personal advantage. The fact that not all revivalist preachers would follow a straight path like Irving never occurred to Antony Oliphant; his implicit faith in such men was to have the most serious consequences upon the life of his son.

Laurence was the Oliphants' only child. Not long after his birth Maria took to a sofa in pursuit of bad health and he only knew her in his childhood as a chronic invalid. In 1837 or 1838 her condition was considered to be so grave that she departed for Scotland, taking Laurence with her and leaving her husband alone at the Cape. They went to the Oliphant family home at Condie in Perthshire. There the landscape changed for Laurence from a foreground bathed in brilliant light into a thing of depth and shadows in which he first discerned the long history of his father's family. Oliphants had always been faithful servants of the Scottish crown from the days when one of their number married a daughter of Robert the Bruce. The anonymous author of a seventeenth-century manuscript in the Heralds' College in Edinburgh spoke for all of them when he described the Lord Oliphant of the day. 'This Baron is not of great renown, but yet he hath good landes and profitable; a house very loyal to the Kings of Scotland, accounted no orators in theyr words nor yet foolish in theyr deedes. They do not surmount in theyr alliances, but are content with theyr worshipful neighbours.'

At Condie Laurence delighted in the dusty corners of the turreted old house, the winding stairs and the cellars that could so easily be made to resemble dungeons. A story was told of him then that showed the early presence of the self-deprecating sense of humour that was one of his most attractive qualities. Certain ladies calling to inspect the laird's sister-in-law, Mrs Antony from the Cape, found the drawing-room empty except for a child. How pretty the mother was they remarked, but what a pity the boy was so plain. 'Ah', said the child dispassionately, 'but I have very expressive eyes.'

Though he was soon sent to school near Salisbury, Lowry was not allowed to forget his filial duty. 'You asked me to speak to you as I used to do', he wrote, aged eight, to his mother. 'I should tell you some more of my besetting sins. One of them is my not saying my prayers as I ought, hurrying over them to get up in the morning because I am late, and at night because it is cold; another is my hiding what I do naughty and keeping it from Mr Parr's eyes, not thinking the eye of God is upon me, a greater eye than man's.' As was often the case in those days, Maria Oliphant took the opportunity, when at home, to obtain promotion in the colonial service for her husband. She was so far successful that, in 1839, he was appointed Chief Justice of Ceylon and given a knighthood. Even so there was no question just yet of the new Lady Oliphant joining her husband and assuming her share of the duties that his high social position now conferred on him: as Chief Justice, he ranked second only to the Governor of Ceylon.

That Sir Antony felt the absence of his wife and child most keenly was demonstrated by a letter quoted by Margaret Oliphant. To Lowry, aged ten, Sir Antony recounted his attempt to confide in a young officer in Ceylon, 'Mr B', whom he had invited to accompany him for a drive. This took place, but when the Chief Justice followed it up with an invitation to dinner, 'Mr B' refused, saying that by mixing in society he was acting inconsistently with his religious principles. Sir Antony's response to this colossal snub was to scourge himself. He hoped that when Lowry was as old as 'Mr B' he would do the same. He expressed his wish that if he should die, Lowry would go to 'Mr B' for guidance about which people to trust. 'And my Lowry must keep this letter which I now write and read it always on his birthday, and if he is able to draw all the morals that it contains and to act as Mr B did, if he never meets Mr B on earth, he will be happy with him in heaven.' And in an excess of self-pity, the Chief Justice continued, 'I write this for my son's welfare, and that mamma may know that there is somebody here who will love and take care of papa when she is far away.'

Louis Liesching, a civil servant in Ceylon, who became a close friend of the Oliphant family, objected to the publication of this letter as showing Sir Antony in a false light. According to Liesching he was, rather, sinewy, active, and energetic, a man of deep religious feeling (as was Liesching), of great mental power, though impulsive and hasty tempered. And he was reckoned to be eccentric; one of his preoccupations being with the experiments then being carried out at Calcutta into the new and startling practice of mesmerism. Liesching drew an idyllic picture of the Oliphants together, the father petted by mother and son, the mother dallying with the son. For when in 1841 Lady Oliphant was at last pronounced fit to join her husband, she was no sooner in Ceylon than she found it unbearable without Lowry. He was at school in England and in the care of relatives; nothing would serve but that he should join her at once.

So, at the age of twelve, he started on the first of many journeys to the East along a route that changed dramatically during his lifetime. He and the tutor his Uncle James had chosen to accompany him, crossed a cold and snowbound France on the high banquette of a diligence that took eight days to get to Marseilles. There was no steamer to Malta in those days, Laurence remembered, the mail being carried by a man o' war that had to suffer the humiliation of taking passengers as well. At Malta they changed for Alexandria, 'where the

East burst for the first time on my surprised senses', he wrote. Alexandria was a much smaller place in those days, with narrow streets in which the carriage as a means of transport was unknown, but just beginning to quiver under the impact the invention of steam was imparting to the world. One of the earliest evidences of this was the direct mail route to India which had just been established by Lieutenant Waghorn. At Cairo, where Shepheard's Hotel had not yet been built, Laurence and his tutor had to put up at a native khan, where they found Waghorn himself, who personally saw to the two wheeled van drawn by four horses in which they crossed part of the desert to Suez. The steamer they boarded there ran out of coal in the middle of the Red Sea, and they had to put into Mocha to take on wood. The Sherif of Mocha received them with ceremony and conversed with the twelve year old about the prospects for the coffee market, the depredations of the Arabs in neighbouring states, and his own bad relations with the Turks.

In consequence of this the ship was weeks overdue when she docked at Ceylon. There Laurence had to exchange his freedom as a traveller, which he had relished, for the close and fond supervision of his mother. His father was much occupied and, it seems, unwilling to exert himself as a parent. Indeed there is evidence that the association between mother and son, reinforced by their years together in Scotland, made his task very difficult and that Lady Oliphant moreover was guilty of undermining Sir Antony's authority over his son. She and Laurence approached him with the kind of teasing affection more suitable to an indulgent uncle and laughed at him behind his back. One of the more serious consequences of this was that, in spite of Sir Antony's remonstrances, Laurence's formal education was neglected since he did not choose to apply himself to books while in Ceylon. This lack of grounding in essential subjects, of knowledge common to others of his age and class – of Shakespeare for example – set him apart and caused some to dismiss him as incapable of intellectual effort, which was very far from the case.

After five years of running more or less wild, at the age of seventeen, being ambitious, he fell in with the idea of going home to prepare for a career in the law, more from the example of his father than from any great enthusiasm for it. No sooner had he unpacked his bags in the Warwickshire vicarage where he was to cram for his Cambridge entrance, however, than his parents arrived in England, Sir Antony having been granted two years' leave which he proposed to spend travelling on the Continent. 'I represented so strongly the superior advantages from an educational point of view of European travel over ordinary scholastic training', said Laurence, 'and my arguments were so urgently backed by my mother, that I found myself to my great delight . . . transferred to the Champs Elysées in Paris.' They all three spent the winter of 1846/47 there, and then in a great, lumbering, comfortable ark of a coach, rolled across France and Switzerland into the little known valleys of the Tirol. There Laurence reflected happily that fishing was more amusing than differential calculus and a knowledge of *patois* likely to be more useful than ancient Greek. That was truer than he could yet imagine; he had an amazing facility for learning languages, though he was afterwards reluctant to reveal which ones he knew, as was only prudent in someone of his profession. He even let his mother believe that he had obeyed her instructions not to learn Dutch at the Cape (she forbade it on moral grounds in support of the Government's attempt to impose English on the Boers). But of course he had picked it up from his Cloete cousins and was to use it to a certain extent in Japan, where it was the only known Western language.

Towards the end of 1847 the family went down into Italy where, as Laurence described it, the revolutionary storm was about to burst and envelope Europe. Momentous events would occur and he would witness them. From that time onward he acquired a taste for such events, a nose for anticipating them and the habit of being present at them. To movement was added excitement, both of which he adored and which had the benevolent effect of temporarily distracting him from the contemplation of his soul. At his age, self-examination was in danger of becoming introspection, and what had been instilled in him as a religious duty ran the risk of becoming an obsession.

In 1848 the people rose against their rulers all over Europe and the shape of things that had existed since 1815 was broken. Italy was the beginning. 'I shall never forget joining a roaring mob one evening', Laurence wrote many years later, 'bent upon I knew not what errand, and getting forward by the pressure of the crowd, and my own eagerness into the first rank just as we reached the Austrian Legation, and seeing the ladders passed to the front and placed against the wall, and the arms torn down.' With dozens of others he dragged the arms to the Piazza del Populo where a lady passing in a coach, who happened to be the Princess Pamphili Doria, was induced to descend and put a torch to them. Laurence then took an active part in the yelling and capering that ensued, 'getting home utterly exhausted and feeling that somehow I had deserved well of my country'. It was his first encounter with the emotion of nationalism which he was never to feel so strongly on behalf of his own country but which he strove to advance for other people with all the fervour at his command. While in Italy he saw the doors of the Propaganda forced by a mob which ransacked the cells, and stood on the steps of St Peter's and saw the tears rolling down Pio Nono's cheeks as he blessed the volunteers going to fight the Austrians in Lombardy. At Messina, where the town was in the hands of the populace, the Oliphants' hotel was bombarded by Neapolitan ships seeking to re-establish the Royal authority, and at Naples itself, Laurence had to take refuge under an arch as Ferdinand II, nicknamed King Bomba, ordered his troops to fire on the crowd rioting in front of his palace.

For a boy of eighteen they were exciting times. And though during the course of these two wandering years he was no more than an onlooker, the experience had a profound effect upon him, not altogether a desirable one. As someone who knew him well in later life observed, the lack of a formal education, of discipline at a crucial age, of contact with other boys and girls and of a normal domestic life left him without a proper sense of proportion. Laurence went on believing that all things were possible because he had not been told the contrary; after all, people around him were achieving what had hitherto seemed impossible, why should he not do likewise in his own life? Most of the time he and his parents spent on the Continent he was perforce thrown back on his own company; his resources were considerable but they required managing and this he never learned to do. He was brilliantly intelligent, perceptive, and intuitive, with a gift of wit and fluent expression, but he was also impulsive, emotional, moody and given to precocious brooding about religion and morality. Even in those days his life swung too quickly from the active to the passive; he had no opportunity of achieving a balance. Nor, though he was living in close proximity to them – too close perhaps – did his parents try to help him, using the pretext of travel to postpone conflict.

After Italy the Oliphants went on to Greece which seemed a haven of calm, though it too was tense. They chartered an old schooner at Piraeus, partly filled the hold with white sand and spread carpets on it. Laurence and his father were delighted with the improvised yacht and planned to explore the islands with a group of friends. Maria objected to the makeshift accommodation and, more reasonably perhaps, to the practice whereby the cook made the salad in his old straw hat. She and the other ladies were left on shore while the rest of the party cruised. Then they went to Egypt and spent a month on the Nile and rode across the desert by the route the Israelites were supposed to have taken. At Suez the intention was that Sir Antony and Lady Oliphant would take ship for Ceylon while Laurence turned his face towards England and Cambridge. His leave of absence from the serious business of getting an education had been extended several times in the last two years, at his own request and his mother's desire; surely it was time for common sense and his father's wishes to prevail? But now it appeared that Sir Antony's indulgence had altogether destroyed his authority; he could not govern his son or silence his wife. Laurence was determined to avoid what he saw as the dull and stifling life of an undergraduate. And so in May 1848, when his parents boarded the steamer for Ceylon he went too. He was just nineteen, not in the least handsome, in appearance hardly prepossessing, but with charming manners and an assurance that belied his years. Louis Liesching recalled the lively speculation among their fellow passengers as to the relationship between the young man, Laurence, and the lady of a certain age, who was his mother.

The next three years in Ceylon were unusual in that it was the only time Laurence had a settled domestic life until he was over forty. He acted as his father's secretary while reading for the Bar, and made himself useful in helping to entertain the scores of official visitors who called on their way to and from India. His assistance was the more necessary to his father since Lady Oliphant fled the heat and humidity of Colombo for a couch on the verandah of the 'Turtle Dovery', a house by the lake at the hill station of Newera Elliya. Laurence wrote daily letters to her there and Margaret Oliphant, who saw them, remarked that he was the centre of everything, 'affectionately contemptuous of papa's powers of taking care of himself, and laying down the law in delightful ease of love and unquestioned supremacy, to his mother'.

The Oliphants were among the first to appreciate the wonders of the climate at Newera Elliya. In 1848 the brothers Baker – John, Samuel, and Valentine – brought assorted wives and children, farm labourers, grooms, a carpenter and a blacksmith, a cow and pigs, with the intention of founding an English village on the elevated plain. Samuel, who was the moving spirit of the enterprise, said he undertook it as a way of having a sporting estate without the burden of paying gamekeepers. But, to Laurence Oliphant, it was the first encounter with an attempt to create an ideal society on virgin land – something that stayed in his mind and was inevitably associated with the happiness he always felt at Newera Elliya. His chief preoccupation there was big game hunting. All round the valley were thickly wooded mountains rising to 9,000 feet, as yet uncleared for the land was too high for coffee. He never forgot the exhilaration of the mountains after the steamy heat of Colombo, the sheer pleasure of a log fire at night and blankets on the bed and waking in the morning to find ice fringing the puddles on the road. Samuel Baker kept two packs of hounds which they followed on foot when the jungle was too thick to ride. They went after anything that moved – elk, pea fowl, elephant, wild boar, cheetahs and alligators. To kill wild boar, Laurence explained, you had to hamstring them when they were not looking, then close in to stab them and watch the death agony that often took half an hour. Alligators you caught by lashing a puppy to a cross shaped piece of wood on a rope and floating it in the pool. When the alligator seized the puppy the wood stuck in his throat so you hauled him to shore and, keeping at a respectful distance, made ball practice with your revolver at his eye. Laurence looked back on this indiscriminate killing with disgust but excused himself with the thought that 'when one is young and excited the idea that animals suffer pain does not seem to occur'.

In those days Ceylon was a hard and raffish place, full of speculators and remittance men drawn by the hope of quick fortunes to be made from coffee and other tropical produce. The conduct of such doubtful business, the clash of flamboyant personalities, and the natural inclination of the Sinhalese to litigation provided ample opportunity for a young lawyer to practise his skill. In 1849 Laurence was called to the Ceylon Bar and, by the time he was twenty-two in 1851, could boast of appearing in twenty-three cases of murder. In 1850 his father was summoned to England to give evidence before a Parliamentary committee of enquiry into the suppression of riots. These had occurred in Ceylon two years before as a result of swingeing taxes imposed to compensate for a collapse in the price of coffee. In 1848 the Oliphants had arrived back just as martial law was proclaimed. Sir Antony had tried some of the offenders but others, equally guilty or innocent, were summarily shot. Laurence was sickened by this demonstration of the inequality of the law, brought home to him in the most direct manner. He was in court attending one of the trials when he heard from outside the rattle of the firing squad. It was the sharpest reminder yet of the unfairness of life; he took it, as he did all such manifestations, as a personal affront. From that time on, though he continued with his legal studies and paid lip service to the prospect of a career in the law, he began to cast about for some other occupation. Though as a result of the Parliamentary enquiry a large number of the civil servants employed in Ceylon were transferred or reprimanded, Sir Antony, whose evidence to the committee was distinguished by a keen common sense, was confirmed in his office. He travelled back to Ceylon in the same ship as Jung Bahadur Rana, whose advent was to acquaint Laurence with his true vocation.

Jung Bahadur was Prime Minister and *de facto* ruler of Nepal, a country largely unknown because of the extreme difficulty of getting there. His visit in 1850 caused a sensation in England. He was the first Eastern potentate to appear in the West and, though the standard of magnificence he and his retinue displayed might be equalled by other Princes during Victoria's reign, it was never surpassed. His conduct was similarly exotic and society was enlivened by the fact that, while in London, the Jung monopolized the attentions of Laura Bell, the most celebrated courtesan of the day. When he met him at Colombo the Jung was so taken by Laurence that he invited the young man to accompany him to Nepal. Laurence was jubilant; 'what a book I shall write', he exclaimed to Louis Liesching. But his parents and their friends were dubious (as well they might have been). 'My approval of your retaining Lowry in Ceylon was never meant to extend to such an excursion which can hardly improve his legal prospects, financially or professionally,' wrote one who was obviously a trusted adviser. As for Lady Oliphant, she expressed her desire that Lowry should stay with her while tantalizing him with the fact that his father said he might go. But it was too late for such manoeuvres to have any effect but that of irritation. In December 1850, having promised his mother to keep in constant touch, Laurence sailed for Calcutta with Jung Bahadur.

His first letter home contained an account of a fellow passenger which is interesting in that Laurence conceived him to be uncomfortably like himself. 'He is a pleasant enough fellow as a companion, but abominably selfish and a thorough charlatan. His faults in the latter respect are something like mine – in fact I saw I might well take warning from him. His interest was the first thing he considered, and he was rather unscrupulous in making everything subservient to it.' At Calcutta he found himself an instant social lion owing to the invitation to Nepal. He was invited everywhere and had to apologize to his mother for enjoying it. It was only for a week and he felt he ought to see as much of men and manners as he could. 'I hope you are not afraid of the gaiety', he wrote. 'I make a point of being alone a good deal in the morning. I hope you will send me a letter of good advice.'

The boy was still a dutiful boy, remembering how much his mother feared that balls and other vanities and perpetual society would imperil his spiritual development, wrote Margaret Oliphant. But Louis Liesching came to a different conclusion; he regretted the invitation for it tempted Laurence away from what Liesching held to be the only true path. From that time forward he believed that Laurence abandoned the Evangelical teaching in which he had been brought up and persuaded himself that he could serve God in the world. Laurence was so facile, so witty, so fascinating, wrote Liesching, that although not handsome he could, like Wilkes, cut out the finest man in the room if only he had a few minutes' start. That sounds wistful except for the mention of Wilkes, which makes it waspish as Wilkes was a notorious womanizer. At Calcutta Laurence's experience of women had scarcely begun but circumstances were favourable to its rapid advance. 'I have taken to making love freely, as I know I am going away immediately', he teased his anxious mother. Yet the quality that most attracted men and women to him throughout his life, as many testified, was his sympathy; a warmth and gentleness that inspired confidence.

When the Jung's party set out from Calcutta, Laurence and the political officer who had accompanied the Nepalese to London, Orfeur Cavanagh, shared a curious kind of coach called a palkee in which there was room for two beds. It was drawn not by horses, but by ten coolies at a time and it took four days and nights to be dragged the five hundred miles to Benares. Mornings and evenings when it was cool they walked beside it, or sat on the box and, if they had a lazy team of men, 'drove it along in the most barbarous way', Laurence confessed. The rest of the time they slept or read. Laurence thought his mother would approve of his selection of books – Guizot's *History of English Revolution*, Boumierre's *Memoirs*,

Lord Mahon's *Life of Condé*, and some small volumes of Paul de Kock that Sir Arthur Buller, a neighbour at Newera Elliya, had lent him. 'Let us hope Lady Oliphant believed these last to be theological treatises', remarked Laurence's biographer. In fact Paul de Kock was a popular French author whose novels of life in Paris concerned what the eleventh edition of the *Encyclopaedia Britannica* called 'equivocal adventures'. When Laurence mentioned them to his mother it was certainly with his tongue in his cheek. At Benares they found the European population green with envy at reports of the elaborate arrangements for the hunting expedition being mounted for the travellers on the borders of Nepal. There were six hundred elephants waiting for them to beat the Terai, Laurence reported to his mother, 'and if they don't get something out of the jungle it's a pity'. The Terai was a vast swamp, famous for its tigers and notorious as a breeding ground for malaria.

'How would you like a Roman Catholic daughter-in-law?' his next letter began. He went on for a page and a half lauding her advantages: she was sensible, clever, and would not be flirted with – which made it dangerous. 'I began by trying to cut out two fellows who were rivals, and I succeeded so triumphantly that it became nearly earnest, to the disgust of one, who cut me dead at last, but we made it up when we killed the tiger yesterday.' After this, and much to the disapproval of Jung Bahadur, Laurence was determined to go elephant catching, something, he said, no European had ever done before and only Sir Henry Lawrence had even witnessed. Disclaiming responsibility, the Jung gave him an elephant with nothing but a sack of straw lashed on its back and a rope to hold it by. 'Taking off cap and shoes I was told to stick to this through thick and thin, throwing myself off the elephant when passing under branches, and holding on with my hands to swing myself back.' Two regiments of Nepalese with a lot of trained elephants had been sent to beat the jungle; when the wild ones appeared Laurence and about a hundred mahouts started in hot pursuit. 'Besides holding on I had to thrash the elephant with a spiked piece of wood. Once [he] came down a tremendous trip on his nose which nearly dislocated every bone in my body.' Laurence swayed about like a bolster, was whipped by branches and tore his hands to pieces on the rope. His pluck was much admired; he said the Jung would have called him a brick if he had a Nepalese word for it. The Jung's English was limited to a phrase, 'You are pretty.'

Sport gave way to ceremony when they left the Terai and climbed slowly and laboriously up to Katmandu. There a Durbar was held to celebrate the Prime Minister's return at which the Jung appeared resplendent in white silk and diamonds, his bodyguard armed with English rifles. Laurence noticed a sprinkling of invited guests in English and French uniforms, 'covered with a good deal more gold and silver lace than their wearers were entitled to'. As for him, he wore his plaid shooting jacket and an old felt hat. The King of Nepal, Laurence felt, was not very pleased to see his Prime Minister, and especially with English rifles at his back. His Majesty had staring eyes, a thin moustache, sensual lips and a bull neck. In the book he wrote, *Journey to Katmandu*, Laurence reported these and other oddities of Nepal; the state rooms of Jung Bahadur's palace where a picture of Queen Victoria's coronation was flanked on the wall by a lady's bonnet and a carpet bag; the dress of the Army Commander in Chief, an ordinary frock coat with large epaulettes, diamond bracelets and a red and white spotted neckerchief; the intricate carving on the houses 'not always of the most proper description'; and the dark temples with their countless images and faded flower offerings. But he seems to have found the splendid scenery of Nepal as uninviting as its politics, and it was not altogether a disappointment when Jung Bahadur, having taken the temperature of his welcome and found it cold, decided that it would not be prudent after all to fulfil the promise he had made in Ceylon that Laurence and his friends should be the first strangers to travel freely in Nepal.

And so they joined with Lord Grosvenor's party which had come to Katmandu independently, and turned towards India and the long hot journey by Agra, Lucknow, and Poona to Bombay. It had to be made in palkees, a dull means of conveyance, Laurence decided, but one conducive to thought. He had neglected the state of his soul he told his mother, but that was hardly his fault. It was difficult to practise habits of self-examination riding on an elephant with a companion always talking or singing within a few feet, but a palkee, he reassured her, 'forces one into oneself more than anything'. After some days he decided that his great weakness was 'flexibility of conscience, joined to a power of adapting myself to the society into which I may happen to be thrown'. And he went on: 'It originated, I think, in a wish to be civil to everybody, and a regard for people's feelings and has degenerated into a selfish habit of being agreeable to them simply to suit my own convenience. I think I can be firm enough when I have an object to gain, and have not even the excuse of being so easily led as I used to think. I am only led when it is to pay, which is a most sordid motive – in fact, the more I see of my own character, the more despicable it appears, a being so deeply hypocritical that I can hardly trust myself; hence arose a disinclination ever to speak about myself.' He hoped there was no humbug in what he wrote, Laurence told his mother. 'It is honest as far as I know, *but don't believe in it implicitly.*'

Laurence found the journey to Bombay wearisome by day and very uncomfortable at night. The dak bungalows at which they were obliged to halt presented a common squalor. Each time they found greasy tables unwiped from the last meal, which the visitors' book showed to have been a month before, an identical couch from which interesting round specimens always emerged, and the same filthy bathroom which the travellers who had preceded them could never have entered. So it was with relief that they camped in the caves of Ajanta for one night, surrounded by 'staring Buddhas and rampant elephants and gods and goddesses making vehement love according to the custom of such gentry'. Laurence made a pillow for his weary head of a little goddess and, in the morning, was reluctant to leave. Ceylon no longer attracted him. His taste of freedom had changed him, Louis Liesching said, finding that his own Evangelical ideas now galled and annoyed the younger man. Laurence's parents found this too, and shortly after his return to Ceylon it was decided that he and his mother would go back to England.

In this decision some question of illness played a part, for a friend who met them at Gibraltar in the autumn of 1851 wrote to Sir Antony as if in contradiction. Lowry looked anything but delicate, this friend said, 'I should judge him a great stout eleven stone fellow able to give me a thrashing.' Margaret Oliphant suggested that it was Maria's health that was once more causing concern and supplying the excuse to abandon her husband. A doctor travelled back to England with her and Laurence, Tom Clark from the 72nd Regiment, who lived with them in London and seems to have exercised constant supervision over Maria. Their first address after landing was the most unlikely one of East Sheen but, for Lowry's sake, they soon moved into more fashionable quarters.

His life in London was governed at first by what he considered the dreary necessity of preparing for a career. In view of his previous experience at the Ceylon Bar it was felt that a year with a barrister in

Lincoln's Inn ought to suffice. He arranged his own reading list; one or two books for acquiring a knowledge of mercantile law, including bills of exchange, together with the laws of evidence – and pleading and real property could take care of themselves. As for eating his dinners, he found stringy boiled beef in the company of three hundred strangers hardly to his taste. But, he told his father, 'by dropping in an unconcerned manner remarks upon a tiger I knocked over here, and a man defended for murder there, talking learnedly about Ceylon affairs etc., etc., [I] incited the curiosity of those whose reserve would not otherwise have allowed them to notice me'.

Things became much more lively with the opening of the season of 1852. As usual it was marked by the holding of a series of levées and Drawing-Rooms by the Queen, at one of which Laurence was presented. She startled him by looking him in the face much harder than he had expected; he returned her gaze with such a will that he forgot to go down on one knee, fell onto both, got up and, finding the backing out process irksome, 'turned tail and fairly bolted'. At about the same time as he received this Royal mark of approbation, a different kind of accolade was conferred on him in recognition of his parents' religious convictions and, not least, connections. He was drawn into the small but influential circle of philanthropists whose leader was the great reformer, Anthony Ashley Cooper, who had lately succeeded his father as seventh Earl of Shaftesbury. Laurence was pressed into service among the poor of the East End of London. His mentor on these expeditions – which neither he nor the objects of them much enjoyed – was Laura, Lady Troubridge, famous in her youth for beauty and gaiety, celebrated in her old age for cold and determined charity. She practised this in the name of an Evangelicalism that drove her to acquaint her grandchildren with early grief and disappointment. This she did by having them got ready for a party. Once dressed and dancing on the step she told them there was no party and sent them back upstairs in tears.

Unlike her Laurence did not believe in mortification – at least for other people. 'I have become a friend of the people,' he wrote to his father, 'think that if they are only trusted they will show themselves worthy of the confidence reposed in them, that nobody has the right to bully them or pull the Crystal Palace down if they wish it to stay up, and that education and kindness, so far from making Chartists, would make loyal subjects.' As for the Crystal Palace which, now that the Great Exhibition was at an end, stood empty and glittering among the trees of Hyde Park, he was one of many who wanted it to stay there. He said he liked the mixture of romping, sedateness, and quiet enjoyment in the crowds that frequented it.

This relaxed and optimistic attitude to the London poor was not shared by strict Evangelicals; Laurence would get into trouble with them in due course. But their acceptance of him at this stage in his life was important to his later career. He became very friendly with the younger members of Shaftesbury's family and through them came to the notice of some of the most influential people in the country. Shaftesbury had married Minnie Cowper, daughter of Emily Lamb whose own marriage to Earl Cowper had produced a number of children, two of which, including Minnie, were thought to be by her lover, Lord Palmerston. After the death of Cowper, Emily married Palmerston who, early in 1852, was temporarily out of office having been dismissed by the Queen from the post of Foreign Secretary the previous December. Consequently Palmerston was much at Broadlands, his family estate near Southampton, where his wife's children and grandchildren were always welcome. One of them, Shaftesbury's second son, Evelyn Ashley, who would become Palmerston's private secretary when he took office again as Prime Minister, was Laurence Oliphant's especial friend. It was through moving in these circles that Laurence came to be known by, and to know, influential people all over Europe. In time they made use of him as an informal and sometimes secret link to convey information that was useful but not always convenient to acknowledge. Laurence's charm of manner, wit, and discretion amply fitted him for the role.

But the most intimate companion of his early years in England was Oswald Smith, a member of the famous banking family; they were friends for thirty-five years. It was Smith's memoir of Laurence Oliphant published in *Time* after his death that gave the most revealing glimpses of his later career – evenings spent tête à tête with Palmerston at Broadlands; conversations with Prince Bismarck at the height of his power in Prussia; companionship with Garibaldi, and the Turkish Commander, Omar Pasha. Of their first encounter in 1852 when he was twenty-three Smith spoke with affection; Laurence, he said, was most popular and a very nice fellow. He was already noted for dash, pluck and energy, Smith said, and remembered how, fresh from Ceylon, he had come down to Kent in the winter and thrown himself into a skating party and, after two days, was better and bolder on the ice than anyone else. He was excitable, impulsive, and fond of amusement.

This restlessness, together with a growing sense of oppression at the length of time it would take to be admitted to the English bar, tempted him to try his luck at Edinburgh. In June 1852 he went there by steamer (accompanied by his mother) and found his anticipation confirmed; looking into the faces of Scottish barristers, he said, they did not express the brieflessness of their English colleagues. In fact his relation, Robert Oliphant, a Writer to the Signet, assured him there had never been such a time for advancement. Laurence determined to cram Justinian for the Civil Law exam which he took and passed on 3 July. In the meantime his uncle, Thomas Oliphant, a noted composer of songs, got him an introduction to John Murray who published his book, *Journey to Katmandu*. This sold well and most of the reviews welcomed it as a promising first attempt. But one of the most influential savaged it. *Blackwood's Magazine* noted that three books about Nepal had appeared at once; they all drew without acknowledgement upon earlier and more scholarly works, the reviewer complained. Orfeur Cavanagh's was the worst in this respect, but Oliphant was guilty too. When helping himself from other people's pages he enriched the extracts with epithets and magniloquent adjectives. Nevertheless, 'when writing of things he himself did and saw there is freshness and merit in his descriptions'.

As he said himself, Laurence was now bitten with the mania of becoming an author but what should he write about? The answer was simple – to go to some out of the way place and do something nobody else had done. And so he decided to go at once to Russian Lapland, an Archangel merchant he had happened to meet having told him that the rivers were running with salmon gasping for a fly, and that you could cross to Spitzbergen to shoot polar bears. It was a sufficiently unusual plan since, by the time he could hope to get there, towards the end of August, most of his shooting and fishing would have to be done in the dark; it was already too late in the season to begin any such enterprise. It is not clear whether Laurence and Oswald Smith, who went with him, knew this before they set out; Smith maintained that they only discovered it when they arrived at St Petersburg. In any case, when they got there the Customs officials imposed such heavy duty on their equipment that they decided to abandon the idea. In the book that he wrote, *The Russian Shores of the Black Sea*, Laurence was uncharacteristically vague about how they came to decide what to do next. Thirty-seven years later, and after Laurence's death, Oswald Smith was a little more forthcoming. He said they had letters of introduction to the English Ambassador, Sir Hamilton Seymour (he did not say from whom). According to Smith, at that precise moment the Ambassador was engaged in discussion with the Tsar about Turkey. These conversations, which turned upon the famous view of Turkey as the 'sick man of Europe', did not become public knowledge until not long before the outbreak of the Crimean War. When they did they caused uproar, as in them the Tsar forecast the imminent collapse of Turkey and invited England to take a share of the spoils, as long as she left Russia to do as she pleased with hers.

It was after their visit to Seymour that the young men disposed of their fishing gear and, unencumbered with luggage, set out for Nijni Novgorod. They said they went to attend the great fair that happened to be taking place at that time, but they at once arranged a passage on the river steamer that towed barges from Novgorod down the Volga. The journey they envisaged was tremendous and its secret purpose exciting. Though they put it about at Novgorod that they intended to follow the Volga down to its mouth on the Caspian Sea, their real goal was the naval port of Sebastopol which lay within an area of the Crimea closed to foreigners. It was known in the West that the Russians had strengthened the defences of the port, but no one had been near enough to see what these were. Their approach to Sebastopol was sufficiently oblique to throw all but the most suspicious off the scent. About a thousand miles south of Nijni Novgorod the Volga came within forty or fifty miles of the River Don before turning sharply east. The plan was to disembark at Dubofskoi, a town on this bend, and cross to the Don, following it down to its mouth at Taganrog on the Sea of Azov. There they would take ship for Odessa which involved sailing past Sebastopol.

The first stage of their journey down the Volga was safe but monotonous as hours each day were spent in one place manoeuvring to free the barges that grounded on the innumerable sandbanks of the broad but shallow river. As no meals were provided they had to lay in stores at Novgorod; bread, potatoes, a ham, and hard boiled eggs. Thirty out of fifty of these proved to be broken or bad, so they would have gone hungry if the captain had not invited them to dinner almost every night. This took place before dark as no lights were allowed on board so there was plenty of time afterwards for thought and sleep.

What Laurence concluded about Russia greatly depressed him; he did not like the evidence of a despotic political system that he saw around him, and he feared the strategic implications of the industrial development that was just beginning. When St Petersburg, Moscow, Odessa, and Warsaw became connected by rail, he reflected, a few days instead of many months would suffice to concentrate the armies of the north and south on the borders of Austria or Prussia. Already, from the evidence of his own and other travellers' treatment by the Russian authorities, he decided that the railways in the Tsar's empire were only made for Russian soldiers.

In *The Russian Shores of the Black Sea* he gave vivid descriptions of what he and Smith saw from the deck of the Volga steamer. But though he found the people who lived by the river picturesque, he made no attempt to establish contact with them; they might have been sheep or cows for all the interest he had in them. This was unusual and occurred partly because of his inability to speak much Russian, but principally because of his antipathy to the country as a whole. Nothing in Russia bore looking into, he wrote; from a metropolis to a police-office a short acquaintance was sufficient. 'No statement should be questioned however preposterous, where the credit of the country is involved; and no assertion relied on, even though it be a gratuitous piece of information – such as, there is a diligence to the next town, or an inn in the next village. There is singular difficulty in getting at the truth.' Possibly his attitude was also influenced by the heat for, as they travelled south, the weather turned unbearably sultry. Piles of melons were for sale at the wood stations where the boat had to stop each day and he and Smith bought some. They had just finished one when the captain appeared and remarked that no stranger ate Volga melons without getting Volga fever, and so it proved. By the time the steamer reached Dubofskoi where they disembarked, both Laurence and Oswald Smith were seized with a kind of ague. In the book he dismissed this as of little account, though he did mention an attempt to describe his symptoms to a doctor, using Latin. But Smith said Laurence nearly died. When they recovered they had to arrange the next stage of the journey. As he went about Dubofskoi Laurence was struck by the immense politeness of the inhabitants. Every respectable looking man took off his hat to every other respectable looking man and they found that to cross the street required at least six acknowledgements of these salutations. The origin of the custom, Laurence remarked, was a desire on everyone's part to congratulate each other on looking so respectable in such an out of the way part of the world.

They were somewhat dismayed when they found that to go by boat on the Don to Taganrog would take weeks. The alternative was hardly less daunting, to buy a carriage and launch themselves across the steppe. Nevertheless they expended £11 on one and set off along the vaguely marked post road. Every fifteen miles or so there was a wooden hut with a sort of kraal for horses behind, Laurence told his mother. 'The country was like the sea, with a heavy ground swell on and a calm surface being covered with short dry grass. Often for miles not a creature was seen: sometimes bullock carts passed us, or a wild Cossack galloped by on horseback, and here and there latterly villages came pretty thick, with round houses like the haystacks with which they were always surrounded.' It was the country of the Don Cossacks who, in spite of their detestation of the Russians, acted as Imperial mercenaries, fighting in whatever part of the vast country the Tsar called them to. It was while they crossed this area that Laurence first obtained information about the war in the Caucasus mountains, two days' journey to the south. For twenty-two years an inspired Muslim leader had held the Russians in check; his name was Schamyl.

After five days' bumpy travelling during which Laurence reflected irritably on the Russians' failure to build a canal (it would link the Black Sea to the Caspian and both via the Volga, to the Baltic), they arrived at Taganrog on the Sea of Azov to find that they had missed the steamer to Odessa by two days. It was the perfect excuse to beg a passage on a German brig bound for Cork in Ireland, but calling on the way at Kertch on the north-east extremity of the Crimean peninsula. The voyage took four days over water that was thick with slime, green and yellow, still and turgid like a marsh, a characteristic that was to earn it the name in England of the Putrid Sea. There was no room to walk on deck which was occupied by pigs and the crew, so they amused themselves by washing their clothes, which scarcely improved them, losing to the pigs in the process two socks and a pocket handkerchief they hung up too low. Landing at Kertch they were at last within striking distance of their target.

There is no better description of the isolation of the place to which they had come than that by Alexander Kinglake at the beginning of his history of the Crimean War. In the middle of the century 'the peninsula which divides the Euxine from the Sea of Azoff was an almost forgotten land, lying out of the chief paths of merchants and travellers, and far away from all the capital cities of Christendom. Rarely went thither anyone from Paris, or Vienna, or Berlin: to reach it from London was a harder task than to cross the Atlantic; and a man of office receiving in this distant province his orders dispatched from St Petersburg, was the servant of masters who governed him from a distance of a thousand miles'. The further South Laurence and Oswald Smith got, the more prosperous the country became, the more primitive was the means of conveyance they chose in an attempt to disguise their presence as strangers. By the time they got to Yalta where the Imperial Household was in the process of building gleaming white summer palaces among the pines, they were reduced to a potato cart. This belonged to a friendly farmer from one of the German agricultural colonies in the neighbourhood. He agreed to take Laurence and Smith into Sebastopol posing as his countrymen. This was not difficult since Laurence at least spoke German fluently. Their disguise was shortly put to the test when they met some Russian merchants with whom they had consorted at the Novgorod fair. They huddled into a corner of the cart hoping that their dishevelled appearance would protect them. In this manner they took the new road from Balaklava to Sebastopol.

Every Russian who spoke of Sebastopol did so with a kind of mysterious awe, Laurence said, so it was with anxious apprehension that he caught sight of it at a sudden turn in the road. He was not disappointed; lofty white houses, frowning batteries of guns and green domed churches gave way to a forest of masts stretching far inland, while the hulks of line of battle ships seemed to be floating in the very streets of the town. Once inside it they felt very uneasy; mystery and distrust pervaded the atmosphere, he reported, and he was oppressed with the feeling that he looked exactly like an Englishman and suspected every soldier in the place of planning to arrest him. Sebastopol was a magazine, literally and figuratively, which might explode at any time, and the only variation in the view was from the mouth of a thirty-six pound gun into that of a sixty-four.

No sooner had they arrived in the town than, they said, they had to beat a hurried retreat. The Tsar was coming to review the fleet and they felt the chances of their being discovered would be greatly increased. So there are not many details of the defences of Sebastopol in *The Russian Shores of the Black Sea*. But the view was expressed that these were not as strong as they appeared; that many of the ships were rotting where they lay at anchor; and that the gun emplacements might collapse under the stress of firing. And there was a conclusion. Laurence remarked that, however well fortified Sebastopol might be from the sea, there was nothing whatever to prevent any number of troops from landing a few miles to the south and taking the town through the undefended suburbs. It was a statement that was to have an important effect, not only on the course of Laurence Oliphant's career, but on the lives of many of his compatriots.

CHAPTER 2

'THIS RESTLESS, SAGACIOUS TRAVELLER'

The Russian Shores of the Black Sea was the first description of the Tsar's vast and mysterious empire to appear for many years. It made its author famous overnight, for it came out towards the end of 1853 when war with Russia already seemed inevitable. By the time it was declared, on 28 March 1854, the book had gone into four editions and earned Laurence £400. 'A mighty handsome spec', declared its equally gratified publisher. This was John Blackwood, head of the Edinburgh firm of the same name, who also published the journal known to its contributors and readers alike as *Maga*. These contributors included many of the most famous authors of the day and Oliphant was to be numbered among them for over thirty years. But his first approach was somewhat tentative owing to the strictures passed upon his account of Katmandu. When Samuel Baker's book, *The Rifle and Hound in Ceylon* appeared, he ventured to suggest that since he had taken part in many of the episodes Baker described, he might try his apprentice hand at a review. And so, in February 1854, 'A Sporting Settler in Ceylon' marked his debut in *Blackwood's Magazine*.

John Blackwood's talent for friendship was remarkable – the most agreeable characteristic of a most agreeable man. In 1854 he was thirty-five, ten years older than Laurence, wiser and steadier, and settled in his place, as in his view of people which, owing to his infinite good will, sometimes bordered on the naïve. John Blackwood gave Laurence warmth and hospitality and constant sympathy. A room was kept for him, as for all his bachelor friends, at his house in Edinburgh; he called it the loose box since, he said, it was an infallible cure for all those who were spavined or galled. Although he sat most cheerfully still at the centre of a web of information and opinion, he sometimes looked rather wistfully at those of his friends whose penchant was for action. Chief among them was Laurence

Oliphant whom Blackwood described as a regular stormy petrel. 'Here's Larrie at last' was his usual exclamation on fishing up a letter from the daily pile. His only quarrel with Laurence's contributions to the *Magazine* was that they were often too liberal and nationalistic for him, retaining as he did a certain admiration for despots like Tsar Nicholas I and the Emperor Louis Napoleon. Apart from that he trusted Laurence completely and confided many personal and business secrets to him.

In turn Laurence introduced many famous writers to the publishing house of William Blackwood and Sons. Chief among these was his friend, Alexander Kinglake, whose first book *Eothen* had been enormously successful. It was Laurence Oliphant who persuaded John Blackwood to accept the outline of his second book. Kinglake was a monstrous clever fellow, Laurence urged, though 'confoundedly fidgety about his work'. And so it proved. It took John Blackwood years of patient encouragement to coax from Kinglake another of the most famous books of the era, his monumental history of the invasion of the Crimea.

In 1853 Laurence and his mother moved their London lodging to Half Moon Street. But although they shared a house Maria began to see less and less of her son who was increasingly caught up in work and society. The first result of the publication of the Russian book was an invitation to him to write articles for the *Daily News*, in those days a rival to *The Times* in the literary field. He got two guineas a column for whatever came into his head and confessed in a letter to his father that it sometimes included 'bosh', which he didn't like doing but couldn't resist if he could think of nothing else – for, as he said, the public was so gullible. Meanwhile he was still active in the philanthropic field where his growing notoriety brought him a larger role. 'On Monday I have to deliver a lecture to what is anticipated to be a crowded audience on reformatory institutions; on Tuesday to make a speech at a public meeting on the Belgravia Ragged Schools; on Wednesday to a large soirée to meet the swells who take an interest in these things.' And then there was the law. He was called to both the Scots and English bar, but as he put it, the world at large seemed a much bigger oyster to open than his neighbour's pockets. So he never went to the expense of buying a wig and gown and, his undeniably frugal soul affronted by the cost of dinners he never ate, he eventually dis-barred himself. That did not matter. Early in 1854 a tide began to flow on which he rose.

At the outbreak of the Crimean War he found himself the master of something no one else possessed – recent information as to the fortifications of Sebastopol. Indeed, according to *The Invasion of the Crimea*, Oliphant's book, with its account of the vulnerable state of the south side of the city, did much to evoke the initial desire for an enterprise against Sebastopol. And on that point it is interesting to note that Palmerston especially was early and enthusiastic in proposing it as the target for the Allies' assault. Afterwards, Kinglake, who was in a position to know since he had sight of the papers of the deceased Army Commander-in-Chief, Lord Raglan, and talked to the other protagonists in the affair, said that at the outbreak of the war neither France nor England was authoritatively informed about the land defences of the port. One plan existed, drawn up by Colonel Mackintosh in 1835, and he further expounded it to the Generals at the Horse Guards in 1854. But it was discounted by them as being out of date. It was from the book of a young Scottish traveller that the Allies derived what knowledge they had, said Kinglake. Mr Oliphant, 'this restless, sagacious traveller', had half divined the war and gone to Sebastopol before the home statesmen had even begun to take the alarm.

Whether Laurence Oliphant's journey to the Crimea was prompted by Sir Hamilton Seymour, or as Laurence always maintained, arose purely by chance, it is clear that he lost no time whilst he was there. When he in his turn was summoned to the Horse Guards in April 1854, he gave Lord Raglan sketches and maps and extracts from his journal and the outline of a plan of campaign which, had it been followed from the start, might have saved many lives. 'They are evidently going to try and take Sebastopol, and I recommended their landing at Balaklava and marching across which I think they will do,' he wrote to his father. He further suggested the seizure of the Isthmus of Perekop – where he and Smith had landed from the Sea of Azov – as a means of isolating the Crimea from the Russian lines of supply. Though he gave the impression in *The Russian Shores of the Black Sea* that he had not had the time to do more than take a cursory glance at the defences, Laurence told Raglan that in the course of a comprehensive tour, he had crossed the high ground to the south of Sebastopol where he had identified the Malakoff Tower as the key to the city – as it proved to be. Among those present when Laurence was interviewed at the Horse Guards was General Sir John Burgoyne, a veteran of the Peninsular War, of the lines of Torres Vedras, latterly

Inspector-General of Fortifications. He was the officer above all others on whose tactical advice Lord Raglan was to rely in the field and he was to make significant use of the information Oliphant provided at this meeting.

The Crimean Expedition was not to sail for some months yet but when it did Laurence was determined to accompany it. He began to learn Turkish and plunged into a study of what came to be known as the Eastern Question. In May 1854 *Blackwood's Magazine* published a long article by him which broke new ground in its assessment of the long term Russian threat. It was called 'The Progress and Policy of Russia in Central Asia' and its theme was that Russia had been engaged in a systematic process of territorial annexation since the time of Peter the Great. Laurence argued that this always began with the use of secret agents to foment disorder within the territory concerned, proceded with a military operation in the name of restoring peace, and ended by swallowing the country whole. Of this process, which he described as destructive of independence and blighting to prosperity, Laurence declared, 'it could not steal over the doomed country too imperceptibly; and, therefore, not until this latter had become sufficiently enervated was the disguise under which it had been acquired thrust aside and the protecting hand of the friend recognized to be the iron grasp of an insatiable giant.' Unless the new found resolution in Europe to oppose Russian aggression against Turkey was successful in destroying this system once and for all, Laurence went on, it would shortly be used against Persia, Afghanistan and India. And so, in this article, he sounded one of the first warnings to Britain of the overriding need to protect the route to India from a Russian advance, and described tactics that the Tsar's heirs do not scorn to use today.

In the light of his confident judgement, Laurence's letters to his father at this time make curious reading, as in them he reverted to the young man of small experience and lowly status, dependent for advancement on the whim of greater men. 'I think Lord Raglan ought in civility to make me his civil secretary. It would be great fun. I met Lord de Ros [another Army commander] this morning and had a long talk with him. I did not mention my anxiety to get out [to the Crimea]. It is very ticklish saying anything about one's self on such occasions, and I must bide my time and qualify myself – be able to answer the lash as you always say.'

He had an eye on two possibilities. John Delane, Editor of *The*

Times, who had been most favourably impressed by the Russian book, proposed that Laurence should go out to Constantinople as the paper's correspondent. So for the first, but not the last time, his fortune came within hailing distance of William Howard Russell, who went instead of him. Laurence kept this offer in the balance until it was too late, as he was hopeful that, at his suggestion, Lord Clarendon, the Foreign Secretary, would send him on a mission to Circassia. There, in the heart of the Caucasus Mountains, Schamyl, the Muslim leader, presided over a theocratic state in which he was both General and Iman. 'Allah is great, Mohammed is his first Prophet and Schamyl his second,' chanted his followers. With the aid of Polish and Hungarian officers Schamyl was waging an effective guerrilla war against the Russians. This remote and mysterious ruler, whose territory lay right in the path of Russia's advance towards India, could not fail to have a singular attraction for Laurence Oliphant. Although in those days he allowed his friends to mock him for it and spoke of it himself with flippancy, he was, none the less, in search of an avatar. Edward Irving had long since died – Laurence never knew him – and he wanted someone to put in his place. He was not content with what he had seen so far of the practice of orthodox Christianity. Only half joking, he and his friend, Walter Pollock (who was to become an eminent judge), toured London inspecting religious alternatives, including even the Mormons who had recently come there from the United States.

Clarendon quite appreciated the sense of Oliphant's political ideas about Schamyl. It would be a great thing, he told the Ambassador to Turkey, Lord Stratford de Redcliffe, to free the Circassians and their neighbours, the Georgians, from the Russian yoke and convert them into useful allies. In April 1854 he gave the opportunity, not to Oliphant, but to a Colonel Lloyd, whom he described as able and enterprising and burning with ardour to help Schamyl. Lloyd apparently represented himself as something Oliphant was not, fluent in Turkish and with great knowledge and experience of the country. It is not clear whether Oliphant was told of Lloyd's mission. But shortly afterwards he accepted an offer by Lord Elgin to accompany him to Washington on special diplomatic service, in the confident expectation that he would be back in time to see action in the East. His good fortune was due to the longstanding connection of the Oliphants with Elgin's family, the Bruces, but more particularly to Maria Oliphant who was close to the Earl's sisters, Lady

Charlotte Locker and Lady Augusta Bruce. And it is likely that Lowry's determination to get to the seat of a war stimulated his mother to get him sent in the opposite direction.

Even without this family connection no young man in his senses would have turned the offer down. The eighth Earl of Elgin and twelfth of Kincardine was one of the heroes of the time. He was Governor-General of Canada where he had first gone in 1847 at the darkest period in her affairs. By drawing down upon his head the anger of the populace against a Bill designed to settle the very dangerous question of the French–Canadian minority – a rebellious minority – Elgin preserved the country from a renewal of the civil war and the constitution from probable repudiation. He quite likely also saved the Empire since his brilliantly tactful handling of the Imperial prerogative during the turbulent years that followed the granting of self-government to Canada, gave her room to breathe and established a precedent for Australia, South Africa, and New Zealand to follow.

In May 1854 Elgin was in London before going to negotiate a Reciprocity Treaty between Canada and the United States, a desperate last resort to preserve Canada from disappearing altogether. Her economy was in ruins as a result of the repeal of the Corn Laws in 1846; farms lay empty, rivers and canals carried no traffic and money was so scarce that Elgin's salary was paid in debentures. Many Canadians saw no alternative in this situation to annexation by the United States. Elgin's answer was to achieve free trade between Canada and the United States. It was as his private secretary in these trade negotiations that he invited Laurence Oliphant to go with him to Washington. The United States Congress had never managed to get round to this not very exciting subject in the past, but there was new hope that summer that it might. The slave question which would provoke the Civil War, was already disturbing relations between North and South. Southerners – Democrats to a man – had no desire to see a lot of dour Canadians added to the existing critics of their particular way of life. So it was to the members of the Democratic party that Elgin addressed himself immediately upon his arrival in Washington.

As his secretary Laurence was present by way of duty at the furious round of parties that began. After several days of festivity the apprentice diplomat thought he began to see what they were driving at. 'To make quite sure I said one day to my chief, "I find all my most intimate friends are Democratic senators." "So do I,"' Elgin replied dryly. This method of persuasion was not only hectic but unorthodox since Congress traditionally frowned upon lobbying by strangers. But Elgin was held in great esteem at Washington where his efforts in Canada were far better appreciated than they were in London and Senators responded to his charm. Society rejoiced at his title while finding him not in the least reserved. 'Lord Elgin is a short, stout gentleman,' reported one newspaper, 'on the shady side of forty (he was forty-three), and is decidedly John Bullish in birth, talk, appearance and carriage. His face, although round and full, beams with intellect, good feeling and good humour. His manners are open, frank and amusing.'

As for Laurence, he took to America and the Americans at once, and they to him. Among the lifelong friends he made on that short visit were the Pringles, plantation owners, one of whose members was US Minister to Turkey. They first inspired in him an abiding interest in the slave question which, with his customary prescience, he at once declared to pose a most serious threat to the continued existence of the Union. Once again, as in the case of Russia, there stands revealed a striking contrast between Laurence's public and his private self. On the one hand, a sureness of judgement on the subject of politics that might be envied by much older men and, by all accounts, an easy confidence in the conduct of diplomatic affairs. On the other, as his letters home showed, guilt, self-doubt, submissiveness; a man of 26 bound to his mother.

Washington, Laurence told Maria, was a howling wilderness of deserted streets running out into the country and ending nowhere, yet it was by no means destitute of civilized amenities and that was troubling him. The Treaty was floated through on a sea of champagne which left Elgin unscathed but Laurence very much the worse for wear. The hangover was increased by the fact that he was enjoying himself very much indeed when he felt he ought not. He was continually obliged to excuse himself to his mother for his proximity to music, gardens, flowers, and bright eyes. 'I did not touch anything else *but* champagne', he told her, 'and stopped at exactly the right moment.' 'I am glad you spoke about the tobacco,' he said on another occasion, 'I have not smoked half a dozen cigars since leaving England, and every one has been a solitary one when I want to compose myself and think. I think it prostitutes tobacco to drink and talk over it.' And so one comes to the true issue between himself, his conscience and his mother. He was continually and increasingly harassed by the question of his relations with women. Regarding those that inhabited the world she knew, his mother never ceased to interrogate him about his intentions, so that he was unable to treat them lightly even if he had so desired. 'It is difficult to define where flirting begins, or what amount of joking and laughing, though perfectly innocent, is not expedient,' he confessed, 'and one gets led imperceptibly on without feeling the harm that is being done to both parties until it is too late.' And he went on, 'as I told you before I am not in any degree involved in anything'. Instead, the solace that his highly sexed nature demanded he sought among women with whom he did not need to get 'involved'. In time his frequent recourse to prostitutes became notorious. It might be said that all he had to do was conceal the truth from his mother while humouring her. But as the future course of his life was to show, he was not capable of that degree of cynicism. He found dissimulation painful and, though he was driven to practise it in self-defence, it left him with a sense of overwhelming guilt. That is what lay behind his often disingenuous behaviour, an inconvenient trait for one who was to follow the calling of espionage.

Margaret Oliphant, who saw his mother's letters to him at this period, described them as anxious prayers, an expression of fear for his spiritual wellbeing, longing for his moral improvement and growth in grace, a continual knocking at the secret chamber of his heart and thoughts to know how his mind stood in respect to religion. Mrs Oliphant remarked that she did not know what Maria's distinctive views were at this time: 'they were, perhaps, a little open to the influence of the prevailing preacher who interested and instructed her, but they were always full of profound and emotional piety and her strongest desire was that her son should be like herself, placing sacred subjects in absolute pre-eminence, both in his thoughts and his life – and that he should tell her so'.

Elgin regarded Laurence's agonizing as a kind of green sickness. 'He sees my twinges of conscience and asked me the other day whether I was going to lay all the sins I seemed so much oppressed with at his door,' said Laurence. After all, Elgin complained, they were only amusing people and if Laurence had anything to repent of he wished he would go away and do it by himself. There were those who wondered how the Earl, 'chief of the can't you let it alone, Melbourne, school of statesmen', would get on with the impulsive, energetic and often melancholy young man, but they liked each other. Laurence thought him much like papa in his way of venting indignation and fuming but never acting impulsively. When the Treaty was signed at Washington Elgin invited Laurence to stay with him as his secretary for the few remaining months he had to serve in Canada.

Because of the notoriety proceeding from his Russian book, and of the new appointment Elgin then conferred on him, Laurence found himself an object of curiosity when they arrived at Quebec, which, since the burning of the Parliament building at Montreal in the riots Elgin had suppressed, acted as the Canadian capital. His elevation made him nervous, Laurence confessed to his parents. 'Know then that I am now Superintendent-General of Indian Affairs, having succeeded Colonel Bruce [Elgin's brother] in that office, and having as my subordinates two colonels, two captains and some English gentlemen who have been long in the service.' The choice of so young a man with no experience of the Civil Service and who had never before set foot in Canada naturally provoked the charge of favouritism. But for the time being Elgin could do no wrong and so the criticism was disarmed. There is no doubt that it was a tribute to Oliphant's energy and ability and, though it was the first time this had been so rewarded, it was by no means the last. Laurence undertook the task entirely seriously; he proposed to reorganize the Department of Indian Affairs and the whole system by which the tribes were managed. 'It must be done with caution and well matured as I suspect the Government will not readily assent to my views which are a little arbitrary and despotic.'

In the high summer of 1854 he began in the only way he could, by visiting his charges. It was a duty eminently to his taste as it involved penetrating into the depths of the backwoods, canoeing on distant and silent lakes or down foaming rivers where the fishing was splendid, the scenery romantic and camp life at that time of year most enjoyable. In fact it was a prolonged picnic with just enough duty about it to relieve him of any feeling of guilt. He inspected Indian schools, held councils, smoked pipes, adjusted tribal disputes and distributed gifts. On Manitoulin Island in Lake Huron he came face to face with thousands of his charges to whom he had to distribute blankets, axes, flour, salt and other useful items supplied by the Indian Department. He was disturbed by what he saw; he said he knew of no nomads – and by that time he had seen Tartars, Kirghiz,

Bedouin, and gypsies – who presented a more poverty stricken and degraded sight than did his red children. The most fruitful source of trouble for his Department at that time was the occupation by Indians of huge tracts of land suitable for settlement by whites. The Indians guarded these hunting grounds jealously but got only foxes and a few musk rats from them, while the Department was forever having to drive off squatters. So Laurence determined to see what he could do about the largest remaining such area, half a million acres on a peninsula in Lake Huron, belonging to the Chippewa. He convened a meeting of the chiefs and, after hours of speeches and what he described as Fenimore Cooper-sounding 'ughs', he was successful in persuading them to cede the land to the Government for what was to them a great deal of money. By means of the revenue derived from the sale of this land to whites, he was able to reorganize the whole financial system of the Indian Department, he said, and save £13,000, for which the Minister responsible at Westminster was so grateful that he offered Laurence a small Lieutenant-Governorship in the West Indies. What happened to the Chippewa who had nothing to buy with their money, he did not say; it was not the fashion of the time to care.

From Lake Huron, Laurence and Viscount Bury, who was to succeed him in the post, paddled across to the head of Lake Superior. There, in view of the future he saw for the country, he bought a town lot in the city of Superior – then consisting of one log cabin and a tent – which he held for many years and sold at a loss just before a land boom. From Superior they went via the headwaters of the Mississippi River to Dubuque, crossed the plains of Illinois to Chicago, and by way of Niagara home to Quebec. It was a tremendous journey which Laurence vividly described in a new book, *Minnesota and the Far West*. The land was still empty, the prairie marked by conical Indian graves not yet torn apart by the plough. But, already, they encountered men moving west, away from the advancing settlements; solitary figures dressed in fox coloured skins, with long steps and flat Indian tread, accompanied by big, sensible looking dogs. Those few people who inhabited Minnesota were keen on slavery continuing, Laurence found. He dismissed English demonstrations against it as hypocritical and futile; soon, he thought, there would be civil war in America.

When the travellers returned to Quebec, Parliament was in session and life became hectic. Laurence reported the role he played in a letter to his mother, which a friend of his described as Laurence 'down to the heels'. 'My life is much like that of a Cabinet Minister or Parliamentary swell, now that the House is sitting. I am there every night until the small hours, taking little relaxations in the shape of evening visits when a bore gets up [to speak]. That keeps me in bed till late, so that breakfast and the drive in (from the Governor-General's residence), detain me from the office till near one. Then I get through business for the next three hours – chiefly consisting of drafting letters, which in the end I ought to be a dab at. I have three bell ropes hanging at my right hand communicating with my two departments and the messengers. I also append my valuable signature to a great deal without knowing in the least why, and run out to the most notorious gossips to pick up the last bits of news, political or social, with which to regale his Excellency, who duly rings for me for that purpose when he had read his letters . . . Then he walks out with an A.D.C. and I go to the House. There I take up my seat on a chair exclusively my own next the Speaker and members (I have made it my business to know them nearly all) come and tell me the news, and I am on chaffing terms with the Opposition, and on confidential terms with the Ministerialists. If I see pretty girls in the galleries who are friends of mine . . . I go up there and criticise members and draw caricatures of them, which they throw down into members' laps neatly folded, who pass them to the original, – by which time I have regained my seat and the demure secretary remains profoundly political and unsuspected. I find nothing so difficult at keeping up my dignity, and when the Bishop or a Cabinet Minister calls, I take their apologies for intruding as if I was doing them a favour. I suppose the dignity of the office was so well sustained by Bruce, that they are scandalized by a larky young cove like me.'

This life ended with the adjournment of the Canadian Parliament on 18 December 1854. Although Elgin's successor asked Laurence to stay on as his private secretary, he declined, faithful to his own axiom that the man who wants to climb a ladder does not rest on the first step. Nor did he wish to go to the West Indies, being still very anxious to see action in the East. In January 1855, therefore, after he had accompanied Elgin home, he was without occupation. The shock of the change depressed him and he found his domestic life irksome and uncomfortable, escaping whenever he could to the haven of the Athenaeum Club to which he had just been elected. While he was in Canada his father had retired and returned to England. Even before he left Ceylon Sir Antony had announced his intention of going to any place in Europe that Lowry might go, as attaché or anything else; 'the wife is buttoned to Lowry's coat tails and I am tied to her apron strings', was how he put it. So determined were Sir Antony and Lady Oliphant to follow their son wherever he might go that they would not take a permanent house in London; in 1855 therefore, they and he camped in temporary lodgings. Sir Antony was something of a trial to Laurence; he was sixty-three, unaccustomed to idleness and not much entertained, either by his wife or the few friends he had in England.

As a means of rescuing himself from this claustrophobic situation, Laurence resorted to his pen and in the spring of 1855 published a pamphlet, *The Coming Campaign*, about the war. This was not going well for the Allies who were bogged down in an interminable siege of Sebastopol. Over in the north-east of Turkey Russian troops were threatening Kars; its fall would not only be a severe blow to the Porte but renew the Russian threat to Persia, Mesopotamia and Afghanistan. In his pamphlet Laurence argued for an expedition to be sent to relieve Kars through Circassia and the Trans-Caucasian provinces; it would consist of Turkish troops under their own Commander, Omar Pasha, or those of the Turkish Contingent, under General Vivian. Privately he renewed his plea to Clarendon to send him on a personal mission to Schamyl, with whom no contact had yet been made, owing to Schamyl's hostility to Christians, and Colonel Lloyd's death from cholera.

In April 1855 Lord Stratford had sent another messenger to Schamyl, one of Her Majesty's consuls, John Longworth. He carried lead and gunpowder as presents and the promise of rifles to come. Ostensibly in search of horses for the Allied armies in the Crimea, he was to ask Schamyl when he reached him what help he wanted from British troops. But in July he was obliged to report that he had failed. The Naib, Schamyl's lieutenant, who controlled the coast of Circassia, had turned him back, being, if anything, more fanatical than Schamyl. Their purpose was to establish a theocratic Empire in the Caucasus independent of Turkey, Longworth reported. But he also said he detected signs of a growing allegiance among the Muslims who were fighting the Russians, to the Sultan, not as ruler of Turkey, but as Caliph, the supreme religious leader, the focus of a holy war. It was this theme that would come increasingly to fascinate Laurence Oliphant, for two reasons. As he grew older he developed a deep interest in all Eastern religion, but more particularly in Islam for whose philosophy he conceived the greatest respect. But he was also one of the first Westerners to foresee the political power that might be wielded by Muslims if they would unite, and the enormous effect their presence could exert on the policies of Britain and Russia in the Middle East and Central Asia.

It is not clear whether Clarendon knew of Longworth's failure when, at the beginning of August, he so far acceded to Oliphant's request as to send him with a letter to Lord Stratford asking the Ambassador, if he saw fit, to speed the young man on his way to Circassia. When Laurence left England he was accompanied by his father like a boy out of school. Laurence was momentarily oppressed at the thought of his mother, 'with the chief objects of her existence both gone', but he comforted himself with the thought of the visits she would pay to kind friends and the ministrations of a favourite niece who had been summoned to her side. On board the ship at Marseilles was the African explorer, John Hanning Speke, now of the Turkish Contingent, who, Laurence said, was dying to go back to Africa and try again to find the sources of the Nile, but he was going to take a turn at Sebastopol first.

When Laurence arrived at Constantinople he found the Ambassador was at the summer embassy at Therapia on the shores of the Bosporus and thither he had to go, leaving his father to fend for himself. Everything depended on his Lordship; nobody, not even the Foreign Secretary, told Lord Stratford what to do. He was already a legend, a splendid figure – the Great Eltchi to the Turks – which meant chief among plenipotentaries, *the* Ambassador. In the course of forty years Stratford had come to exercise complete supremacy over the Sultan, Abdul Mejid. His career at Constantinople went back to 1810, to the days when Napoleonic France was supreme, when, as a young attaché aged 24, his Ambassador having departed to greener fields, he was left in charge by the Foreign Office and forgotten. He was fond of remarking that the most important dispatch Whitehall sent him in those years concerned certain manuscripts thought to be hidden in the Seraglio. Single-handed he had formulated policy, conducted negotiations and concluded treaties on behalf of his sovereign, but with such a concern for Turkish interests that French influence soon gave way to English throughout the Ottoman Empire. This ascendancy was not pleasing to Russia; Tsar Nicholas I came to regard the Great

Eltchi as his particular foe, an attitude that was wholeheartedly reciprocated.

Stratford disposed himself very favourably to Laurence Oliphant, whose Russian book he approved and whose company he found amusing; Laurence was invited to stay at the Embassy and in due course offered the post of private secretary to the Great Eltchi. Years after he remarked that, at Therapia, he had come into contact with a more brilliant group of men than could be found in any other diplomatic circle in Europe. In their separate ways three of them became noted Orientalists; Percy Smythe, later Lord Strangford, was a scholar; Charles Alison, the diplomat *par excellence*, became a distinguished Minister to Persia; Lionel Moore, known as the Irish Arab, was a wanderer and a wit, and became a cherished friend of the Prince of Wales. Odo Russell (inevitably nicknamed O don't), a much loved man, held diplomatic posts all over Europe and, as Lord Ampthill, ended his days as Ambassador to Berlin. He shared Laurence Oliphant's fascination with experimental religion; they became fast friends.

Towards the end of August Stratford decided to go to the Crimea in order to distribute medals and see for himself how things were going. 'All the flower of the Embassy will accompany me', he wrote to Clarendon, adding that he would take Oliphant, and very glad to do him a service. The Ambassador was doubtful of the wisdom of risking anyone else on the mission to Schamyl which was proving so vexatious, but he was much in favour of the diversion in the Caucasus, and he sympathized with Omar Pasha who was fretting at being detained in the Crimea when his troops could be more usefully employed in saving Kars.

The Black Sea was crowded with vessels of all kinds making their way towards the Crimea and while Laurence travelled in comfort with the Ambassador, his father joined the ranks of non-combatants hurrying to be in at the fall of Sebastopol which was soon expected. As the ship approached Kamiesch Bay in the darkness all Laurence could detect of the land was the distant flashing of guns and the sullen reverberation which followed. In the daytime he hardly recognized the road from Balaklava which in 1852 he had followed into Sebastopol seeing hardly a soul on the way. Now it was a muddy confusion of men, animals, guns, and the other appurtenances of a prolonged siege. It was nearly a year since the start of the Allies' attempt on Sebastopol. They had landed to the north of the port, not to the south of Balaklava as Laurence had recommended, and from the north they had come down upon the city following their victory at the battle of the Alma. There they were checked by fortifications and the indecision of the French, whose commander, Marshal St Arnaud, was deperately ill. It was then that Sir John Burgoyne had recommended a flank march behind the city to the south to occupy ground dominated by the Malakoff Tower. Having got that far the Allies waited for the siege train to be brought up. The delay was just sufficient for the brilliant Russian engineer, General von Todleben, to organize the strengthening of the defences. Now a year later, finding himself seated next to Burgoyne at Army headquarters, Laurence asked him if he had not been right in his report of the defenceless state of Sebastopol? Yes, Burgoyne replied, and he regretted the delay in attacking once they had arrived to the south of the city. But no one could have foreseen the improvising genius of a Todleben.

As the author of *The Russian Shores of the Black Sea*, and the advocate of what was now acknowledged to have been a sensible plan, Laurence was given a very cordial reception in the Allied camp. Having assured himself that Sir Antony was safely accommodated, he found himself a place to sleep in a capacious Indian hut which was the home of his very old friend, Valentine Baker, now in command of the headquarters' escort. With a member of the Royal Artillery he made an expedition to the most advanced trench whose shelter, to his unprofessional mind and unaccustomed nerves, he said, was meagre to a degree. He found it strange to rig himself out in ball costume in order to dine with the Ambassador and the Admiral on the flagship, *Royal Albert*, in Kamiesch Bay, and to sit over coffee at the stern watching shells explode. Somewhere in the trenches he encountered Charles Gordon of the Royal Engineers who, like him, was soon to go to China. What with these excursions, the ceremony of the distribution of the medals and an exhibition of camp cookery by M. Alexis Soyer, he found plenty to pass the time. But he was not sorry when Stratford de Redcliffe, having decided to send Alison along the coast to Circassia to make contact with Longworth, gave permission for Oliphant to accompany him. The fall of Sebastopol was only a matter of a few days and the Allied commanders had at last turned their attention to the campaign to follow it. Sir Antony Oliphant, having thoroughly inspected the captured city, took himself home to England.

For his son the next few weeks were a joyful muddle of adventure,

'THIS RESTLESS, SAGACIOUS TRAVELLER'   39

exertion, excitement, and companionship. Laurence acted as an unofficial liaison officer to Omar Pasha whom they found at Trebizond, waiting for his troops to come up from the Crimea. He and Oliphant got on well together and Laurence's Turkish improved to the point where he could tell jokes and the bawdy stories Omar adored. Kars fell to the Russians before the Turks could reach it, so there was a lot of fighting to do in the very remote provinces of Abkhasia, Mingrelia, Imeritia, and Gouriel. Much against the inclination of Lord Stratford who had a diplomatist's dislike of the Press, Laurence turned journalist for the duration of the Trans-Caucasian campaign, sending regular articles to *The Times*, for which he got £50 and a favourable mention of *Minnesota and the Far West*, which was not selling well.

In search of copy he plunged into the thick of whatever action was in progress. It suited him; he was much happier when he was active, he told his mother. 'When I just say my prayers and read a text earnestly and then go and gallop about and am in hard, healthful exercise, I feel much better in mind and body. I feel my mind much more innocent and less bothered and perplexed; but I am afraid this is wrong, and that one's occupation ought to be God's work, and not what papa calls playing one's self.'

Since the Naib was still implacably hostile and Omar Pasha was not disposed to help him, Laurence's mission to Schamyl was given up. In any case, in October 1855, Clarendon told Stratford he had had reliable confirmation of what he had long suspected, that the Russians had made a pact not to harass Schamyl if the guerrilla leader would refrain from helping the Allies. (The Russians kept this promise while it suited them and then seized Schamyl and imprisoned him.) It was when all question of Schamyl was officially at an end that Captain Richard Burton the African explorer serving with Beatson's Horse, came riding into the affair. He said that Lord Stratford had suggested to him that he should contact the guerrilla leader but would not allow Burton to offer him men, money, or arms. Whatever the truth of this, it would not have pleased Oliphant, nor did the long letter Burton wrote to *The Times* the following year which read as if he were the only person ever to have though of a diversion in the Caucasus. Later on, when Burton and Oliphant were involved in the Speke affair, Oliphant's actions were explained as arising from a great dislike of Burton. If that were true, it is likely that it was originally inspired by Burton's intrusion over Schamyl and the Caucasus, a subject which, as we have seen, Oliphant regarded as of the first importance.

Towards the end of 1855 the weather in the Caucasus which had been ideal for the campaign, turned suddenly bad. It rained without stopping, the tents leaked, clothes and bedding were soaked and there was little to eat but biscuits and rice. Laurence's mood altered with the conditions. He was seized with what he called a sulky fit of devotion. 'My religion at these times is not of a happy character,' he wrote to his mother. 'I am gloomy and disgusted when I am trying to go to religion for comfort. Somehow or other something ought to come of it all for I am always thinking of the subject in some shape or other. My conscience is never satisfied with my conduct nor my understanding with my belief; so that altogether I am in a state of internal conflict and argumentation.' Laurence found these fits of black depression very difficult to shake off without some powerful means of distraction and they occurred more frequently as the years went by. On this occasion in Circassia his low state of mind coincided with physical exhaustion and perhaps because of that he fell victim to an acute attack of fever. As soon as he could travel he was obliged to go home to England.

He only meant to stay there until he had quite recovered his strength for, as letters to John Blackwood written in the early part of 1856 show, he had every intention of taking up the offer of becoming the Great Eltchi's secretary and was even prepared to forgo the pleasure of writing about his experiences in deference to the Ambassador's aversion to journalism. But in March 1856, in common with a great many other people, his plans were upset by the sudden and quite unexpected conclusion of peace in the Crimean War. This was done at the instigation of the Emperor of the French who was contemplating helping Italy against her overlord, Austria, and wanted Russia on his side in that affair. Laurence regarded this peace as a monstrous betrayal, and from that time forward nourished a lively detestation for Napoleon III. In particular he resented the fact that, although the granting of independence by Russia to Circassia had been included in Palmerston's terms for any peace, this was ignored in the French haste to conclude a treaty with the Tsar.

Laurence's reaction was extreme; he pronounced himself entirely disillusioned with great men and determined that henceforth he would make his own way in the world. It was an aspect of his character that he could not help, which was to cause him pain and distress throughout his life – that he felt his personal honour touched by matters that were beyond his control and took upon himself responsibility for conditions that he could not hope to alter. And so he turned down Lord Stratford's offer and spoke instead of standing for Parliament.

This impulse towards a settled career in England probably arose from the possibility of his marriage. That he had found someone he wanted to make his wife seems likely, though the girl's name is not known, and the only reference Laurence made to the subject in later years was to say that the season of 1856 had a special attraction for him. It ended without the announcement of an engagement but when in September he departed for the United States, it was with the avowed intention of making a lot of money in a very short time – something that had never concerned him in the past. How he proposed to do it remains a mystery.

He travelled in the company of Delane who was going in order to observe the Presidential election. Their visit began in a most convivial manner as American newspapermen and writers flocked to meet the Editor of *The Times*. Oliphant was by no means in his shade, owing to his growing reputation as a writer and traveller, and to having established friendly relations with the Press on his previous visit. In New York they held court together; among their visitors were the writer and philosopher, Ralph Waldo Emerson, Horace Greeley, Editor of the *New York Tribune*, and the mystic, Henry James Sr. In late September they made a tour of New York State together and stayed with friends of Delane at a house on the Hudson River. In October they parted, Laurence to go south to study the question of slavery which, as he said, was now driving the union to disaster. He was by no means hostile to slavery himself, as he saw it practised on the plantations where he stayed. The Pringles, for instance, whom he visited, were benevolent masters; slavery to them was a form of paternalism and the only means of working land where, for half the year, whites had to flee the heat and the fever it brought. It seemed impossible that things would ever change in the quiet back country of Georgia and the Carolinas through which Laurence travelled in the autumn of 1856. This mood prevailed until he came to New Orleans and stepped into another adventure.

Men were being recruited there to fight in Nicaragua where a young and impatient journalist from San Francisco, William Walker, was engaged in setting up a private state, with himself as dictator, his friends as the new ruling class, and the existing native inhabitants as helots. Walker's recruiting agent at New Orleans for this amazing enterprise, referred to as a filibuster, was Pierre Soulé, a flamboyant lawyer and erstwhile United States Minister to Madrid. Soulé invited Oliphant to go to Nicaragua with the next consignment of arms and men for Walker and he agreed, ostensibly because it would make a very good subject for a book. But it is possible that his involvement in the affair was not accidental, and that he had been sent by Palmerston to find out what was going on.

Nicaragua's shape and position on the map dictated the Prime Minister's concern which was shared by the President of the United States. Nicaragua is a narrow country south of Mexico, with indented bays and a vast lake in its middle, connected by rivers to the Atlantic and Pacific Oceans. For many years it had been the site preferred to Panama for a proposed canal, and after gold was discovered in California in 1849, the American millionaire, Cornelius Vanderbilt, had established a Transit Company to take prospectors across Nicaragua to the Pacific. When Walker's mercenaries started to arrive, there were frequent clashes between them, the men of the Transit Company, and troops from neighbouring Costa Rica which was opposed to Walker's filibuster. The eastern end of the Transit was at Greytown, the capital of the native Kingdom of Mosquito which occupied the coastal fringe of Nicaragua and was a British protectorate. Palmerston, who had never acquiesced in the Monroe Doctrine by which the United States sought to exclude all influence but her own from the New World, was alarmed by the unrest in the area and determined not to relinquish Mosquito.

Laurence Oliphant's version of his part in this tangle was that Soulé offered him a grant of land in Walker's Nicaraguan empire in return for his assurance to the British Government on his return that Walker was not the means by which the United States proposed to annex the small republics of Central America, and that, on the contrary, his object was to weld them into a new Anglo-Saxon state. Of this project Laurence remarked that though it was undertaken by a single man, it was not more immoral than similar enterprises were when undertaken by governments, and one which was calculated to benefit not only the Central American states themselves, but the cause of civilization generally. How this cause was to be advanced by the re-introduction of slavery, on which Walker's state would depend, Oliphant did not say; apparently he believed that freedom might be subordinated to economic progress for a time when the people concerned were backward – Indians or Negroes.

With three hundred heavily armed 'emigrants' he embarked at New Orleans for the voyage to Greytown which Walker had seized. On board were Englishmen who had been private soldiers in the Crimea, Poles who had fought in the last Polish insurrection, Hungarians who had been with Kossuth, and Yankees who had been fighting Indians in Kansas. Now they proposed to fight, first the employees of the Transit Company, next the Costa Ricans. But, when they arrived off the coast of Mosquito, they found a squadron of the Royal Navy there and when a boarding party came out to inspect the 'emigrants', Laurence having rashly opened his mouth, was identified as a British subject in a place where no British subject ought to be. He was hauled before the Admiral who demanded to know what it was all about. Laurence was the more forthcoming as the Admiral turned out to be his cousin.

According to the book he wrote about this episode some years later, *Patriots and Filibusters*, Laurence became the Admiral's guest on shore at Greytown, a position which put an end to his plan of joining Walker in the interior. He stayed there until the arrival of the mail steamer that plied to Colón in Panama and then took passage on her, escaping with relief from the great heat and incessant rain of the Kingdom of Mosquito. The fact that he chose to go south and not back to New Orleans was capable of a perfectly innocent explanation, that as a writer Laurence wanted to explore an area that was attracting great interest in Europe and the United States as the site of a proposed seaway between the Atlantic and the Pacific Oceans. But it is highly likely that he had one particular interest in mind, that of the British Government, and that his journey to Panama was an extension of the mission which had brought him to Central America in the first place.

Colón was the eastern end of a railway built at the time of the California gold rush by the same company as operated in Nicaragua. For some reason which he did not explain, Laurence had a free ticket for it, and so he made the four and a half hour journey between two oceans at Vanderbilt's expense. Arriving at Panama town on the Pacific shore he spent some days inspecting the harbour. He concluded that for those whose goal was California – most of the American travellers – the best and shortest route was still through Nicaragua. The real importance of Panama was to Britain as a staging post on the new route to Australia and New Zealand which had begun to attract thousands of emigrants. The port of Panama consisted of two islands, two and a half miles off shore where deep water ships could anchor. Laurence went out to them and pronounced them to be capable of being developed into a far better naval station than the existing one at Valparaiso. In these circumstances it was vital to discover whether Panama might be the object of a filibustering expedition such as Walker's which the United States government could use as a pretext for annexation. Precisely what Laurence reported to Palmerston on this subject cannot be known, but the fact that he did so can hardly be doubted.

From Panama he returned to the Atlantic coast through Honduras which was also a candidate for the seaway. In that country he travelled in the same railway carriage as a priest who, after several days in his company, and upon discovering his connection with Walker, proposed to him to join in a conspiracy to promote a revolution in Honduras. If Laurence would help, said the priest, he might become War Minister in the new government. Laurence said he went so far as to learn a secret sign from the pious conspirator in case he ever needed a friend in the new regime. 'After all,' he wrote in *Patriots and Filibusters*, 'he was only proposing to me to do on a small scale in Honduras what a clerical deputation five years afterwards proposed to the brother of the Emperor of Austria to do in Mexico on a larger one, and which that unhappy prince accepted as a religious duty.' Five years later Laurence Oliphant was summoned to an audience with the prince in question, the Archduke Ferdinand Max, before he left for Mexico to reign as the ill-fated Emperor Maximilian. From the knowledge gained in 1856 Laurence warned him that Central America was not the place for any man who had a position to lose or a conscience to obey.

Nor was it a place for a young man to linger. Laurence found its climate oppressive, the scenery monotonous and society, such as it was, very dreary. And though the events he had witnessed might affect the fate of governments and the balance of power in an increasingly significant area of the world, they gained more excitement in the telling than they afforded in reality. Neither was the process of getting from place to place any more inspiring. Even as early as 1856 and in so remote a place as Central America, steamships and trains were on hand to carry Laurence almost anywhere he wanted to go; their pace might be slow but their arrival was guaranteed.

Nevertheless, when he returned to England in the early part of 1857 he found that rumours of his adventures had preceded him and lost nothing in the telling. It was even said that he had been executed – which was Walker's fate in the end. At the first party that Laurence went to, his partner, a charming young person whom he was very glad to see again, put out two fingers by way of greeting, raised her eyebrows in mild surprise, and said in the most silvery and unmoved voice, 'O, how d'ye do? I thought you were hung.'

CHAPTER 3

MISSION TO CHINA

IF, as seems likely, this cool young lady was the girl Laurence hoped to marry, the question arose as to how he was to support her. By that time his books and articles were bringing in a reasonable sum, but his chief hope for the future, as he saw it then, was to enter Parliament and quickly obtain office, a career for which his talents especially fitted him, and in which he was already expected to do extremely well – or so his friends and relations thought. Suddenly, in March 1857, the opportunity arose and he grasped it. Quite unexpectedly, Palmerston called a general election over the question of China. Laurence stood as Liberal candidate for the Stirling burghs, a constituency in which his family was well known, and where he was considered to have an excellent chance of getting in.

But then, surprisingly, his health broke down, so that he was obliged to withdraw in the middle of the campaign, and shortly after announced that he had accepted an invitation from Lord Elgin to accompany him to China. The illness was unspecified, but a letter survives in which he told Mrs William Ashley, Shaftesbury's sister-in-law, that it was so grave that, for a time, he was forbidden to read or write. So anxious was he to quit the country that he insisted on joining Elgin's expedition, even though, ten days before it was due to sail, he told Mrs Ashley that he had only just been allowed out of bed.

Though there is no direct evidence of a broken engagement, the impression remains that this was what lay behind the affair. It is reasonable to suppose that some great shock contributed to Laurence's collapse since there were other occasions in his life when his state of mind was seen to have an adverse effect on his health. If this were the case, it caused him once again to turn his back on England, and embark upon a tremendous journey lasting two years, which offered moments of distraction but did him no good: it condemned him to long periods of inactivity and solitude which he always found hard to endure, and which contributed to the corroding sense of insecurity that would eventually upset the balance of his mind.

If he had indeed intended to marry, the collapse of his plans was tragic for though he appeared content to warm himself by other people's fires – being a frequent and popular guest on the long country house visits customary in those days – there can be no doubt that he wanted a hearth of his own. In no other way could he permanently cast off the stifling embrace of his parents and, at the age of twenty-eight, become his own master. It was the sad fate of this brilliant and lovable man to appear to flourish in the most sophisticated society, while suffering the inward pain of an unusually disturbed, and unnaturally prolonged, adolescence.

Elgin's expedition, for which Laurence was invited to act as private secretary, was the result of Palmerston's victory at the general election. It was a Liberal landslide that would undoubtedly have swept Laurence with it into the House of Commons. Palmerston had called the election after losing a vote of censure for his support of Sir John Bowring, Governor of Hong Kong. In retaliation for a Chinese insult to a British vessel, the lorcha *Arrow*, Bowring had attacked Canton. This incident, which took place in the autumn of 1856, was the culmination of a long period of struggle between the British merchants who wanted to trade freely in China, and the Chinese, particularly the Commissioner at Canton, Yeh, who was determined to make them submit to humiliating restrictions. The *Arrow* incident provoked a bitter conflict involving murder and the destruction of property, Yeh offering thirty dollars apiece for the decapitated heads of foreign barbarians. In April 1857, newly confirmed in office as Prime Minister, Palmerston enlisted the support of France, Russia, and the United States for Elgin's mission. It was to force Peking to agree to a sweeping reform of the regulations that had inhibited trade.

When the expedition left in May, Laurence took with him the warm wishes of the Liberal electors of the Stirling burghs who bore him no grudge for his withdrawal, though he had found it extremely embarrassing. While the five thousand troops that were to provide the teeth of Elgin's argument went round the Cape of Good Hope, the Earl and his suite, including Oliphant, went via the Mediterranean to Egypt. There they found themselves crossing the desert in the first train ever to carry passengers to the central station at Suez. When their ship eventually docked in Ceylon they encountered General Ashburnham, who brought the first news of unrest in the plains of

Upper India and discontent among the sepoy troops. This caused Elgin to hesitate, fearing its effect upon his mission to China. But having no men as yet, he decided to go on to Singapore to meet them. It was an inauspicious beginning to a journey that was memorable for its discomfort. The smell from 1,500 boxes of opium carried in the hold gradually pervaded the ship as if a bottle of laudanum was held under their noses. They were fagged, headachy, sweaty, sad at the separation from their families, and unaccustomed to the cramped conditions. Elgin stayed in his cabin, reading blue-books, increasingly appalled at the magnitude of the task that faced him and hopefully sipping sherry laced with quinine in an effort to escape fever. Oliphant was in a curious mood, lecturing the other members of the staff, whom he had only just met, about a new belief he had encountered in America; he called it spiritualism.

At Singapore they heard that Indian mutineers had murdered Europeans, seized the forts and treasure of Delhi, and proclaimed the son of the Great Mogul. There soon followed a desperate plea for help from the Governor-General, Lord Canning. With no prospect of advice from London, Elgin had only the members of his suite with whom to discuss the dilemma. Laurence's views must have carried a good deal of weight, for he had had practical experience of India during his visit in 1851. Moreoever, the fact that his uncle, James Oliphant, was a recent past Chairman of the Court of Directors of the East India Company, meant that his information on the subject was likely to be as up to date and detailed as that of anyone else not on the spot. But to answer the immediate questions that the news from India posed hardly needed special knowledge. Should the success of the China expedition be jeopardized by directing the troops to India? Would Elgin not lose face by arriving at Hong Kong alone and with no certainty of when his army might appear? This was a serious consideration, but there was really no choice, for British prestige throughout the Far East depended on her holding India. Messages were therefore sent to divert the approaching troop transports to Calcutta, while Elgin, Oliphant and the rest went on to Hong Kong.

When they got there they found that Yeh was only too pleased to gloat over their lack of force. Moreover the other plenipotentaries from France, Russia and America were not to arrive for some weeks yet, so Elgin decided to risk a quick return to India in order to help raise the morale of his hard-pressed friend, Canning. (They had been at school and college together.) The Governor-General was dangerously isolated in India, accused of lack of experience and weakness which had already earned him the contemptuous name of Clemency Canning. Elgin determined to take with him to India his most effective weapon, the magnificent warship *Shannon*, whose sixty-eight pound guns were meant to intimidate the Cantonese. The voyage to Calcutta took three weeks and Laurence found it almost unbearable. The *Shannon* had no poop and he had to clamber on the rail if he were to see the sea and breathe a little air. At Singapore, on hearing of the massacre at Cawnpore, they paused only to take on 400 tons of coal and extra troops. When the *Shannon* sailed, 1,100 men crowded the shut-in decks and the thermometer stood at 90 degrees.

The tension rose as they approached Calcutta, for at Diamond Harbour they learned the rumour that a considerable force of mutineers was marching on the city. And so the *Shannon*'s passage up Garden Reach to Calcutta was one of the most dramatic moments in the history of the Indian Mutiny. Vividly Laurence recalled it in his book, *Elgin's Mission to China and Japan*. The excitement on board was matched by exhilaration on shore, he wrote. 'Our stately ship suddenly burst upon the astonished gaze of two European gentlemen taking their evening walk, who, seeing her crowded with the eager faces of men ready for the fray, took off their hats and cheered wildly; then the respectable skipper of a merchantman worked himself up into a state of frenzy, and made us a long speech, which we could not hear, but the violence of his gesticulations left us in little doubt as to its import, then his crew took up the cheer which was passed on at intervals until the thunder of our 68 pounders drowned every other sound, shattered the windows of sundry of the "Palaces", attracted a crowd of spectators on to the Maidan, and brought the contents of Fort William on to the glacis.'

Canning was able to tell them that Calcutta stood in no immediate danger. But panic was near the surface, and many feared that the approaching Muslim festival of the Mohurrum would be the signal for a massacre. The *Shannon* turned her huge guns on the Maidan, but her troops were hurriedly sent up country towards the besieged city of Lucknow. Elgin decided he could stay until after the Mohurrum and he and his secretary moved into Government House. Laurence wrote a long account of the state of affairs to Mrs Ashley, using the gold pen she had given him as a farewell present. No one had any doubt that the China force had saved Calcutta, he told her.

Canning had entirely lost the confidence of the community; he did himself great injustice by his extreme reserve and reluctance to trust his subordinates. No one doubted his courage or honesty, but they did his judgement. Meanwhile Elgin was asking for more troops to be sent urgently to Hong Kong; 'it would never do for the world to suppose that we cannot manage two Eastern difficulties at the same time', Laurence wrote.

As outsiders at Calcutta the members of Elgin's mission experienced a sense of alienation from the European population that was to remain with them for the rest of their time in the East and was greatly to increase the stress of their position. The narrow interests and social pretensions of the British merchants were something Elgin and Oliphant both despised; at Calcutta they were also sickened by the cruelty that fear of the mutineers inspired even in practising Christians. 'It is a terrible business this living among inferior races,' Elgin told his wife. 'I have seldom from man or woman since I came to the East heard a sentence which was reconcilable with the hypothesis that Christianity ever came into the world. Detestation, contempt, ferocity, vengeance, whether Chinamen or Indians be the object.' When British commissioners told mutineers under sentence of death that their bodies would be flung to the dogs so that their souls would not rest, Canning dismissed them. Laurence was present at a dinner shortly after when a clergyman bitterly attacked Canning for having done so, saying that the mutineers deserved their souls to suffer, and that he would have them tortured before they died. This and other similar remarks were deeply shocking to Laurence who took them very much to heart; they put him out of temper with clergymen for the rest of his life.

At the end of August Elgin, Oliphant, and the rest of the suite returned to Hong Kong to wait for the new detachment of troops and the French, Russian, and American diplomats. For fear of typhoons the mission's ships had to anchor off shore, which meant spending days cooped up on board for lack of energy or inducement to go ashore. Hong Kong was beautiful but there was absolutely nothing to do. In *Elgin's Mission* Laurence explained that there were two walks, one to the right along the shore, the other to the left. If you went further and scrambled up Victoria Peak you risked an attack of fever, which with boils and dysentery was a common complaint.

There was no female society, and a large bachelors' dinner was the height of gaiety, he remarked. That was as far as he went in describing their tribulations in the book. But in a letter to Delane he was more candid. Here they all were in the harbour of Hong Kong, he wrote, in a state of petrified disgust, feeling as if they had been condemned to the hulks. Elgin acted the philosopher, reconciling himself to the life of a captain of a merchant ship, but Laurence was ready to commit suicide for the sake of a woman, even a Chinese one with bound feet. 'Pity me,' he gasped. Deprived of sex, he stimulated himself with thoughts of religion – increasingly he confused the two. He longed for a creed to which he could commit himself whole-heartedly, he told his mother; he wanted it to be powerful enough to govern him completely. 'It must invade with overwhelming force a man's whole nature, obliging him by its purity and the strength of its appeal to his convictions to recognize the truth.' This mystical approach to religion would in time come to govern his life and, in later years, he was very careful about talking of it. But at that time in China he was still willing to be teased about his belief and went about striking attitudes – playing himself, as his father put it. He was to be seen on board ship kneeling before an embarrassed sailor in whom he pretended to recognize a spirit, and drawing his companions into endless discussions about religion. In this he was superficial in theory, said Mrs Oliphant, but heroic in his determination to follow out his conclusions to whatever end they might lead.

At last the troops and diplomats assembled. When, at the end of December, Commissioner Yeh refused to accede to Elgin's demands, they had to proceed to the bombardment of Canton. Elgin hated the idea; when he looked at the city from the ship, he told his wife, he felt as if he was claiming for himself a place in the Litany after plague, pestilence, and famine. The consequence of his distaste, which Laurence shared, was that Canton escaped lightly. Laurence obtained permission to watch the capture of the city from a hill outside the walls which was found to be a cemetery. This turned out to be useful as he was able to take shelter from the flying balls in a deep little grave. Chinese warfare was dangerous, Laurence complained. 'If you are alone in the midst of a silent turnip field, you are as likely to be shot as if you were immediately under the walls with an attacking party, for they have no idea of taking aim, and their rockets go flying about in all conceivable directions.'

Within a very short time he saw the scaling ladders put up and the British forces clustering like bees into a hive. He bolted down to join them and stood upon the city wall looking down on a vast expanse of roofs, a labyrinth of winding lanes, pagodas, temples, all devoid of people and entirely silent. Yeh turned out to be an enormous, dirty, insolent, and ferocious man, who boasted that he had worn the same coat for ten years and, in the same breath, that he had had hundreds of thousands of people decapitated. He was removed to a ship and then to Calcutta, where he defiantly died. The mission stayed at Canton for the shortest time possible, until order was restored. Laurence was disappointed because he could find no decent specimens of porcelain at a price he could afford. Mrs Ashley had proposed they enter into a joint speculation as porcelain collecting was all the rage; he offered her fans instead.

The capture of Canton left the Imperial Government unmoved. It would not treat with Elgin direct, nor entertain discussions about relaxing the restrictions on trade. He therefore determined to make a show of force as near the capital as he could get and, in April 1858, set out in HMS *Furious* for the mouth of the Peiho River which led up to Peking. He arranged with Admiral Seymour, commanding the British naval forces in the Far East, to send after him as many gunboats of shallow draft as he could spare, and as soon as possible. Privately, Seymour did not approve of Elgin's foray to the north, but he assured him that the boats would be sent. At Shanghai where they stayed on their way to the Peiho, the mission found the merchants very angry at the mildness of the treatment Canton had received. Elgin and his entourage were assailed by hostile comments which they had to endure as best they could. Laurence made up for this in his letters home when he castigated the citizens of Shanghai for their fear and greed.

He was not sorry, therefore, to escape from Shanghai for a time by taking a letter containing yet another request for negotiations from Elgin to the Governor of Kiangsu Province. He lived at the ancient and beautiful city of Soochow, where no foreigner had ever before been openly received – a few had been smuggled in in disguise. Laurence approached the city by boat and entered it by a water gate, for Soochow, like Venice, stood on a network of canals, crossed by rialto-like bridges, and enclosing fragrant gardens. He was received with ceremony but again to no avail. The Imperial Government would not treat with Elgin.

Even Soochow with all its crumbling charm did not appeal to Laurence. With the exception of Singapore, which he had found delightful, the East so far struck him as a desert. Much worse was to come. On 14 April *Furious* dropped anchor eight miles out from the Chinese coast in the Gulf of Pechili, which was as near as she could get to the mouth of the Peiho River owing to the shallow water. Laurence thought it very like the Sea of Azov, though the water was not quite so thick. Gales kept the Gulf in a condition of boiling pea soup, he said. As the coast was so flat they could only see the Taku forts defending the mouth of the river outlined against a brilliant sunset, and for most of the time it was depressingly overcast. For weeks they lay waiting for the gunboats of shallow draft which would be able to cross the bar. 'Cutting north-east gales swept over the dreary waters of the Gulf, and whistled dolefully through the shrouds, ill preparing us to meet the sudden transition; blasts of hot air, charged with impalpable dust from the deserts of Gobi, not only completely obscured the horizon but cracked our lips, parched our throats and concealed itself in the innermost recesses of our clothing, or served as a general pepper to our food.'

Elgin was at his wits' end, he told his wife. He had no authority to order Admiral Seymour to send the gunboats – he had nearly withdrawn from the expedition for that very reason – but he could do nothing without them. He had no definite instructions from England and he had heard a rumour that the Government had changed. He did not even know if his policy was still approved. The only person who gave satisfaction in this irritating situation was apparently Laurence Oliphant for, once again, Elgin promoted him over other men's heads. When Frederick Bruce, his brother, went home, Laurence took his place as acting Secretary of Embassy. He himself found a congenial companion in the captain of the *Furious*, Sherard Osborn, already famous for his expedition to the Arctic in search of the explorer, Sir John Franklin; like Oliphant Osborn was a Fellow of the Royal Geographical Society, and an aspiring writer. Laurence was also very friendly with Wingrove Cook, *The Times* correspondent who was travelling with the expedition. Elgin did not approve of their association. Cooke's dispatches were inclined to echo the criticism of the way in which Elgin was conducting the approach to the Chinese. He feared moreover that, as an erstwhile contributor to *The Times*, Oliphant's loyalty might be divided. In fact, though he gave no secrets away to Cooke, Laurence, as we shall see, eventually provoked a huge public row when he wrote about Admiral Seymour's tardiness.

At last, after five wearisome weeks, Seymour and the gunboats arrived. The Admiral's delay caused great loss of face to Elgin who had intended his arrival at the Peiho to take the Chinese by surprise. The Taku forts would have been destroyed at once and a passage up the river forced as far as Peking, where the right of foreign Ambassadors to reside in the capital would have been firmly established. Instead, Elgin had been obliged to lie off shore in full view of the Chinese, unable even to stop the hundreds of junks taking tribute grain up to the capital. The unsuccessful attempts by what boats he and the French did have to pass the bar at the mouth of the river provided a source of mirth to the defenders of the forts, and, while the mission kicked its heels, the cool weather vanished to be replaced by mercilessly hot and brilliant skies which added greatly to the discomfort of the campaign.

So, by the time the Taku forts had been taken with the help of the French, and the river lay open to the Allies, Elgin and all his companions were heartily sick of the affair. Theirs were the first foreign ships ever to follow the sinuous curves of the river into the heart of China. The countryside was flat and brown and dusty and reminded Laurence of the south of Russia. He watched from the deck as each successive mud village gave up its inhabitants who ran and bowed to the strange vessels that needed neither wind nor current nor sail to continue on their course. Having done that the peasants squatted in a thin, blue, wondering line all along the bank. At Tientsin, fifty miles from Peking, Elgin was met by Imperial messengers at last offering negotiations. As the Chinese hoped he would, he halted there to await the high ranking Commissioners who would conduct the talks.

Laurence was present at them. It was a momentous occasion, for out of them came the first agreement to allow foreigners to trade and travel wherever they wished in China. Trade was certainly needed, Laurence thought, as he explored the stifling streets of Tientsin; the mills of Manchester could be kept busy clothing the Chinese. But how would they pay for it? He was shocked by the poverty, filth, and indifference to suffering he encountered, and retreated to the shade of the temple which was the mission's headquarters to play skittles with the soldiers on guard.

These troops seemed fated to be always in the wrong place for, while he was at Tientsin, Elgin received word that renewed disturbances had broken out at Canton which threatened Hong Kong. He was obliged to send all the soldiers he could spare south at once and to prepare himself to follow. He decided to leave the details of the treaty to be thrashed out later at Shanghai where the Imperial Commissioners agreed to go. He and his entourage had to cancel their visit to Peking where Elgin was to have had an audience with the Emperor. At the end of June, much to the relief of the Imperial Government, Elgin, Oliphant, and the remainder of the mission, turned their faces to the south.

The weather at Shanghai was hotter than anything Laurence had ever experienced; the sky leaden, the river airless and crowded with merchant ships waiting hopelessly for a cargo. Once again he was reduced to spending hours in his cabin, trying not to scratch the boils and bites that afflicted him, and picking fretfully at the condition of his soul. He was miserable, he told Mrs Ashley, he had been away from England so long everyone would have forgotten him. His unhappiness was shared by his companions. And so it was with the greatest delight that they all heard that Elgin had decided to employ the weeks that must elapse before the Chinese Commissioners could arrive with their new instructions by going to Japan. The mission had with it a yacht, a present from Queen Victoria to the ruler of that country. When *Furious* put to sea on 31 July they rejoiced, not only in the movement and the cooler air, but in the prospect of adventure.

Japan was the most fantastic, most exciting country in the world; more remote than Africa, as mysterious; an ancient Empire with a half remembered civilization that had been closed to foreigners for over two hundred years. It was only four years since Commander Perry with his black American ships had prised the oyster open, and less than two since the diplomat, Townsend Harris, and his secretary of Dutch origin Henry Heusken, had been grudgingly allowed to install themselves in a temple on a cliff at Simoda, a small port one hundred miles from Edo, the capital of the temporal ruler, known as the Shogun, or Tycoon.

Townsend Harris had spent those years in a patient attempt to get the Shogun's government, known as the *bakufu*, to sign a Treaty with the United States, granting access and providing for trade. A draft had existed for several months. When the Japanese heard of Elgin's success at Tientsin, they hastily signed the US treaty in the hope that it would shield them from harsher demands by Britain, whose naval power they feared. For, though the Japanese people were rigorously prevented from gaining knowledge of the outside world, the *bakufu* had a listening post on the island of Deshima in Nagasaki Bay. There, in return for submitting to a surveillance that was humiliating in its demands, the Dutch had been permitted to retain an entrepôt. They were required to submit annual reports to the *bakufu* on the state of the outside world; Dutch became the only means of communication between the Japanese and all foreigners.

The first landfall *Furious* made was the island of Iwoshima which gave evidence of civilization unknown in China. A flagstaff on its highest point conveyed news of their approach to the mainland. They did not know it then, Laurence wrote, but cannon placed at intervals along the six hundred mile route to Edo passed on this signal so that, by the time *Furious* dropped anchor in Nagasaki Bay, the Shogun knew it. As the ship steamed gently up the long inlet that led to Nagasaki, she passed rows and rows of cannon on the cliffs, pointing seaward. Alongside were sham batteries made of painted canvas. They came to the place where all foreign ships had to anchor, where the Dutch, waiting for permission to proceed, spent the time collecting all Bibles and prayer books into a chest which was nailed down and handed to the Japanese to keep until they left. Christianity was anathema to the Japanese, and had been ever since the seventeenth century when Christian converts were accused of conspiring with the Portuguese to overthrow the Shogun, one of the events that led to the closing of the country. The channel into the harbour was blocked now by one official boat, on the roof of whose cabin a gentleman sat, reading and fanning himself. Lining the rails of *Furious* the mission held its breath to see what he would do; he looked up and waved them back with his fan. As the ship held on her way regardless, he fell to reading again. That, said Laurence, was symbolic of the way the Japanese dealt with them throughout their visit; they were vehement as long as they thought it possible to carry out their instructions from the government, but they had a marvellous facility for accepting a situation once it was forced upon them. In 1858 this held good for the duration of their short stay, but three years later, when Laurence became Secretary of Legation at Edo, he was to discover just how vehement the Japanese could be.

As soon as *Furious* reached anchor, Laurence set off for Deshima. He found its one narrow street as neat and clean as a village in Holland; unassuming houses lined the street with verandahs seaward, looking 'with large hollow eyes into each other's interiors in a dismal sort of way, as if they were quite weary of the view'. Through their open windows women were to be seen, the only native Japanese allowed to stay in Deshima after the Dutch merchants were shut in at nightfall. The Japanese considered foreign females more dangerous than their male counterparts, so no Dutchwoman had set foot in Deshima for two hundred years. Although the Dutch merchants of Deshima were strictly watched and searched whenever they went across the only bridge to Nagasaki, Laurence encountered no check or search. Braced for the usual noise, smells, confusion and dirt of a Chinese city, he was enchanted to find broad, clean, gravelled streets running up into wooded hills, a population friendly and relaxed, anxious to help the barbarians at whom they hardly stared. Light wooden screens were pushed back giving glimpses of cool gardens behind; half clothed men and women languidly watched over their entirely naked children. In the heat of the day the women wore nothing above the waist, the men when boating affected two small triangles of cloth, one over the loins, the other on the bridge of the nose, an area held to be particularly vulnerable. At the end of the day the whole population emerged outside its front door to wash. At this the mission flinched a bit; as Townsend Harris remarked, he could not account for such an indelicate proceeding on the part of a people so generally correct. Laurence soon became accustomed to the sight of both sexes clothed 'in nothing but the Japanese equivalent of soap'.

The Vice-Governor of Nagasaki, on the other hand, was most elaborately dressed. He was a plebian looking man, Laurence wrote, with an extremely smiling countenance and extremely short legs. When he bowed, which he did often, his two swords cocked up behind him like a double tail. He wanted Lord Elgin to make the Queen's yacht over to the Governor of Nagasaki, but Elgin, who depended on the yacht as an excuse to go as far as Edo, declined.

In Nagasaki harbour Laurence saw the beginnings of the ship repairing yard which the *bakufu* had directed to be built, using Dutch engineers in charge of Japanese workmen. So strong already was the desire to learn Western ways that several feudal overlords – *daimyo* in Japanese – had obtained the Shogun's permission to learn to use a lathe and other tools, and could be seen in the machine shop or at the drawing board. Chief among these enthusiasts was the greatest lord of all and the most independent minded, the Prince of Satsuma, whose domain lay across the strait from Nagasaki, and with whose secret agents Laurence Oliphant would have a great deal to do in the years to come. Satsuma had already established an electric telegraph between his palace and his capital of Kagoshima, a distance of three miles; he also had glass factories and cannon foundries.

On leaving Nagasaki, *Furious* and her escort weathered a prolonged storm and put in at Simoda, altogether a smaller and poorer place than Nagasaki. The mission descended on the bazaar to buy lacquer and other locally made goods. Perhaps because of the storm, Laurence laid in a stock of waterproof greatcoats made of wax paper, 'so completely effectual in a storm of rain as the best mackintosh ever made'. They were very light and portable, their only drawback being a tendency to tear but, and this is what appealed to his Scots soul, at eighteenpence apiece, they were only half the price of a pair of white kid gloves.

As soon as *Furious* arrived at Simoda, Henry Heusken came off to her with offers of hospitality and assistance. Landing to inspect the temple where he and Townsend Harris had spent two long years, Laurence did not envy them their solitude in spite of the books and the spectacular view. Harris told Elgin that the *bakufu* had sent word that they were prepared to negotiate a treaty with the British; he offered Heusken as interpreter in these talks. Elgin accepted with pleasure; he found the young man congenial and obliging. Laurence made fast friends with him and, during the time they were together, drew from Heusken the detailed knowledge of Japanese history and customs that he, with his unrivalled knowledge of Dutch and Japanese, had been able to acquire. *Elgin's Mission to China and Japan* contains a great deal of information contributed by Henry Heusken, who died before he could set down his own record.

With Heusken on board the *Furious* proceeded to the capital, where Elgin was determined to go in spite of the fact that no foreign ship had anchored in Edo Bay since before the country had been closed to strangers. Even Commander Perry had not gone so far but halted at Kanagawa. The day after they arrived at Edo the Commissioners appointed to negotiate the treaty came on board. Laurence made friends with one in particular, Higo no Kami, with whom he talked every day for the rest of their stay. Higo was most anxious to learn English, as his great ambition was to be chosen for one of Japan's first embassies to go abroad – something that was now considered inevitable. In fact Higo no Kami was the principal mover behind the drafting of the treaty with Townsend Harris, a very able diplomat and a great enthusiast for Western ways. He carried a series of fans in his bosom on which he noted his English vocabulary. At luncheon he asked Laurence the names of the dishes, wrote them on his fan and fell to. The Japanese did not jib at European food; ham, champagne, paté de foie gras, curaçao and strawberry jam all went down well – and champagne especially well. Mindful of its diplomatic uses, Elgin had thoughtfully brought a plentiful supply.

As they awaited the invitation to land they contemplated Edo Bay. Five island forts parallel to the shore protected the approach – at least the *bakufu* hoped they did, for they were the result of recent moves to strengthen the coastal defences and had never been tested. They were made of large square blocks of stone surmounted by large and useful looking guns. Houses stretched along the low shore backed by gentle wooded hills on most of which stood temples. A pagoda rising among trees in the centre of Edo marked the Shogun's palace. Over it all towered the white spectacular cone of Fujiyama, a mountain of whose existence and spiritual significance Laurence had not even known until it broke upon his view at Simoda.

They landed on 17 August, Lord Elgin in full dress leading the way in his barge to the strains of 'Rule Britannia', played by the ship's band. Thirteen ships' boats paddled after him, each with a brass cannon in the bow and ensigns flying. Scores of little boats came bobbing out to meet them, circling round this splendid and interesting procession. At the landing place they encountered their first Japanese conveyance called a *norimon*; it was a kind of sedan chair, but a very uncomfortable one, as the occupant could not see out and had to sit cross legged while swinging about far too close to the ground. It was all right for the Japanese, said Henry Heusken, they tucked their legs under them, but Western pants were too tight and Western muscles too stiff to make this possible. Laurence preferred a horse, but regretted the choice. The saddle was knobbly, the stirrups too long, the horse too fresh, and he cursed China for the scourge from which he suffered – boils.

Unlike the blasé inhabitants of Nagasaki, the people of Edo went wild with excitement at the mission's approach. Crowds ran alongside the procession and men and women rushed to see them, dripping from the bath. At intervals the street was barred by a huge gate so that one section of the population was left peering enviously through the bars at the next crowd to gather. Laurence noticed that the cross streets were closed by ropes that nobody attempted to pass. Their lodging was in the state apartments of a Buddhist temple and the English were touched to find there European chairs, tables, and beds. These were copies of Townsend Harris's furniture which the Japanese, with exquisite courtesy, had had made secretly at Simoda before he came to Edo to negotiate his treaty.

The only irksome thing about their apartments was the constant surveillance they were under. There were people who watched them officially, and people who watched them unofficially; these last were sometimes reduced to poking holes in the flimsy paper walls that separated the temple from its neighbours. Everyone in Japan was expected to keep an eye on everyone else; that is how society was arranged. There were two occupants of each official post who had a duty to spy on one another. The Japanese saw nothing strange in this and, from the evidence of the dual title of the British head of mission, concluded that others managed likewise. Elgin, they said to themselves, performed the outward and visible ceremonies, while Kincardine did his part so skilfully that he was never seen.

Laurence spent the following days exploring Edo. In consequence of the enforced residence there of the *daimyo* and many thousands of their retainers – in this the Shogun emulated Louis XIV – the city was vast, sprawling, and densely populated. The *daimyo*'s life of luxury and obligatory idleness was also responsible for the number of large and opulent shops stocked with all manner of goods – silks, lacquer, and porcelain. In the heart of Edo was the citadel, a huge moated enclosure, eight miles round, containing lakes, gardens, and, reportedly, some 40,000 inhabitants. Here the Shogun lived, as jealously secluded as the spiritual ruler of Japan, the Mikado, who was shut away at Kyoto. The Shogun never went out, except on state occasions. 'It was a cruel satire on this unhappy potentate to present him with a yacht,' Laurence wrote, 'one might as well request the Pope's acceptance of a wife.' The mission was not allowed to see him. Instead, he sent his compliments to Lord Elgin and a ceremonial dinner which they found laid out on the floor when they returned to their quarters. There was a good deal of seaweed about it, Laurence found.

Discussions with the Japanese about the details of the treaty were a great deal easier than those with the Chinese at Tientsin. Higo no Kami was forever making jokes, and the atmosphere was markedly friendly and relaxed. No difficulties arose or, it might be more true to say, were made, and so the treaty was ready to be signed by 26 August 1858. It was similar to the American agreement; its most important provision was to permit the establishment of a British Diplomatic Agent at Edo and to open the ports of Nagasaki, Kanagawa, and Hakodate to trade immediately; Osaka, Niigata, and Hiogo were to follow by 1863.

The next day the yacht was handed over to a twenty-one gun salute; the first the Japanese Navy had ever fired. It was time to pack and go. Box after box of china, silk, ivory, gold ornaments, and lacquer piled up on the deck of *Furious*. Swords too arrived on board, though it had proved curiously difficult to persuade the Japanese to part with any; they seemed to regard them with veneration. On top of this came unexpected gifts from the Shogun – silver models of storks for Elgin, a china bowl for the commander of the yacht, and dozens of thickly padded robes. These, said Laurence, were each as large as a German duvet and as warm. Their enormous dimensions occupied half the quarter deck, 'and threatened to produce serious effects upon the mind of the first lieutenant'. The ship's stores had to be ransacked to meet this challenge which no one had foreseen. The Commissioners seemed quite pleased with the flannel, soap, and chocolate produced, but more especially welcomed several rifles. The parting was marked by demonstrations of affection on both sides. They sailed on 28 August, pausing only to land Henry Heusken at Simoda.

Of that short summer encounter in Japan, Laurence wrote many years later, 'Those travellers who first saw it painted it in its gala dress. A population nude, peaceable and contented, a landscape of fairy-like beauty, a sky unrivalled even in Italy and they left before they had recovered from the charming surprise.' All the same he had had time to see beyond the charm, courtesy, and quaintness; he had sensed the shock of the encounter with the West and his judgement of the Japanese character was shrewd. The people were obedient to their superiors, courageous and honest. But they were also notoriously vindictive, superstitious, haughty, exceedingly tenacious of their honour, and unsparing in their mode of protecting or revenging it. So it was more than probable, he thought, that as England's relations with Japan were extended they would become less amicable. The overbearing and insolent manner of a certain class of Englishmen in their relations with semi-civilized races would provoke antagonism among the Japanese and the very dissimilar modes of thought of the two races would give rise to strain. The amiability of their reception at Edo was the mask which a somewhat shallow diplomacy led the

Japanese to assume to meet a danger they thought imminent and which they dared not fight. 'They fancied they saw impending on them the fate of India, and they believed the only alternative was to grant us concessions such as we had already wrung from China,' Laurence concluded.

On their return to Shanghai they had to prepare for the arrival of the Imperial Chinese Commissioners to complete the Treaty of Tientsin. Two of them, Wang, a provincial Governor, and Sieh, a provincial Judge, were chosen by Peking to settle the details of tariffs and trade, a vital part of the treaty. The British representatives named to take part were Laurence Oliphant and Thomas Wade. The latter was to be a lifelong friend, one of the very few with Laurence at his lonely death. In 1858 Wade was already fluent in Chinese and experienced in diplomacy; he was destined to become a most distinguished Minister to Peking. Each day Wade and Oliphant were carried in chairs through the hot, reeking streets of Shanghai to a building four miles distant where they found Wang and Sieh waiting for them. Business was transacted in an airy upper room with an extensive view over crazily tilted roofs; it was attended by a prodigious consumption of tobacco, and copious relays of almond and other tea. When it was over they were regularly pressed to dine, an experience they sought to avoid if possible as it involved the consumption of much grease and many unknown viands. When politeness insisted they accept, the dinner always ended in a drinking match of hot samshu with Sieh, a man with a naturally jovial temperament and a very strong head.

Their discussions had great significance for the future of trade between west and east, for they fixed a reasonable duty on goods going into China and prepared the way for the celebrated Chinese Maritime Customs service which Horace Lay, who was a member of Elgin's mission and attended the trade talks as an extra interpreter, was destined to direct for many years. Most controversial was the agreement to legalize the opium trade. Laurence knew that this would be opposed in England, and explained to Mrs Ashley that it was the only way to stop the abuses of the illegal traffic. Unlike other goods which might be carried into the interior of China by foreign importers, opium was to come under the control of the Chinese government as soon as it had been landed at the open ports.

When this business was completed at the end of October, Elgin announced his intention of proceeding up the Yangtse Kiang where no foreigner had ever been, 'to create a wholesome moral impression on the minds of the people upon her banks'. And so, while signing the Treaty of Tientsin in a temple on the outskirts of Shanghai they could see *Furious* in the river, snorting and pawing like an impatient racehorse, puffing off sharp jets of steam and lashing the water with her paddles. Four other warships accompanied them when they set off into the unknown. It took them six weeks to sail as far as Nanking and back; their progress much hampered by sandbanks and actively opposed by the Taiping rebels who controlled the country through which they passed. Wherever they landed Elgin adopted great ceremony and was met with politeness that concealed much curiosity. At Nanking, which was the centre of the rebellion, Laurence tried to discover the tenets of the Taiping religion. So far as they were expounded at all, he remarked, he found them an extraordinary jumble of Jewish polity, Christian theology, and Chinese philosophy. He could speak with some confidence of all three since he had already begun the study of comparative religion which, towards the end of his life, came to obsess him.

When the expedition returned to Shanghai, Elgin found letters to say that his brother, Frederick Bruce, had been appointed Minister to Peking. For several weeks they waited for him to appear, revisiting Canton, which was calm again, and calling at the islands of Hainan and St John where Laurence tried to find the tomb of Francis Xavier. When, by February, Bruce had not appeared and the flow of official correspondence had all but dried up, Elgin concluded that they might leave. And so in March 1859, with inexpressible relief they turned their backs on China. At Galle they found Frederick Bruce, and with him the news that Sir Antony Oliphant had died of a sudden heart attack.

This was the first serious blow Laurence had ever encountered, and it struck him at a time when he was most vulnerable – cooped up on board ship and disposed in any case to brood. He had already spent long hours contemplating the wilder shores of religious belief; now this shock propelled him further down the path of spiritualism. As so many of his contemporaries did, he turned to it because it promised that the loved one was not gone beyond recall. There was a story concerning him that received much currency at this time, and which Margaret Oliphant repeated in her book. According to this, before he had been told the news, he came on deck one night and announced to his friends that he had seen his father, and that he was dead. The date was taken down and later found to be correct, 'which would be a remarkable addition, if sufficiently confirmed, to many stories of a similar kind which are well known', Mrs Oliphant wrote.

CHAPTER 4

PRIVATE DIPLOMACY

LAURENCE now had an urgent reason for desiring to get home, and his impatience was shared by his colleagues since the mission had lasted far longer than anyone could have foreseen. As captain of *Furious* Sherard Osborn ordered the fullest possible steam ahead and, on 19 April, only ten days from Galle, she dropped anchor inside the great black rim of the Aden crater. There an encounter took place that was to end in one of the most famous and tragic quarrels in the history of exploration, a quarrel in which Laurence Oliphant would play the part of catalyst, as he was so often strangely fated to do. It is this episode which is called to mind whenever Oliphant's name is mentioned today; its effect upon his reputation has been misleading and unfair.

On 16 April a coasting vessel from Zanzibar had landed at Aden two explorers newly emerged from the remote and mysterious lake region of Central Africa. They were Richard Burton and John Hanning Speke who had been gone for two years looking for the sources of the Nile. Speke was convinced that the river rose in the great lake only he had seen, which he called Victoria Nyanza. Obviously such a romantic and exciting discovery would arouse the greatest interest in England. Elgin offered both men a swift passage home, but they had to make up their minds at once as *Furious* would sail as soon as she had coaled. Speke accepted, Burton declined. He had been very ill with fever; he said he chose to remain at Aden to recover. To Speke he said, 'I shall hurry up Jack, as soon as I am able.' Speke's answer, according to Burton was, 'Goodbye old fellow; you may be quite sure I shall not go up to the Royal Geographical Society until you come to the fore and we appear together. Make your mind quite easy about that.' These are famous words and the last the two are supposed ever to have exchanged. Speke's promise was not kept; the reason being, it was said, that Laurence Oliphant persuaded him to break it.

According to Burton's wife, Isabel, on the way home from Aden, Oliphant told Speke that Burton was a jealous man and being chief of the expedition would take all the glory of the Nyanza for himself. If he were Speke, Oliphant said, he would go to the Royal Geographical Society at once and get the command of the next expedition (to trace the Nile down from its source). He, Oliphant, would back him and get others to do so. This is what happened in the end and it is quite likely an accurate account of Oliphant's opinion of Burton. The question is how did it come about?

At the time of the great quarrel it was widely remarked that Oliphant detested Burton and had seized the opportunity of the voyage home to poison Speke's mind against him. Isabel Burton said that Laurence Oliphant was driven by caprice to break up friendships. And in our own time the charge has been made that he was a homosexual who desired to make Speke his lover and that jealousy of Burton drove him on. But judging from Laurence's previous experience of Richard Burton, and Speke's frame of mind on leaving Africa, the truth of the matter seems likely to have been much less dramatic and much less damaging.

Laurence Oliphant had good cause to judge Burton capable of the theft of someone else's ideas. In 1855 in the Crimea Burton had twice tried to steal his own thunder – over the mission to Schamyl and the diversion in the Caucasus. As for Speke, it is known now that he went on board *Furious* in a state of nervous distress and antagonism towards Burton that had festered ever since the discovery of the Nyanza and was the worse for having been suppressed. One facet of Speke's character which had a tremendous influence upon his conduct was that he conceived grudges against people which he concealed at the time, only to reveal them later, often to the public discomfort of their subject. In this case Speke knew that Burton did not accept his claim to have discovered the source of the Nile; it is likely that he feared others would not either. For though he passionately believed that the great river rose in the lake he had seen, he had not proved his theory; he had not followed round the shore; he knew that a second expedition would be necessary before the prize was his. When he met him on board *Furious* it is likely that Speke found Laurence Oliphant no more than a sympathetic audience for these fears.

They were already well acquainted, having travelled out to Constantinople together in 1855. They shared a fascination with the

Caucasus, where Speke would have gone but for the invitation to Africa from Burton in 1856. And they concurred in the desire to promote a larger purpose in Africa than exploration or trade. Precisely when Speke conceived his plan for a nation to be established in the fertile uplands stretching, as he thought, from east to west across the continent, is not known, but its emphasis upon the moral and spiritual regeneration of the African race was something that Laurence was deeply interested in and which, as we have seen, he had already envisaged as applying to the Indians of Central America. Whether it was he who put it into Speke's mind, or Speke's own plan, hardly matters; it was bound to bring them together.

Concerning the charge of homosexuality, the truth cannot be known, but it seems very unlikely that this influenced Laurence Oliphant's advice to Speke on the voyage home, or his subsequent conduct regarding the choice of leader for the second expedition to the Nile. Towards the end of his life, people who had felt wronged by Oliphant accused him of committing homosexual acts, but the charge was prompted by malice and the evidence for it is, at the very least, inconclusive; it will be discussed in its place. But Speke may have raised the subject with Oliphant at the time, for it is known that, on his return from Africa in 1859, Speke in private indulged in hysterical denunciations of Richard Burton, and these – to John Blackwood and others – contained the allegation that, during the expedition to the lakes, Burton made advances to him.

On 27 April Elgin, Oliphant and the rest of the mission, with Speke, left *Furious* at Suez for the last time and boarded the train for Port Said. As Laurence remarked, so fast was their progress that they had the satisfaction of being the first people ever to breakfast on the Red Sea and dine the same evening on the Mediterranean. They landed at Plymouth on 7 May 1859 to a heroes' welcome, having been away from England for almost exactly two years.

We do not know how Laurence was greeted by his newly widowed mother; no doubt she was overjoyed to see him and gratified by the good report Lord Elgin gave of him. We may be sure that whatever efforts Laurence made to retain a sense of his father's nearness would be fully matched by hers. Lady Oliphant's pleasure at seeing her son again was only tempered by the knowledge that he would not stay long at home for they both now accepted that his career lay in the diplomatic service. But the trials that Maria faced in regard to this were the lesser ones of moving house, since she remained determined to follow Laurence to whatever permanent appointment might be his. The difficulty was that, although everyone spoke of Oliphant as a coming man, all his activity so far had been outside the official diplomatic sphere; now he had to persuade the panjandrums of the Foreign Office to recognize him. The means, he believed, lay close at hand; as in the case of *The Russian Shores of the Black Sea* he felt that a successful book about China and Japan would greatly smooth his path. And so, in the early summer of 1859 he settled happily to writing.

But he did not forget Speke for whom he was in a position to do a great deal. Laurence's reputation stood high with the Royal Geographical Society, of which he was a Fellow, and to which he had sent lively but scholarly papers at regular intervals during his absence in the East. The latest, describing the voyage up the Yangtse River had been read for him at the Society's March meeting and aroused much interest for its graphic account of the effect of the Taiping Rebellion on the Chinese towns. As soon as he arrived back in England, Laurence was elected to the Society's Council and made a member of the influential Expedition Committee. And on his return to London Speke went round to the Royal Geographical Society and told its President, Sir Roderick Murchison, all about the discovery of the Nyanza. Murchison was so impressed that, according to Speke, he declared 'we must send you there again'.

When Burton arrived in London towards the end of May, he said he found the question of the second expedition already settled. Moreover he complained that even his cherished plan of entering Africa through Somaliland was dismissed as unworthy of notice. But, as the records of the RGS show, the matter was not so cut and dried and Oliphant, though he was in a most influential position, seems – on paper at least – to have acted in an even-handed manner as between the two. An *ad hoc* sub-committee was set up consisting of John Crawfurd, Francis Galton, and Laurence Oliphant to consider alternative plans from each explorer. Burton and Speke were called to present these plans at a meeting of the sub-committee on 21 June. Although Speke afterwards accused Burton of copying his idea, what each proposed to the meeting was quite different. Speke intended to follow the previous route inland from the coast to the west shore of the Nyanza. Burton reverted to his old theory that snow capped mountains feeding the sources of the Nile lay somewhere in the unexplored and dangerous country of the Horn of Africa. He proposed to go there disguised as an Arab merchant and, from Harar, strike west towards the Nyanza.

The report that Laurence Oliphant, as spokesman of the sub-committee, presented to his colleagues judged that both expeditions were equally desirable and stressed the high regard they all had for both explorers. But it declared that Speke's expedition was the more urgent since he deemed it essential for a caravan with advance supplies to set out for the Nyanza from Zanzibar no later than November 1859, he to follow some months later. If Government finance was to be obtained the RGS ought to lose no time in asking for it. Burton's journey did not call for a similar urgency in carrying out preliminary arrangements and the state of his health meant that he could not himself fix a time when he would start. The report concluded that the Society should go ahead at once with arrangements for Speke's expedition. Its application to the Government on behalf of Burton might be made as soon as he was able himself to report that his health was so far recovered as to enable him to enter upon the arduous task which he had undertaken. Surely that was fair enough? Burton's plan was not dismissed, as he said, nor was it stolen from Speke, as Speke said. Nobody who saw Burton in the summer of 1859 could have supposed it possible for him to go straight back to Africa. Isabel Burton said he had had twenty-one attacks of fever and was a mere skeleton with brown-yellow skin, so weak that he could hardly stand.

As it turned out, the most valuable service that Laurence Oliphant rendered Speke was to introduce him to John Blackwood with the recommendation that his Central African Journal be published in the *Magazine*. This was hardly precipitate; Laurence did not approach Blackwood until after the Council of the RGS had ratified the sub-committee's recommendations on 27 June. When he met him Blackwood conceived a great admiration for the young explorer as a fine specimen of an Englishman, 'unpretending, simple hearted but determined'. The publisher wrapped Speke in the same genial warmth he gave to all his contributors and, in addition, turned upon him the avuncular eye that Laurence had enjoyed at the beginning of his career. When Blackwood discovered how dilatory and awkward a writer Speke was he enlisted Laurence as sub-editor and general overseer in the preparation of the articles that appeared in *Blackwood's Magazine* later in the year. This was a task that Laurence performed with skill and for many other writers, including Sherard

Osborn, who produced an account of his experiences during Elgin's mission to China, and John Petherick, yet another African explorer. Oliphant's facility in writing was the envy of his professional colleagues – words flowed on to the page, ordered and exact; though his style appeared effortless it did not lack tension.

Though Laurence was intent upon finishing his own book as soon as possible he did not let it interfere with a hectic social life. With the glamour of China and Japan fresh upon him he was hardly less of a lion than Speke and a great deal more engaging. Witty, kind and charming, not yet thirty and unmarried, with the certain prospect of a brilliant career before him, all doors were open to him and more especially in those houses with marriageable daughters. If Laurence ever regretted the loss of his earlier love he never referred to it, but he now sent his mother his usual tantalizing letters. From one house where there were several pretty sisters he announced himself as deeply in love with them all. From another he sent a more sober account of the young woman in question, concluding that she would suit his mother perfectly as a daughter-in-law but, 'as for myself I despair of finding anyone; probably when I do she will be anathema to you'.

For the most part his letters to Lady Oliphant were good natured and affectionate, with their accounts of dancing until 3 a.m., then waking so fresh at seven that he wrote his book until the others struggled down to breakfast at eleven. 'Charming women at hand when I am inclined for a cosy chair in the drawing-room and a touch of the aesthetic. Any amount of game merely for the trouble of strolling through a few turnip fields . . . Any number of horses to ride – all the more to be appreciated after two years of filth, heat and absence of social and intellectual enjoyment.' But he was no longer responsive to his mother's continued demands to share his 'serious thoughts'. Gently but firmly he told her not to pry, there were certain things he would not disclose. He warned her that there was a dark side to his life; as he put it, while he could dispose of his time between innocent recreation and profitable employment he was happy. When he was idle he was apt to become low spirited and then he turned to much less innocent pursuits.

In September Laurence and Sherard Osborn and Speke lectured to the British Association meeting at Aberdeen. From there Laurence went on to stay with Sir James Clark, the Queen's doctor, now retired, at Birkhall near Balmoral. On 24 September Queen Victoria noted in her Journal that it was a quite mild evening and Mr Oliphant and Sir James had dined, 'the former a pleasing clever young man, who has been Lord Elgin's secretary and has written clever books'. That was the only Royal reference to Laurence Oliphant at that period. But indirectly it is clear that the freedom he was given from then on to move in Royal circles all over Europe stemmed from the high opinion Prince Albert in particular formed of him. And it was because of the contacts he made in these circles, added to the people he had come to know through Palmerston and Shaftesbury, that Laurence possessed an unrivalled source of information about European affairs and a means of access to many of the men who conducted them.

What service he had rendered to earn the approval of the Royal Family is not known, but their regard for him endured until the end of his life. He was an especial friend of the Queen's third daughter, Princess Helena, who in 1880 told the Earl of Beaconsfield that she had known Laurence Oliphant since she was a child. Their acquaintance probably came about through Lady Augusta Bruce, Lord Elgin's sister and the Queen's close friend. Lady Augusta was very fond of Laurence and in some measure acted as his patroness. But his popularity was such that it soon gained a momentum of its own. From Birkhall he went to shoot at Cortachy Castle, the Scottish home of the Earl and Countess of Airlie. Blanche Airlie and Laurence shared a fascination in the practice of spiritualism then taking England by storm. She was the second of the five Stanley girls. In December 1859, Laurence was invited to spend a week at their home, Alderley, where her three unmarried sisters were Maude, Kate, and Rosalind.

His longest sojourn was at Broomhall for serious conversations with Lord Elgin about his book. The question to be settled was how much of the dispute between Elgin and Admiral Sir Michael Seymour over the tardy arrival of the naval force at the Peiho in 1858 ought to be allowed to appear. Sherard Osborn, Delane, and Wingrove Cooke hoped that Laurence would tell it all. It would be the book of the season, Osborn told John Blackwood; he only hoped Oliphant would not allow the canny Earl to cut out all the bone and gristle. 'Over finesse is the Earl's failing; he always flinches at a climax,' Osborn said.

This time the Earl's caution was tempered by his lasting resentment at the humiliation in China. When it appeared, the book provoked a furious public row over its revelation that at the moment of the Allies' first confrontation with the Chinese, when face was all, the whole might of France was represented by two gunboats inside the bar of the Peiho River and that of England by two despatch boats run aground on top. Seymour, by then a Member of Parliament, and Elgin in the Lords, went at each other hammer and tongs with newspapers joining in. 'A very pretty quarrel in which everyone seems to be in the wrong,' *The Times* remarked. Then, in the Commons, Lord John Russell, the Foreign Secretary, let fly at Laurence Oliphant, accusing him as a public servant of betraying the confidence of those with whom he worked. This called forth a vehement but anonymous letter in *The Times*. Lord John's proposal that Seymour and Elgin shake hands while 'poor Mr Oliphant' as scapegoat be driven forth from public life might be politic but it was neither generous nor just. If Oliphant published confidential information supplied by Elgin that was his Lordship's fault, not his. Why should Oliphant incur the lasting condemnation of the Foreign Secretary who was the arbiter of his future career? Laurence who, if he did not write the letter himself, probably inspired it, heartily concurred. 'Why can't he hit a man his own size?' he asked John Blackwood. 'He is like a monkey that I knew on board ship, who when the men thrashed him, used to turn and bite a boy.'

Nevertheless he knew he must proceed with more caution. The first edition of *Elgin's Mission to China and Japan* had sold out by the end of February 1860, not a little helped by the row, as Laurence was well aware. In March he was holding back the preface to the second edition because it contained reflections on 'that mean beast, Johnny' which he would have to cut if, as he hoped, Russell appointed him to a permanent post within the diplomatic service. For a week or so his fate teetered in the balance. The Chinese settlement had collapsed – mainly as a result of Elgin's failure to press on to Peking – and a second punitive expedition was ordered out to China to restore the Allies' prestige. No one who had been on the first expedition wanted to repeat the experience but Elgin was finally prevailed upon once again to take the lead. Laurence was 'horribly discomposed' at the thought that his first official post might land him back on the mud of the Peiho River, and cast about for a decent way of escape. 'I have imposed high conditions as the price of my services', he told John Blackwood. These conditions, which Elgin put to Lord John Russell without comment, were audacious in one so young and apparently inexperienced. Laurence said he would not go to China unless he were appointed Secretary of Legation. On 6 March, to his enormous relief, he heard he was not to go.

He always maintained that what he did next was entirely on his own initiative, a private intervention in the cause of international justice, and a way of revenging himself on the Emperor Napoleon III for the 'betrayal' in the Crimea. It was exceedingly rash in one who depended on the goodwill of the Foreign Secretary to further his chosen career. At the end of March 1860 Laurence Oliphant added himself as an active agent to the most explosive mixture in European affairs – the unification of Italy. As he described it many years after, he proposed nothing less than to try to prevent Nice and Savoy from being handed over to France. Told where he was going John Blackwood offered him special terms for his account of his adventures.

Nice and Savoy were the price of French help for the Kingdom of Sardinia in obtaining Lombardy from Austria in the war of 1859. The bargain had been struck in great secrecy between the Emperor Napoleon III and the King of Sardinia's Minister, Count Cavour. By early 1860 rumours of it had been circulating for some time. Although there was much enthusiasm in England for the Italian cause, public opinion was aroused against the proposed transfer. Lord John Russell was one of those who privately found it most distasteful that the inhabitants of Nice and Savoy should be moved about like puppets for such a man as Louis Napoleon Bonaparte. But he and the Prime Minister, Lord Palmerston, had to take a longer view and decide if it was worth going to war to prevent. Their correspondence shows that they feared that France would push her frontier right down to the Simplon Pass, and that the Swiss were also very alarmed at the prospect of France taking over Chablais and Faucigny, two districts of Savoy bordering on the Lake of Geneva which, under the Treaty of 1815, shared in Swiss neutrality. Although their incorporation into France threatened the balance of power, Palmerston eventually decided there was nothing England could do to stop the Emperor. 'He will make a great mistake,' he told Lord John Russell, 'he will destroy all Confidence in his Intentions of future Policy and he will combine all Germany in a hostile league against him.'

On 24 March 1860 the Emperor announced to deputies summoned to Paris for the purpose that a plebiscite would shortly be held in Nice and Savoy to decide their future. On their way home to set the vote in motion who should join them but Laurence Oliphant? 'Imagine my coming from Paris in the same railway carriage with the Savoyard deputies,' he wrote to Abraham Hayward. His choice of Hayward as the recipient of his frequent letters on this and many other excursions into European affairs was carefully premeditated. The post from the Continent was not secure; letters were opened and sometimes went deliberately astray. Hayward was a writer, a mutual friend of Kinglake, and habitué of the clubs that Oliphant attended. But his importance lay in the fact that he was a famous purveyor of news and gossip, having the ear of politicians like the Duke of Newcastle and Lord Palmerston. Hayward's access to the Prime Minister was made easy and unremarkable by his role as Lady Palmerston's 'chief of staff' in social matters, so that he was constantly at Cambridge House and Broadlands.

By the time Laurence wrote to him, on 30 March, he was already in Geneva, having made a tour through Chablais and Faucigny with the Savoyard deputies. He had made a careful assessment of the way in which the vote was likely to go. Though the great mass of the people favoured Switzerland and neutrality, French intrigue and bribery would win the day, he told Hayward. He evidently did his best for Switzerland; at a dinner in Belleville, capital of Faucigny, he so stirred up those present with promises of English support that they proposed a demonstration on the spot. But Laurence felt the moment was not ripe – or safe – and was obliged to dissuade them. 'There's nothing more to be done here and I am off,' the letter ended.

The only other letter written by Oliphant to have survived from this time was sent from Turin on 3 April to Lord de Grey and Ripon. Though he was a personal friend of Laurence, he was also Under Secretary for War. In his letter to de Grey Laurence apologized for sending nothing to him from Savoy, pleading pressure of affairs. He gave a similar account of French intrigue to win the vote in Savoy as he had to Hayward, and confessed that his own efforts in support of the Swiss had come to nothing. Yet he was convinced that the people were really seven to one on the side of the Swiss. Laurence said he hoped there would be a European Congress to settle the question, and that England would take her stand at it upon the necessity of annexing Savoy to Switzerland. Otherwise French intrigue and the Italian desire for unification at whatever cost would win the day. 'These mad Italians will imperil their new Kingdom by allowing France to rest upon the Simplon for the prospect of gaining Venetia,' he told de Grey, 'they are afraid to offend the Emperor though they admit him to be a blackguard.' Cavour was in the same category, Laurence said; he was sacrificing everything to the idea of a united Italy and was quite unscrupulous. He explained that he was writing in the midst of a fearful hubbub consequent upon the opening of the new Italian Chamber and must break off to attend the first day's proceedings. He would send a fuller account of his activities in ten days at the latest. 'Will you kindly post the enclosed as no letter to this address is allowed to pass through France,' he asked de Grey. It is tantalizing not to know the identity of this person, or the details of the message to him or her, but Laurence's letter to de Grey does at least show that the movements of this apparently independent young man who was dabbling in the affairs of more than one foreign country were being monitored in Whitehall.

According to Margaret Oliphant, it was Laurence's acquaintance with diplomatic society that procured him an invitation to dine with Cavour, whom he described as 'a thick set solid man with a huge square head and spectacles, an able, mathematical, practical sort of head without chivalry, principle, or genius.' To have obtained such an invitation in the very first days of the opening session of the newly elected Chamber of Deputies argued the highest possible diplomatic influence. When with Cavour, Laurence said, he made no allusion to the question of Nice, which was his next private concern, but he was convinced that in his secret soul Cavour would have been pleased at the success of a conspiracy which would have saved Nice for Italy, if it could have been made plain that he had no complicity in it.

Just such a conspiracy was now on foot, the whole purpose of which was not revealed. Laurence put it about at Turin that it was his idea as an eccentric young Englishman to try to influence the vote at Nice against the French. For that purpose he applied to the English Minister at Turin, Sir James Hudson, for an introduction to the most famous Nizzard of all, General Garibaldi. Hudson remarked to Lord John Russell, 'I told [Oliphant] neither he nor Garibaldi could do anything for the Nizzards who were already bought and paid for . . . and that he would find Garibaldi who was full of talk would end by doing nothing.' Something of this mission to Garibaldi, though not the whole story, was published by Laurence Oliphant twenty-seven years later when most of the actors were dead and there was no longer any indiscretion in referring to it.

According to this, Laurence arrived at Turin on 3 April with letters of introduction to the Deputies from Nice who had gone to Turin in the hope of thwarting the transfer of their province to France. On 4 April he was summoned to a meeting in a large room at the top of a house reached by a long dark stair. Some fourteen men were sitting at a table at the head of which was a red-bearded, slightly balding man in a poncho who was General Garibaldi. The point at issue when Laurence entered was whether the Nizzard Committee (for such it was) should try by opposition in the Chamber to delay the plebiscite due at Nice in ten days' time, or resort to organizing a riot in the town itself. Garibaldi was all in favour of the riot; although a member of the new Chamber he despised constitutional methods. Time was short for either course. Suddenly, Garibaldi turned to Laurence who, not unnaturally, had been keeping quiet, and asked him what he thought. He said he ventured to suggest that constitutional methods be exhausted before recourse was had to violence. As an Englishman, and, therefore, an authority on parliamentary procedure, he was instantly requested to formulate the motion to be laid before the Italian Chamber. The gist of it was, he said, that the Franco-Italian Convention which provided for a plebiscite to be taken at Nice should be submitted to the Turin Chamber before the vote was taken, as it seemed contrary to all constitutional practice that a Government should make arrangements with a foreign Power by which two valuable provinces were to be transferred to that Power without the Chamber of the country so deprived having an opportunity of seeing the documents so disposing of them. For the first time, but by no means the last time, Laurence's legal skill was used in the service of foreign powers.

It took some time for Garibaldi to get the point at issue into his head and when he did he was not very excited about it. But it commended itself to the majority and, finally, Garibaldi consented to speak to it, though in such a half-hearted way that Laurence did not have much confidence in the result. On 12 April Laurence went to the Chamber and spent more than an hour coaching Garibaldi whose parliamentary debut it was. But, according to him, Garibaldi would not take a note or prepare his ideas; he told Laurence several times what he would say but never said the same thing twice and always missed the principal points. With its patriotic sentiments and glowing enthusiasm and muddled criticism of Cavour, his maiden speech brought down the house, but the motion was lost, for Garibaldi did not speak to it.

That night another meeting of the Nice Committee was held in the upper room at which Laurence was again present. The plan then formed, he said, was simple. It was known that on the day of the plebiscite, the following Sunday, French and Sardinian troops would be withdrawn from Nice to avoid the appearance of intimidation. So the coast would be clear for a 'small scale popular movement'. All that was intended, according to Laurence, was to wait until the vote was taken and then smash the ballot boxes so that the result could not be known. Friends of Nice at Turin would persuade the Government to have the vote taken again later, trusting to a change of heart to swing it against the French. Garibaldi invited Laurence to join this enterprise which many of his associates denounced as foolhardy. Smashing ballot boxes in someone else's country was hardly the sort of thing the Foreign Office liked its diplomats to do. But, apparently indifferent to the impression his behaviour must have produced upon his prospective employers, Laurence joined the train for Genoa on 13 April, sharing a carriage with Garibaldi and an aide-de-camp, and a huge bundle of letters which the General read and then tore into little bits. At Genoa they parted, Laurence with instructions to engage an empty diligence that would pick up ten conspirators on the outskirts of the town and take them to Nice. They would prepare matters there for Garibaldi's arrival by sea with 200 men the following Sunday, 15 April.

Thus far the details of the plan are well known. But in a letter to John Blackwood, hitherto unpublished, Laurence indicated that the real purpose was to proclaim Garibaldi President of an independent state of Nice. Whether this was ever Garibaldi's intention or a figment of Oliphant's imagination one cannot say. And if it were true, there is nothing to suggest who thought of it – Garibaldi, Oliphant, Cavour, or even Lord John Russell. But it is interesting that before Oliphant had left London, the Marquess of Clanricarde had told the House of Lords that the municipal authorities of Nice, rather than be considered a threat to France as part of a greater Italy, would prefer to be declared neutral. And privately, Clanricarde furnished Russell with letters from Nice to show that Cavour had been approached on this point and had agreed.

In any case events in Sicily overtook the adventure before it had really begun. Finding it difficult to persuade a suspicious clerk at the diligence office that even an Englishman required six horses and fifteen extra seats to take himself and his portmanteau innocently to

Nice, Laurence retreated to Garibaldi's hotel on the waterfront to think up a more convincing excuse. He found the place in uproar. Messengers were pouring in from Sicily with news of the insurrection that had broken out on 2 April. Garibaldi announced that he and all the volunteers he could collect must start at once to join in. Warmly he urged Laurence to go with him. Laurence, who rightly suspected that the torn up letters in the railway carriage had had something to do with Sicily, regretfully declined. He said he had been away from home almost as long as he was able and that affairs at the *London Review*, a new magazine in which he had a financial stake, required his presence. It may have been so but it was curiously out of character. For it meant that he gave up the chance of being the only foreigner in at the start of the famous conquest of the Kingdom of the Two Sicilies that fired the imagination of the whole of Europe. Moreover Laurence was a long standing advocate of the cause of a united Italy and found it easy to sympathize with Garibaldi's personal philosophy with its echoes of the utopian socialist doctrine of St Simon and Fourier. And what a marvellous book he would have written!

Instead he went home, calling on the way at Nice on the day of the plebiscite. In the absence of Garibaldi he found no one with either the ability to organize, the courage to execute, or the authority to control a movement against the vote. And so he said he took the only revenge he could upon a populace so weak and easily misled. Illegal though it was he procured a ballot paper and voted himself for the Nizzards' annexation to the hated France.

At the beginning of May 1860 John Blackwood was glad to hear him safely back in London and, as he put it, 'not at Cayenne'. In the same letter enclosing payment for two articles for the *Magazine* roundly denouncing the French, Blackwood told Laurence that Speke had gone off back to Central Africa, ignorant of the fact that Burton had attacked him in his newly published book *Lake Regions of Central Africa*. Laurence, who proposed to review the book (which condemned Speke's field work on the first expedition and the conclusions he drew from it), was urged by Blackwood to 'pitch in to the hound'. The whole style of Burton's remarks, said Blackwood, was in striking contrast to honest Speke's punctilious reticence and delicacy in saying nothing (in public) about the man he disliked and despised most in the world.

Society and two leaders a week kept Laurence busy for the rest of the season. He half wished he had not meddled with the *London Review* which required too much office work; he was rather of a sporting disposition, he told John Blackwood. In August came a chance to gratify this in the most exalted manner; he was invited to shoot deer by the Duke of Saxe-Coburg-Gotha, Prince Albert's elder brother, and, according to Laurence, one of the most liberal and enlightened of the German Princes. While staying at Gotha, he told Blackwood, he went over to Salzburg to assist at a meeting between the King of Bavaria and the Emperor of Austria, a spectacle he found both interesting and brilliant. He also gleaned details of a conversation one of his princely fellow guests had had with Napoleon III at the military camp at Chalons on a subject of perennial interest to him – the French Emperor's Eastern policy. And from the ducal castle Laurence wrote to Edinburgh asking his publisher to send copies of *Elgin's Mission to China and Japan* to the Duke of Coburg and Prince Albert.

By that time the book had proved a great success; according to Blackwood its style was singularily pleasant and readable, the matter not only interesting but put in a very sound judicious style. It was this capacity for judgement and the ability to express complicated issues in a succinct manner that made Laurence so valuable to his masters. For there can be little doubt – though there is no proof – that in those years, as perhaps much earlier, he was already acting as a secret agent for the British Government, using as cover his articles in *Blackwood's Magazine*, and the fact that his natural gregariousness and popularity opened many doors to him. John Blackwood must have long since guessed the truth since Laurence could not refrain from dropping hints, but he was always discreet.

At the end of August Laurence departed from Gotha to Vienna ostensibly on a visit. As travelling companions he had the Earl and Countess of Airlie and Lord Edward St Maur, son of the Duke and Duchess of Somerset. The Duchess was one of Laurence's greatest friends; she and her sister, Mrs Caroline Norton, Sheridan's daughters, were renowned in society for their brilliance and beauty. After spending a week in Vienna, Laurence and Lord Edward wandered on through Hungary staying at country houses owned by Magyar nobles. The purpose of this journey was almost certainly to assess the likely response in a part of the Austrian Empire known to be discontented, should Garibaldi land troops on the Dalmatian coast. Such a move would be designed to create an opportunity for Italy to gain what she really wanted from Austria, the province of Venetia. By the end of September Laurence had reached Belgrade where he stayed with John Longworth, his old friend from Circassian days, now Consul-General. From there he wrote a letter to Abraham Hayward in which he forecast a revolt in Hungary, Croatia, Wallachia, and Serbia, against Austria should Garibaldi invade.

Austria had only herself to blame for the disaffection in Hungary and among the Slav minorities on the borders of the Empire, Laurence reported. The whole Hungarian section of the Austrian army, some 100,000 men, were expected to desert in the event of a popular movement. 'The Croatian frontier levies consisting of 80,000 men are equally unfaithful and in the event of Garibaldi's landing on this side would in all probability join him.' Having delivered that interesting information and assisted at the installation of Prince Michael, the new Serbian head of state, Laurence told Hayward that he proposed to ride across the country to Montenegro, and to cross to Italy to call on Garibaldi.

He and Lord Edward St Maur set off through Bosnia and Herzogovina, wild and turbulent mountain regions, 'abounding in brigand bands, enchanting scenery and fleas', with the added charm to two young men of perpetual risk to life and limb consequent upon its chronic state of guerrilla war with Turkey. They emerged at the coast and crossed to Corfu where they were joined by young Mr Herbert of the Legation at Athens. When he left them there, Laurence said goodbye to them for the last time. 'I little thought when I parted from my friends to embark on board the steamer for Ancona,' he wrote, 'how tragically their young lives were to be terminated – Lord Edward to fall a victim to a bear while shooting in India and Herbert to be held to ransom by brigands and finally murdered by them near the plains of Marathon.'

Once in Italy he rolled for three days and two nights to Rome in a diligence and then to Naples. Garibaldi received him with affectionate cordiality but what, if anything, Laurence told him about the state of Austria–Hungary he never disclosed. In the hope of seeing fighting he went to Capua but found that the serious work had all been done by, among others, English volunteers, one of whom was Evelyn Ashley. His Hungarian friend, Eber, General in Garibaldi's army and correspondent of *The Times*, invited him to his headquarters at Caserta, to the vast and splendid palace Bomba had owned. Laurence was assigned the royal bedroom and found the royal bed so thickly festooned in gold, lace and satin that he doubted Bomba had ever slept in it. But he would not be fussy and got straight in.

Then, at last, Victor Emmanuel arrived to claim a kingdom at the hands of the sailor from Nice. Watching them together on the balcony from the square below Laurence recalled the day twelve years before when he was one of the mob fired on by Bomba's orders and identified the gate where he had taken refuge. Now he was listening to the voice of the deliverer standing with bowed head and in red shirt. 'Thus did United Italy owe its existence to a combination of opposite qualities in the persons of its two greatest patriots who would not work together; for it is certain that Cavour would never have created it without Garibaldi, or Garibaldi achieved success without Cavour.'

From Naples Laurence went home to resume the familiar round of pleasant excursions into society and congenial work as a journalist; success and popularity were seen to attend him. But inwardly he was just as consumed with guilt and doubt as he had always been. The difference now was that he professed to have found an answer to his longing for self-improvement and a consolation for the death of his father. This was spiritualism, which he and a great many other people affected to believe could transform their lives, as well as keeping them in touch with the dead. Some evidence of his preoccupation with the new faith appeared in letters written at this time by a friend of his, young Kate Stanley, Blanche Airlie's sister. (Kate married Lord John Russell's eldest son and became the mother of Bertrand Russell.) 'Mr Oliphant sat here for 1½ hours yesterday', she wrote, 'discoursing vehemently on spirit wrapping (sic) in which he firmly believes and he did tell us some wonderful things; a man who had never seen him before (a medium) at New York wrote a letter before him as if fr. his grand mother and signed it with her name. I cannot explain in writing but as I do not believe Mr Oliphant lies I cannot understand how it could be done.' And Kate went on, 'at present I do not feel it would be possible for me to believe in Spirits and tables etc: poor Landseer is going nearly mad from it.'

The bond of spiritualism between Lady Airlie and Laurence was one that Maria Oliphant shared. From Italy Laurence had written to her, 'I hope you will go and see Miss Fawcett. She may tell you some interesting things about Harris. I was sure you could not see him now but I am glad you have got a promise for the future.' Miss Fawcett was a very old friend of the Oliphants, a fellow Scot, and an ardent spiritualist. Vague though it was, the letter was already significant in its suggestion that the man, Harris, was both mysterious and withdrawn. It was the first mention of one who was to have the most profound influence on the life of Laurence Oliphant.

But that was not for some time yet. At the end of 1860 events in China produced a sudden shift in the log jam of his diplomatic career. In October, de Norman, First Secretary of the British Legation in Japan, who was temporarily attached to Lord Elgin's second Chinese mission, was, with others, tortured and brutally murdered. In revenge for their deaths Elgin took the controversial decision to burn the Summer Palace at Peking. In London Lord John Russell, faced with the necessity of replacing de Norman, submitted Oliphant's name to the Queen. Though he was warm in praise of de Norman, Lord John had nothing to say of Oliphant to Her Majesty beyond the dry comment that his account of Elgin's mission to China and Japan had been given with much ability. But if it was not openly expressed, Lord John's confidence in Oliphant must have been considerable and suggests that he was far from displeased at his adventures in Italy. Sir Rutherford Alcock, Minister in Japan, had applied for two years' leave; it was understood that Oliphant would act as chargé d'affaires whilst he was away. 'An exceptional appointment in one so young', commented *The Times*. (Laurence was thirty-one). It was not quite what he would have liked – though rather more than some people thought he deserved. John Blackwood was doubtful; Japan was so far away. Lady Oliphant was absolutely determined that, if Laurence went to Japan, he would not stay there long without her. There were all sorts of dangers, not least the prospect that, with little else to do in his spare time, he might marry the first available girl.

As for Laurence himself, Kate Stanley gave a candid account of his state of mind. He disliked going very much, she told her brother, Lyulph, and looked for an end to it after two years when he hoped to get an appointment in Europe. He was very anxious that Japan should not be thought his 'spécialité', so he would not learn the language. He would write another book and make large collections of stuffed birds for the British Museum. Then in a postscript Kate was moved to exclamation and underlining. 'Just think what a ridiculous report has just got about that Maude [her sister] is going to *marry* Mr *Oliphant* and going to Japan with him. Blanche was congratulated about it and Mr Oliphant also. Too ludicrous.' True or not – and one does not know – Maude Stanley never married becoming instead, as Bertrand Russell testified, the perfect aunt.

Laurence entered into the customary polite wrangle with the Foreign Office over who should pay his passage to Japan. As it was his first official mission he argued that the FO should pay, especially since the fare would cost him £200 of the £300 allowed for his outfit. Correspondence between Edmund Hammond, Permanent Under Secretary at the Office and Lord John Russell produced the decision that the Foreign Office would pay to Shanghai only, and Oliphant would have to bear the cost of Bligh, his servant. His salary was to be £800 a year, not large in comparison with those paid at Legations in Europe, but more than it appeared, for the Japanese Government, the *bakufu*, allotted coin to diplomats in greater proportion to their needs than it did to merchants. In consequence there was a profitable black market in money inside Japan.

Laurence arrived at Shanghai in early June, just missing Sir Rutherford Alcock who had gone back to Nagasaki from which port he intended to ride the 600 miles overland to Edo. This was a brave but foolish enterprise, the first time any Westerner had tried to penetrate the interior of Japan for 200 years. Alcock intended it as a demonstration of his government's determination to enforce the right of passage given under the Treaty of 1858. But, though the Western signatories did not know it, the Mikado had not yet ratified it; moreover he was unlikely to do so for all foreigners were beginning to meet with hostility and violence from the Japanese. Just as Laurence had foreseen in 1858, the shock of opening the country had produced a violent dislike of strangers. The Japanese had suffered from inflation and lack of food after the coming of the merchants and resented their arrogant behaviour. Savage attacks were made upon foreigners by swordsmen who inflicted terrifying wounds. In January 1860 the slaughter of Henry Heusken, Townsend Harris's secretary, provoked the most serious crisis yet. Poor Heusken was only twenty-four; all that remained of his remarkable knowledge of Japan was in Laurence Oliphant's book.

After Heusken's murder Alcock led a retreat from Edo by foreign diplomats to the relative safety of the port of Kanagawa (Yokohama). Townsend Harris refused to go, preferring to rely on the Japanese to protect him, thereby earning the undying gratitude and esteem of the *bakufu* and the lasting hostility of Sir Rutherford Alcock. During the months spent at Kanagawa the British Minister appeared harassed, tired, and extremely nervous. From Kanagawa, in October 1860, he wrote to Hammond hoping that the Foreign Office would send out a good Secretary of Legation so that his leave might not be long delayed. 'You little know what a life this is to lead away from all civilizing influences in a state of most utter isolation,' Alcock complained; 'no man can bear it for many years without deterioration both moral and physical.' This letter arrived in London nearly three months later, when arrangements were being made for Laurence's journey to Japan. Lord John Russell's reaction to it was that Oliphant had better catch the first available boat.

The Foreign Secretary's concern was well founded; Alcock's state of mind undoubtedly contributed to his decision to ignore the advice of the *bakufu* against venturing into the interior of Japan. By the time Laurence arrived at the Shogun's capital at the beginning of July 1861, Alcock had left Nagasaki and was travelling slowly across the islands towards Edo. The British Legation where Laurence was to live was accommodated in the temple of Tozenji near the great Imperial highway into Edo, the Tokkaido. It was a vast and scrambling place in a valley surrounded by trees, dense as a jungle and very difficult to defend. But the diplomats had recently returned there from Kanagawa having had copious assurances as to their safety from the *bakufu*. Laurence, who found the country sadly changed, considered that the conditions which the envoys would be obliged to endure raised serious questions as to the advisability of their return. He saw at once that issue would have to be raised with the *bakufu* over it. He described the very irksome restraints in a letter to the Duchess of Somerset. There were 300 guards round the temple; eight followed him wherever he went and prevented him from talking to people. 'If my servant runs after a butterfly a two sworded official runs after him.' Most galling was the attitude they were expected to adopt. As long as they were respectful towards the *daimyo*, the barons, and the *samurai*, the swordsmen, they were safe. Humility was the thing, Laurence decided. 'A true Christian who exercised the highest of Christian graces might live here in perfect safety all his life.' He did not openly pose the question how long he thought he, or anyone else, could stand it, but occupied himself in the days before Alcock's return by starting a collection of rare insects destined for the British Museum. Bligh was useful in this, having once had a master versed in such things. By the time Alcock arrived there was a substan-

Laurence Oliphant in 1854, aged 25

Laurence Oliphant on the Quarter Deck of HMS *Furious*, 1858. Photographed by the Captain, Sherard Osborn

Laurence Oliphant as Lord Frank Vanecourt. From the drawing by Richard Doyle for *Piccadilly*, (1870 edition)

tial collection, impaled on pins, laid out on the table under the window of Bligh's room.

The members of the Legation sat up late the night Alcock returned. There was much to discuss and Alcock and Oliphant had not met before. The journey across Japan had been fascinating but odd. Screens of cotton cloth were erected in all the villages through which Alcock passed, blocking the view down every street. Crowds of people came to stare at him, not in the more remote parts where it might have been expected, but as he and his retinue were on the Tokkaido, drawing near to Edo. As they approached Tozenji they noticed that all the tea houses were closed. Besides these strange events, Alcock told him that his friend from his previous visit, Higo no Kami, had committed ritual suicide as one of the officials responsible for opening Japan to the detested foreigners.

So, when Laurence went to bed it was not to sleep. As he lay in the dark a dog began to growl and the watchman's rattle sounded from an inner courtyard. Seizing the nearest available weapon, a heavy hunting crop, Laurence jumped over the dog into the narrow corridor leading to the main rooms of the temple. Out of the darkness came a black and silent figure that cut at him with a long two handed sword. Yelling for help he struck out with the whip trying to entangle the sword in its lash but he felt a blow bite into his shoulder. Another encountered his left arm raised to protect his head and inflicted a very severe wound on his wrist. A flash and a loud report behind him signalled the arrival of a colleague, George Morrison, who fired point blank at the assassin. The bullet glanced off his sword. A second Japanese appeared at whom Morrison fired and missed; he received a cut across his head. As silently as they had come the swordsmen departed. Bleeding profusely Laurence and Morrison reeled into Alcock's office where they found him unhurt, with two other members of the staff, and Bligh, who had crashed head first through the paper wall. Two swordsmen had climbed in at his window but he had been saved because they stepped with bare feet onto the pins of his insect collection. By then the Legation guards were aroused and the sound of cutting, slashing, and screaming approached. Faint with loss of blood Laurence urged his colleagues to escape into the garden but they refused. Suddenly the noise stopped to be followed by the appearance of smiling, bowing Japanese officers congratulating them on their fortunate escape. In the dining-room where the principal encounter had taken place a severed head lay under the sideboard, the body in the middle of the room; another had its face shorn off. Staggering barefoot across the room Laurence trod on something like an oyster; it was a human eye.

The rest of the night was spent on the alert; great bonfires were built in the temple grounds and the guard reinforced. In the morning Laurence discovered that his life had been saved by a beam in the ceiling of the corridor on which the assassin's sword had caught. At midday a detachment of British sailors arrived, sent in haste from HMS *Ringdove*, lying providentially off Kanagawa. With them came the French Minister, 'pour partager les dangers,' he said. Laurence was removed to *Ringdove* which anchored in Edo bay. For three days he was in acute discomfort, red as a lobster with prickly heat. It hurt to lie on his side because of his wounded arm and on his back because of his boils. To make matters worse ophthalmia attacked both eyes. In a temperature of 93 degrees, with mosquitoes whining maddeningly out of reach, he lay in the dark and endured. And being Laurence he pondered the object of it all. The answer he found was reassuringly simple, 'whatever is, is best. I have such a profound feeling of being in God's hands and having nothing to do with my fate that gratitude even would be presumptuous.' This, he told his mother, was his creed or philosophy. Tested by his nearness to death he found it quite satisfactory.

> 'Live I, so live I,
> To my Lord heartily,
> To my Prince faithfully,
> To my neighbour honestly,
> Die I, so die I.'

If only he could have left it at that.

Laurence did not blame the Japanese for the attack but he recognized that it would have very serious repercussions. It was the outcome of England forcing herself on a people who had never wanted her; the upshot would be a war or a summary withdrawal. 'If we are withdrawn I shall feel very much my tail between my legs; if we go to war I shall go in for looting *daimyos*' palaces and feel a blackguard.' Most unusually the Shogun took notice of the attack and, to prove his sympathy, sent Alcock some ducks and a pot of sugar. The Legation had in fact been invaded by 29 men; two were killed outright, and three committed suicide when tracked down the following day. One was captured and executed, the rest escaped. On the body of one of the dead in the Legation was found a paper which read; 'I, though I am a person of low standing, have not patience to stand by and see the sacred Empire defiled by foreigners . . . This time I have determined in my heart to undertake to follow out my master's will . . . If this thing . . . may cause the foreigners to retire and partly tranquillize the minds of the Mikado and Government I shall take to myself the highest praise. Regardless of my own life I am determined to set out.'

Although there were rumours that the instigator of the attack was the xenophobic Prince of Mito, the most persistent rumours blamed the Prince of Tsushima. This was the most likely explanation, Alcock told the Foreign Secretary (now Earl Russell). Russians had lately landed on his island and to revenge their depredations some foreigner must be killed. The choice fell on Alcock who was known to be at Nagasaki, the nearest port to Tsushima. But he departed for Edo before the Prince's assassins came up with him and they could not attack him on rival *daimyo* territory. The next chance was between Kanagawa and Edo on the Tokkaido, which explained the crowd of people who stared at him there and the fact that the tea houses were closed. But it too was missed. So the Prince's retainers set upon the Legation itself.

Laurence's wounds healed rapidly. But Alcock, who had started his career as a doctor, was concerned that the cut on his wrist might deprive him permanently of the use of his hand. Although he knew it meant postponing his own much needed leave of absence, he recommended that Laurence should go home for treatment. But first there was secret and urgent work to be done, word of which Laurence must carry to the Foreign Secretary in person. Alcock knew that if there was to be war with Japan it would require careful preparation. The alternative, summary withdrawal, was unthinkable since it would almost certainly mean abandoning the country to the Russians. And to keep an eye on Russian movements in the Far East had been the principal object of his secret instructions on being appointed Her Majesty's first Minister to Japan. For the time being at least some sort of accommodation would have to be reached with the *bakufu*, the Shogun's government. Fortunately the *bakufu* proved to be of the same mind, so that Laurence came to be present at one of the most curious and historic meetings in the history of Japan.

Until after the attack on the English Legation in July 1861 the foreign envoys in Japan had been groping in the dark; as Alcock put it, fighting with shadows. Behind the shadow they knew was a substantial power but they could not discern its shape. They looked upon the Shogun at Edo as the effective temporal power and upon the Mikado at Kyoto as nothing more than a puppet of ceremony. They had not yet realized that under the stress of foreign intervention the country had begun to turn away from Edo towards Kyoto and, though they were suspicious, they did not know for certain that the Mikado had refused to ratify the treaties under which the country had been opened to the hated foreigner. Now for its own ends in the struggle with the Mikado, the *bakufu* determined to reveal something of the true state of the country. On 4 August therefore, Alcock, Laurence Oliphant and Admiral Hope, commander of the British naval forces who had just arrived, rode in state with a detachment of marines through the streets of Edo, 'densely crowded with scowling multitudes', said Laurence, to the Ministry of Foreign Affairs. There for the first time the two Japanese Ministers responsible for Foreign Affairs sent away their retainers, the Vice-Governors and the official spies and, with one interpreter, sat down to talk directly and fairly frankly to the three Englishmen. In his *compte rendu* of the meeting Laurence noted how relieved the Ministers appeared at the absence of their entourage.

They asked for the postponement of the opening of three ports to foreign trade due under the 1858 treaty. They feared that if this were not granted there would be further discontent among the people; they needed seven years' grace to soothe them and to grow more food. They explained how the Shogun had fought his way to the temporal throne in the sixteenth century; since then, they said there had been only small disturbances until the present day – 'this is the first time anything important has taken place'. To open Osaka and Hiogo would be especially dangerous since these ports were near Kyoto, the Mikado's capital. The Mikado lived shut away from the outside world and only communicated through women who misinformed him, they explained. Here Alcock asked them point blank if the Mikado had ratified the treaties. No doubt he had, was the equivocal reply, but now he knew how unsatisfactory things were and was very much dissatisfied. 'He has some very unruly subjects,' they said; 'this is a secret,' they hastened to add. If Osaka and Hiogo were opened to trade there was no saying what collision might be brought about between the Mikado and the Shogun. This was the crux of the matter. Alcock refused to consider any postponement so the Ministers announced that a special embassy would be sent to

Europe to put their demand directly to the Western governments.

They then broached the very delicate subject of the Russian presence on Tsushima. The island occupied a very important strategic position between Japan and the Korean peninsula. In March a Russian frigate had landed men there on the pretext of doing repairs; there had been clashes with the local people, and now the captain refused to go away. If the English would give help against the Russians, the Ministers said, the *bakufu* would open a port on Tsushima to trade. Alcock was nothing loath, seeing a chance for England to gain a very useful advantage over the Russians. But he hastened to add in a confidential despatch to the Foreign Office that this could only be contemplated as part of a general plan in regard to Japan and other Powers. So delicate was the matter that Alcock promised that Laurence Oliphant would repeat what he could not write on his return, which was to take place at once.

When, towards the end of August, Admiral Hope set out for Tsushima in his flagship *Ringdove*, Laurence Oliphant was on board. At Fatchio, capital of Tsushima, Laurence found the Prince's officials reluctant to admit the presence of any Russian ship. After some prodding they confirmed the substance of the *bakufu*'s story but declined to say where the Russians were. So *Ringdove* went exploring; as she rounded the island so the reason for the Russian venture at once became clear. Forty miles away across the strait the highlands of Korea were clearly visible, the southern tip of the huge peninsula to whose northern frontier the Russians had already advanced. Now, unless she received some check, Laurence thought she would undoubtedly take over all of it. Cruising along the coast of Tsushima *Ringdove* found a broad inlet. Inside it they looked with amazement at a perfect skein of narrow channels overhung with huge trees; the water was deep and very still, now and again the channel broadened out into a large pool. Whole fleets could be safely hidden at such an anchorage.

Rounding a corner, spars appeared among the trees and, behold, the Russian frigate, *Possadnik*, moored to the shore with a gangplank down and bamboo pipes bringing water on board. Her master, Captain Barileff, though no doubt shattered to see *Ringdove* at the entrance to his hiding place, received Laurence with commendable *sang froid*. In answer to the question of what on earth he was doing there he said he was completing a hydrographical survey. 'Looking through the cabin window from which was visible a farmyard with a cow and poultry,' Laurence wrote, 'I asked him if he combined agriculture with hydrography.' Barileff was forced to admit he was doing a little farming but, he insisted, only to pass the time. Walking about on shore Laurence found a flagstaff with a Russian flag, substantial buildings including a sick bay, a brick kiln, and the beginnings of a 'Russian steam bath'. This greatly worried Admiral Hope since he thought it meant the Russians were preparing to spend the winter there. A strong diplomatic protest was made to the Russian fleet commander at Olga Bay and in due course *Possadnik* cast off her agricultural responsibilities and sailed.

In his report of the incident to the Foreign Office Laurence remarked that the *bakufu* had obviously been frightened by the Russians and had only offered the port on Tsushima to placate them and everyone else. Tsushima was useless said Laurence, but Chusan across the straits would make a capital port. Not only was there a vast natural harbour but the hinterland was very rich. What better way to frustrate Russian designs on Korea than to plant an open port on the very coast they desired? He was years ahead of his time, for Korean resistance to Western penetration was, if anything, stronger than that of Japan. But he offered the suggestion as another move in that great game which, long familiar to those facing Russia in the West, was now to be played with increasing vigour in the East.

From Tsushima Laurence started on the long journey home. He reached England in October 1861, delivered a letter from the Shogun to the Queen, and was immediately invited to stay with Palmerston at Broadlands. There was no doubt in anyone's mind that he would return to Japan as soon as he was fit – his wounds had healed but he had lost the use of several fingers. On the way home he had called at Canton and talked to the Consul, Harry Parkes, with whom he had become friendly during Elgin's Mission. Parkes wrote to his wife about Oliphant. They had discussed the possibility that Alcock might resign. If the post were offered to Oliphant he could hardly refuse, as it was 'a post of danger', although Lady Oliphant would be much against it. He would be the right man in the right place, Parkes thought; 'he is very able and has already mastered a most complicated and difficult subject'.

CHAPTER 5

SECRET AGENT

EVEN though he was still convalescent, Laurence remained at the bidding of the Foreign Secretary. The time he had to rest at home was very short; events in Italy caused Lord Russell to call upon him for a special purpose. On 4 January 1862 Russell wrote to Oliphant, 'You told me when I saw you that you would be ready to undertake any journey in the public service which I should think useful.' He would much like to have a trustworthy account of the state of feeling in Italy, said Russell, especially in the Centre and South. He would like Oliphant to go through Venice and Trieste and thence to Corfu and Naples, consult General La Marmora, the Commander-in-Chief of Victor Emmanuel's forces at Naples and in Calabria, and return via Florence, Bologna and Turin, where Sir James Hudson was still Minister. The Foreign Office would afford him enough money to pay his expenses, Russell assured him; he must set out within a fortnight.

Russell and his Under-Secretary at the Foreign Office, Austen Henry Layard, were particularly bothered about Italy that winter since there were rumours that reaction had set in against further unification. People were reported to be aspiring to preserve Venetia to Austria, and it was thought opponents of the cause had even infiltrated Victor Emmanuel's army. Oliphant would make a special attempt to determine the strength of the contending parties at Trieste and Ancona, centres of the disaffection, Russell told Layard. On a larger scale, whatever happened in Italy was likely to affect the precarious balance of the rest of Europe.

In his familiar guise of an idle, well to do, inquisitive, and eccentric young man, reinforced by a new aura of interest resulting from his wound, Laurence set out on the first stage of his journey which was announced as part of his convalescence. How fit he was after his Japanese experience we do not know, but he did not recover the use of his fingers for a very long time. At Vienna he stumbled across the best possible cover, though the risk he ran in adopting it was acute and not only for himself. The twenty-year-old Prince of Wales was at Vienna on his way to the Near East. Laurence was invited to join him as far as Corfu, which meant that he would be a member of the Prince's suite during his visit to Venice and Trieste, the areas in which Russell was most interested. He promptly announced the invitation in a letter to his friend, Madame Blaze de Bury (a Scot married to a Frenchman; a writer, and acquaintance of Kinglake). After Corfu he would go on to Southern Italy in the hope that Lord Russell might have 'something for him' as he was tired of idleness and sport, Laurence told Madame de Bury. As an attempt to conceal from the Austrians what he was up to in Venetia this was audacious but, quite likely, effective since Madame de Bury was a close friend of the Austrian Foreign Minister, Count Rechberg.

The Prince's journey took place at the Queen's command in the bitter aftermath of the Prince Consort's death, six weeks before, and Russell, for one, had hoped that she would not be so cruel as to insist upon it. The Prince's Governor who was travelling with him, was Elgin's younger brother, Robert Bruce. He knew Laurence Oliphant from the days of Elgin's Governor-Generalship in Canada, and now he seized upon him as a means to distract the sad and bruised young Prince from his grief. In this Bruce was more successful than he could have hoped since it was the beginning of a lifelong friendship between the two. The Prince appreciated Laurence's ease of manner and wit and, as the years went by, found distraction in the contemplation of his friend's increasingly odd adventures. Denied access to matters of state by the Queen's command, Albert Edward nevertheless came to be passionately interested in foreign affairs; with his wide experience and shrewd judgement, Laurence Oliphant was one of those on whom the Prince relied for his information. And apart from more serious matters, they shared a weakness for attractive women. Whenever he was in England Oliphant stayed often at Sandringham, dined at Marlborough House, and was regularly in the Prince's company at the Cosmopolitan Club.

At this, their first encounter, Laurence expressed an opinion of the Prince of Wales that neither the Queen nor his other acquaintances shared, but which came to be recognized as wise and farsighted. He suggested that the Prince was rarely done justice to in the public estimation. 'I think his development will be far higher than people anticipate. Then his temper and disposition are charming. His defects are rather the inevitable consequences of his position which never allows him any responsibility or forces him into action.' From Corfu Laurence wrote to Lord Russell hoping that he would not disapprove of his having joined the Prince. It had given him an opportunity to visit Venice without exciting suspicion, and he had been most circumspect about gathering information while in such a delicate position. When the Royal party went on to Trieste they were invited to the nearby castle of Miramar by the Archduke Ferdinand Max, who was shortly to leave for Mexico, there to reign as the ill-fated Emperor Maximilian, and confirm the truth of Oliphant's warning about the dangers lurking in Central America.

After taking leave of the Prince of Wales at Corfu, Laurence crossed to Albania and made for Scutari its capital. He had heard strong rumours of a landing by Garibaldi on the Dalmatian coast, he told Russell, and had also had reports of organized disaffection in the Slavonic and Greek provinces of Turkey. Scutari was a good place to investigate these rumours. French and Russian agents there were stirring up the Christian population against the Turks, and the Turks would only be able to cope with the unrest by using such methods as the rest of Europe would condemn (these were prophetic words). In this all Laurence's sympathy was on the side of Turkey; he regarded it as essential to keep her strong whatever the cost, in order to counter-balance Russia. Scutari, he discovered, was also a centre for the revolutionary movement against United Italy, so he did his best to find out where the armed bands he had heard of were to land on the Italian coast, at the same time as pursuing the possibility that United Italian groups had been formed to foment discord in Turkey – to the detriment of Austria. 'What a curious tangle!' he exclaimed to Layard, and urged him to appoint a good man as Consul at Scutari.

Then, in obedience to Russell's instructions, he went back to Italy and wandered through the provinces that had passed to Victor Emmanuel as a result of Garibaldi's triumph at Naples. It was a remote and primitive country through which he and Bligh travelled. At Manfredonia, which even he described as an out of the way place, Laurence was diverted from the collection of information about conspiratorial landings by an unexpected invitation to tea, marked 'old English style', which was delivered by a little girl in the name of a Miss Thimbleby. Politely accepting, he found an extraordinarily old woman in the darkness of a tumbledown and deserted palazzo in the centre of the sleepy town. Trembling with excitement and pleasure, speaking half Italian, half English, she told him she had come there with her brother when he was appointed Consul in 1804. Her sister had been Mrs Jordan, mistress of William IV. Miss Thimbleby asked Laurence where he was staying and received the name of his hotel with satisfaction – that was where the English always stayed, she said. Why, he replied, he didn't know the English often came to Manfredonia? 'Oh yes', she said, 'there was an English family staying there in 1829.'

This curious encounter was followed by an even more extraordinary event, for as he resumed his journey and drove into the little town of Salmona he was met by a band, flags flying, women waving handkerchiefs, and crowds lining the streets. In the square where his carriage stopped, the band struck up 'God Save the Queen' and the Mayor advanced to welcome him. Laurence, bewildered, suggested they had got the wrong person, to which the Mayor replied that they were well aware he wished to travel incognito but could not regard it seriously. 'We could not allow Lord Palmerston's nephew to pass through our town without making some demonstration of respect in token of the gratitude we feel for your illustrious relative.' To argue would be not only useless but impolite, Laurence felt. So, promoting an unsuspecting Bligh to be his secretary, in which capacity he was taken in charge by a group of polite men in swallow-tailed coats, they passed through a lane of applauding spectators to the town hall where fifty of them dined on champagne and other delicacies. When the speeches began, compliments were lavished on England in general, and Palmerston in particular. Laurence never gave any hint of how he supposed this glorious mistake had come about. It is possible that the townspeople confused him with Evelyn Ashley who had been at Naples in 1860 and worn the red shirt; it is also possible that, for reasons known only to himself, Laurence made use of his name. However it occurred, the address the town of Salmona directed to Palmerston reached him safely, to his Lordship's great amusement.

By the time Laurence reached Naples his official and private roles were thoroughly confused. His instructions there had been to see General La Marmora, Commander-in-Chief of Victor Emmanuel's army, and to make a report on the state of feeling in the army and among the civilian population of the area it controlled. But he found that La Marmora had received no word of this, nor did Laurence carry letters of introduction – for obvious reasons. So, he told Russell, he had had to approach La Marmora on the basis of his personal acquaintance with him. The General had commanded the Sardinian contingent which fought on the side of the French and English in the Crimea; it is possible, therefore, that Laurence met him before Sebastopol in 1855. Otherwise he must have made contact with him at Turin or Naples in 1860. As a result of the General's intervention Laurence was able to move freely in Calabria and Sicily and was received with kindness and given information wherever he went. He was horrified, therefore, when, having sent his report to Turin for transmission to the Foreign Office in London, Sir James Hudson proposed to show it to King Victor Emmanuel. Laurence begged Russell not to permit this as it would be a poor return for the frankness and civility he had been shown; he might bear the opprobrium such an act would incur, he told Russell, but not the slur on his honour. 'I entirely approve his conduct', the Foreign Secretary minuted.

What use was made of the knowledge collected on this uncomfortable and sometimes dangerous journey is not known. Laurence did not even extract the usual amount of material for *Blackwood's Magazine*; he told its publisher he had had many adventures, but on this occasion must consider his pen at the disposal of his masters. But one proposal he made as a result of it so impressed Russell that he put it to Palmerston. 'I quite agree with you,' the Prime Minister replied, 'that there can be no Harm in letting Oliphant try his Hand at Vienna to persuade Austria to acknowledge the Kingdom of Italy. If that could be accomplished without any conditions the Italians could reasonably object to it would be a very good thing. But Austria would naturally require some engagement on the Part of the Italian Government tending to secure to Austria the quiet Possession of Venetia and possibly Austria might also ask some stipulation in favour of the temporal Power of the Pope over Rome.' And so, on 14 July 1862, Lord Russell presented his humble duty to Queen Victoria and told her that he proposed to send Mr Oliphant to Vienna on a private mission without any ostensible character. Mr Oliphant would ascertain the views of the Cabinet of Vienna about the recognition of Italy but not make any definite proposals. 'Lord Palmerston concurs in the opinion of Lord Russell in respect to Mr Oliphant', the Foreign Secretary told the Queen, but sadly neglected to record what that opinion was.

On his way to Vienna Laurence delivered a letter on the subject of Italy to King Leopold of the Belgians but was not received, as the

King was ill. In any case, Leopold wrote to Russell when he had recovered, the subject was so difficult that, try as he might, he could do little to reconcile the opposing parties. There is nothing in Oliphant's own hand to show what arguments he put to the Cabinet at Vienna but there is a hint of what they might have been in a letter from Russell to Julian Fane, Secretary of Embassy at Vienna. It would be a great pity, Russell told Fane, if the Austrian Foreign Minister, Count Rechberg, refused to recognize Italy; it was not too much to say that Austria would probably lose Venetia by such obstinacy. If the Emperor Franz Joseph would recognize the greater part of the Kingdom of Italy and give over the civil government of Venetia to the ex Grand Duke of Tuscany with the title of Duke of Venetia, telling him to employ none but Venetians in civil affairs, 'there would be some chance that Venice would be preserved to the House of Hapsburg'.

It was not to be. His mission completed, however unsuccessfully, Laurence was at liberty to do as he pleased. It was August, when the fashionable world dispersed to the ends of Europe. He went to Bad Homburg with Algernon Mitford, later Lord Redesdale, who seemed to think that he was still weak and in need of care after his experience in Japan. Redesdale, who described Oliphant as just then becoming interested in spiritualism which afterwards played such a large part in his life, summed him up as 'a mystic in lavender kid gloves'. The Victorians used the phrase, lavender kid gloves, to signify someone who was over fastidious and languid – a curious view of Oliphant considering his active life and close acquaintance with the more savage parts of the world. But a similar impression of him at this time is given in Henry Adams's account of him; it may be that Laurence was in the grip of one of his recurring bouts of depression and this was how it appeared to others.

In December 1862, Adams, who was the son of the US Minister to the Court of St James, was invited to Fryston Hall in Yorkshire by Monckton Milnes, writer, politician, Fellow of the Royal Geographical Society and bibliophile (his collection of erotica was celebrated among those who knew of its existence). It was a cold and foggy time and Mrs Milnes was away, so the five men present, Adams said, had nothing to do but astonish each other. He described a man of thirty with his arm in a sling whom he had already seen at Lady Palmerston's. Oliphant's figure and bearing were sympathetic – almost pathetic, and he had a certain grave and gentle charm. He seemed exceptionally sane and peculiarly suited for country houses where every man would enjoy his company and every woman would adore him. Also present was Algernon Swinburne, like a tropical bird, high crested, long beaked and quick moving, with rapid utterances and screams of humour. Dinner was easy and informal, and during it Oliphant told the story of his Japanese experience simply; after that, and far into the night, Swinburne dominated the proceedings. Adams then became friendly with Oliphant who, with Evelyn Ashley, helped to get him elected to some London clubs. 'All the world knew and loved Oliphant,' Adams concluded, 'but he disappointed in the way that all the world knows.'

That was to come. For the moment Laurence was still very much sought after in society. Redesdale described how he was one of the few young men privileged to be admitted into Lady Palmerston's inner circle at her famous Saturday parties at Cambridge House and, in December, there was another glimpse of him in Lord Palmerston's diary. They were both guests of Lord Broughton; one cold morning they rode together to Stonehenge.

In the New Year this gentle way of life suddenly changed. Simmering unrest in Poland, inspired by progress towards freedom in Italy and similarly fomented by Napoleon III, broke out into open revolution. On 22 January 1863 thousands of young men faced with conscription into the Russian Army took to the woods and swamps instead. Factions which had worked secretly and in isolation for years, like mercury coalesced under the threat of Russian force. The Poles looked to France to make good her promise and to England, above all to Palmerston, to act in their support. To many it seemed the time had come to break the power that Russia, Prussia, and Austria between them held over land that belonged to no one else but Poles, but whose geographical position made it Europe's hostage. Bismarck took the Russian side and, in February, concluded an agreement allowing the Tsar's soldiers to pursue rebellious Poles across the Prussian border. Austria held back and in those parts of Poland under her control exercised authority less harshly, or perhaps just less efficiently, so that Cracow near the Galician border quickly became the centre for the political organization of the revolution. Bands of partisans were formed there, arms and money collected there. It was to Cracow that Laurence Oliphant went first.

Needless to say, as in the case of Italy in 1860, he maintained that he went on his own initiative. This time he waxed philosophical about the purpose of his going, presenting himself as a student of revolutions at large, as an explorer of men's motives at such a time. 'Instead of plunging into the centre of Africa to discover the sources of the Nile like Speke and Grant why not dive into the sources of revolutions? Why confine exploration to physical geography when there are so many moral and political geographical problems yet unsolved?' he demanded. In fact, as the Royal Archives show, he was sent to Poland by order of the Foreign Secretary. The Poles suspected as much; *Czas*, a newspaper published at Cracow, remarked that his object in being there must be known to Palmerston. That was so. On 27 March Oliphant took the opportunity of a safe courier to send Lord Russell an account of the situation. He said he had arrived in Cracow the day after the defeat of the insurgent army under the popular leader Langiewicz. He foresaw that the fight would be carried on by guerrilla warfare which was likely to succeed since the Poles were undismayed and the Russian Army demoralized. But the Poles lacked arms and were confused by the attitude of the Austrian authorities which was hostile one minute and lax the next. Three days later he sent Henry Layard a detailed account of the strength of the guerrilla leaders on the frontier with Austria and reported that he was off to Lemberg to investigate rumours of insurgent activity there. Lemberg, which he reached after a ten hour journey by train, was in the grip of driving snow and a bitter wind. Apart from the fact that the Poles were all dressed in black to signify mourning for their country, you would scarcely know a revolution was in progress, Laurence said; it was Easter and the insurgents had gone home for a few days. But soon he was in touch with the people organizing the bands of partisans. What help he brought them we do not know but the message he gave to them was to beware of French offers of help and not to trust the Emperor Napoleon. It was Palmerston's fear that Napoleon III would make use of the Polish insurrection to create mischief wherever he could, and more specifically to move French troops across the Rhine.

From Lemberg Oliphant went to Warsaw which he reached with difficulty since the bridges had been destroyed. There he made contact with members of the clandestine Central Committee. These insurgent leaders moved so often and so fast that it took the Russians fifteen months to catch up with them. (When they did the revolt was finally and bloodily suppressed.) Laurence wrote admiringly of the way in which the Central Committee conducted its affairs under the Russians' noses. It made use of the Government telegraph for the transmission of its information, the Government machinery for the promulgation of its orders, and the Government police for carrying out its decrees – in fact of almost everybody in Poland except the Russian Army, the peasants of certain districts, and Marquis Wielopolski, the Russian-appointed Polish Governor, a fat and forceful man who reminded Laurence of a cross between Yeh and Count Cavour. Since everyone was in the secret anyway, Laurence made little attempt to preserve his incognito, but adopted a pair of coloured trousers and a hat; as no native Pole would be seen dead in either at that particular time, he hoped that this attire would protect him from the attentions of the Russians and the police. Among the Poles who helped him, the only one he named was Count Adam Potocki whose family had large estates in the east and were hereditary Governors of Brody.

One of his contacts made it possible for him to visit a group of partisans in hiding. In order to do this he had to pretend he was leaving for Berlin. He got his passport stamped and boarded the train with his friend. At a small and isolated station they got off and found a springless cart drawn by two fresh horses waiting for them. This bounced and shook them down a rough road and through a town inhabited solely by Jews, to a pine and beech forest into which they plunged. At a farmhouse in a desolate clearing they found the band, romantic looking men on high-mettled horses, with flags waving from their lances (rifles were scarce) and tricolour ribbons floating from their square fur caps. They wore long jackboots and massive spurs and broad belts garnished with revolvers, and swords jingled at their sides. They moved at night, falling upon the Russians and carrying off their weapons. By day they retreated deep into the forest where they built great roaring fires and, said Laurence, comforted themselves with warmth and tobacco. That was something he well understood being all his life a very heavy smoker. They paid for their supplies with drafts upon the elusive Central Committee which were always honoured without question. To hear them sing the Polish national anthem was to be deeply moved, said Laurence, who found the keen imagination, courage, and energy of the Poles irresistible.

But though his mood was, as always, quickened by the unfamiliar surroundings and people, and elated by the prospect of action, and his mind engaged by the complexities of the situation, he was under no illusion as to the horror facing the Poles. He attended the summary execution of a peasant suspected of collaborating; he met mothers whose sons had been killed or deported; he watched his friend's wife entertain the partisan leaders, white with anxiety at the risk they brought with them – 'but no words escaped her lips except those which were kind and hospitable'. Laurence conceived an intense admiration for the women of Poland, whose tenderness was mixed with sympathy for the cause, and inextinguishable patriotism. This led them to acts of increasing devotion and self-sacrifice. It was with these images in his mind that he wrote to Layard pleading for help to be given to the Poles; they had fixed their eyes and their hopes on England and he trusted they would not be disappointed. Those hopes were never realized, for though the English government eventually sent a strong protest to Russia about their treatment of the Poles, Palmerston would not be persuaded to do any more.

Although he returned to England in April, Laurence kept a close watch on events in Poland. During the summer, which he spent in the usual agreeable manner, he heard that one of his closest Polish friends had been placed in solitary confinement, that the leader of the band he had visited in the forest had been captured and shot, that women who had offered him hospitality were in prison and threatened with flogging, and that the Archbishop of Warsaw with whom he had discussed the rebellion had been exiled to Siberia. So it was in no light mood that he prepared to return to Poland in September. This was again on orders from the Foreign Secretary, who wanted to discover the truth of reports of Russian atrocities against the Poles in Ruthenia, and of claims that the country would shortly rise against the Tsar.

Laurence's travelling companion on this occasion was Evelyn Ashley. Ruthenia was a far distant country, beyond railways, even without regular arrangements for travel by coach. After days in the train spent crossing a large expanse of Europe, they arrived at Lemberg at the end of the line, with the vast and largely trackless Russian plain before them. At Lemberg they bought a carriage and hired a Russian-speaking servant.

Before they set out Ashley wrote to his step-grandfather in terms that must have given Palmerston cause for regret if not for a change of mind. The Poles were now in the depths of despair, Ashley said, and accused England of abandoning them. 'Hope of (England) has buoyed them up; what was written and spoken encouraged them to go on and now they are left in the lurch and abandoned to atrocities.'

The Austrian government, which in the beginning winked at the doings of the insurgents, now brought her whole might to crush them. In Cracow insurgents had been shot and the prison at Lemberg was crowded with people suspected of hiding rebels. Austria's harsh action was attributed to the line taken by the English Government, and Russia's excesses also to English policy. 'The Poles now say if (England) would help us, recognize us as belligerents. This will prevent Russians and Austrians from shooting us like dogs and will enable us to raise a loan, will give us opportunities for getting arms and with this we shall get through the winter.' Ashley said that he and Oliphant had visited farmhouses on the Galician border and seen the numbers of wounded men being tended by Polish women. One of those they met was Countess Augusta Potocka; Palmerston might recall sitting beside her at dinner at Windsor Castle.

From Lemberg they went a night's journey to Brody near the frontier which stayed in Laurence's mind as a town of Jews who buzzed and swarmed in the arcaded market square, strange in their numbers and in their distinctive attire; long coats, long beards, long curled locks and stiff black hats. Though he spoke of them with the unthinking contempt that was the fashion in those days, Jews had always claimed his attention wherever they were. Now he was to come to know them better, for the region he and Ashley were to traverse was the centre of their European homeland. It was his fate to go back to Brody nearly twenty years later when he would be hailed as Moses come to lead the Jews to their new Promised Land.

Four skinny ponies dragged their big carriage painfully across the sandy plain towards the Russian frontier. Progress was slow and soon the sand was so deep they had to get out and walk. At the customs house on the Russian side they were halted altogether. Laurence said the Russians were determined to find some excuse for refusing them entry. They began by accusing their servant of having a criminal record but abandoned this when an inspection of their baggage revealed altogether more damning evidence. This was a metal pin in the shape of a Polish eagle, a map of the country they hoped to cross, and a *Bradshaw's Railway Guide*. For eight hours Oliphant and Ashley sat in their carriage under a blazing sun while the custom house talked to Kiev by telegraph. Soon they were as keen to leave Russia as they had been to enter it – which in the course of several visits, Laurence said, he had always found to be the case. At last their expulsion was decreed. The map was considered much too dangerous to leave in the hands of customs officials, and instructions were given that it should be sent to Kiev. The pin and the *Bradshaw* were given into the custody of a Cossack who was to escort them to the border. There he presented them to the travellers with as much form and ceremony, said Laurence, as if he were returning their swords, 'while we, once more armed with our Railway Guide bade him a reckless and defiant adieu and hugged to our grateful bosoms that true evidence of an enlightened country in an advanced state of civilization'.

It does not seem that their purpose was greatly affected by this summary rebuff. Enough information existed on the Austrian side of the border to give them a clear picture of the country they had come to inspect. So they turned their thoughts to the next stage of their mission and rattled and jolted south in the dust and lingering heat of the great central plains to Jassy in Moldavia. There they embarked upon the most delightful of adventures; one that Laurence enjoyed far more than any other at the time, a charming account of which he gave in his book, *Episodes in a Life of Adventure*, published in 1887.

According to this, he and the Hon. Evelyn, meeting by chance a nun in their box at the opera in Jassy, were invited by her to visit her convent in the Carpathian mountains. And so, we are asked to believe, with no more ado, they embarked upon a tour of all the numerous and ancient religious establishments in that wild and beautiful region. It was no ordinary tour. Wherever they went their arrival was known in advance; fires were burning in the guest rooms, feasts were ready prepared and the most important members of the community drawn up to receive the two young men. Their appearance in the secluded Carpathian valleys aroused both curiosity and respect, for as Laurence recounted in tones of surprise in *Episodes* everyone was convinced that they were commissioners sent by England to enquire into the confiscation of ecclesiastical property decreed by Couza, ruler of the Principalities. That is very likely what they were. England and Turkey and France and Russia had been at odds among themselves for many years over Moldavia and Wallachia, whose misfortune it was to occupy that interesting space on the map separating Russia from Turkey. England and Turkey had opposed turning the Principalities into the state of Romania, but France and Russia together had brought it about. In 1861 Prince Couza had come to power helped by Napoleon III, whose interest in that region made Palmerston nervous. Hence his close eye on

Couza's attempt to despoil the Church in the manner of Thomas Cromwell.

There was a decidedly pre-Reformation air about the monastic establishments of Moldavia. Discipline was relaxed, food abundant, and comfort prevailed. Instead of cells the monks and nuns lived in small cottages surrounded by flowers. The nuns, Laurence said, were happy, pleased, and natural which, in his case, meant coquettish. As always in the company of women he was charming – gently teasing, respectfully flirtatious. For his part he was amused to see the signs of fashion in their habit, a pale yellow border to a hood and an expanded hem to a skirt. Crinoline fever, raging in Europe, had not spared the nuns of Moldavia in spite of the Metropolitan's best endeavours in confiscating the 'cages' that held out their skirts. All the nuns were addressed as 'mother' no matter what their age. This was quaint but pleasant, Laurence thought. To be called 'son' by a girl of nineteen gave him the impression of having inspired an affectionate interest. He found the ceremony of parting even quainter but no less agreeable. The nuns lined up in a row, 'we reverently kissed their hands and they bent over and kissed our heads'. It was difficult to imagine how strong the temptation was to linger by one and hurry past another, he said. 'Persons who have never known before what it is to have a great many pairs of lips, some fresh and ruddy others old and wrinkled pressed in rapid succession on their foreheads, will be conscious of a sensation of numbness on the scalp at last; arising probably from a conflict of emotions; nor, if the head be bald as mine was, will it be possible to prevent its becoming red.' He was young to be bald but he does not seem to have minded; his friends always worried more about his appearance than he did.

Emerging from the mountains they posted to Bucharest where they interviewed Prince Couza, whom Laurence described as an unscrupulous adventurer. After a brief and mysterious hunting trip in Transylvania they went to Pest where Ashley boarded the train for home. Laurence was vague about what he did next. In *Episodes*, the only account of his movements at this time, he said he visited friends in Hungary and then 'worked his way' into Silesia where he went to stay at Primkenau with the Duke of Augustenburg. If coincidence was an art that he consciously practised, perfection was now achieved for, as soon as he arrived at Primkenau, the King of Denmark died. The consequence of that was a crisis in the affairs of

Europe, the prospect of an unlimited war over who should rule in Schleswig and Holstein, the Duchies lying between Denmark and Prussia. Primkenau was the fulcrum of this crisis, for as soon as news of the death was known, on 16 November, the Duke of Augustenburg renounced his claim to succeed in the Duchies in favour of his eldest son, Prince Frederick.

The Augustenburgs were well disposed towards Laurence Oliphant. Frederick was the same age. An ambitious, intelligent, and amiable prince, he was married to the daughter of the Queen's dearly beloved half-sister, Princess Feodore, and his younger brother, Prince Christian, was soon to marry Victoria's third daughter, Princess Helena (Laurence's especial friend). It is not clear how Oliphant came to be introduced to them, but it was possibly due to Prince Albert, whose elder brother, Duke Ernest of Saxe-Coburg-Gotha was an intimate friend of the Augustenburgs. Frederick's other warm supporter, who was also near him in age, and shared his liberal views, was Crown Prince Frederick William of Prussia.

In the discussions that took place with a view to placing Frederick on the ducal throne, Oliphant played an undetermined but important part, probably as the personal emissary of Queen Victoria. He attended the ceremony at which the prince was declared Duke of Schleswig and Holstein and accompanied him to Frankfurt to drum up support from the rulers of the Confederation of German states and their ministers who were assembled there. A confrontation seemed inevitable: Denmark's new king, Christian IX (who was the Princess of Wales's father), indicated that he would tighten his hold on both Duchies.

Palmerston told Russell that the Schleswig–Holstein question was more intricate than the riddle of the Sphinx and more difficult to untangle than any Gordian knot. 'It however divides itself into Two Branches,' he explained to Russell, 'the one about Holstein, the other about Schleswig.' The difficulty was, he went on, that 'the Queen and Paget [Minister to Denmark] are at Cross Purposes, and while Paget writes about Schleswig, the Queen writes about Holstein'. However flippant, that was essentially true, for if the question was to be considered in the light of the broad national aspirations of the people in the Duchies, those to the north in Schleswig were mostly Danish speaking and those in Holstein mostly German speaking. Queen Victoria's sympathies were with the German side, which she considered to be coerced by Denmark, and her interest in the affair was wholly engaged by the fact that Prince Albert had once made an attempt to find a solution for it.

From Frankfurt Prince Frederick, accompanied by, among others, Laurence Oliphant, went to Gotha where Duke Ernest helped him to set up a provisional government and supported it with money, arms, and political advisers of a suitably liberal flavour. This served to deepen the crisis which came at a difficult time for the peace of Europe. The Polish revolution was not yet suppressed, the threat to Austria from Italy not yet resolved. People had just begun to realize that, if the ambition of the Emperor Napoleon were suspect, it might be more than matched by the questionable aims and rising strength of Bismarck. In those circumstances everyone asked what England would do and everyone acknowledged that much would depend on what public opinion in England wanted her to do. But, as Laurence Oliphant wrote at the time, English public opinion was often incapable of understanding complex questions and Ministers were left floundering without a clear policy. It was his role in the affair to attempt to sway that opinion towards a particular policy – the recognition of Prince Frederick.

It was not an easy task. Although the Augustenburg claim to the Duchies was wildly popular in Germany and Prince Frederick was applauded wherever he went, in England public opinion was all for gallant little Denmark and its most visible representative, the beautiful and newly married Princess Alexandra (whose wedding to the Prince of Wales Laurence had been invited to attend). It was in order to redress the adverse balance of opinion in England that on 16 December Duchess Alexandrine, wife of Duke Ernest of Saxe-Coburg-Gotha, wrote to her sister-in-law, the Queen of England as follows. 'Dearest Victoria, I write these lines to you at my Ernest's request. He asks me to say that in view of the false reports in the English papers, and of the inadequacy of what the English government hears about feeling in the Duchies, it is essential that a competent agent should be sent there to report on the situation. My Ernest says that he considers Mr Oliphant to be the most suitable person; that he is known to you and was much valued by Albert; and my Ernest likewise thinks highly of him. He is an impartial, truthful and able man.' The Duchess asked the Queen to get Lord Russell's approval for Oliphant's mission to the Duchies, thereby hoping to win the English Foreign Secretary over to the Augustenburg side.

At Gotha the tension of the moment together with the strain of the past months spent endlessly travelling in sometimes hard conditions, suddenly told on Laurence. In a letter to John Blackwood on Duke Ernest's writing paper with the coronet somewhat perfunctorily blacked out, he confessed that he would not be able to deliver an article promised for the *Magazine*. Whether he had 'put on too much steam', or his stomach was to blame, he could not say, but he was *hors de combat* with racking headaches. It was perhaps a recurrence of the illness that had attacked him prior to his departure for China; these headaches were to plague him increasingly.

He recovered in time to take part in the talks at Gotha between Duke Ernest, and Prince Frederick and his political advisers which led to immediate action. On 30 December 1863 Prince Frederick, an aide, and Laurence Oliphant quietly and without luggage boarded a steamer at Harburg on the Hanover shore of the Elbe; it dropped downsteam through blocks of floating ice to Gluckstadt on the Holstein side. There they were met on the pier by one or two gentlemen who had been forewarned of their coming. At first the town of Gluckstadt took no more notice of them than Harburg had done. But as the party entered the market place Prince Frederick was recognized. 'Suddenly a sort of electric shock seemed to thrill through the town,' Laurence wrote afterwards, 'people began to run towards the market place,' and Frederick and his companions found themselves surrounded by an enthusiastic and excited crowd who hailed him as their lawful sovereign.

When they reached Kiel, the capital of Holstein, it was white with snow and red with the glare of torches carried by crowds ceaselessly chanting the anthem, *Schleswig Holstein meer umschlungen*. Once again Laurence found himself in a square looking up at an aspiring ruler, not on the balcony of a palazzo this time but at a window of the Bahnhof Hotel. But Frederick, though he was to provoke more disturbance in Europe than even Victor Emmanuel had done, was destined never to reign. For the moment, however, Laurence was profoundly moved. After the miles and miles of Russia and Austria and Poland and Romania he had traversed in the past year, after the Slavs and the Magyars, the Serbs and the Greeks whom he had struggled to understand, he felt suddenly at home with these people who looked like English farmers. After all, he asked himself, was not Schleswig-Holstein the cradle of the Anglo-Saxon race; their oldest songs preserved, not in their country but in his, and the most authentic records of their history to be found in the chronicles of Bede?

Now he who had witnessed all the national uprisings in Europe since 1848 – with the sole exception of Greece – welcomed the Augustenburg claim as the latest manifestation of that feeling which was often the true religion of his time and which he, personally, was to attempt to translate into a mystical experience.

It was at Kiel that Antonio Gallenga, *The Times* correspondent, found him and remarked that Oliphant's name was on everyone's lips. Gallenga already knew Laurence, by reputation and probably in person. He was Italian by birth, a follower of Mazzini in the early days, a close friend of d'Azeglio, the Piedmontese Minister in London who had the ear of Palmerston. Who had not seen or heard of Oliphant? Gallenga wrote. 'Mr Oliphant the writer, the great traveller, the aspiring statesman, the semi-official diplomatist, a pleasant acquaintance, not to be passed by.' A certain dryness of tone in this may be explained by the fact that Laurence was in possession of most of what Gallenga wanted at Kiel – information as to the movements of Prince Frederick, access to him and his political advisers, and permission to interview the various deputations that came into Kiel from the surrounding country.

Although tension between Copenhagen and Berlin was growing hourly, the trains were still running, and Laurence's next move was to go north to spend some hours pottering unchallenged round the forts of the Dannewirke, the ultimate line of Danish defence. Describing this excursion in an article published in *Blackwood's Magazine* only two months later, he said there was nothing to stop him going from the Danish batteries down to the office of the Prussian commander, but the liberality and lack of suspicion of the Danes was so great he did not choose to abuse it. That may have been so but the local commander was not the only Prussian within Laurence's reach. Though from the Dannewirke he returned to Kiel and amused himself for a day or two skating out to sea down the hard ice that bound the vast harbour, he shortly departed for Berlin. There, with the information as to the state of Denmark's defences fresh in his mind, he had a series of interviews with the Crown Prince of Prussia and Bismarck, the Prussian Chancellor. Crown Prince Frederick's view of the affair was one of straightforward support for the Augustenburg claim but Bismarck's was far more devious. From the beginning he wanted the Duchies for Prussia, not least the strategic harbour of Kiel. Bismarck so manipulated matters that he made the Danes believe that England would fight on their side; this belief – which was not backed by any decision by England – led the Danes to stand firm against an ultimatum from the German states, and that provided the pretext for Austria and Prussia to march their men into Schleswig-Holstein early in 1864. (In this campaign the Duchies fell to Prussia, leading to war between Austria and Prussia in 1866, which ended Austrian influence in Germany for ever.)

If, as is likely, Laurence Oliphant had a part in this tangle, no hint of it remains, but he learned enough at Berlin to be back at Kiel in time to witness the invasion by Austrian and Prussian forces. This invasion, though not unexpected, occurred far sooner than anyone had thought it would; his presence at it indicates the possession of inside knowledge. Moreover, something he did at this time so upset Palmerston and Russell that he was never employed by them again. It is possible that Oliphant, who was brought into the affair by the Augustenburgs with the tacit approval of Queen Victoria, was used by Bismarck to Prussia's advantage. Palmerston was very irritated by Victoria's behaviour at this time; he complained that she was following a policy of her own in opposition to that of her Ministers, and perhaps Oliphant was a tool in this.

The ostensible reason for Laurence's disgrace at the Foreign Office was the article he wrote for *Blackwood's Magazine* for March 1864 which contained the account of his inspection of the Dannewirke. That was reckless but there was worse to come. The article contained a bitter and contemptuous attack upon Palmerston's whole approach to foreign affairs as Prime Minister and Russell's conduct of them as Foreign Secretary. It was inspired by Laurence's passionate belief that England had betrayed the sacred cause of nationalism, a belief made urgent by the things he had seen over the past few years, above all in Poland. England stimulated the Poles to act by popular clamour, Laurence wrote, and then deserted them. 'We have irritated Russia to such a degree that she does not consider the insults she subsequently heaped upon us a sufficient compensation for our interference. In Italy we are proverbial for barren sympathy; in France we have of late done all we can to increase the national antipathy. The only Press more bitter against England than the German is the Danish, so we have failed to conciliate the one million people for whose sake we have offended forty. The only friends remaining to us in Europe,' Laurence concluded, 'are a few Mussulmans.'

The effect of this article (and of his actions?) was disastrous. 'I am in tremendous hot water,' Laurence told John Blackwood, 'cut right and left by members of the Government.' They accused him of ratting and he reflected that he had lost all hope of Government employment. But he was unrepentant; he told Blackwood he knew he was in the right. 'When you remember that I watched the affair through at Frankfort from the beginning where I know all the leading politicians; that I have talked this matter out with Bismarck; that I know from him ... that we really were the cause of the Austro-Prussian army being in Schleswig-Holstein when all the efforts which were made to prevent it were thwarted by the English policy; when, as I lived with the Duke of Coburg, I know what those efforts were; when ... I have been let in behind the scenes by the Crown Prince of Prussia, who had evidently opposed Bismarck, and by the Duke of Augustenburg, his personal enemy; and when at this moment I am in possession of information of which our Government is totally ignorant – I write with an amount of knowledge and certainty which I know will not be appreciated by the ignorant public, and I am quite prepared to see the paper [*Blackwood's Magazine*] hostilely contradicted and abused. Nor inasmuch as much of my information is based on conversations, can I defend it.' There were only three people who publicly advocated the right course in Schleswig-Holstein, Laurence remarked; himself; Robert Morier, *en poste* at Berlin (and a close friend of the Crown Princess of Prussia); and Alexander Kinglake, who had been making valiant speeches in the Commons. Blackwood, who rather wished he had not published the article, tried to console Laurence. In any worthwhile position, he remarked, the reputation of being able to do anything damaging to a Ministry was about as useful as being able to help it. But, 'they must be in a funk or they would not be so touchy'.

On 28 February Laurence Oliphant was summoned to an audience at Windsor. According to the Queen's Journal he told her that hatred of Prussia in Germany was intense and the feeling against England unfortunately also very strong. It was hopeless to expect a union of the Duchies with Denmark but he suggested there might be a division of Schleswig, giving the Danish part to Denmark and the other half with Holstein to Germany. 'Dearest Albert had always thought that the only way to settle the question', the Queen noted. Bismarck wished to get the Duchies for Prussia but his rule could not last long, or so Mr Oliphant thought. Afterwards, somewhat cryptically in the circumstances, the Queen wrote to her daughter, the Crown Princess of Prussia, 'You never told me you had seen Mr Oliphant. He is such an agreeable clever man'. She forgot, the Crown Princess replied, equally cryptically; 'we like him so much – clever and agreeable with a remarkable talent of understanding foreign countries and their conditions'.

In the spring of 1864 a conference of European powers was held in London to try to settle the Schleswig-Holstein question. Very precise, and at the same time witty accounts of what took place at it began to appear in the columns of the *Owl*, a new satirical weekly, whose authors were unknown. The *Owl* was all the rage, especially among diplomatists who derived a good deal of pleasure from the parodies of Lord Russell's dispatches which also appeared in it. Both the reports of the conference and the parodies were written by Laurence Oliphant. Even his closest friends thought this foolish since his connection with the paper could not be long disguised. But it was a lighthearted prank, the plaything of a number of rich and well connected young men; among them Evelyn Ashley; Algernon Borthwick, later proprietor of the *Morning Post*; and Henry Drummond Wolff. They charged 6d a copy for the Owlbum, as they called it, and had only the printer to pay. So they spent the rest of the profits on dinners for pretty girls at which the table was laden with presents. Once they went for a day to Paris, dined up a tree in the Bois de Boulogne, and sang their heads off.

Laurence was often in Paris in 1864 and in the company of the Augustenburgs. He was hand in glove with half the potentates and conspirators in Europe, John Blackwood told Charles Lever, but there was no humbug about him: 'Oliphant is a good fellow and a good friend'. When he was in London Laurence visited the Prince of Wales almost every morning. George Smith of Smith, Elder, publishers, whose office was nearly opposite Marlborough House, said he was 'a sort of human and animated newspaper'. His conversation was remarkable – full of leaks from Cabinet and gossip in high places. After giving the Prince the news of the day Laurence would call in on Smith, who described him as fascinating, with 'beautiful eyes'.

In March 1864 Laurence accompanied John Hanning Speke to Paris and introduced him to the Ambassador, Lord Cowley, in an attempt to further his bid for French support for his African colonization scheme. On that occasion Speke went so far as to tell the members of the Société de Géographie de Paris that the Africans wanted an Emperor more than the Mexicans (referring to the ill-fated

Maximilian). If one could be found by the French, Speke said, no one would be more pleased than the English. One takes leave to doubt the truth of that. Although the task of moral regeneration of the Africans appealed to the Empress Eugénie, neither Louis Napoleon nor the French geographers were attracted by Speke's division of the region he had come to regard as his own; the French being offered a route inland from the west coast up the Gaboon River while the English monopolized the Nile. By the time they were together in Paris Laurence had come to act as a watchdog to Speke whose letters show that he was in dire need of one. Even before he and his companion, James Grant, returned to England in the summer of 1863, having traced most of the course of the Nile down from its source – but not the crucial stretch – Speke's letters showed signs of hysteria, of an unreasoning obsession with what he regarded as Richard Burton's misdeeds. John Blackwood, who had Speke under observation at his house in Scotland for many weeks in the summer of 1863 while he coaxed him to finish his *Journal of the Discovery of the Source of the Nile*, became increasingly concerned that the public would misunderstand his remarks. He refused to publish one part of the book, referred to as 'the tail', in which Speke accused Burton of incompetence, cowardice, malice, and jealousy on their expedition of 1857–9. When Speke insisted that the 'tail' be printed for his family, both Blackwood and his nephew and partner, William Blackwood, were terrified that it would become public. John Blackwood confided in Laurence Oliphant; 'Pray speak to him and prevent him from putting his foot in it as much as possible,' he begged. At the same time Blackwood urged Oliphant to attack Burton in the review of Burton's account of the Nile affair he was writing for the *Magazine*.

When it came out this article only added to the mounting bitterness of both sides. And so, according to Isabel Burton, when Oliphant raised with Burton the invitation to debate the Nile affair with Speke at the September meeting of the British Association (which traditionally acted as the summer meeting of Fellows of the Royal Geographical Society), Burton was goaded into accepting. Speke invited Laurence to stay with him for this meeting but he had been summoned to attend upon the Augustenburgs. It was while at Primkenau that he saw in *The Times* news of Speke's death by shooting on the eve of the meeting with Burton. On 22 September Laurence wrote to John Blackwood about Speke. 'Poor fellow, one of the last conversations we had when we were living together in the spring in Paris was on the subject of death. He said that since having made his Nile discovery, life seemed so utterly flat and uninteresting to him that after knocking Burton down he felt he should no longer have any object in living. He talked altogether in the most indifferent way of existence and would not have looked on death as a misfortune.'

As for Laurence his Ruritanian way of life was drawing to a close. Probably because of his conduct in the Schleswig-Holstein affair, and certainly owing to his connection with the *Owl*, which had become common knowledge, a career in the diplomatic service no longer offered the prospect of rapid advancement. Nor, after the assassination attempt in Japan, was it to his mother's liking. He decided once again to stand for Parliament. Over the last four years he had served other people's aspirations to the best of his ability and with all the passion at his command. Now it was more than time that his own brilliant promise should be transformed into reality.

CHAPTER 6

THE BROTHERHOOD OF THE NEW LIFE

AT the next general election in July 1865 he stood in his old constituency of the Stirling burghs, and this time a high Liberal tide floated him into Parliament. His prospects for advancement within the party appeared good, for Gladstone was Chancellor of the Exchequer and the Elgin family friendship they both enjoyed would surely serve him there. That was the view taken in the clubs where Laurence's newest career, like everything else he did, was the subject of interested comment and where the coolness between him and the leaders of the party, Palmerston and Russell, was not immediately remarked. Laurence himself had already formed a plan; he proposed to take an independent line on foreign affairs and be very submissive on home matters, he told John Blackwood. It was just as well for someone who had been as little in England as he had been over the past ten years.

Although Parliament would not reassemble for six months he was not without occupation. As Joint Secretary, with Clements Markham, of the Royal Geographical Society, he worked very hard. The Expedition Committee on which he once more had a seat, was now concerned with preparations for Dr Livingstone's last and greatest journey to the African interior. Laurence was diligent in his attendance at this and other committees. He also read and evaluated papers submitted for publication in the *Geographical Journal*, and contributed to debates on subjects of which he had first hand knowledge, subjects as far apart as the proposed ship canal across the Isthmus of Panama and the best way of approaching the opening of Korea to western trade. Then, in the summer, *Blackwood's Magazine* began publishing instalments of a brilliant new satire, *Piccadilly*, which aroused a good deal of attention and flattering speculation about its author. Many names were mentioned and one man publicly claimed the distinction; in fact it was Laurence Oliphant.

Piccadilly was an exposé of the more venal side of London society in which, behind a facade of wealth, power, and self-righteousness, Laurence affected to discover greed, vanity, and fear. The tone he adopted was just as scathing as that he had used in his celebrated article denouncing England's foreign policy. In *Piccadilly* Lady Broadhem is ready to sell her daughter to the highest bidder, the 'Hindoo converted millionaire', Mr Chundango. Lady Mundane milks the middle class Mr Bodwinkle of thousands of pounds for persuading society to go to Mrs Bodwinkle's ball, and little Spiffy Goldtip deals in misleading information on the Stock Exchange. Yet, though the world in which they moved might be corrupt, it remained as Laurence described it, most desirable; warm, gay, luxurious, full of attractive women, pleasure and excitement. The centre of this world was Cambridge House on Saturday night where carriages queued for Lady Palmerston's party in spite of the pouring rain. 'Horses with ears pressed back, wincing under the storm; coachmen and footmen presenting the crowns of their hats to it; streams running down their waterproofs and causing them to glitter in the gaslight; now and then the flash of a jewel inside the carriages; nothing visible of the occupants but flounces surging up at the windows as if they were made of some delicious creamy substance and were going to overflow into the street.' Laurence, in the person of the hero, Lord Frank Vanecourt, prepares to join the wearers of these delicious dresses by fixing the smallest of white bow ties over the pearl stud at his neck, thrusts two right hand gloves into his pocket by mistake and drives to Cambridge House. There tête-à-tête in a remote corner with Lady Veriphrast, he explains that he proposes to write a book about civilization. He meant about what he had lately come to think of as wrong with civilization.

He begins with a swingeing attack upon all organized religion. The clergy preached a doctrine that could save the world – Christianity – but they did not practise it, so why should anyone else? The priesthood, once an inspiration, had become a trade, wrote Laurence bitterly; the Church without inspiration was a grate without fire. Catholic, Protestant, Dissenter – he spared none from the accusation of humbug and hypocrisy. But he saved his most contemptuous blow for the people he knew best, the Evangelicals whom he now accused of practising a religious quackery that he could only despise. In the person of a muscular Colonial Bishop, Joseph Caribee Islands, he lampooned the missionary fervour of the evangelical upper class that he had once been content to share. Having seen their activities in the world outside Exeter Hall his was one of the few voices then raised to suggest that these were not always perfect; that they might sometimes be misguided, ineffectual, or downright harmful. He invented a phrase, the 'worldly holies', to describe those people who formed a select and exclusive society with its vanities and its excitements, its scandals and jealousies, which kept itself aloof from the 'wholly worldly' on the grounds that it represented a religion of love. But, 'by constantly toadying and flattering each other they irresistibly foster that air of subdued arrogance which is so displeasing to society at large'. The religious world in London, wrote Laurence, wanted religious lawyers and religious bankers and religious doctors. 'They like to get their wine from somebody who holds sound views, but I think they cease to be so particular about the principles of those from whom they get their bonnets.'

And so he indulged his talent, his quick observation, wit and wide experience to turn upon the world and the people he knew – the Shaftesburys, Ashleys, and Troubridges who had befriended him. But if the wit and style and knowledge of the world displayed in *Piccadilly* belonged to Laurence Oliphant, the inspiration was that of someone else, someone very strange; a preacher from America called Thomas Lake Harris whose influence upon him was to be very long-standing and quite disastrous. Because of him Laurence would forfeit his career in Parliament, his reputation, and some of his friends. Far graver than that, his lucid mind, his quick observing eye, his judgement, even his compassion, would all be strangely smothered so that his very identity was put at risk.

Thomas Lake Harris's first visit to England occurred in 1859 (significantly the year of Sir Antony Oliphant's death) when he delivered a number of sermons at the Marylebone Institute. The Oliphants, mother and son, were among those who attended and, in common with many others, asked to make Harris's closer acquaintance. But, as we have seen in the letter Laurence wrote to his mother from Italy in 1860, Harris refused. It was his practice with aspiring disciples to hold them at arm's length so that their enthusiasm increased, and until he could make sure that they were sincere, worthy, and, above all, likely to be useful. As it was revealed in the sermons, his doctrine, which was to prove so attractive to so many people, was a powerful mixture of Christianity, spiritualism, and utopian socialism. It took its first direction from the eighteenth-century Swedish mystic, Emmanuel Swedenborg, with whose teaching his English audience was probably fairly familiar, but it contained aspects that were not discussed by Harris at these gatherings which arose from his peculiar emotional needs and a soaring ambition.

As a preacher Harris was compelling; as a person interesting; as a man outwardly attractive, with a fine natural gift for manipulating people. The evidence of *Piccadilly* which contains not only the broad outline of his revealed doctrine and his famous call to 'live the Life', but also a long quotation from one of his poems, suggests that he was again in London early in 1865 when Laurence was writing it. By then, it is clear, he had quite a following. His first visit in 1859 had come at the time when England was invaded by a succession of revivalist preachers from America, thrown up by the movement that had swept that country the previous year, referred to by some as a 'great awakening'. Of all these men Harris was by far the most extraordinary. Those followers he did accept into the Brotherhood of the New Life, as he called it, were expected to offer up faith, obedience and all their worldy goods. To mark the break with the outside world the newcomers were given private names known only among themselves. What these were, and how the Brotherhood lived, will appear.

So far there is little in this to distinguish the Brotherhood from the many other movements that arose in the United States from the early nineteenth century onwards. The Shakers; the Owenites at New Harmony; the Oneida Community; the Mormons; all these movements which Harris claimed to have studied, began as groups of people united by an unusual individual, who were prepared to turn their backs on ordinary life. Whether they professed celibacy or polygamy, poverty or a decent competence; waited for the Second Coming or the End of Time; they did it in the manner that seemed best to them, and were beholden to no one else. They were expressing a belief in the American dream – the arrival of Utopia in the New World; the only difference between them and the rest of the country was that they looked for it to appear rather sooner than most other people did. There were places, however, where the appearance of religious enthusiasm was so frequent that it came to be unwelcome. These were the so-called 'burned over' districts of upper New York State. For a long period of years extending from the 1820s almost to the outbreak of the Civil War, small communities mostly west of the Hudson River were shaken by the appearance of itinerant preachers or the uprising of home-bred adepts, quite often women. As the

Thomas Lake Harris in his study at Vinecliff, before 1875

Miss Jane Lee Waring in her late fifties

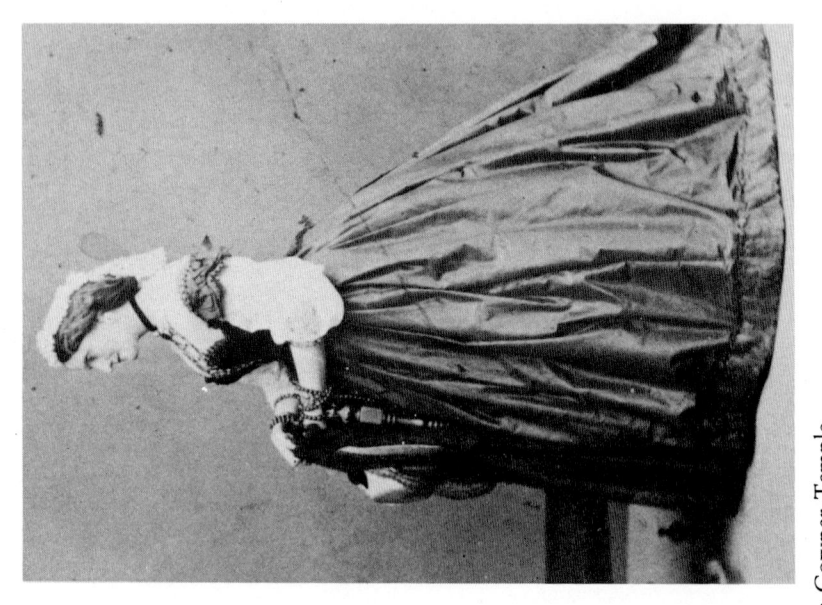

William and Georgiana Cowper-Temple

chapels were the largest and most frequented places for miles around, the intrusion of a sometimes frantic enthusiasm into the practice of an austere religion kindled a spreading fire. Before this died out it could destroy the allegiance of a congregation to its minister, damage family relationships, and sometimes irreparably upset the emotional balance of certain individuals. It often became apparent in these cases that the chief purpose of isolation was to consolidate the power of a particular leader over his newly gathered flock.

It was in this place and at this time that Thomas Lake Harris grew up. He was born in England in 1823 at Fenny Stratford, but his parents left for America when he was five. They settled in Utica, in New York State, where Harris senior kept a grocery store. According to Thomas Lake Harris – the only source of information about his family – his father was a strict Baptist, a severe and intolerant man; all the love and care came from his mother. Her death when he was nine, and his father's remarriage shortly after bore very heavily on him. He said his stepmother was unkind and, as an unhappy adolescent, he took refuge in dreams and imaginings about his dead mother who came to represent all that was pure and noble. In time his imagination broke its terrestrial bonds and set his mother among the angels in heaven. When he was still very young he discovered a facility for preaching. Thin, poorly dressed, with burning eyes and a hacking cough, he tramped the country round Utica receiving board and lodging in return for his sermons. People who heard him sometimes complained that instead of theology his sermons were full of poetic images, but they praised his delivery and they responded to his enthusiasm. After a while he came under the wing of the Universalist Church, so-called because its members believed that Christ had died to save all mankind, not only the elect. They offered him the post of minister of a church in the Mohawk Valley. His fame soon spread beyond that place as he was a frequent contributor of long mystical poems to the Universalist magazines which had a wide circulation. In 1845 he married, but his much loved wife, Mary, died, possibly in childbirth. This second tragedy shook him very deeply and was probably the cause of much that happened later. Now, in his mind, wife and mother inhabited a celestial sphere.

In 1848, in a small town called Hydesville in the 'burned over' district of New York State, mysterious rappings were heard in a house in which there were two young daughters, Margaret and Katherine Fox, aged 13 and 12. These rappings they were able to interpret and soon to manipulate with the command, 'Hear, Mr Splitfoot, do as I do.' Word spread and crowds came to marvel, tremble, or mock. Though the idea of communicating with the dead had already been advanced, by Swedenborg among others, the means to do so had been lacking. Now suddenly the Fox sisters seemed to have found a way. When P. T. Barnum signed them up to give public demonstrations of their control over the rappings, spiritualism was propelled into spectacular prominence. One of its first and most widely respected exponents was Andrew Jackson Davis, the 'Poughkeepsie seer', who was particularly responsive to hypnosis. Davis, who professed to be in touch with Swedenborg, gained influence over people – and made money – by a series of brilliant diagnoses of illness which he produced while under hypnosis. In 1848 Thomas Lake Harris became a disciple of Davis, as did other clergy. Harris lectured up and down the country on Davis's beliefs and practised mediumship on his own behalf. He always maintained that spiritualism was of dual origin. One was God-given, the other evil and in the wrong hands it could do untold harm. The concept provided him with a motive for his own actions and an excuse when things went wrong. This they soon did. Davis who, like many another seer and prophet of that time inclined towards free love, was accused of stealing another man's wife. Harris broke off relations with him at once since he considered him to have defiled the female sex.

In 1850 certain people in Auburn, New York (where Brigham Young was once a journeyman painter), believing themselves to be in communication with the Twelve Apostles, decided to withdraw to a place apart the better to hear the message. A community of about 100 people was set up at Mountain Cove, Fayette County, Virginia, which was to be Christian, spiritualist, and socialist; all the members believed implicitly in the Fox sisters. Harris and a man called James Scott were the leaders of this community. At Mountain Cove it was understood that the Day of Judgement was soon expected and until then all property was to be held in common; so said the Apostles. The trouble was that they said it to each member of the community in a different way, so that things got confused. To order them better Harris and Scott decreed that, henceforth, the Apostles would speak only to them. That did not work either; squabbles broke out and some members left; the Day of Judgement had to be postponed. Moreover the enterprise was broke and though Harris and Scott tried to salvage the deeds of the land, some 10,000 acres, they do not appear to have been successful. In any case, Harris explained later, 'a dark magnetic cloud of death descended on Mountain Cove'.

He wandered south preaching to small groups in the backwoods of Georgia, South Carolina and at New Orleans. There he married his second wife, Emily Isabella Waters, an ardent spiritualist. In about 1854 he returned to New York and set up an independent congregation called the Church of the Good Shepherd. There he preached his own particular brand of Christian spiritualism, socialism, and Swedenborgism. This, while it was based on a searching analysis of the Bible – such as Evangelicals could only approve – was unlike their belief liberal and optimistic, affirming that man was at liberty to progress and capable of doing so. In fact Swedenborg's voluminous writings contained ideas attractive to all manner of reformers and seekers after truth, who drew strength from the Swedish mystic's wonderfully assured view of man's role in creation. Among his admirers in the United States were Ralph Waldo Emerson; Henry James senior; George Ripley, founder of Brook Farm; and Horace Greeley, celebrated editor of the *New York Tribune*.

From Swedenborg's cornucopia of ideas Harris made two his own. The way he interpreted the first caused great and lasting offence to members of the New Church into which Swedenborg's most faithful disciples had organized themselves. The way he used the second to manipulate his own followers was evil and ruined the lives of several, including Laurence Oliphant. The first idea was that it had been given to Swedenborg to interpret the meaning of the spiritual world – that the answer to all man's religious questions lay in his *Arcana Coelestia*, an enormously long commentary on Genesis and Exodus. In 1857 Thomas Lake Harris produced the *Arcana of Christianity*, also an enormously long and, in spite of much repetition, vague book. When the New Church members took its message in, they were scandalized. Harris paid passing tribute to Swedenborg for breaking ground on spiritual matters. But it was he, Thomas Lake Harris, to whom had been given the far greater power of interpreting the celestial world.

The second idea adopted from Swedenborg undoubtedly had a particular attraction for him in view of his history. It was that God was both male and female, and that each human being, male or female, had a counterpart of the opposite sex. Love, Harris came to believe, was only desirable between counterparts and then it could be the source of divine power capable of regenerating the world. The difficulty – a large one – was that one's counterpart was rarely, if ever, one's existing husband or wife. It followed that marriage as an institution was superfluous, not to say actively harmful. This was the more so because its conventions stood in the way of an exercise that in the right hands might lead to one's counterpart sooner than otherwise. If Harris held a member of the Brotherhood of the New Life in his arms, she (with him it was always a female) might be granted a glimpse of her ordained counterpart and the love of Christ would flow down to them. Harris's own counterpart was not Emily but a being called the Lily Queen who lived mostly in heaven. He celebrated her in a poem written in 1854 called 'An Epic of the Starry Heaven'.

> Here find thy mate, forever, two in one,
> Circle from star to star, from sun to sun,
> In language liquid as the bliss of love,
> Repeat below the truth revealed above.

This doctrine of counterparts and the divine power conferred by the union was not casually revealed, it was the central mystery of the Brotherhood and the dark side of Harris's philosophy. It put into his hands the power to break existing marriages, to prohibit others and to withhold from those who believed it the hope of any normal life. Its first victim was Emily Harris who was forced to live a celibate life within marriage; it drove her to the edge of insanity.

One of the most prominent members of Harris's congregation in New York was Horace Greeley, who professed great admiration for him in the beginning both as a preacher and a poet. Greeley was a famous journalist and editor, widely liked and respected though freely admitted to be a little odd. He was a great campaigner for the abolition of slavery and for temperance and one of the first Americans to take to his heart the ideas of Charles Fourier, the French utopian socialist. Greeley had a farm on which he practised some of Fourier's ideas, and about which he wrote at length in the *New York Tribune*. He was prone to let his enthusiasms run away with him and was aided in this by his wife, a nervous, ailing woman. It was at her invitation that the Fox sisters spent some months in the Greeley household after their public début. Greeley opened the columns of the *New York Tribune* to accounts of experiments in alternative religion and the utopian socialism that so often accompanied it. In 1858 these were again the subject of popular interest as a new wave of religious enthusiasm covered the country. It was probably Greeley who ensured that when Harris announced his intention of going to England in 1859 he received a warm invitation to stay with Garth Wilkinson. It meant that Harris could count on the visit being a success.

Wilkinson was a fashionable London doctor, one of the leading practitioners of homoeopathy and a founder member of the Swedenborg Association. He had translated many of Swedenborg's works from Latin into English and when still very young had published a first edition of William Blake's poems at his own expense. Wilkinson was an outspoken, independent, liberal minded man, who had much endeared himself to Henry James Senior during the latter's sojourn in England. Wilkinson was a friend of Carlyle, and of Emerson, and a regular contributor to the *New York Tribune*. Thanks to his good offices crowds came to hear Harris preach in London, drawn by his known advocacy of spiritualism. Society was in two minds about this. On the one hand it was a fashionable game in which even the Queen and Prince Albert joined. Rapping, table turning, levitation, séances were the amusement of the hour. On the other hand it made a very serious claim to be a newly revealed religion with the promise of extraordinary things to come. This last view was best expressed by Robert Dale Owen; like his father, Robert Owen, a forerunner of socialism, a student of spiritualism. He wanted passionately to prove its scientific origins; otherwise he wrote, 'how heart sinking, how utterly unworthy the conception that, under the Divine Economy, that grand privilege of progress to which man owes all he ever was, or will be, is denied to the Science of the Soul inhering in every other'.

There were many members of the English upper class who wanted to agree with him but who, in view of the crude sensationalism and commercialism that bedevilled the subject after Barnum secured the Fox sisters, kept their interest to themselves. If they came to hear Harris it was ostensibly in a spirit of enquiry. They found that he preached what they wanted to hear and his very first sermon rescued them from their dilemma. His assertion that spiritualism could be good or evil depending on how it was used and by whom, went far to reconciling what one might call the parlour aspect of it with its more serious claims. The fact that Harris warned his audience to shun the tricks practised by certain mediums only reinforced this view. After that his message was one of the greatest hope and promise. If

Christianity could shake off the fetters imposed by sectarian clergymen mankind could conquer sin. Sin, Harris declared, was in the most literal sense the cause of disease, insanity, and death. But he did not offer a definition of sin in these sermons or explain the doctrine of counterparts.

Lady Oliphant and her son were not the only persons of consequence attracted by this millennial message, as we shall see. But in her biography of Laurence Oliphant, Margaret Oliphant was at pains to represent Harris's attraction as limited to the humbler members of society. His lectures, she said, were a little florid in phraseology, 'as was perhaps necessary for the class to whom they were addressed'. It was one way of covering up a great deal that might afterwards have become embarrassing. She labelled Harris an impostor and a charlatan and then, being an honest woman, found herself at a loss to explain how Laurence and his mother had been taken in by him. Apparently she did not know that Laurence's father had been a disciple of Edward Irving (which is strange considering that she had written Irving's biography). Louis Liesching thought that Sir Antony's adherence to Irving went far to explaining Laurence's submission to Thomas Lake Harris.

Garth Wilkinson was not deceived by Harris. Very soon after he met him something turned him against him. Whether he sensed an underlying flaw both in his personality and his doctrine, or objected to his sweeping claims to be wiser than Swedenborg, or was affronted by the description of the Lily Queen among her 'fays' in Harris's verse, is not known; but he quickly became an enemy.

After a few weeks in London, Harris and Emily withdrew to Yorkshire where the Prophet, as he now liked to be called, meditated upon the importance of isolation to spiritual regeneration and produced a commentary on the Apocalypse of St John. This was published in the magazine he wrote and his adherents circulated, the *Herald of Light*. It was from Glasgow where they went next that news of the founding of the Brotherhood of the New Life went forth in the *Herald of Light*. Harris had been moved by the scenes of poverty he had witnessed in the North. Only by establishing the nucleus of a new society that could perfect itself in isolation from the distractions of the world could the evils he had seen be overcome. Henceforth the idea of utopian socialism dominated his teaching, if it did not govern his behaviour.

When Harris and Emily returned to London they were no longer welcome to Garth Wilkinson so they rented a house in Queen's Terrace not far from the hall where Harris was again to preach. Wilkinson was still pestered by people wanting introductions to Harris – among them Lola Montez – which he refused to give. When Laurence Oliphant came to ask the same favour Wilkinson begged him not to go near Harris. We do not know whether this was due to a professional judgement about Harris's effect on Laurence's mental condition or whether Wilkinson merely wanted to preserve a friend from an unrewarding experience. However, Laurence made his own way to Queen's Terrace where, by his own account, he spent a long time walking up and down outside before he decided to ring the bell. It would have been far better for him if he had gone away instead.

Nevertheless, as it was first presented, there was a good deal to attract him in the Prophet's message. One as tortured as he was by self-doubt and the constant prying of his mother must have welcomed the Universalist belief that no matter what he did, or how he lived, God would save him in the end. From earliest childhood Laurence had had thrust upon him by his parents' Evangelical teaching a sense of responsibility not only for himself, but for all mankind. The grace with which he bore this appalling burden was part of his charm, but the strain it imposed must have been almost intolerable. Now here was Harris, exhorting him to 'live the life' and ready to tell him exactly how to do it. No wonder Laurence embraced this optimistic faith; its tenets, greatly enhanced by his own sincerity and compassion, were embodied in *Piccadilly*, though as yet without any hint of the dark side of Harris's philosophy; no mention of the secret belief that the origin of sin was sex and the penalty for it insanity.

When in the summer of 1861 the American Civil War broke out, Harris made for home. He anticipated chaos, he explained in the *Herald of Light*, and in chaos he foresaw golden opportunities for spiritual regeneration that he must be on hand to direct. He collected a group of the faithful in New York and went with them to the comparative isolation of Wassaic in Dutchess County about eighty miles up the Hudson River. There the members of the Brotherhood of the New Life, by 'breathing together' would become a centre of divine power and, ultimately, regenerate the world. Or as Harris put it in his own words, 'the new respiration, imparting a simultaneous vibration to all beings, will attract, through the operation of Divine affinity and cement the bonds of a perfectly reliable and permanent fraternity in which civil discord will be impossible'. In order to achieve this divine respiration – which was an actual physical reaction – each member of the community must purify himself by manual labour. And if Harris was to defeat the forces of evil that would surely attack, absolute obedience to his will must be practised by all. He assumed the title Father Faithful, and began to look out for more recruits and land on which to plant vines.

About sixty people joined him, many of them women. A high proportion had already suffered illness or misfortune; one was a cripple, two others had tuberculosis. The Reverend Buckner and Dr Martin with their wives and children were refugees from the devastation of the Civil War and the attentions of the Ku Klux Klan. James Requa was a banker who had gone broke. In religion they were mostly Baptists, but there were two Shaker couples who did not stay long, and a Quaker who did. In 1863 the Wassaic land was sold and a larger acreage bought at Amenia further up the valley. With it went a grist mill and next to it was established the First National Bank of Amenia, with Harris as President and Requa as Cashier. It was a one roomed shack with a pot-bellied iron stove blasting out heat in the winter. There President and Cashier sat, feet on stove, waiting for depositors. Both mill and bank, essential to any small American town, were part of Harris's scheme; through them he hoped to gain a hold on a wider community and attract useful recruits. Later he started an hotel and explained that the 'germs' of the New Life were transmitted in the food.

In 1863 Violet Fawcett, who was probably the link with the Oliphants, and her fiancé, Arthur Cuthbert, came to Amenia where they were married by Harris. Cuthbert was to be Harris's faithful disciple and apologist for the rest of his life. First, though, he had to be disciplined, and shortly after the marriage he was sent away to work as a lumberjack. The reason given was that Cuthbert's 'states' interfered with Father's gallant struggle to establish divine respiration. Unfortunately, eager as they all were to co-operate, no one had the slightest idea what was going to upset Father next. Pitt Buckner, one of the boys who grew up in the Use, as they called their life, told how, often in the middle of the night Father would decide that everyone must change their beds in order to improve their 'states'. Pitt was in charge of knocking up the sleepers and conducting them out of their carefully arranged warmth into empty and freezing cabins. Sometimes Father decreed that everyone sit up all night to pray for a particular individual assailed by 'infernals'. They all had to concentrate hard until the evil appeared to take a concrete form and then pray frantically aloud, 'Bind him, Lord, bind him'. The person was only deemed to be free when their breathing became deep and sustained. People's nerves in such a situation being what they were, it often took days, weeks even, of communal struggle during which time the chosen one was allowed almost no sleep.

Usually Father battled alone against 'infernals', an activity that alternated with the writing down of revelations, both of which occurred at night so that he was often too exhausted to go out during the day and much too spent to think of doing any manual work. On these occasions his orders were conveyed to the community by Jane Lee Waring, described in the newspaper reports about the Brotherhood as Harris's secretary. After Harris, Miss Waring was the dominant personality at Amenia. 'She was very bright, very beautiful; a big grand woman, happy all the time.' She was also very rich and reportedly brought Harris half a million dollars. Jane was an able woman; in due course she took into her hands the management of the viticulture business that was to be the Brotherhood's only commercial success. She was popular with the Swedish hired men who had to be taken on to deal with jobs the Brothers fumbled. One of them, Israelson, remembered her as 'lovely and nice. She smoked like a trooper lying on her couch.' She smoked the clay pipes that Harris cast off.

Many years later Laurence Oliphant drew a picture of Harris as Masollam in the novel of the same name. 'There was a remarkable alternation of vivacity and deliberation about the movements of Mr Masollam. His voice seemed pitched in two different keys . . . When he talked with what I may term his "near" voice, he was generally rapid and vivacious; when he exchanged it for his "far-off" one, he was solemn and impressive . . . His eyes were like revolving lights in two dark caverns, so fitfully did they seem to emit dark flashes, and then lose all expression. Like his voice they too had a near and a far-off expression, which could be adjusted to the required focus like a telescope, growing smaller and smaller as though in an effort to project the sight beyond the limits of natural vision. . . . The general cast of countenance, the upper part of which, were it not for the depth of the eye-sockets, would have been strikingly handsome, was decidely Semitic; and in repose the general effect was almost statuesque in its calm fixedness.'

The first indication that Harris might have a vital role to play in Laurence Oliphant's life came at the end of *Piccadilly*. By renouncing the heroine, Lord Frank Vanecourt reduces the worldy holies to floods of tears and all the characters wallow in repentance. Vanecourt returns exhausted to his rooms, sinks on the bed and sends for a doctor. One 'whose name cannot be divulged' enters and, lifting him from the bed with a single touch, announces his intention of taking Vanecourt to America. 'My heart leapt within me for its predictions were verified and the path lay clear before me.'

In 1865 Laurence was more disposed to seek a drastic solution to his problems that he had been six years previously when he had first met Harris. In spite of his success at the election, the fame that *Piccadilly* brought him, and the continuing enjoyment of a brilliant social life, he was harassed, possibly sick, and almost certainly frightened of becoming insane. *Piccadilly* abounds in references to madness. 'People call me odd,' Laurence had Vanecourt say. 'I wonder really whether the conflicts of which my brain is the occasional arena are fiercer than those of others. I wonder whether other people's thoughts are like clouds as mine are – sometimes when it is stormy grouping themselves in fantastic forms . . . again consolidating themselves, black or lowering till they burst in a passionate explosion.' Fits of depression reduced his mind to the condition of white paper and the world to that of a doll stuffed with sawdust. At times like these, as always when inactive and brooding, the sexual urge bothered him greatly; as he put it, 'the law of my members is moved into activity', and this time he made no move to resist. Margaret Oliphant referred in guarded terms to rumours of his promiscuity at this stage of his life; the current may have run more high, she said, 'the impetus of existence at its fullest force have carried him further than conscience approved'. Now, at such a time, was the inner meaning of Harris's doctrine made plain to him. Promiscuity was sin, Father taught; sin was punished by disease and insanity. And superstition apart, there may have been a physical explanation for his mental stress; then and after his death rumours abounded that he was in the grip of syphilis.

Yet he did not seek a permanent sanctuary at Amenia; the sacrifice would have been too great as the promise of a brilliant career was near at hand. In September 1865, with a view to finding a theme for his maiden speech in the House of Commons, he went to America where he planned a journey through the Southern States to see for himself the havoc wreaked by the Civil War. But he went to visit Harris first and at Amenia suffered a recurrence of the blinding headaches that had come upon him at Primkenau in 1863. This time they were so bad that his family and friends were gravely worried; apparently at his request, his mother rushed to be with him at Amenia. What happened then was never known but, by the time Laurence had recovered and, in December, gone on his way to New Orleans, Lady Oliphant had decided to stay with Harris. She liked life in the new country, she told John Blackwood; she had not felt so well for many years.

In 1865 Maria Oliphant was 54, and had been a widow for six years. She seems to have had few friends; those people who spoke of Laurence Oliphant with affection mentioned her rarely, except to hint at her clinging attachment to him and her undue influence over him. The cautious remarks that do survive suggest that she was a self-centred, neurotic woman who exacted great indulgence from all around her; the cause of whose semi-invalidism lay in her mind; who sought, not so much guidance from the religious mentors she was notorious for pursuing, but attention. No doubt like many other women, she was drawn to Harris both as a preacher and as a man; the prospect of an ordered and sheltered life under his supervision must have seemed good to her who had suffered from loneliness and anxiety during Laurence's frequent and deliberate absences. Now her acceptance into the Brotherhood of the New Life meant that Harris had a powerful new means of bringing her son within his grasp. For the time being he remained free. At the end of December, apparently entirely recovered from his illness, he returned to England.

When Parliament reassembled in February 1866 two subjects only occupied both Houses; a ruinous outbreak of cattle plague and the more than usually disturbed state of Ireland. So dangerous had the activities of the Fenians become that the Government moved to suspend *habeas corpus*, a necessity that the Commons found both alarming and very distasteful and which John Bright, the Radical MP, condemned in a grave and moving speech. It was known that men, money and arms were flowing into Ireland from the United States and various proposals were made to approach the American Government asking for the aid to be stopped. It was also known that Laurence's maiden speech was to be on this subject, so that there were disappointed shouts of 'Oliphant, Oliphant' when the Chancellor of the Exchequer was called instead. So he was assured of a large and attentive audience when at last he caught the Speaker's eye. What followed was a disaster. Laurence described the Fenians in America as a joke and dismissed the fears of the House as to Ireland with attempted flippancy. He misjudged its mood and, in the manner of his earlier attack upon Palmerston's foreign policy in *Blackwood's Magazine*, recklessly condescended to his seniors. The speaker who followed rebuked him for his attitude and there were none of the usual plaudits for a maiden speech recorded in *Hansard*.

A week or so later he was in very hot water with his own party and, more particularly, with Gladstone. At the election the previous July, the Liberals had promised to bring in a new Reform Bill. Gladstone was in charge of it but suspected of dragging his feet as there was no timetable for it. Laurence put down a motion for debate on 10 April calling for a Royal Commission to gather statistics and other data on which to base a revision of boundaries and a redistribution of seats. This motion, commented the *Illustrated London News*, was more officious and obnoxious than the more direct hostility of the Conservative opposition; 'Mr Oliphant, we should mention, is a Liberal.' He, a mere back-bencher, was undertaking to do the Government's work and, the paper thought, it would have to fight or yield. It yielded. Laurence agreed to withdraw his motion, protesting that he had had no intention of embarrassing the Government; his object was solely to 'countermine those undermining it'. He got the procedure wrong to the sardonic amusement of his own side of the House.

This was less well disposed to him than had at one time seemed possible. Russell, who had become Prime Minister at Palmerston's death the previous autumn, and Gladstone, had to face considerable opposition from within their own party from factions either supporting or opposing the controversial issue of the new Reform Bill. Laurence was a nuisance to them in that he chose to follow John Bright, who advocated the widest extension of the franchise. Throughout his time in Parliament Laurence was passionately in favour of reform, the issue over which the Liberal Government fell in 1866. When, in April 1867, Gladstone tried to water down measures proposed by Disraeli in the Conservative version of the Bill, Laurence Oliphant was a leader of the Tea Room revolt of Liberals against their own party leaders. Although this meant that, in the end, Disraeli's Bill was far more generous in its extension of the franchise than Gladstone's would have been, the Tea Room revolt was a move that Bright, for one, did not approve.

In spite of his Parliamentary duties Laurence was still active in the diplomatic sphere and able to bring considerable influence to bear; influence that was to have an important effect upon the future of Japan. In July 1865 two secret envoys had arrived in England sent by the Prince of Satsuma, one of the leaders of the *daimyo* who had begun to question the authority of the *bakufu*, the Shogun's Government at Edo. When they arrived in London the envoys, Matsuki Koan and Godai Tomoatsu, went straight to Laurence Oliphant. On their behalf he wrote to Henry Layard who was still Under Secretary of State for Foreign Affairs, explaining that Satsuma and the other *daimyos* hostile to the Shogun wanted Britain to open trade directly with them. Laurence remarked that this could hardly be done without the knowledge and consent of the *bakufu*, but suggested that pressure be brought to bear through Harry Parkes, the British Minister who had replaced Sir Rutherford Alcock. Unless the Shogun's monopoly of trade was broken, Laurence argued, dangerous discontent would lead to an explosion. In 1865 Layard apparently did nothing about this approach as it was still Foreign Office policy to back the Shogun. In March 1866 Laurence sent a memorandum to Lord Clarendon, once again Foreign Secretary, on behalf of Matsuki Koan and Godai Tomoatsu who were still in England, arguing that Britain should support the independent *daimyo*. The memorandum foretold the fall of the *bakufu* and proposed a group of independent lords to take its place, in structure resembling the recently established North German Federation (a body Laurence knew well from his Schleswig-Holstein connection). Clarendon had three meetings with Matsuki Koan and sent the memorandum on to Harry Parkes. From then on Parkes began to shift British support in the direction of Satsuma, Choshiu, and other dissidents, so that when the *bakufu* did collapse in 1868, of all the treaty powers Britain was in the closest and most influential position *vis-à-vis* the restored Mikado's Government.

Laurence Oliphant's leaning towards the Prince of Satsuma was reported to the *bakufu* at the time. Throughout 1866 Oliphant was in contact with two separate groups of young Japanese sent to study in England. One of these groups came from the Satsuma and Choshiu fiefs and was under the supervision of Matsuki Koan and Godai Tomoatsu. Its members had been smuggled out of Japan in the ships

of the Scottish merchant, Thomas Glover. He was one of the first
Europeans to settle at Nagasaki where he actively promoted business
deals with the independent *daimyo*, above all Satsuma. Glover's
family at Aberdeen looked after some of the Japanese students who
came to Europe in this way before travel abroad was permitted to
Japanese citizens. One of them was Kanaye Nagasawa, who did well
at school in Aberdeen and then found his way to Thomas Lake
Harris at Brocton.

The other group of young Japanese to visit England in 1866 was
sponsored by the Shogun and, as such, came under the official care of
the British Government. It appointed a naval chaplain, a Mr Lloyd,
to be in charge of them. It was Lloyd who became suspicious of
Laurence Oliphant and refused to let any of his charges near him. But
some of them went secretly to hear about the Brotherhood of the
New Life and Harris, whom Laurence presented to them as a living
Confucius. These Japanese went in fear of their lives if they were
found out for, as Laurence explained to the Hon. William Cowper,
'When I asked Lloyd to allow them to come and see me he perempt-
orily refused on the plea that I was trying to get up a plot with the
Satsuma people against the Tycoon' – which, of course, was exactly
what he was doing.

Of all the people to keep his secrets, William Cowper was the best.
He and his wife Georgiana became Laurence Oliphant's closest
friends. The bond between them was Harris – 'no-one ever attracted
William more', Georgiana wrote. Although they were involved with
spiritualism and acquainted with the philosophy of Swedenborg, it
was Harris's preaching of Christian socialism that particularly drew
the Cowpers to him. They invited Harris to stay at Broadlands,
introduced him to many of their friends and protegés, including John
Ruskin, and gave him money. The extent of their involvement with
him was not known at the time nor has it been since. It would have
caused widespread comment, ridicule even, for it was a remarkable
association between a revivalist preacher from the backwoods of
America, whose motives people were already beginning to question,
and a Minister of the Crown, a man born into the Whig oligarchy,
whose mother was the beautiful, amusing, and clever Emily Lamb,
whose first occupation in politics had been as private secretary to his
uncle, the Prime Minister of the time, Viscount Melbourne. William
Cowper was Palmerston's step-son – some said his natural son –
who inherited Broadlands, the great house in Hampshire and, after

his mother's death, added Temple, Palmerston's family name, to his own.

Laurence and Georgiana Cowper had in common the recent death of a parent when they first met. As was so often the case she turned to spiritualism for comfort and in her memoirs rather shamefacedly admitted that she had frequented the séances of D. D. Home, the celebrated, later notorious, medium; 'so alluring, so bewildering, so utterly disappointing, but still furnishing to the material mind a new basis of belief', argued Georgiana. According to her William was drawn to spiritualism for her sake and never endorsed Home – a point of some delicacy for though he was not detected in physical fraud his ambition became suspect. Laurence was not involved with Home either – though he was invited to his séances – believing the subject far too serious for what he regarded as vulgar parlour tricks.

William and Georgiana Cowper and Laurence Oliphant suited each other; they were all three odd and remarkable people who shared a desire to set the world to spiritual rights. In William this took the form of a passionate ecumenicalism; he enquired diligently and hopefully into religious beliefs of every sort, worshipped in churches, chapels, and halls belonging to every creed, and kept open house for clergy of all possible persuasions and some improbable ones. His family regarded him with a certain alarm; Lambs and Cowpers were not religious and it bothered them that William was; they feared that he might lose all sense of proportion and become a Roman Catholic. He did attend Mass once in a 'Romish' church and found the experience exhilarating. 'We came to a part which shocked me very much, addressed to the Virgin,' he explained, 'but then I left off looking at the book.' In some ways William was close to Laurence's definition of a 'worldly holy'. He moved in the same circles; Shaftesbury was his brother-in-law (and did not quite approve of William); frequented fashionable preachers; went to prayer meetings, and sat on committees doing various kinds of good. There was a certain arrogance and self-regard in this. 'How I should like to be a Reformer,' he wrote, 'how I should welcome the scorn of the frivolous, the hatred of the selfish, the hostility of the worldly which should prove to me that I was doing my duty.' His accomplishments were practical rather than spiritual though none the worse for that. In 1866 he had been Commissioner of Works for six years, during which time he presided over measures in Parliament to preserve England's commons and London's open spaces. He was responsible for saving Epping Forest from the speculative builder, for placing the Royal Courts of Justice in the Strand and, more controversially, for building the Embankment on the Thames, which sadly, forever banished London's riverside into a painting by Canaletto. This was the more regrettable since William had a keen appreciation of painting. He was a friend of William Morris, to whom he gave a contract to decorate St James's Palace, and an early patron of Dante Gabriel Rossetti.

Like Laurence Oliphant, William Cowper was popular in society; like him attractive to women and attracted by them. He loved the form and colouring of women and their clothes. 'Danced with Lady Seymour', he wrote in his journal, 'gorgeous in a train of red velvet studded with diamonds.' In his youth (he was born in 1811) 'beautiful Billy', as Lady Holland called him, was much in demand as a dancing partner for the young unmarried Queen. With him religion and society did mix; unlike Laurence he felt no guilt at indulging in worldly pursuits. William saw nothing incongruous in a day that began with a visit to Beamish, the fashionable preacher, went on to hear poor children reciting the catechism, and finished with 'a little Palace dinner of 80'. He did not bow to criticism; when the London Mission attacked him for the insult they imagined he had delivered to them by presiding at their anniversary meeting in Exeter Hall during the day and dancing at night (a picture of him at it had appeared in the *Illustrated London News*), it was God's world he told them, not the devil's; 'we must subdue it to its lawful King, not abandon it to the enemy'.

Yet he was vulnerable to criticism of his behaviour and judgement. As Commissioner of Works he had in his gift the appointment of clergy to certain churches and though he did not make bishops, he was very close to those who did – Shaftesbury and the Prime Minister himself. So in 1860 he offered St Peter's, Vere Street, to F. D. Maurice and persuaded Palmerston to give Christ Church to his friend – like Maurice a Christian socialist – the Reverend Llewellyn Davies. These were appointments for which, Georgiana remarked, he was considerably abused. How much louder would the cries have been if his critics had known of his close and lasting attachment to Thomas Lake Harris and the Brotherhood of the New Life? Of this he wrote that it was 'an experiment as important to mankind as that of St Benedict and the founders of monasticism, the Lutheran Churches which organized themselves without an episcopate, the

THE BROTHERHOOD OF THE NEW LIFE

Quakers who dispensed with a ministry, or the Reformers who rested on the foundation of justification by faith alone'.

As for Georgiana Cowper, she endorsed this view wholeheartedly. Georgiana never did anything by halves; she was large, warm, impulsive, and dangerously naive. In spiritual matters it was she who chased after phantoms, drawing William irresistibly in her wake. Palmerston took fright at her early in their acquaintance and warned the family: 'just the sort of person the RCs would get hold of'. To Laurence Oliphant as to John Ruskin, she gave the sort of undemanding kindness that he had never had, becoming in time a substitute mother. According to the writer, Logan Pearsall Smith, Georgiana never grasped the difference between right and wrong: 'when no cruelty existed she could not see why people should not do as they liked'. Georgiana always did exactly as she liked. In 1866 she was already acting as go-between for Ruskin and Rose la Touche whose tortured love affair Rose's mother bitterly opposed; Georgiana was the means by which the two met. Ruskin had seen Georgiana from afar in Rome in 1842, and worshipped her; 'statuesque severity and womanly sweetness joined', he wrote in *Praeterita*. By 1866 she had grown stouter and, to some people, had become a figure of fun. As with Lady Ottoline Morell, society accepted her hospitality which was lavish and laughed at her for it behind her back. Archbishop Benson reported her dressed in a garment apparently designed by Ruskin, 'with the sort of smile that comes from having been told for many years that your smile is like a sunset or a strain of music'. 'Green was her colour', wrote her devoted admirer, Edward Clifford, 'and her dress generally had some look of costume. She seldom bent but met her friends at her full height with a radiant smile.'

Georgiana was the youngest daughter in a family of twelve children. Her parents' immense wealth came from sugar plantations on Antigua and there was a tropical abundance of feuds and intrigues in the family history. In order to inherit under the will of a distant relative they changed their name from Halliday to Tollemache and briefly occupied Ham House, that beautiful and romantic place beside the Thames where nothing had been altered since the Jacobean age. Georgiana's father died when she was very young; her mother retired from society and she came under the care of her flamboyantly Evangelical sisters, who hardly ever allowed her to go out or to meet people. She was rescued from this nightmare by the curiosity of the

Queen who, seeing her at the opening of Parliament and struck by her appearance, invited her to a Court ball. William met her on the way to church, appropriately enough, and married her in 1848.

When in the spring of 1867 Harris, Emily and Jane Lee Waring again arrived in England, they saw a good deal of Laurence and the Cowpers. Harris was now manoeuvring to get all three more closely involved in the Brotherhood of the New Life. The reason for this was money. He had his eye on a large tract of land at Brocton, which he re-named Salem-on-Erie, about three hundred miles north-west of Amenia on the shores of the great lake. It was fertile land, ideal for growing grapes, even though the winters were very hard. But the price was high owing to the aftermath of the Civil War and the fact that some of the farmers did not want to sell. They asked absurdly high prices and were amazed when James Requa, who was conducting negotiations, closed with them without argument. The money he had was Lady Oliphant's who remained at Amenia, very enthusiastic about the new venture. But, as she did not have enough for all the land that Harris wanted, new sources had to be tapped.

Laurence was now more than ever vulnerable to the Prophet's influence. As far as his everyday life was concerned, something was badly wrong. It was rumoured that he was being pursued by a woman, probably a discarded mistress whose behaviour was causing him such distress that he contemplated suicide. This, coupled with his early troubles in the Commons, may have been the reason for his continued failure to shine on the floor of the House. In 1867 there were no more light hearted speeches, no expert intervention on foreign affairs, not even an effort at speaking on behalf of his Scottish constituents. He confined himself to brief comments on matters of little importance and the tabling of questions whose chief purpose, one suspects, was to mark his presence at Westminster. He told his first wife, Alice, that as a condition of accepting him into the Brotherhood, Harris imposed silence on him in the place where it hurt the most. That may have been true; it certainly formed part of the Oliphant legend, and it would have been an ingenious way to dispose of his career, a serious impediment to Harris's plan. But it should be remembered that Laurence was prone to dramatic explanations, particularly where Harris was concerned. *Hansard* shows that he was not altogether silent, merely ineffectual.

Whatever the truth of this, Harris certainly ordered him to perform other tasks. Chief among them was a daily measure of sewing, the idea being that, in the Use, the most menial tasks were the most rewarding and the surest way to the necessary humility. So when he was not at the House, the Athenaeum, the Royal Geographical Society or dining out, Laurence sat in his rooms hemming petticoats. 'I find the greatest benefit from it,' he told Georgiana Cowper, 'it induces calm and if not actually devotional, at all events a contemplative state of mind such as I have never been in the habit of cultivating – my life having been one of intellectual and bodily excitement.' As the months went by calm became harder to maintain. Laurence was increasingly ill and wretched; so great was the strain that he even disappeared for a time so that his mother, frantic with anxiety, appealed to Delane to have *The Times* help find him. Afterwards, to William and Georgiana Cowper, Laurence expressed his deepest gratitude for their help at a terrible time: 'I had all the symptoms in my head of softening in the brain', he told them. His letters were now signed Woodbine, the Use name Harris gave him. It was perhaps the most absurd of all (though Lady Pink Ears for Emily Harris came close). Margaret Oliphant forbore to mention it in her biography of Laurence, fearing ridicule. Of the others, Jane Lee Waring was Lady Dovie, Lady Oliphant was Viola, and Georgiana Cowper was Lowly (a rather incongruous description). Harris never addressed her husband as anything more fanciful than Dearest William. Mrs Requa, a special favourite, was Golden Rose and James, her husband, Steadfast. The choice of Woodbine, like everything else Harris inflicted on Laurence, was intended to humiliate him. 'The sight of the abject human being', Harris was to write, 'moves me to reverence and awe.'

As far as Laurence's spiritual life went, in 1867 he believed he was at the parting of the ways. Somehow he had to bring himself to leave the world so as to devote the rest of his life to the service of God. The decision was acutely painful. As *Piccadilly* shows Laurence loved the world, craved excitement, pleasure, women; all of which he thought he was obliged to renounce. How hard it was to go out into the street for half an hour each evening to watch the carriages setting out and then to go back to his sewing. He believed it was necessary to be humbled in this way. Harris 'was better able to bully me than any man I had ever met', he wrote. 'I had to be broken in and Harris was the chosen instrument.' Apart from the Cowpers and Margaret Oliphant very few people yet knew how Laurence's life had altered. John Bright was one. On 8 May he wrote in his diary that Laurence had called on him and talked at length about 'his change of views and life and Mr Harris, American spiritualist, very curious and interesting'. Bright was fascinated by spiritual matters and, as a lifelong member of the Society of Friends, naturally sympathetic to religious minorities. A few days later he was invited to dinner at Laurence's lodgings where he found five young Japanese. Bright said that two of them had already been with Laurence to visit Thomas Lake Harris; these were probably Matsuki Koan and Godai Tomoatsu. Japanese were still rare enough to Western eyes for Bright to record their appearance carefully in his diary. He thought them robust and intelligent, with heads of more than average breadth and power.

The Japanese talked at length about Harris and his doctrines and in return Bright explained to them the Friends' belief in the idea of Inner Light and direct communication between the spirit and the human soul. His account is invaluable since it is almost the only one by a sympathetic but independent witness. It shows clearly that, in the Japanese experience, the practice of 'breathing together', of transmitting Christ's love through human contact was innocent of sexual innuendo. This is very important since such practices were inevitably susceptible to a different interpretation and were the source of scandalous allegations, in the first place against Harris, later against Laurence Oliphant.

The Japanese told Bright that they had thought Christianity was one of the superstitions of the world, useful perhaps in England but no more true than other superstitions. When Harris preached to them in America they were strangely moved and one of them cried. Harris grasped their hands and the one who had not cried felt his right arm tremble and, for many weeks, it was affected by a nervous trembling he could not explain. 'When away from Mr Harris, on a visit to Canada, they could think of nothing but him. They call him not Mr Harris, but Faithful, and seem to regard him as their deliverer from their ancient state of ignorance and darkness . . . They are what, in the language of the high Spiritual school, is called "open" and are affected strongly by the "states" or conditions of those about them.' Bright's diary continued, 'This theory of theirs, and of Mr Harris, is founded on a belief that it is possible for Christ, in His spirit to take possession of the soul, and to become almost physically incorporate with man. They feel some change in their breathing as if He filled their lungs, and they have at times a certain fluttering or trembling of the heart, as if their whole system were touched by the influence of His presence in them'. Harris's idea, Bright went on, was that the

Japanese were a very sensitive and receptive race and would receive the new religion with ease and fervour. He found the evening pleasant and instructive, though he confessed it was difficult to comprehend the true nature of the change the Japanese had undergone. Afterwards he walked home in the cool night air and read *Paradise Lost* before going to bed.

Throughout the spring and early summer of 1867 Laurence waited for a summons from America. Georgiana Cowper tried to bring him and John Ruskin together, anxious that her other protégé find relief from torment in the Prophet's message. As a writer Ruskin jibbed at Harris's style. He used too many fine words without understanding them, he told Georgiana, and this was important in forming a judgement about him. 'Men have been even more deceived by their favourite words than ever by their favourite sins.' It was not until two years later, when Ruskin met Laurence with the Cowpers at Denmark Hill, and when he was more unhappy and vulnerable, that he was brought by Laurence's eloquence to concede there might be something in Harris after all.

In July the summons came at last and Laurence was allowed to leave England. Margaret Oliphant described him as characteristically cheerful and light hearted with 'that sense of the humorous which, living or dying, never forsook him'. In her view he went from no sense of failure or disappointment; she blamed only Harris, the wretched fanatic, the vulgar mystic, as she called him, who had ensnared him for an evil purpose. Alexander Kinglake, too, expressed the hope that Laurence's charm and cleverness would rescue him from the redoubtable Harris. Very few others knew where he had gone. The Cowpers went to Liverpool to see him off and gave him a dressing-bag. Laurence was touched and hoped that he would be allowed to write to them. He charged William with the care of his belongings, including his diplomatic uniform, the payment of his subscription to women's suffrage, and the finding of a pair for the next session of Parliament. This, together with the fact that he made no move to resign his Secretaryship of the Royal Geographical Society, suggests that he had every intention of coming back.

And so, one day in the summer of 1867, he arrived at the railroad depôt at Amenia, a tall Englishman in a high hat, blue broadcloth suit and gloves, with a cane, gold watch and massive gold chain. He must have looked strange to the Amenia people and even stranger beside the Harrisites who came to fetch him. Years later an old inhabitant remembered the men, 'like Russians, all whiskers'. They had boots, overblouses and flowing patriarchal beards. They only came down to Amenia in a covered wagon to peddle flowers and milk; the Brotherhood grounds were closed to outsiders and the townspeople had to get permission to enter them. For Laurence the end of his long journey from Mayfair was an empty shed with a pile of wooden crates out of which he had to construct his bed, a table, and something to sit on. His meals were sent over to him in a basket and he was not allowed to speak to more than one or two people. He was able to watch his mother going about her domestic duties, but they could not gossip together, Laurence explained in a letter to the Cowpers, without the danger of their 'states' passing over to Faithful. Harris had drawn up a programme for Laurence who was to start at once. He got up in his shed at 5 a.m. and spent the entire day cleaning out the stables and carting manure. In this way he was supposed to be purifying himself from his old habits in the world. As the sin, so the remedy, Harris explained, and, in case the significance of this was not appreciated by the others in the community ordered them all to anoint themselves with a highly pungent nostrum for syphilis.

If that was crude and unpleasant there was worse to come. Since childhood Laurence had struggled to reconcile a highly sexed nature with the taboos imposed, generally by his Evangelical upbringing and particularly by his mother. The subject was hopelessly confused in his mind with religion and morality; early in his life he wrote that an interest in religion, a preoccupation with things spiritual seemed to arouse him sexually. In an undoubted cry for help he said, 'If a divine power is necessary to overcome the depravity of human nature, a divine revelation is necessary to enable one to discover wherein that depravity precisely consists.' Sadly, there was nobody to answer that crucial question but Harris. Depravity, the Prophet proclaimed, was sexual intercourse; it was original sin, the reason for the Fall, the source of evil in the world and, to turn the knife more sharply in the wound, the literal cause of insanity. It was this demented doctrine that henceforth prevented Laurence from seeking relief from sexual desire, that caused him to live a celibate existence even when married, and that almost drove him insane. How tragic it was that he found no one to counter this advice before it was too late. Even if Lady Oliphant had been wise enough and willing to do so she was kept away from him, cooking, cleaning and washing handkerchiefs to the greater glory of the Use.

Jane Lee Waring could have helped him had she been so inclined. She knew how prone Laurence was to the influence of the woman nearest to him; she boasted of it. Her story was that he had come to Amenia for her sake alone, having fallen in love with her at an earlier date. She said she rejected him, believing him to be afflicted with syphilis and dissolute, his ambition 'like that of other Englishmen of his class' being to know a thousand women. But she was totally committed to Harris, believing him capable of inflicting death on those who crossed him, and quite unconcerned that he might do so.

After the transfer to Brocton, which took place in the early winter of 1867, Harris's claims to spiritual power grew. They were the reason why Horace Greeley ended his visits; 'he wants to be Pope, and I don't like Popes' he explained. At Brocton the Prophet built himself a thirty-room house on the edge of the lake, with pillars in the Grecian style, which he called Vinecliff. To ensure privacy he got the townspeople (who refused to call the place, as Harris wanted, Salem-on-Erie) to agree to re-route the public highway which ran too near the house. He was able to do this since he now owned most of the site of the town, having invested some 250,000 dollars, half of which came from the Oliphants. At Vinecliff Harris lived in style, surrounded by books, pictures and flowers and with all the working parts of the enterprise – barns, stables, and sheds, removed to a decent distance. Women only shared this abode; as Laurence explained to William Cowper, 'it is a sad reflection on all of us men that not one of our "states" is sufficiently advanced to enable Faithful to bear us living with him yet'. In the house with Harris were Lady Oliphant; her maid, Constance; Jane Waring; and Mrs Requa, otherwise known as Golden Rose. Harris doted on Golden Rose. It was in her arms that he most often reached the Lily Queen; because of this she was deferred to by all the members of the community, not excepting Jane Waring.

Shortly after the move to Brocton her husband, James Requa, fell ill, apparently of rheumatic fever caught on the long journey from Amenia. Though he lingered for weeks he was only attended by Dr Martin, whose medical skill Harris usually did not trust, sending for outside doctors at the slightest hint of illness. Rumours about the death circulated for years afterwards. Before he fell ill, though in good health, Requa had had a premonition of death and put all his business affairs in order. According to the local paper, 'when taken sick he stated to his friends that he was not to get well, and so it proved'. Harris comforted Golden Rose with the thought that Steadfast had been called to his counterpart in heaven, and himself, no doubt, with the fact that, although Requa, once a millionaire, was a declared bankrupt, many of his assets in New York had been safely transferred to his wife.

As for his own wife, Emily, she now lived apart, closely watched. 'Mrs Harris is very quiet as long as she keeps employed in small uses but easily excited', Laurence explained to the Cowpers. Her task was to weed the long lines of larch seedlings sent over by William Cowper that were to provide support for the growing vines. Whenever she went out two Use boys followed her to make sure she did not try to commit suicide. Levine, one of the Swedish workmen, told how she asked, watching the wind on the lake, 'will you go and tie up the trees, they blow like the devil himself?'

The first winter that Laurence spent at Brocton was very hard. Vividly he described the daily activities to the Cowpers. 'To get up at half past four these cold winter mornings, the thermometer below zero and a gale of wind blowing that obliged you to shut your eyes, to clean up the stable and horses with hands and feet so cold that no amount of work warms, to take a lantern and a sled with a lot of barrels and go a quarter of a mile to haul water for washing the linen of all the Use who are here, every drop freezing as it falls and all one's clothes coated with ice, to handle these icy barrels with bare hands, to breakfast at six a.m. and then face the freezing blast all day – once I got frostbitten on my nose – to load and unload bricks in storms of sleet and hail, to get stuck in drifts by oneself, to have the harness break in critical places and no-one to help.' This was not a complaint; he never uttered one word of criticism about the life he was obliged to lead. But what on earth did he think about as he toiled in this dismal way? How did someone who thrived on warmth and excitement and rejoiced in excellence, intellect and wit tolerate the cold darkness, the icy hills, the grim living conditions, the megalomaniac and his broken down disciples?

Occasionally things did become too much for him. Once when the horses got restive he threw away the reins and lay down in the bottom of the sled kicking and shouting as the townspeople rushed out of their houses to see him disappear in a flurry of snow. No wonder stories about him circulated in the little town. Brocton people thought him very peculiar looking and could not believe anyone could know so little about horses. 'He used to hitch up a team; instead of doing it like anyone else, he would hitch it up wrong end in', they said. If he was sent up a hill to get wood on a sled, he had to take the horses out and turn the sled round himself. 'Any American boy could have done it easily, he was funny at it and people laughed.' But they were not unsympathetic; they liked him. 'He was the best of them, if he had stayed loyal the community could have survived', they said.

Laurence's lack of skill as a teamster was more than matched by the ineptitude of the other members of the community. According to Dr Martin's son Robert, 'each member of the community devoted himself to what he knew least about'. Those who had been servants were put into positions where they were ill at ease, while people with professional qualifications struggled with menial tasks. The result was that things were badly and extravagantly done. Inexpert milking dried up the cows. The packages they tried to make to ship grapes in were a joke, 'though every stick was cut with a prayer and every tack hammered in with an invocation'. Things only got better when Pitt Buckner, son of the Baptist minister from Georgia, got old enough to take control. Pitt, whose Use name was Earnest, developed a lifelong attachment to Laurence Oliphant. He was competent at farming matters. 'If there was a sick cow, a broken down horse in Brocton, they came to sell it to the community, but since I've been in charge, they can't sell us such.' According to him and to Robert Martin, the second generation saw through Harris. One day Pitt was ordered to leave Brocton as his 'states' threatened to kill Father. Greatly fearful Pitt walked round and round Vinecliff in the night, hoping and expecting that Father would die. In the morning when he saw that Harris was still alive, Pitt gave up his faith and ultimately transferred his devotion to Laurence Oliphant.

In those circumstances the community could not prosper for long; money had still to be got from outside. Early in 1868 a wealthy English family, the Ruxtons, proposed to hand over a very large sum to Harris for which Laurence and William Cowper were to be joint trustees. The invitation to the Ruxtons was to prove a mistake, as it was through them that criticism of the Use first became outside knowledge, leading to attacks upon the movement as more odious than that of Brigham Young. Besides repeating rumours about unorthodox relationships between men and women and the undisputed fact of the repudiation of marriage, the Ruxtons advanced most serious charges about the ill-treatment of children. This came at a time when the local paper had already reported the case of a Use child found crying for its mother from whom it had been forcibly separated. Laurence was obliged to answer at length a series of difficult questions from Georgiana Cowper who was very fond of children. He could see nothing cruel, he said; they were well looked after in a house by themselves called the Bird's Nest. Familial ties had to be broken to allow for the process of spiritual regeneration; love for mankind must replace love for individuals. 'Our work is to rear hero-martyrs.' The Cowpers appear to have accepted this. Robert Martin, one of the inmates of the Bird's Nest, afterwards remarked that the deliberate neglect of the children's education was the worst sin Harris committed. Robert remembered Laurence Oliphant with affection; he said he told the children marvellous adventure stories without putting on airs.

During the winter of 1867/8, Harris's hold on Laurence became more complete. The Cowpers were concerned at the tone of his letters and anxious about his seat in Parliament. They wrote urging Laurence to return to England and live with them; they were too late. On 17 February 1868 Laurence wrote: 'Faithful saw that in my present condition, to return to Parliament would not only be most injurious to me spiritually, but as the Divine Protection would be withdrawn, might be attended with fatal natural results. Nor could I find the slightest internal indication that I had any use there, while I felt the strongest conviction that I was in my right place here. Under these circumstances Faithful saw when the time for decision had come, I had not a moment's hesitation and I felt justified in pleading my health as a reason, as I am morally convinced that I could not have lived through the session.'

In April 1868 he applied for the Chiltern Hundreds. His constituents accepted his plea of ill health in good faith and with genuine regret. And so ended a career that once had seemed most likely to lead to high office. But perhaps he was altogether too fastidious to succeed as a politician. Voters were like playing cards, he once remarked, the more you shuffled them the dirtier they got. 'When it became clear to me that, in order to succeed, party must be put before country, and self before everything, and that success could only be purchased at the price of convictions which were expected to change with those of the leader of the party, my thirst to find something that was not a sham or a contradiction in terms increased.' Laurence urged William Cowper to follow his example; to remain in Parliament was no longer the way to achieve reform. Everything in England must crumble into dust before it could be raised up on new foundations. William must abandon his fellow men now and sort out his own spiritual problems in readiness for the future. 'My dearest friends,' wrote Laurence to both Cowpers, 'you must begin to pull up some of the roots that hold you away from us who love you so much. We can't go to you, you must come to us.' Though, as she told Ruskin, Georgiana was sorely tempted, William Cowper held back. His refusal aroused echoes of a cooler age. He knew he was useless where he was, but he might do good some day, he said. One of Lord Melbourne's maxims came to his mind, 'whenever you don't see clearly, stand still'. 'My dear, dear friend', William wrote to Laurence, 'I look to you to help me to see clearly.' But he declined to pack his portmanteau.

Nevertheless he remained anxious to do what he could for the Brotherhood. Laurence instructed him to smooth the passage to America of the Japanese remaining in England. Owing to the stress of civil war at home some of them were experiencing difficulty with money. Laurence asked William to invite them to Broadlands and, if necessary, to advance them the passage money to America. He urged William to go about this in secrecy and above all to keep it from Garth Wilkinson. He was especially anxious about the young Japanese in the care of the Glover family at Aberdeen; one of them was the son of the Prince of Tosa, another the son of the chief minister of the *daimyo* of Shimonoseki. They were miserable, 'these merchants care for nothing but money', Laurence complained. This enterprise of bringing the young men out of the closed society of Japan straight into the Brotherhood of the New Life was surely one of the strangest Laurence Oliphant ever embarked upon. At least three of the Satsuma delegation who went to Brocton subsequently held very high office under the Meiji Restoration. They were Matsuki Koan, first Japanese Ambassador to London, Foreign Minister and Governor of Kanagawa; Mori Arinori, Minister at Washington in 1871, Minister of Education in 1885, founder of the modern system of education in Japan, and Hisanobu Sameshima, first Japanese Ambassador to France. All three were lifelong Harrisites. Only one of the Shogun's delegation who met Harris in 1865 seems to have been at all anxious to join him, but he was Fukusawa Yukichi, destined to become the most famous teacher of Western culture in Japan, founder of one of the earliest and greatest of Japanese universities, a very influential figure in the Meiji Restoration. It is not certain that he actually went to Brocton but he was one of those who risked discovery by going secretly to visit Laurence Oliphant in 1865. Arthur Cuthbert wrote that Harris looked for great things from the Japanese as Shinto worship centred on the Divine Mother enthroned on Fujiyama, just as the Lily Queen was Sovereign over the Use.

As for the Japanese, they grew wary as their eyes became accustomed to the light of modern day and they learned more about the Use; a few who made the long journey from Japan via San Francisco turned round without staying. As Kuroda Kiyotaka, one of the Commissioners of Foreign Affairs, put it, when they first heard of Harris all in the Brotherhood seemed good and holy; then they discovered the superstitions connected with it. 'Mr Harris talks too many spiritual wonders', they said. By the middle of 1868 even those who would always remain faithful to Harris felt obliged to go home to be present at the birth of the new nation. No doubt it was with relief that they relinquished the menial work they had been obliged to perform – hauling water, carrying bricks, cutting vine poles – work that to men of the *samurai* class, as most of them were, bred in the most rigidly hierarchical society in the world, must have seemed a harsh penance.

Laurence's other attempts at proselytizing were less obviously successful. Georgiana was told she might talk to Lady Elcho (Lord Elcho had been to hear Harris), and to Lady Airlie as long as she was careful what she said. William was asked to send a copy of Harris's works to John Bright in Laurence's name and to others anonymously. As far as society was concerned, it was not quite true, as was said afterwards, that Laurence had entirely disappeared; his letter of resignation to his constituents was dated from Brocton and had been published in the Scottish papers, but very few people knew what it was all about. So when an enterprising reporter got into the community, his story of Harris the Prophet, 'Lord Oliphant', the English MP, and the 'dusky pagans' (the Japanese), created a sensation. In England the *Daily News* was moved to write a leading article on the subject of why so many people deliberately disappeared (curiously enough, Speke's brother had just been retrieved from a self-inflicted limbo). The disappearance of Laurence Oliphant, whom it described as an easy writer, a fluent speaker, a gentleman of graceful manners, was the most remarkable of all.

Thomas Lake Harris was equal to reporters. Whenever he had

anything to do with them a most favourable picture of the expanding wine business, the recently established hotel where travellers were served by ladies from the most socially prominent American families, and the generally thriving condition of the Use appeared in the papers. The means by which the Japanese got to Brocton was not explained. It was inferred that Harris had connections in Japan: soon he was usefully confused with the United States Minister to Edo of that name. Though this error was often made in the years to come, neither Harris nor Laurence ever bothered to correct it. Of the dark side of the Brotherhood of the New Life nothing was revealed.

CHAPTER 7

WAR CORRESPONDENT

In all that strange time Laurence had written nothing. Then, towards the end of 1869, John Blackwood was startled to receive a contribution to the *Magazine* called 'Dollie and the Two Smiths'. This was a satirical description of life in a remote lakeside community of Upper New York State which lacked nothing of the old bite and drive. The farmers of Salem-on-Erie as Laurence presented them were just as venal as their vastly more polished counterparts in *Piccadilly*, and he regarded their antics – wheeling and dealing in small town affairs, dickering for horses, land or wives – with the same sardonic eye. But a kinder note had crept in, as though the hardship of the life they led, of which he had now the most intimate and bitter experience, explained and in some part excused their human failings.

As he described it Salem was a village with a single street, three churches, an equal number of dry goods stores, a schoolhouse, two taverns, a blacksmith, and a billiards saloon. White clapboard houses looked across the lake to the half-cleared, newly settled farms. Parlours, with their ornaments of dried fall leaves, were kept carefully closed as life went on in the kitchen. Lizer, the German servant girl, worth no wages till her English improved, had to share the attic with apples and empty trunks. When she woke, homesick, in the middle of the night, she heard the unmistakable sound of the New World – the howl of the locomotive as it tore past the depôt at the head of the lake.

Lizer and her mistress, Dollie, so Laurence informed his sedentary readers in the clubs and country houses of England, did everything by machine – washing, sewing, knitting stockings, paring apples churning butter, canning sweet corn and tomatoes. The amazing Dollie, besides, milked cows, baked bread, preserved fruit, and saved wood ash for soap. But on Sundays she turned out to go to meeting in a chignon and a long train, 'as neatly chaussée and gantée as if she lived on the Boulevards instead of Beaver Lake'. Her questions to

Elder Fisher on abstruse matters of theology greatly embarrassed that worthy and, Laurence remarked, were slowly eroding his authority in the minds of many of his congregation. Dollie's opinions were radically independent and greatly in favour of women's rights; she allowed no one but herself to fetch her letters from the post. In short, she was a symbol of the New American woman. She was also, one may suppose, in her energy and poise, a portrait of Jane Lee Waring, done with the characteristic teasing affection that Laurence was famous for bestowing effectively and undiscriminatingly on the female sex; an approach which the Prince of Wales described with approval as 'sugar doodling the ladies'.

The bizarre realities of life at Salem-on-Erie, or Brocton, as its uninstructed inhabitants would persist in calling it, did not enter into the article. But its appearance indicated that matters there had come to a crisis, as did the fact that, shortly after the article reached Edinburgh, Laurence himself re-appeared in London. As in the case of Cuthbert, exile from the Brotherhood was part of Harris's method of discipline, but to send Laurence back to the scene of his former life, subject him to the amused inspection of society whose interest had been titillated by the recent newspaper articles, was a refinement of cruelty. On a practical level Harris sent Laurence back to London in order to earn money. This was the more necessary because of the Ruxtons' defection and the bad publicity resulting from it which dried up the flow of offerings. Obediently, Laurence set about his task. As with his Brotherhood name, Margaret Oliphant found the details too odd and distressing to publish. Laurence paid a leading London tailor £500 to teach him the trade in the earnest belief that the making of clothes for the needy poor was a holy occupation. And so, in the early spring of 1870, Woodbine once more sat sewing by himself. This time Harris was not impressed; 'Try something else', he wrote.

That was not easy. In the eyes of the world Laurence was now no more than an erstwhile diplomat, a failed MP, a not so young man who had publicly succumbed to the very odd ideas of a charlatan. But apparently he did entertain hopes of a return to some significant occupation. How realistic these hopes were depended on what view of him was taken by those who had employed him in the secret service of the government in the early 1860s, on their judgement of his continuing reliability. They had not baulked then at his known predilection for seers and spiritualism, but it remained to be seen whether this cover could still be useful, or had become so important in itself as to destroy their confidence in him.

In spite of these difficulties, Laurence was very glad indeed to be home. Margaret Oliphant, who met him shortly after he landed, noted a kind of holiday happiness about him, a restlessness and exuberance which spoke of a new zest for life. He stepped back into society with astonishing ease. Nobody had forgotten him. 'He was too piquant in his personality, and amused society too much to fall aside out of its favour,' wrote Mrs Oliphant. He had hardly any money and was obliged to live in the poorest lodgings and travel third class by train. This made for a certain awkwardness on country visits as the carriage sent to collect guests from the station had to wait for Laurence to arrive from the furthest end of the platform. It was rumoured that he was disenchanted and depressed, as befitted one who had sold his birthright and, far more, his career, for very much less than a mess of pottage. This was not so, according to Mrs Oliphant; she said Laurence remained convinced that, as she put it, the narrow and undistinguished community at Brocton represented the very ideal of society. As everything that was wonderful was said about the Brotherhood of the New Life and Thomas Lake Harris (and not without reason), the questions put to Laurence were sometimes ludicrous. To these, wrote Mrs Oliphant, loyally and rather desperately, 'he knew how to respond with a laugh, a jest or winged word that went through the foolish questioner like an arrow'. Nevertheless the ridicule hurt.

Some people's questions had to be answered. At dinner at Marlborough House, Princess Alexandra asked if it was true that Laurence had hawked fruit along the railway line in Amenia. Yes, he said, he did it because it was necessary, and to keep his pride down. For that, the Prince of Wales remarked, all *he* had to do was step across to Buckingham Palace.

A sudden end to this existence came with the outbreak of the Franco-Prussian war which took almost everyone by surprise. On coming into office as Foreign Secretary on 27 June 1870, Lord Granville declared that not a cloud obscured the prospect of peace. So it was like a clap of thunder in a summer sky when, following the incident of the Ems telegram engineered by Bismarck, France declared war on Prussia on 15 July and marched her troops into the Rhineland. This was the work of the devil, Laurence declared, and set off at once to join in. At first his efforts met with little success. He applied to Lord Granville for a job. The Foreign Secretary promptly invited him down to Walmer Castle where, Laurence said, he was 'kind and civil and disappointingly vague'. The truth may be that it was Laurence who was vague, and Granville did discuss some plan with him. Otherwise the invitation to someone in Laurence's reduced position at a time when the Foreign Secretary was extremely preoccupied, is hard to explain. However, immediately after his return from Walmer, Laurence fell in with Delane who, as unprepared for war as everyone else, was feverishly recruiting special correspondents for *The Times*. He offered Laurence a well-paid job writing letters for the paper from Lyons and the South of France where Republican antagonism towards the Emperor Napoleon was already manifest. Laurence departed at once but made haste very slowly. From Tours on 25 September he wrote to the Duchess of Somerset to explain his sudden disappearance from London. 'I have just come off a 36 hours journey along railways encumbered with wounded men and soldiers hurrying to some army which does not yet exist. The whole country seems to be rising, nothing to be seen but soldiers.'

Laurence was caught up in the second French mobilization which was just as slow and chaotic as the first. In late July and August the wild confusion on the French railways had put paid to the hopes of the Emperor. While the German, on being called to the colours, found his arms and uniform near to hand, a French soldier might have to travel across Europe, or even from Algiers to join his regimental depôt. Consequently, in less than a month, the Germans over-ran the North of France. On 1 September, Sedan fell, Napoleon and one of his armies being taken prisoner there. Bazaine and another were shut up in Metz. The Empress Eugénie fled to England and a Government of National Defence took over in Paris. On 19 September the Prussian-led armies joined hands around the city at Versailles without firing a shot. At Tours, Laurence talked to Lord Lyons, the British Ambassador, who, he told the Duchess, saw nothing for France but a siege of Paris and a fight to the bitter end. Much to the fury of the remaining British residents, the Ambassador did not stay in Paris, but fled the city just as the Germans closed the ring. Now the new French government was raising an army to be controlled from Tours by republican delegates. They were about to acquire a leader in the person of Léon Gambetta, who on 7 October escaped from Paris in a balloon. From Tours, Laurence travelled slowly and uncomfortably towards the South of France. There he discovered that a far uglier and more tragic storm was brewing. In Lyons and Marseilles extreme Republican agitation provoked by, among others, the future Communard leader, Cluseret, and the Russian anarchist, Bakunin, foreshadowed the dreadful civil war to come. Laurence arrived in Lyons in time to witness the scene on 28 September as Cluseret harangued great crowds from the balcony of the Hôtel de Ville. That time the National Guard stood firm and, for the moment, the reds were forced to back down. 'Cluseret's principal claim to being considered a French patriot', scoffed Laurence in *The Times*, 'consists in having become a naturalized American!' Curiously, Cluseret's sojourn in America included a spell directing those Fenians whose activities Laurence had so belittled in his maiden speech as a Member of Parliament.

France was now a dangerous place for foreigners: the English were particularly disliked, their neutrality seen as a betrayal after the French, by fighting side by side with them in the Crimea, had 'saved' India from the Russians for them. On his way to Lyons, Laurence had already been accosted as a Prussian spy. Now a far more dangerous incident occurred. In Lyons, Laurence was challenged by a man suspicious of his appearance. Taking him aside, Laurence explained his business as *The Times* correspondent. The man, Leroy Beaulieu, then offered his services as a guide. By this means, Laurence found his way to a meeting called to set up a committee of public safety, which, as its name implies, was full of ardent revolutionaries. Beaulieu having talked indiscreetly, Laurence's presence became known and the company's mood very angry. *The Times*, it was commonly said in France, had been bought by Bismarck, so what was its correspondent doing there? 'A yelling, cursing crowd all looking for you, all crying vengeance on you', wrote Laurence, 'was a truly terrifying sight.' For a time he sat, petrified, in its midst. Then, as people rose to search him out, Laurence and Beaulieu rose too and, 'loudly humming the Marseillaise', edged towards the door.

For the next week or so they drove about the steep streets in almost the only private carriage to be seen. For although the administration remained in the hands of the legitimate authority, the mood was one of extreme republicanism. Lyons was full of defeated soldiers of the line, whose officers were prisoners in Germany – these and hundreds of unemployed weavers proved fertile ground for revolutionary attitudes. Hatred of foreigners and the bourgeoisie was rife; 'the day of denouncements' was near, Laurence feared.

He did not stay to see it. An urgent message from Mowbray Morris, Manager of *The Times*, directed him to apply for permission to join the Prussian Army Headquarters at Versailles. This was in response to a *cri de coeur* from Delane who had originally planned to send Captain Henry Hozier, who had reported for the paper during the Austro-Prussian war of 1866. (Hozier married Blanche Airlie's daughter and became the father of Clementine Churchill.) The War Office refused permission on the grounds that Hozier was a serving officer. Upon reflection Delane decided that that was all to the good. Oliphant must go instead, he told Morris. This was in spite of the fact that *The Times* already had William Howard Russell there, who was on familiar terms with the staff and dined often with the German princelings at the Hôtel des Résérvoirs. It fell to Morris to explain to an irritated Russell, that Oliphant enjoyed a special relationship with King William of Prussia, but that was not the only reason why Delane and Morris wanted him there. They had in fact just received an ultimatum from Russell that he would not stay to witness or chronicle the bombardment of Paris. This 'silly resolution' wrote Delane in October 1870 was dependent on an event that would not occur: he was assured by Prussians he trusted that there would be no bombardment, the defences of Paris would be attacked separately; 'bombardment don't answer'. Nevertheless, it was as well to have a replacement for Russell in mind.

After receiving Morris's instructions at Lyons, Laurence was out of touch with the newspaper for some time. Afterwards it transpired that his response – an unusual one – had been to cross the French frontier to Berne in order to telegraph personally to Bismarck via the German Legation for permission to go to Versailles. Morris, when he heard, was aghast. All that was necessary was for Laurence to apply for an ordinary Army pass. 'Try to get in somewhere to see something,' he urged. There was bitter competition among foreign newspapers to place correspondents with the Germans, either with their armies in the field, or at Versailles. This was because, from the beginning of the war, the French had denied all access to their troops by order of the Emperor. Himself an erstwhile journalist, Napoleon III was conscious of the way vital information reached the enemy through the Press, and determined to prevent it. *The Times*, which might be said to have invented war correspondents in the person of

William Howard Russell, thundered in vain against this edict. Various undesirable consequences flowed from the French decision. Their self-denial often meant that information was needlessly coloured by the Prussian channels through which it went. And the system was dangerous for correspondents. For instance, Morris ordered Laurence to find out from the Germans full particulars of the movement of the French armies of the Loire and the Vosges. The Germans must have the information, said Morris, and 'you need not scruple to publish it'. But if the French discovered that Laurence was the source, they might well shoot him.

Before that could happen he had to get to Versailles. Once again he went off at a tangent. He went to Frankfurt where he may have sought out Rudolf von Lindau, an old friend from Japan, then working for the *Frankfurter Allgemeine*. Lindau had connections with the Berlin Foreign Office and sometimes acted as Bismarck's mouthpiece in the Press. If Laurence asked him for help with the Chancellor it was of no avail. For on 22 October he wrote to Odo Russell at the Foreign Office in London from Darmstadt complaining that he was still without the necessary pass. In Darmstadt he was comfortably lodged at the British Legation whose chief was another old friend, this time from Schleswig Holstein days, Robert Morier. Laurence gave Odo Russell a long, gloomy, and most accurate account of the state of France and the ever increasing likelihood of civil war.

It was not until early in November that Laurence arrived at Versailles. Probably not without a certain satisfaction, William Howard Russell reported to Mowbray Morris that he was still without papers. 'he is *mal vu* here and he attributes it to two causes – his absence in America and his odd opinions, but the fact is that he is only remembered as a very ultra liberal, a *friend* of *Morier* when he was last in Berlin.' It was decidedly not the time for liberals. Bismarck's response to Laurence's various approaches had been so abrupt and negative that Laurence now feared to approach the Chancellor direct. Sadly, his apprehension was shared by all those liberal Germans with whom he had been most closely associated during the Schleswig Holstein affair, to whom he now appealed for help. Roggenbach, Minister of the Duke of Coburg, though he had promised to intercede with Bismark's secretary at Versailles, shirked sending a letter. Even the Crown Prince of Prussia felt obliged to send an aide to pump William Howard Russell on Laurence's reasons for being at

Versailles. Apparently satisfied, he invited him to dinner. At this dinner Laurence's description of the revolt in Lyons and Marseilles greatly heartened the Prince, who hoped it would spread to Paris and so compel surrender before a decision had to be taken to bombard the city into submission. Crown Prince Frederick was firmly opposed to this, both on humanitarian grounds, and because he knew how unpopular it would be in England. But, as William Howard Russell pointed out to Mowbray Morris the Crown Prince was *persona non grata* with the Prussian High Command and his marriage to the Princess Royal was deeply unpopular; his views were hardly likely to carry much weight.

The question of Laurence's papers had still not been resolved when the French suddenly offered him a way out. On 9 November, the republican Army of the Loire, under General d'Aurelle de Paladines, won a much needed victory by driving the Germans out of Orleans, thus posing a threat to the whole German position round Paris. Hastily, the Grand Duke of Mecklenburg Schwerin was ordered to block the French advance. Men, arms and equipment poured out of Versailles and with them went Laurence, pretending that the confusion was the only reason for his lack of a pass. In true Oliphant style he described his departure as dramatic, dashing off literally at a moment's notice in a fiacre hired from the nearest public stand. But it was careless of him to depart in this precipitous manner as his presence at the Orleans campaign had been planned by William Howard Russell and Morris at least a week before. Much to his annoyance, he was just too late to observe the battle of Coulmiers which the Germans lost. Their defeat propelled the campaign right into the centre of the stage, as d'Aurelle de Paladines was suddenly felt to be capable of raising the siege of Paris.

Laurence, who was the only English correspondent with the Army, now sent home a series of brilliantly evocative articles describing the impact of German troops upon a quintessential part of France. As such they are timeless and may stand, not only for 1870, but for 1914 and 1940. At this moment in 1870, public opinion in England was shifting from its earlier approval of Germany and condemnation of France towards keen sympathy for the conquered. These articles, from which Laurence tried to exclude his own growing disquiet at German behaviour, nevertheless did much to strengthen the anti-Prussian mood in England. The Germans were guilty of pillaging, Laurence told the Duchess of Somerset, but he could not say so for fear of being sent away from the Army. Part of the trouble lay in the Prussian habit of quartering its army directly upon the civilian population. Tents were not carried and bivouacs made only when all else failed. In the towns the Prussian Intendant based his demands on the tax returns – so and so many people must provide so much food, beds and fodder. In the villages of the Beauce and Eure et Loire, where Laurence followed the Army, the first thing to be taken over was the oven, on which a guard was placed, then the butcher and the blacksmith. Tickets were issued to soldiers and civilians alike for bread and meat. Flour was scarce for the corn lay unthreshed.

Laurence became intimately acquainted with the fear and anger of the peasants at the military requisitions. As he had no papers he was obliged to fend for himself in the matter of food and lodging. That often meant dining off a loaf of bread and sleeping in the carriage. Sometimes, though, it meant clean sheets and a dinner 'quite artistic in its excellence'. Though his dispatches did not say so, Laurence shared his varying fortunes with a German correspondent and a French servant he had picked up in Frankfurt. They were his only companions as there was not much love lost between him and the Grand Duke's staff. They were supercilious and arrogant, he grumbled, and could not understand how a newspaper correspondent could be a gentleman. For their part, the Germans were increasingly concerned at the sale of arms to the French by free lance Birmingham manufacturers and some of the odium rubbed off on Laurence. But there was a more serious reason for the friction. William Howard Russell's correspondence with Mowbray Morris shows that the Germans thought Laurence's French servant was a spy. General von der Tann, commanding the Army, sent a furious telegram to the Crown Prince at Versailles complaining about Laurence and his servant. Orders were sent at once for the man to be arrested and sent to Germany. 'Was it not strange for Oliphant to take a Frenchman who had been hanging about Frankfurt to the HQ of a Germany Army,' commented Russell. 'What could he mean?' Russell could not explain. Dining with the Crown Prince that night, he reported him 'not as jolly as usual'.

After that Laurence spent a good deal of time either ahead of the Army, or at a distance from it. To follow it was to risk becoming trapped in the lengthy convoy of supply wagons. 'It was high treason to cross or disrupt the line of march.' So he and his companion went off by themselves, making a good six miles an hour on the smooth, hard roads, often arriving at a village dangerously soon after the French had left, but in front of the Germans. As they travelled over the swelling cornfields, the huge, dim outline of Chartres Cathedral rose like a lighthouse in the distance. The French were shy of coming to battle and had to be hunted down. For a time it was almost pleasant, a late November sun shone and the roses were still out in some of the loveliest country in France. Here again were villages with but a single street, a blacksmith's and a tavern. But this time they were ancient, stone-built, with a chateau at one end and a horse pond at the other. Surly men in blouses hung about in knots, and frightened old women stood at cottage doors in front of the young ones, who were forbidden to come out. The franc-tireurs had become more active in recent weeks, drawing down upon the country people German reprisals: suspects were shot and houses burned. Round Orleans the priests were ordered to preach a crusade. Laurence was indignant at the risk their action placed the people under. He described their plight with compassion, with that gentleness towards people in trouble he always showed.

As the weather turned sharply cold, fighting began in earnest. Laurence followed its course, from the edge of woods, across ravines, behind stone walls, and, most advantageously of all, from the steeples of village churches. This was dangerous; he risked being taken for a sniper by either side. He acquired a reputation for foolhardiness. 'He was not an ideal war correspondent,' wrote Alexander Innes Shand, 'he risked himself too freely ... even the Zouaves blamed the Englishman's rashness.' In December the French began to lose battles. At Artenay the dead froze, jammed in the furrows, and the wounded died of cold in the night. 'The German soldiers made pilgrimages between the straw they slept in in the barns and huge fires of unthreshed wheat straw at which they warmed themselves.' In England committees were formed to collect seed corn for the next season's sowing, for there would be none in the Beauce.

Laurence was getting tired. 'There is something awful about getting up every morning and going to a battle as regularly and calmly as if one were going partridge shooting,' he remarked. After writing despatches at the end of the day, he found that his head gave him warning that he had used it enough. The destruction of Châteaudun particularly upset him. 'In the midst stood the remains of a hotel, little left to mine host but his white paper cap and coat, and, as he stood in his kitchen with a huge shothole over the chimney and a soup ladle in his hand, I begged him in my character of conqueror and fellow Christian to give me food and lodging.' Many of the three hundred houses burned down in the town had been set on fire by hand.

The Germans re-entered Orleans on 4 December. Laurence was there almost too soon, forced to take shelter in the suburbs at night as the artillery wagons dashed past like fire engines and the troops doubled along the pavé. The German bombardment had been frightening in its intensity. Hozier, who was there as assistant military attaché, confided to Russell that, if no one had been looking, he would have bolted from the shells. The ruins of Orleans reminded Laurence of Canton after the English attack; M. le Maire had tried to resist and the city had been punished for it. The Germans made a noisy jubilee of their return, drums rolled, bands played, trotting cavalry jingled past, soldiers sang. They were watched by French prisoners, cold and bored, huddled around the statue of Jeanne d'Arc in the centre of the Square. The weather was still bitter, the Loire carrying down masses of ice. Four small gunboats each had a little brass gun trained on the quais.

After the battle of Beaugency, Laurence went back to Versailles. The reason, Russell reported to Morris, was that his German companion had been ordered away by the Grand Duke, who objected to the content of his dispatches. According to Russell, Laurence felt he could not carry on without his friend. Although Russell paid generous tribute to the brilliance of Laurence's campaign articles – Delane and Morris were delighted with them – he did not conceal his irritation at Laurence being granted complete freedom of movement while all the other correspondents were under his control. Russell made it clear that he thought Laurence not only incapable of working alone, but unstable to such a degree that he could not live without society and a companion to talk to. That would hardly have been surprising in a normal person returning from a close acquaintance with the scenes of a bitter war, but Laurence was still under the strain of his duty to Harris: no wonder he appeared pinched and cold on returning to Versailles, and walked in his sleep. Morris told him to stay for Christmas to rest and recuperate.

He did not lack company of the most diverse kind there. William Howard Russell saw him talking earnestly with the Duke of Coburg; he dined often at the Hôtel des Résérvoirs with the bored and idle members of the so-called 'ornamental staff'. Shortly after his return he was happy to greet his old friend, Odo Russell, whom the Foreign Office had sent on a special mission to Bismarck concerning an apparent Russian threat to the Black Sea. Alexander Innes Shand was another friend who wrote for *The Times* and was destined to be one of those who sustained him in the last years of his life. Then there was Lord Adare, a raging spiritualist who, in the intervals of chasing young men, wrote articles for the *Daily Telegraph*, which the Crown Prince of Prussia thought extremely hostile. There was D. D. Home, 'Mr Sludge the medium', who prowled about Versailles, courtesy of the *San Francisco Chronicle*, pinching stories from the journalists and capitalizing on the King of Prussia's known interest in spiritualism. He was *persona non grata* to the French, since his influence over the Empress Eugénie at the birth of the Prince Imperial had been so great as to make Walewski, the Foreign Minister, threaten to deport him as an Italian spy. In 1870 there were still many people in England, on the Continent, and in America who believed that they had seen Mr Home float gently and horizontally out of a window towards a rhododendron bush, returning, by another, with a flower. Lord Adare certainly did. Laurence believed it to be possible, but felt it to be trivial.

The person who saw most of Laurence that bitterly cold Christmas at Versailles was W. H. Russell with whom he shared rooms. It is clear from Russell's diary that Laurence confided in him about Harris and the Brotherhood of the New Life. Russell was intrigued and not unsympathetic, though he often found Laurence's presence irksome. He was himself exhausted, bored and jumpy. He complained that Laurence disturbed him, never stopped asking unimportant questions, and consulted him on all points. On Christmas Day his irritation boiled over. 'I tried to write but "New Life" is a nuisance. What would the "New Life" be? It would monopolize all it wanted – sticks its legs across yours on a cold day obscuring the fire, be immensely vain, also lecherous in an odd sense – very willing to intrigue for ends – very cautious in money matters, a deceiving yet practical life with eyes to main chance.'

Circumstances were making them all jumpy. On 31 December a group of English correspondents, Laurence among them, were gathered to see the New Year in. It was clear and cold and very silent: the Paris forts had not fired for hours. But, as the clock struck twelve, on the very last stroke the great guns of Mont Valérien shattered the calm. On 4 January Russell got a hint that something was about to happen at last – the German bombardment of Paris. True to his determination, he refused to watch it and handed over the arrangements made for him to Laurence. Fog on the day obscured everything. Morris was upset, both by the lack of news and by Russell's behaviour. 'Are the kitchens and cellars indifferent at HQ?' he enquired sarcastically, 'or is it the bombardment turns your stomach?'

Morris now determined that Oliphant, not Russell, should enter Paris whenever the siege was lifted. Russell, who was feeling old, tired, and ill, acknowledged the sense of this but with reservations. Oliphant was a writer of immense power, he told Morris, but during the years of isolation with his sect in America he had come to doubt his own ability. And at that particular moment he was in a highly nervous condition, walking in his sleep and appearing very unhappy – 'moony melancholy' was how Russell put it – at the prospect of being sent back to the continuing Loire campaign without a companion. Odo Russell feared for his friend in this event and urged that Laurence ought not to be left alone. As it happened he was not, for another correspondent volunteered to accompany him. This was Alfred Austin, a 'queer, proud little man', who Russell feared would be a drag on Laurence in the field. Austin never travelled anywhere without a foot warmer in the carriage and insisted on clean sheets and a decent bed every night. However appropriate for a future Poet Laureate, these were hardly the thing for a war correspondent. This time Laurence went better prepared; he even acquired a sort of uniform consisting of a frogged coat, a gold band to his hat, and Russell's Indian medal as a defence against spy catchers. As well as the medal, 'which pleased him very much', he carried Russell's Chlorodyne against everyone's common enemy, diarrhoea. As he followed the German Army to the surrender of Rouen, Jules Favre arrived in Versailles to negotiate an armistice, which was signed on 27 January. Paris was starving and in flames. From their strongholds of Belleville and Montmartre red republicans threatened the Government of National Defence.

Morris sent at once to order Laurence into Paris only to find that he had already set out. There were more than fifty correspondents at Versailles clamouring for permission to enter the city, but Bismarck refused to allow them in; he did not want any more useless mouths to fill while food was short. A way had to be found to circumvent the guards. The first to succeed was Alistair Forbes, whose brilliant dispatches to the *Daily News* had regularly scooped *The Times*. He got in on 31 January but left almost at once. On 1 February, Laurence and a friend set off in a one horse shay stuffed with food – cold turkey, tongue, paté, sausages, bread, biscuits and chocolate. For public consumption Laurence's story was that, in the queue at the Pont de Neuilly, they persuaded an old woman to ride with them posing as their mother, and so bluffed their way across. Privately, he told John Blackwood, he went in 'in the diplomatic bag'.

Once in Paris there was much to do. During the armistice France had to elect delegates to a Constituent Assembly to sit at Bordeaux. Having established his headquarters at the Hôtel Chatham on the Champs Elysées, Laurence set out to take the political temperature. He did not like what he found. Paris was in a dangerously unstable state and there was no one really in control. 'Those who are discreet and able are weak and irresolute. In its present mood the nation cannot appreciate talent unless it is combined with passion. Unfortunately, it even seems to prefer the passion without the talent.' Every political meeting Laurence went to ended in a shouting match and, as he climbed the steep sloppy streets of Belleville, he collected pocketfuls of candidates' lists.

Many observers felt that the unbearably frivolous Parisians deserved all they had got. They deplored the inaccuracy of the French press which, throughout the war, had consistently exaggerated victory and dismissed or ignored defeat. Now *Le Figaro* justified this: 'It is necessary to gild our misfortunes and to fall with grace and to wreathe our memory with garlands.' A patriotic government would have covered it with ashes, remarked Laurence. So far his published comments, if acid, had been restrained. Then, on or about 10 February, he went to a theatrical representation of the fall of Châteaudun. As one who had seen the ruins he was deeply upset: the performance disgusted him: it was parody, indecency, buffoonery, he stormed: disaster had hardened the French, they were near the brink of the abyss and seemed to feel no humiliation. 'At this moment France is in need of a Prophet, rather than a President', he declared in *The Times*.

Morris could not have this. 'Highly as we esteem your opinion,' he wrote, 'we must not forget that a correspondent's first duty is to give information.' Laurence must not be so harsh on the Parisians. But Laurence was listening to another voice. On 10 February he wrote to

Morris that he was thinking of returning to Brocton; he warned the Manager that his departure, when it came, would be sudden. It seems that he had letters from America that were causing him considerable disquiet.

Morris took the threat of his departure with amazing calm considering that he had nobody to fill his place at such a crucial time. Delane did not trust Hardman, the previous incumbent, and there was something wrong with William Howard Russell, whom Laurence had taken to referring to privately as the 'decorated doctor'. In early March, Morris wrote to Russell that he would take no responsibility for his further movements; 'all your recent letters to Delane and me have been written in such a tone that we agreed that it was desirable you should return home at once'. Morris offered Laurence Russell's brougham and pair and recommended him to take a central apartment for the sake of comfort and privacy and in order to receive visits from people who did not like being seen in hotels.

Shortly after this Morris was relieved to hear that Laurence would stay on in Paris, at least for a time. He had become immersed in tracing the course of the threatening civil war, risking his life by roaming the streets in search of events: as usual never more happy than in action, excitement and danger. And as always, he dressed the part. Gone was the silken top hat and black frock coat of everyday wear. Shand saw him bustling about the disturbed quarters of Paris 'in a flexible felt and a suit of tweeds'. Often the rappel, with its terrifying echo of the great Revolution, was beaten at night and men marched to the sound of drums. Laurence got up then and went out to see the National Guard gather. Among the peaceable portion of the inhabitants he sensed a kind of restlessness that reminded him of cattle stirring before a storm.

On 15 February, *The Times* carried a dispatch by him which identified the danger posed to the French government by growing disaffection among the National Guard. Throughout the siege they had drawn money and rations and, as working men, had never lived better. Now the siege was over money would stop, and work would not be available. Then, Laurence foresaw, would come the pressure which would drive these men to adopt the political methods of Félix Pyat, the most extreme Communard leader; 'and inasmuch as when this movement begins, it will possibly spread under the influence of an organization which ramifies all through Europe, disturbances in Paris may be the signal for a sympathetic action wherever labour and poverty are synonymous words ... the social revolution will be most complete where the extremes of poverty and riches have been most striking.' Karl Marx could hardly have expressed it better. Once again Laurence foresaw events lying far in the future. Of that particular harvest the Commune was the seed.

On 19 February the delegates at Bordeaux voted overwhelmingly for Adolphe Thiers to become the head of the new government. In *The Times* Laurence wrote that many people expressed doubt and dismay, for Thiers was a persistent advocate of war and 'however remarkable his talent for conversation and his power of historical observation, those who know him intimately must feel that, with the best intentions to serve his country he possesses neither the nerve or judgement which will fit him for the leader of a nation in this last extremity'. This was harsh, but it was consistent with Laurence's attitude towards Thiers throughout the time he remained as Paris correspondent.

As the time for the German entry into Paris approached, great fear was expressed about the reaction of the populace. Laurence shared it: it only needed some half drunken man or fanatical woman to fire a pistol to provoke a terrible disaster. But it must take place. If the Germans did not enter the French would say they were afraid. Yet when the day came the entry was quiet, almost unnoticed, few Parisians being allowed on the Champs Elysées to see the Germans march around the Arc de Triomphe. Statues in the Place de la Concorde were draped in crepe; the French were not displaying their usual taste, Laurence felt. Russell watched the review at Longchamps before the Emperor William and then left by special train to forward the news to London. Laurence remained to observe the German departure on 3 March. What he saw would never be forgotten or forgiven by the French. This time the Germans marched straight under the Arc de Triomphe: 'as the head of each battalion came under the Arch the mounted officer leading it reined up for a moment, cast one look up at the list of victories inscribed overhead, one glance back to their men, then, waving their helmets high above their heads, gave the signal for a ringing cheer'.

The German departure released a surge of talk, of movement on the boulevards and in the clubs and cafes. If talk could save a country there would be no fear for France, Laurence thought. But the relief was short-lived. Paris was an armed camp with the disaffected National Guard facing Thiers's soldiers. And wherever a barricade was to be built, or a police agent damned, there were the women, more excited and dangerous than the men. At night Laurence explored Montmartre, a horrid waste of shanties, crumbling walls and ruins, with only one steep approach road. Up this road on 26 February, the National Guard had dragged two hundred cannon to save them from the German entry. Now these guns dominated the rest of the city. Very early on 18 March Laurence got wind of a Government order to the Army to retrieve the cannons. He arrived at Montmartre at 5 a.m. in the rain, slipping through a line of artillery horses. There he found bloody chaos, the barricades manned, the soldiers mutinied, two Generals massacred, and the National Guard about to march on the centre of the city. By evening the Thiers government had fled to Versailles and the red flag of the Commune flew over the Hôtel de Ville.

Paris was now exceedingly dangerous but Laurence went on reporting for *The Times*. He was not popular with the Communard leaders: of Félix Pyat he had written that he suspected he was a raving lunatic. Mowbray Morris was anxious for his safety and on 21 March wrote to ask him to take care. The following day Laurence and Furley, another *Times* man, went to observe a demonstration called by the Parti de l'Ordre in the Place de l'Opera. Laurence was much struck by the fact that those members of the party present were of apparently high social standing. They were unarmed. As it moved towards the Rue de la Paix the crowd was met by sentries of the National Guard who hesitated and fell back. 'Thus encouraged, with loud cheers and waving of hats, and frantic applause from the windows and balconies the great procession of black coats and hats moved on,' wrote Laurence in *The Times*. But there came a check and the crowd moved back as its leaders perceived a barricade at the Place Vendôme manned by National Guard. Laurence and Furley were pushed into the door of a bank and went upstairs for a better view. They saw a young officer seize a tricolour, the flag of Thiers, and lead the unarmed people towards the barricade. Some National Guard reversed their arms; others fired point blank into the crowd.

Bodies were everywhere, a man and a dog lay bleeding side by side. Not all were dead: 'many lay in a line behind a lamppost or quite under the arch of a door'. A bullet shattered the window of the bank and a splinter of glass lodged in Furley's hat.

That bullet did more than break a window, it provided the most powerful impetus to the legend that had begun to grow about

Laurence Oliphant and the Prophet Harris. The story went that Laurence took it as a sign that Harris wanted him to return to America and that his life would be forfeit if he disobeyed. To the disbelief and scandal of the assembled Press Laurence left Paris that evening for the United States. He never explained or elaborated upon his strange action. But the letters of William Howard Russell to Mowbray Morris of *The Times* provide an answer to the riddle of why Laurence left his post at such a critical time.

These letters show that Laurence had received disquieting news from America during the previous week which had almost prompted him to leave at once. He confided in Russell. 'He was very unhappy and irresolute as to his purpose of staying and at last said he could be trifling with his conscience after having had a warning if he stayed, as he had a clear intimation of what he ought to do and only wavered about the time of going.' After some thought, Russell said, Laurence decided to stay another week while Russell went to London taking with him a telegram to Thomas Lake Harris announcing the date of Laurence's departure for America. On the morning of the demonstration by the Parti de l'Ordre Laurence had had further letters from America which meant he must depart that evening. He was in much distress of mind, Russell reported to Morris, and regretted the fact that he appeared to be throwing *The Times* over. In spite of the story about the bullet, Laurence made arrangements with Mowbray Morris for his post to be covered during his absence and told him the date of his expected return.

So why did he go? The reason was his mother. Lady Oliphant was very ill, 'an absolute breakdown of health and strength was threatened', wrote Margaret Oliphant. Her penance at Brocton had been longer and harder than that of her son and not merely in the unaccustomed manual labour she had been obliged to undertake. Her sacrifice was Laurence himself. She had not been allowed to say good bye to him when he left in 1869. Throughout all the months of the war she had been allowed no letters from him. 'She who had broken her heart over every parting, she who had lived upon his letters and desired to share every serious thought,' wrote Mrs Oliphant, 'she was kept without information or consolation.' She was afraid of exile, of the discipline that no one, not even Jane Lee Waring, escaped. It was said of her by the other members of the Brotherhood that if she were asked to leave Vinecliff she would get no further than the gate where she would lie down and die.

She was not alone in this fear and, while Laurence was at sea on his way from Paris to Brocton, the Brotherhood was shaken by the fate of another outcast. James Fowler was a man of feeble constitution and weak nerves, whom Harris ordered to leave. Fowler obliged but, after a time of aimless wandering, crept back to Brocton and shot himself. Robert Martin remembered how Mrs Fowler had been made to wait at table at the hotel, where people pointed her out as the wife of the man who had killed himself the day before. This death could not be concealed and contributed towards the unease about the Brotherhood that had been growing for some time among the local inhabitants. Newspapers like the *Mayville Sentinel* and the *Fredonia Censor* gave much space to Fowler's suicide.

When Laurence arrived at Brocton Harris surprised him with the announcement that he proposed to hand back all the property given to the Brotherhood by its members. This was in consequence of the Ruxton affair, which had been followed by the departure of some families and almost all the Japanese. According to Harris, Laurence wept, and pleaded with him to keep the land, arguing that the law did not allow foreigners to own it. Whatever the truth of that – and Harris was still in possession of the land ten years later – his control over the members of the Brotherhood was clearly under strain. In the aftermath of the Fowler affair he proposed to take Mrs Requa and Jane Lee Waring on an extended trip to Europe, staying first with the Cowper-Temples at Broadlands. Laurence also returned to Paris, taking his mother with him. Though he did not openly question Harris's behaviour towards her, he was deeply upset at her condition.

In Paris he and Lady Oliphant moved in to a house in the Rue du Centre. Laurence had been away less than two months. On 16 May Valentine Chirol, then nineteen, came across him in the street, watching the destruction of the Colonne Vendôme – 'a tall Englishman with a long flowing beard'. Recognizing Chirol to be English, Laurence warned him that to be present at one of the Commune's madder acts of historical revenge was hardly safe. On 21 May 1871, Thiers's army entered Paris and savage retribution was exacted from the Commune, which took a week to die. Fires were still burning and prisoners being marched through the streets when Thomas Lake Harris, Jane Waring, and Mrs Requa arrived in Paris following their visit to Broadlands. It was not the time for tourists. But, as with the upheaval of the American Civil War, Harris professed to see great opportunities for spiritual regeneration arising out of the bloody shambles that was Paris. 'The sphere of opposition to divine order is much weaker than in England.' Illness came between the Prophet and his task. He succumbed to a series of fits that induced temporary paralysis. Jane Waring's letters home described these fits with such a marked lack of concern as to suggest that they were not infrequent. It is possible that this was the reason why the members of the Brotherhood gave Harris a wide berth whenever they detected certain signs. It was decided that the party should go on to Switzerland so that Father could find 'peace in high places'. And the newspapers there would make better reading than the *Mayville Sentinel* and the *Fredonia Censor* which would keep harking back to Fowler's death.

Laurence was privately relieved at their departure; 'Father's presence is an awful pressure, though it is a blessed one'. His life was hectic enough without Father. Far from dismissing him, *The Times* had made him Chief Correspondent in Paris at a salary of £1,200 a year. He earned it. He wrote brilliantly and knew everybody; as Edmond de Goncourt remarked, he was treated like an Ambassador rather than a journalist. John Blackwood, who visited him in the summer of 1872, marvelled at the life he led. 'Everyone, from the Duc d'Aumale (the Orleanist leader) down consults him and there is a constant frenzy of comings and goings. Yesterday at déjeuner a card was sent in for him and he disappeared upstairs to see von Arnim, the Prussian Ambassador. Then, a very fine looking fellow who proved to be Prince George Solms, a cousin of the King of Hanover (a fierce Russian hater) was shown into the room. In addition there were the Vicomte de Calonne of unknown principles and M. and Mme de Blowitz.'

Laurence, who was to be the means of introducing Blowitz to *The Times*, met him at the house of a mutual friend, Frederic Marshall. Marshall was a business man who had lived for twenty years in France and lost all his money in the war. During the siege he wrote articles for the *Daily Telegraph*. John Blackwood thought him interesting, if odd. In 1872 he had for a long time been a sort of teacher and guide at the Japanese Embassy in Paris, and Blackwood learned a good deal about him from long conversations with the Japanese Minister, Hisanobu Sameshima, one of the Japanese Laurence had taken to Brocton in 1865 who remained a faithful follower of Thomas Lake Harris. Blackwood found this out to his cost when he and his wife, 'indiscreetly' as he put it, expressed their regret in front of Sameshima that Laurence remained a disciple of that faith.

Laurence and Blowitz came to know each other very well while sitting at the bedside of Frederic Marshall's daughter, who had consumption. That was in the summer of 1871 when Blowitz was Thiers's poodle. His acquaintance with Thiers went back to 1848 when, a wanderer of unknown origin, uncertain fortune and unproven ability, Blowitz arrived in Paris at the age of about twenty-three from somewhere in Bohemia. Eventually, as a rather unlikely professor of foreign literature, he had come to rest at Marseilles, Thiers's birthplace and political stronghold. In April 1871 when an insurrection threatened Marseilles, Blowitz had rendered invaluable help to the Prefect and in consequence had been sent to Versailles to be congratulated by the President of the Republic. From then on he had had daily access to Thiers.

In July Hardman, Laurence's assistant, was to be away. Frederic Marshall suggested that Blowitz should step into the breach. Laurence agreed, sensible of the value of easy access to Thiers. Blowitz had never even seen a copy of *The Times*, so Laurence spread the paper on the floor and explained the rudiments to him. In this way was the 'Prince of Journalists' born. According to Blowitz, Thiers was pleased since he saw the appointment as a means to use *The Times* to his advantage. But Blowitz soon disillusioned him. 'The intercourse between M. Thiers and myself was at times less candid, for I had to give news which embarrassed him instead of the one sided information which he communicated to me to help his policy.'

In August 1871 Blowitz' appointment with *The Times* was extended. It was about this time that Edmond de Goncourt told a curious story about Laurence Oliphant which, though his memoirs are untrustworthy, seems plausible. Goncourt said that Blowitz was the means of introducing Oliphant into Versailles during peace negotiations between the French and the Prussians from which all newspaper correspondents had been excluded. The Prussian delegate was Count von Arnim, Ambassador in Paris. Thiers proving obdurate, von Arnim declared, 'to hear you talk you might have won the battle of Sedan'. At this, Thiers burst into tears and accused von Arnim of taking advantage of a fallen adversary. Thereupon von Arnim refused to have anything more to do with him, and it was Oliphant, conveniently at hand, who, after consultations with Thiers, drew up the agreement with von Arnim. In fact, talks about reparations did take place at Versailles in August 1871, between von

Arnim and Thiers. And it was in August that year that Laurence was offered the Legion of Honour which he refused, almost as if it had been a badge of servitude. Moreover, he could hardly be persuaded to meet Thiers after that and, when he did see him, was irritated and haughty, and treated the President of the Third Republic with something like contempt.

In the summer of 1871 Blowitz and his wife came to share the house in the Rue du Centre with Laurence and Lady Oliphant. They became acquainted with the name and history of Thomas Lake Harris. Blowitz did not admire him and told Laurence that his philosophy was based on pride. In spite of this the two men got on well together; they respected each other's ability and shared each other's work. Though Laurence was a superb writer of articles about subjects that appealed to him, he was clumsy at composing short telegrams and bored by the routine of gathering news. Blowitz was good at both and almost too good at sniffing out information, so that *The Times* was accused of being in Thiers's pocket. As Chief Correspondent Laurence was concerned at these charges, but told Mowbray Morris he could counter them by the independent tone of his articles. His own independence and sense of equilibrium rapidly returned in the absence of Harris, who went back to America at the end of 1871. Margaret Oliphant, who stayed with Laurence and his mother at about that time, was gratified by the change in him since his first re-appearance in the world. He was sobered out of his first elation, she thought, and profited greatly from resuming work which, while it was not all that he once might have hoped, was yet worthy of him and his training. That Laurence once more had a home, Mrs Oliphant thought, had a lot to do with his increased confidence and tranquillity.

It was at this moment of tranquillity, when he was forty-two, that Laurence at last met the woman who was to become his wife. On her would depend the maintenance of that tranquillity, the continuation of his life in a normal groove. Because he was always vulnerable to the personality of the woman nearest to him, her influence would be paramount. His life had already been extraordinary, and, at the same time, wasteful; it would take a remarkable woman to separate him from the redoubtable Harris and salvage what remained of his brilliant promise. This *was* a remarkable woman and her influence upon Laurence had extraordinary results. Their life together was not tranquil, but very curious and sad.

CHAPTER 8

ALICE

'SHE is twenty-six and according to my taste very pretty,' Laurence wrote to a friend in March 1872, 'but that has nothing to do with it.' As her portrait shows, Alice was more than pretty; she was enchanting. Poised and slender with dark hair and wide dark eyes in a pale and delicate face; an air of fragile beauty was belied by the mouth and chin: the mouth was full, the chin determined. Her gaze was forceful, mocking, and surprisingly sly. Her voice was low and musical, yet clear and deliberate, so that people who heard her were doubly attracted. Robert Browning called her 'a perfect flower of womankind'. In Margaret Oliphant's opinion, Alice displayed all those attributes necessary to the wife of a distinguished man. 'A young woman of an ancient and long established race with all the advantages of a fine and careful training, and that knowledge from her cradle of good society, good manners and notable persons, which is an advantage beyond all estimates to the mind qualified to profit by it ... one of the most attractive and charming of God's creatures ... full of brightness and originality, sympathetic, clear headed, yet an enthusiast.' It was this last quality that was the key to Alice's character and the arbiter of her fate. No one knew this better than Margaret Oliphant who portrayed Alice in the most sympathetic light and yet contrived to suggest to those prepared to read most carefully the reason for a marriage which, to people who were acquainted with Laurence's history and beliefs, seemed unlikely and unsuitable, and to Alice's relations at first simply horrendous.

She was descended from a Norfolk family of the sort that was so very old and distinguished that titles were superfluous. For complicated reasons of inheritance, her father's full name was Henry l'Estrange-Styleman Le Strange. He was squire of Hunstanton and master of an ancient rambling house. After an unsuccessful attempt to enter Parliament in 1847, he gave himself up entirely to his first love, the decoration of churches. He was both a scholar and an able painter, and fortunate in the time which allowed him to practise both to their best advantage. For it was the period of ecclesiastical embellishment and Henry Styleman Le Strange had the finest to work on. In 1856, the Dean and Chapter of Ely Cathedral invited him to decorate the roof of the nave. He spent two years in research before he began to paint. In 1860, he was invited to assist Butterfield in drawing up plans for St. Albans, Holborn. In July 1862, he collapsed and died. His designs, wrote his son, Hamon, 'were the fruit of much learned study and great religious enthusiasm'. It was in this atmosphere of dedicated scholarship and High Anglican celebration that Alice was brought up. When her father died she was sixteen, and everything changed.

Her mother, born Jamesina Stewart of Inverness-shire, married again. Her second husband was Charles Wynne Finch, sometime M.P. for Caernarvon. By all accounts he was a devoted stepfather, and Alice and her two sisters, Jamesina and Ada, were often at Voelas, his family estate in the mountains of Wales. But never for long. Although she entertained at Voelas, the second Mrs Wynne Finch was not enamoured of its beauty, wildness and freedom. Her heart lay in Paris, in the life of the salons, and it was a measure of her sophistication and intelligence that she moved in that difficult world with ease, and became fast friends with one of its leading lights, the small, fuzzy haired, short skirted, witch-like and eccentric Madame Mohl, herself a Scot. As Mary Clarke, she had been born in Edinburgh in 1790, but brought up in France in close proximity to Madame Récamier and her constant companion, Chateaubriand. After her marriage to Julius Mohl, a distinguished Orientalist, her salon became a fashionable centre of opposition to Louis Napoleon. Among its French habitués were Montalambert, Renan, Guizot, Mérimée and Barthélemy St. Hilaire. Her friends among English society included Florence Nightingale; Dean Stanley and his wife, Lady Augusta; Lady William Russell and her sons, Odo and Arthur; Nassau Senior; Kinglake; and the Brownings. The Le Strange children, especially the youngest, Guy, were much petted by Madame Mohl and it was Guy's privilege always to make the tea.

However stimulating the conversation and distinguished the company at Madame Mohl's, this was hardly the life to satisfy Alice. By 1872 she had been for nearly ten years a grown woman in her mother's shadow, and Mrs Wynne Finch, no less a beauty than Alice in her time, was by all accounts not an easy person to get on with. By then Alice's sisters were married; and it was a little surprising that the beautiful, kind, charming, and fairly rich Miss Le Strange had not spread her wings before. The reason was her inability to compromise: if she could not soar, she would not fly. Alexander Kinglake who, like Browning, knew both Alice and her mother well, saw in her two things that do not often go together; imagination and force of character. He said that Alice yearned to make an alliance between mind and soul and liked to wield the faculty of close reasoning; 'but her glorious eyes showed all the time that imagination was the dominant gift'. Margaret Oliphant shrewdly remarked that Alice was a little weary of admiration and tired of unprofitable life. She longed for something better and higher than she had yet found. The opportunity of practising charity offered by life in the country could not compensate for the boredom of living there, and the calm and indulgent Christianity she generally encountered left her wanting something more magnanimous and, at the same time, exacting and authoritative; in short, 'her slight shoulders longed for a cross to be laid on them and her impatient heart for some great thing to suffer or to do'.

Ironically, it was Lady Oliphant who was responsible for bringing Laurence the wife she had always feared to encounter. Left to her own devices in Paris while he worked all hours, she took to going for drives and Alice, as a neighbour, was invited to accompany her. It was not long before Lady Oliphant imparted to her all the details of their life at Brocton. Her story seems to have had upon Alice the effect of a revelation. By her own account she was fascinated by the idea and almost immediately attracted to the disciple. For the first time, she said, she saw someone who not only held the highest views she had ever imagined on the subject of one's responsibilities, but had found it possible to work them out into a life much purer and more full of use than anything she thought compatible with the human nature she saw around her. As she took in how that life had become possible to him, so she began to know that she was falling in love with him. For a time she was disturbed, fearing to wrong Laurence, but once her initial doubts were resolved, she was excited and uplifted by the world unfolded to her, and deeply stirred by the promise of sacrifice and suffering it held.

As for Laurence, he cleaved to Alice as to nobody else in the whole of his life. From the beginning he had the very highest respect for her qualities, as well as a very natural pride in her appearance, however he tried to disguise it. She was to be all in all to him; wife, mother, child and, not least, goddess. Their union, he explained to Alice, would renew his being and almost double his powers and faculties. Alice would have to keep down that part of her nature that she most relied on – her reason – in order to allow the development of her emotions on which he would rely. 'The great dual principle of the world is love and wisdom and the latter can only be developed by the former. The intellect is wholly dependent on the affections.' In short, Alice was to be Laurence's counterpart; with her he would attain that union of male and female which was divine. Through her he might aspire to reform the world and restore woman to her rightful place in it. It was a tribute to Laurence Oliphant's resilience and faith in the human race that, after so much suffering, he could perceive only this magnanimous vision in the distorting mirror held up by Thomas Lake Harris.

At Brocton, news of the engagement sounded an instant alarm. Although it seems that Harris had lifted the prohibition on Laurence marrying some time before, he had apparently not foreseen someone like Alice; a helpmate was all very well, but a rival was not to be born. That was the gist of a message delivered in a letter Jane Lee Waring wrote to Lady Oliphant. 'When Father left word that Woodbine was no longer to hold himself from seeking a wife, we of course understood that he knew how terrible marriage was, and that unless through weakness or inability to stand alone while passing through regenerative training, some had to marry, the rapid way to victory and use was through purification first and marriage afterwards and he [Harris] never dreamt of Laurence's loving anyone until he had been thoroughly tested by the discipline of the life.' And, in an implied threat Jane Waring continued; 'if this dear girl can give him up utterly to God and enter upon whatever discipline is before her, [God] will bring them together when and as He will, *if they are for each other*'!

Contrary to their expectation, the 'dear girl' did not flinch at this message but rather rejoiced at the promise of adversity thus early fulfilled. But Laurence was thrown into an agony of doubt, apprehension and frustrated longing for the wife he feared to lose. The letters that tell of this have been lost or destroyed and exist now only in the pages of Margaret Oliphant's biography. Those parts of them touching upon his reaction to Harris's opposition to the marriage apparently showed him in so poor a light that Mrs Oliphant considered it necessary to paraphrase most of them. According to her, his efforts to conciliate Harris came near to grovelling; his involving Alice was distasteful; and the arguments he used to justify the position to her, specious. Laurence asked Alice to pretend that the decision to postpone the marriage, taken in obedience to an order from Harris, was theirs alone. 'It would be so satisfactory to be able to answer those who accuse [Harris] of tyranny, and us of a blind and servile obedience by saying that from first to last we have acted not under his dictation but according to the promptings of our own conscience.' He held to this explanation even in a most private letter to Odo Russell, whom he addressed as a brother enlisted in the same cause. Russell knew that marriage was not the end with them but a means to further the 'great work', Laurence said. He and Alice both had the great lesson to learn of loving the cause better than each other. Until the 'selfish element' in their affection was removed, they must not marry. As this was a reason impossible to tell the world, Laurence wrote, they were open to all sorts of misconceptions – 'which chiefly take the form of my being married elsewhere'. That this rumour was widespread is clear from another letter which he wrote to Elgin's brother in law, Frederick Locker, asking him to deny that he had ever been married in America.

All this bore very heavily upon relations between the Oliphants and Alice's family. Her eldest brother, Hamon Le Strange, was also very worried about the fate of her capital in such a marriage. Laurence refused to enter into the arrangements normal in such cases: he insisted that Alice must remain in control of her own money and do with it as she saw fit. Once she arrived at Brocton, she saw fit to hand it to Harris, as Hamon Le Strange had feared. Alice's mother, Mrs Wynne Finch, now either withheld, or withdrew, her approval for the marriage which was fast becoming an item of scandalous gossip. Something had to be done. It was then that Georgiana Cowper-Temple came to the rescue with the offer of her London house as a refuge. Provided that they did not mind dispensing with the customary celebrations, there was nothing to stop Laurence and Alice from marrying almost at once. When Laurence wrote to Mowbray Morris asking for leave of absence from *The Times* for the occasion, he begged him to say nothing about the fact that it would take place earlier than planned. Morris agreed to keep the secret, but rather dryly pointed out that he alone could hardly keep the news from leaking out. In the event it did not, and Laurence and Alice were married at St. George's, Hanover Square on 8 June 1872. The only people present were Maria Oliphant, Georgiana and William Cowper-Temple, and a mysterious Mr J. Henry Johnson. Their address in the marriage register was put as Curzon Street, the Cowper-Temple's house.

Their married life began, as it would continue, on two different levels. One was that of the outer world, to whose forms and conventions they paid every respect. The other was private, inward, spiritual and exalted. In both these worlds Laurence and Alice proceeded on a basis of mutual respect, admiration, sympathy, and love. As Margaret Oliphant put it; 'it was their belief (as they thought, quite novel and wonderful, but, in fact the faith of all religious mystics both Catholic and Puritan) that even in loving each other, the chief thing to be considered was the service each could do for God and for the benefit of the world, and not any selfish happiness of their own'. It was to an apparently successful and absorbing outer life in Paris that the Oliphants returned from London. Laurence resumed his activities as *The Times* correspondent, and he and Alice settled down at the Rue du Centre. They had rooms with Lady Oliphant on the first floor of the house, while Blowitz and his wife occupied the second. With a touch of asperity Blowitz described the ménage. They took their meals together, Madame de Blowitz being in charge of the arrangements as the anxieties and practical difficulties of the management of a household were, he said, beyond Lady Oliphant. 'Like so many English ladies who have spent much time in the colonies she had always been in the habit of shifting the responsibility of domestic and household worries upon others.' Apparently Maria felt no call to glorify the Use so far from Brocton, and Alice had not yet found her feet.

In August 1872, Laurence and Alice set off on a journey into Spain. He gave out that they had no settled objective, no itinerary for what was supposed to be a belated honeymoon. Imagine their surprise when, at Bilbao, they ran across the King who invited them to sail with him in a magnificent iron clad frigate along the coast of Spain! A coincidence, Laurence called this, but it was of the special Oliphant kind which habitually delivered him to the source of potential trouble or actual upheaval. Bismarck's backing of a Hohenzollern prince for the vacant throne of Spain had brought about the Franco-Prussian war. When it was over, in 1871, Amadeo, second son of Victor Emmanuel of Italy, had been elected to fill the dangerous gap: England, France and Prussia kept a close eye on him. In 1872, there were signs already that the task was beyond him. His advent had done nothing to settle the disturbed state of the country where

Carlists drilled in the mountains and Republicans in the market square. Amadeo was surrounded by time servers at court and he and his Queen were met by open and deliberate rudeness as they went about the country.

Laurence Oliphant's interest in the affair is maddeningly unclear, but he corresponded with Austen Henry Layard who was then British Minister in Madrid and, in May 1872, wrote to the Prince of Wales suggesting that a visit from him would help to bolster the shaky young monarch. The Prince turned this idea down with the remark that it was none of his business to go about Europe consolidating dynasties. Nevertheless, it appears that some assistance was considered to be desirable. When Amadeo's frigate arrived at Corunna with the Oliphants on board, they found seven ships of the Royal Navy there. Laurence and Alice were invited on board the Admiral's flagship for the four days of 'festivities, saluting and smoke' consequent upon the Royal visit to the Fleet. When it ended they sailed back to Santander with the King. Laurence told Georgiana Cowper-Temple how much he liked the King and how unworthy the Spanish people were of their monarch. Alice, who was the only lady on board the frigate, saw a good deal of Amadeo, having sat next to him at dinner every night for a week. And, since Mrs Cowper-Temple was of their world, Laurence confided to her that it was odd they should have been able to make such great friends with the King; 'we have wondered what design Providence may have in it as affecting the Use'. The answer to that was none; Amadeo abdicated in 1873.

On board the Admiral's flagship at Corunna, Laurence and Alice found Lieutenant Charles Le Strange, one of her brothers. After four days in their company, in Laurence's words, Charlie became convinced that, in all family affairs, Laurence and Alice had been actuated by honest and pure motives. This easing of the strain was followed by a thaw in Paris. Writing to Mrs Cowper-Temple in December 1872, Alice remarked that her mother and stepfather, who had just arrived in the city, 'after a little preliminary shyness have settled down with easy, not *very* intimate, but entirely amicable and agreeable relations'. Writing to Georgiana in her turn, Lady Oliphant was not quite so coolly sanguine. Although she felt that the Le Strange family would soon be reconciled to Alice's 'sad fate', in her opinion Mrs Wynne Finch was the one most difficult to appease. Maria was not called upon to sustain a truce with Jamesina for long; at the end of the year Father called her 'home' to Brocton.

She went gladly, in the knowledge that Laurence and Alice would follow. Laurence was coming to the end of his usefulness to *The Times* and his obligations to it had become a burden to him. Henri de Blowitz, who had a lively affection and respect for Laurence, nevertheless perceived his shortcomings which were increasingly serious. He was a good correspondent while describing war and revolution, Blowitz said, but once the country was recovering he felt himself, as it were, humiliated, at having to do the work of a peacetime hack. He became sulky and irritated and began to shirk the job. 'He threw the bridle on my neck, approved in advance of all my communications and received them rather with the pleasure of a reader than with the attention of a correspondent called upon to make them public', said Blowitz. Watching Alice, he thought she did nothing to dissuade Laurence from this course. 'His young wife whose aspirations were more elevated than his, and more romantic, could not be satisfied by this daily task, a little too exactingly regular so that she was not likely to induce him to love it anymore.' From Printing House Square came a barrage of complaints where once there had been praise. Towards the end of 1872, Mowbray Morris was obliged by illness to be absent. John Macdonald, who replaced him as Manager, began to tighten the reins. He was not nearly so well disposed towards Laurence as Morris had been and began to rebuke him for sundry acts of negligence. In February 1873 he sent a furious complaint about a scoop the *Daily News* obtained as a result of Laurence's laziness. The latter's response was to send a letter of resignation to Delane. Among the reasons he advanced for this was that news from his mother in America meant he must go back there for a time. France was then peaceful and *The Times* could do with a new eye on affairs. Warmly, Laurence recommended Blowitz for the job – he did not get it until later – and asked for a salary increase for him. Rather wistfully, he told Delane that he would return at once if there were any special service he could do; he would not have thought of leaving if the reason had not been serious. The postscript was a cry for help. 'Besides the fact that there seems very little to write about, I am the more reconciled to the prospect of leaving by the more frequent recurrence of my headaches which warns me that two years and a half of pretty steady work is beginning to tell upon my head.'

The prospect before him was enough to make it ache. Harris, it seems, had recalled him in order to reassert his hold over him and to extend it to Alice. Once again Laurence had to relinquish the world he enjoyed and his friends to submit to the orders of a man he now acknowledged oppressed and frightened him. Condoling with Frederic Marshall about the loss of a friend they would both sorely miss, John Blackwood exclaimed, 'Did he give you any idea as to his future plans or is it just to be as his spirit or that of Harris moves? I do hope he is coming back. It is one of the most curious cases that ever was and it is most distressing to think of such a man and that charming wife in such a position as they must be out there.' How difficult that position was is revealed by the lengths to which Laurence went to ensure that Alice would be acceptable to Harris. At his prompting she wrote a letter to the Prophet before they left Europe, which was remarkable both in the confident and dispassionate view she took of her own nature and position in the world, and in her willingness to placate Harris.

She explained to Harris that she had suffered years of spiritual doubt caused by horror of suffering and her inability to understand how a God of love could permit it. Although she had tried to work for others, she had been hampered by doubt of its effectiveness and suspicious of her motives until, she said, she met Woodbine. Now she was ready to submit to the discipline he had undergone. Work did not frighten her; she did not cherish ease or comfort, money or property. The incomprehension and disapproval of her friends would not worry her. 'One thing only has been a terrible pang to me, the giving over of my own judgment in questions of moral judgment to any human authority.' To shut her eyes and leave the seeing to Harris, Alice said, was like putting out the one clear light that had been given to her for guidance. But she knew she must.

Harris intended to make sure that she did. At Brocton she was subjected to trials hardly less testing than those Laurence had undergone in 1865. The story that she was obliged to spend time regularly buried up to the neck in earth to ponder the transience of beauty was, one hopes, apocryphal, though it would not have exceeded Harris's power of invention or his desire to inflict humiliation. The irony was that, under these trials, Alice flourished. While she rejoiced in her decision to accept humiliation, she was not capable of feeling any such emotion: unlike Laurence she was armoured in self esteem. As for the work she was made to do, she liked cooking and learned to excel at it; she did not flinch from washing, mending or gardening. She went at rearing poultry with a will, directing Lady Oliphant's efforts, and writing to her mother for a treatise on how the French hatched chicks. Soon the cottage where they lived was surrounded by coops and struggling broods of small yellow things. In fact, as it turned out, Alice was altogether wonderful at managing, though she had the sense to hide this from everyone but Lady Oliphant at this stage. But, as she became more confident and more positive, so friction developed between her and Jane Lee Waring. The two women were in striking contrast; Alice dark and fragile beside Jane's blonde and robust person. There was nothing unpleasing about Alice to console Jane. At the beginning of her life in the Brotherhood she appeared gentle, modest, and pliant; the other disciples liked her, the Swedish hired men adored her; Pitt Buckner worshipped her. So did her husband, and that was all he was allowed to do.

Harris had recalled Laurence to Brocton to set his seal on the marriage and this he did without delay. Though Laurence had feared Harris would part him from Alice, he did not do this at first; he did something infinitely worse. He allowed them to live together as man and wife in the eyes of the world and he forbade them to sleep together. This was for the simplest and gravest of reasons: he said they were not counterparts. It was a command they obeyed without question. In Laurence's case this cruel circumstance achieved an almost final break between love and sensuality, both of which he craved, complimentary emotions which his mother's influence had split apart for him. Alice's presence was the opportunity for these to be reconciled in a person wholly devoted to him, and the tragedy was that she was capable of it – in Brotherhood terms she could have become Laurence's true counterpart. That may even be why Harris acted as he did, but Alice's position is not so clear; one does not know enough about her. Perhaps it was in her nature, as it was not in Laurence's, to be relatively unconcerned by the cost of such a sacrifice. There is some evidence from later years to suggest that this might have been so, though the strain upon Laurence was immense. To his second wife, Rosamond, he explained; 'We lived as sister and brother . . . It was difficult . . . But it did not prove to be impossible. Presently, when my health failed for a short time, my physician ascribed my breakdown to my continence.' In the circumstances it was sad that the first enterprise Laurence was involved in after his marriage concerned a place called Heart's Content.

This was the Newfoundland end of the submarine cable laid by the *Great Eastern* in 1866 after ten years of tremendous effort against storms and accidents, and the expenditure of a frightening amount of money. The laying of the cable was the realization of a dream, one of the great romances of the era. It was due to the vision and tenacity of three men: Cyrus Field, an American millionaire; Charles Bright, a brilliant English engineer; and John Pender, also an Englishman, a no less brilliant entrepreneur. By 1873, their company, the Anglo-American Telegraph Company, had enjoyed seven years of monopoly in telegraph traffic between the New World and the Old. It was Laurence's purpose to end this monopoly.

Newfoundland was a vital link in the traffic. In 1854, Cyrus Field had obtained the exclusive right to land cables on the island. In the uproar that followed Laurence's intervention, Field was to argue that nothing short of such a monopoly would have attracted capital to such a risky enterprise as the Atlantic cable appeared to be in 1854. The right was to last for fifty years, with a break clause after twenty. In 1874, the Newfoundland legislature, if it wished, could pre-empt the right and take all lines, cables and other installations into its direct control. In March 1873, a rival to Anglo-American was founded. Its purpose, indeed its mission, was to end the monopoly and so bring telegraph rates down. Among the directors of the Direct United States Cable Company, as it was called, was Henry Labouchère (always a sign of the drive, if not always of the probity, of an enterprise), E. T. Lushington, a former Financial Secretary to the Indian Government, and Viscount Bury, who had followed Laurence as Secretary for Indian Affairs at Ottawa in 1855. Its London Manager was Heinrich von Chauvin, son of the General who commanded the Prussian Army telegraph system during the Franco-Prussian war. The Direct US Cable Company gave Siemens Brothers a contract, their first, to lay the cable, and they commissioned a special ship, the enormous *Faraday*, to do it. But the enterprise would have been a large and risky speculation had not someone discovered – or remembered – the break clause in Anglo-American's contract. That this was known to the directors of the new company from the start is clear from the fact that, on his way from France to Brocton, Laurence Oliphant had called at Newfoundland. In an article he wrote for *Blackwood's Magazine*, published in July 1873, which was ostensibly an account of the history and geography of a remote part of the Empire, he took care to spell out the implications of the break clause, and to represent the people and Government of Newfoundland as ready and anxious to take over the cable traffic. After that, the issue acquired an impetus of its own and came to dominate the campaign for election to the Legislature due to take place that autumn.

Laurence went back to the cold and slithery streets of St. John's in November and set about persuading the electors to vote for those members who favoured exercising the right of pre-emption. Alice provided an intriguing glimpse of his purpose in a letter to her brother, Guy Le Strange. She said that Laurence, 'as a mere paid servant of the G', was preparing the way for the laying of a cable the following year. What was G? Was it Government? If so, which Government was paying Laurence Oliphant to break the monopoly of Anglo-American?

The argument advanced by the Direct US Cable Company – and evidently the one favoured by Laurence – was that freedom of communication would be substantially served by the ending of the monopoly and the consequent lowering of cable rates. In Newfoundland itself a more cynical view prevailed. Speculators in cable shares were trying to 'bear' them, and this was behind the frenetic campaign now launched to bring about pre-emption. Pamphlets were issued, meetings were held, articles were written and money flowed like water. According to the historian of Newfoundland, Judge D. W. Prowse, this went to buy the opinion of influential lawyers, journalists, and politicians, that Anglo-American's installations could be taken over at little cost as so much wood and iron, and that a handsome annual income could be got from the companies which would flock to land their separate cables on the island. The amiable judge did not even exclude himself from the list of people thus persuaded. When Laurence Oliphant arrived in St. John's, Anglo-American shares, known as Dogs, stood well above par on the London Stock Exchange. Then, at the crucial moment, it was made known that Newfoundland would indeed pre-empt and Dogs dropped £9 a share. According to the judge, the ring of speculators made £400,000.

Later, and as Anglo-American fought back, the mood of euphoria evaporated. Newfoundland was a cold, harsh, poor, and underpopulated country. How could the fishermen who made up the greater part of its workers, and the lawyers and journalists who sat in the Legislature, find huge sums for compensation to Anglo-American for the loss of its assets? Compensation was the cry that defeated the Direct US Cable Company's first assault. But, the counter argument also went, was not the cable a passing dream?

Judge Prowse thought so. Newfoundland could not afford dreams, except in its names. Besides Heart's Content, there were Harbour Grace, Rich Point, Fortune Bay, and the Bay of Exploits. When the new Government came in, it was decided not to pre-empt.

Temporarily defeated in his higher purpose, though if Judge Prowse is to be believed somewhat richer, Laurence returned to Brocton to ponder the situation. The solution, when he found it, owed nothing to the Prophet, but it was inspired, and the row it produced nothing short of transcendental. He devised a Bill, the Marine Telegraphs Bill 1874, whose apparent purpose was to regulate the hoped-for growth in cable traffic to and from Canada and the rest of the world. But Section 15 was aimed exclusively at Anglo-American. Under it, no company that had exclusive rights to land cable anywhere else in the world, was to be allowed to continue to land cable in Canada, unless it granted reciprocal rights to every other company. And, Anglo-American's cables would only be permitted to remain in use until another company was ready to take over the service. In April 1874, Laurence and Alice Oliphant arrived in Ottawa, he to urge this truly amazing piece of legislation upon the Canadian Government. In a letter to John Blackwood, he explained what he was about and remarked that he and Alice were staying with the Governor General, the Earl of Dufferin; at his invitation, was the implication. But, in her published diary, Lady Dufferin was at pains to describe the meeting as purely accidental. Dufferin walked down into town, she said, and there met the Oliphants in the street. 'He, very pleasant, she a sweet, pretty little woman, very chatty.' Such condescension, used to her face, would not have pleased Alice, who practised it herself on, among others, Georgiana Cowper-Temple and her own mother-in-law. In the baffled, but determinedly fair minded manner that afflicted all those who met, and tried to understand, the Oliphants, Lady Dufferin described their beliefs; 'she says in the community, no one ever speaks about religion, everyone believes what he likes. Harris is a moral doctor. They believe he suffers physical pain when his followers offend. They know when they do anything [wrong] themselves by a peculiar sensation in the throat.'

If he was not already aware of it before going to Ottawa, Laurence found the political climate there favourable to his Bill. The British North America Act of 1867 had transferred control over the greater part of Canadian affairs from the Imperial Parliament at Westminster to that in Ottawa. Moreover, the Macdonald Government had just

Laurence Oliphant in 1870

Portrait of Alice Le Strange
by Madame de Rechten

Hunstanton Hall, King's Lynn, Norfolk. Photograph taken c.1910

been brought down over allegations of corruption in the placing of contracts for the Canadian Pacific railway. Monopolies were unfashionable, particularly those held by foreigners; Canadians wanted to control their own assets. The Marine Telegraphs Bill was taken up by Robert Blake, an upright, austere, and highly respected figure, who had done much to expose the Canadian Pacific scandal. Although he had refused office in the new government under Alexander Mackenzie, he was highly influential. The result was that the second reading of the Marine Telegraphs Bill was moved in the Senate on 13 May 1874, and that was the first Anglo-American heard of it. Even then, the news was passed to them in London by their own Superintendent of Telegraphs who extracted it from what was a private communication. There was very little Anglo-American could do at this late stage; Cyrus Field, who was supposed (by the other side) to have had advance warning of the Bill, was away in California with, of all people, Charles Kingsley. It fell to a director of the Company, Lord Monck, to do his best. As a former Governor General of Canada, his influence was considerable, though whether he ought to have exercised it in this case was another question. He succeeded in persuading Lord Dufferin to reserve the Bill for the Royal Assent, thus taking the decision as to whether it should become law away from Ottawa to Westminster. This move brought a reluctant Lord Carnarvon onto the scene. As Secretary of State for the Colonies it fell to him to advise the Queen. The pitfalls were glaringly obvious; this was the first Bill so reserved since the British North America Act, and Carnarvon felt it was a bad issue on which to re-assert the Imperial Government's control over Canadian affairs. He and Dufferin conducted an anxious correspondence, in the course of which Dufferin acknowledged that a monopoly of cable traffic was highly undesirable and remarked that Anglo-American's control had been disadvantageous to the Canadian Government. Whether this indicates a deliberate attempt by that Government, through Laurence Oliphant, to get the monopoly broken, one cannot say, but it does show that his intervention was not unwelcome in certain high circles. In the end, Carnarvon decided to send the Bill back to Ottawa with no recommendation. It was re-introduced in the session of 1875 and with the support of Mackenzie, the Prime Minister, passed. In London, a pamphlet claimed that it was an act of confiscation directed against men who had spent £5 million to realize a dream of great benefit to all mankind. Of the Bill's author and promoter, Laurence Oliphant, the pamphlet could not speak too critically.

He now became New York Manager of the Direct US Cable Company, which set about building up a rival traffic to Anglo-American. Though his salary, and other money he might earn from writing, went to the Brotherhood of the New Life, his days as an acolyte in the Use were over. Harris made him live henceforth in the 'real' world as a businessman and entrepreneur. Details of his life from 1875 and for the next few years are sparse; it is known that he crossed the Atlantic many times in the service of the cable company. Kinglake saw most of him, and described Laurence as sitting in his hotel room talking to his wife and mother by telegraph. He was not enjoying himself and he hated the separation from Alice. A distaste for commerce informed all his remarks about this time and he represented himself as trying to make a living among ruffians and hypocrites. A show of innocence, he felt, was the best weapon against them. 'All the mysteries of Rings, the fraudulent manipulation of Stock etc, are becoming familiar to me. I am at this moment making four contracts with four separate companies, all managed by, not to put too fine a point on it – swindlers; at least according to my unsophisticated mind I should have so considered them; they are only called smart here. My only weapon is a guileless innocence which disarms them.'

He laboured the point of this apparent innocence at a meeting with the chief wizard of them all, the railway king, Jay Gould, against whose cleverness he had been warned. According to Margaret Oliphant, he went to Gould and told him he was not his equal in financial affairs so Gould could crush him if he would. Instead, said Mrs Oliphant, Gould treated Laurence with kindness and consideration. Laurence did not reciprocate it. Gould, he told John Blackwood, had an island on Lake Erie, specially as a sanitorium for invalid parsons, presidents of Young Men's Christian Associations, Sunday school teachers, secretaries of charitable associations and founders of theological seminaries; 'who are kept there free of expense on condition they force his wild cat railway bonds down the throats of their congregations'. Quite oblivious of any parallel with another community on Lake Erie, Laurence told Blackwood, 'I was thinking of showing it all up in *The Times*, but have been too busy.'

During this time, Alice remained at Brocton. Laurence described her as well and happy, but others were doubtful. John Blackwood wrote in 1876, 'Kinglake says that she, by the inspiration of Harris, is devoting herself to the rearing of poultry and moralized over the mysterious power that kind of saint has in knocking the mind out of the most intelligent women'.

By the time he wrote that a change had come to the Use which was to have far reaching effects, not least upon Laurence and Alice. Though Harris still ruled at Brocton, he did so in the spirit only for, in 1875, he had put the vast width of America between himself and most of his disciples. With Jane Lee Waring and Golden Rose and two Japanese as an advance party, he went to California. According to him, he was moved to establish the religion in virgin territory, 'open' to his teaching. According to Kanaye Nagasawa, one of the Japanese, he went because he had read an attractive account of growing vines on the West Coast, but above all because he could not stand the Erie winters. Reading this, one remembers the thin young man coughing his way round the Mohawk Valley and wonders if the central ritual of the Use, 'breathing together' had not something to do with Harris's weak lungs?

In 1875 there were few people in California, only Indians, Spanish missionaries, and a few forty-niners turned farmer or shopkeeper. The Brotherhood of the New Life was very nearly the first of the sects to take root in that productive soil; only the Mormons preceded Harris. The country was empty and beautiful, as Harris described it in a series of letters to William Cowper-Temple. He had bought land in a valley near the sea in the vicinity of a small town called Santa Rosa. It was ideal for growing vines; the temperature was 85 in the middle of the day, cool at night with breeze and dew. The open country ran for miles on every side without a fence, wild horses abounded descendants of the ones the Spaniards introduced. If 'dearest William would come to stay at Fountain Grove, as the new home was christened, he and "dearest Lowly" (Georgiana Cowper-Temple) could have a wooden house and Japanese servants to look after them.' Harris told William he needed £1,000 for the interest on the purchase of the land and a further £1,000 for a building for guests. He would repay the money over three years. It appears that William provided it.

At Brocton, in the summer of 1875, Alice, her mother-in-law, and the widow of poor James Fowler, were left in the charge of a Mrs Clark who had strict instructions as to their regimen. This Mrs Clark was Constance, Lady Oliphant's maid, whom it was said Laurence had 'wronged'. She had married a member of the Brotherhood and now governed every detail of her former mistress's life. All three women were kept short of food and not allowed to wear shoes. Levine, the Swedish hired man, showed Alice a path through the bushes to his house where she sat, barefoot, in the kitchen, eating bread and jam and regaling Mrs Levine with stories of her previous existence. What Mrs Levine most liked to hear was how Alice, before coming to Brocton, had never dressed herself in her life.

Alice was still at Brocton when business for the Direct US Cable Company and certain other matters took Laurence to London. There he was much in the company of her brother, Hamon Le Strange, who had long ago made up the quarrel between them. Laurence dined often with him at his club, and stayed with his family at Hunstanton Hall. Hamon's diary records Laurence's growing apprehension about the future of the Direct US Cable Company which was under attack by Anglo-American. All sorts of unfair tricks were played, including the circulation of a report that the *Faraday* had been lost with all hands; an attempt to prevent her laying cables in Trinity Bay, Newfoundland; and even the deliberate sabotage of cables. Towards the end of 1876, John Pender made a determined effort to take the company over. After a long and furious struggle he finally succeeded in May the following year. Long before that, Laurence had begun to prepare for another enterprise. Throughout the summer of 1876 he drew up plans which, if they succeeded, would put him into a position of great influence in one of the largest, richest, and most crucial areas of the British Raj.

The princely State of Hyderabad was a Muslim stronghold in the heart of Hindu India. In view of the disturbed condition of Muslim countries at the time, notably Turkey, and the designs of Russia upon another, Afghanistan, it was only prudent for the British rulers of India to keep a closer eye than usual on Hyderabad. So when Laurence Oliphant was invited to preside over a council whose object was thought to be to make Hyderabad an independent Muslim state, the Viceroy, the Secretary of State for India, and the Queen wrote letters to each other about it. Power in Hyderabad lay with the Nizam's Chief Minister, Sir Salah Jung, who was the originator of Laurence's invitation. By astute management over the years he had restored the fortunes of the State which had been almost entirely dissipated by the previous Nizam. In 1861, the British government had been obliged to rescue Hyderabad from certain bankruptcy, the price of which was control of its most prosperous region, the Berars. In 1876, Salah Jung was determined to get the Berars back. He was a very able, impressive, and cunning man, who well understood the English character and how to manipulate it, and his prestige stood very high in the rest of India. Sir William Gregory, then Governor of Ceylon, described the effect he had upon the Durbar of 1875. All the Indian potentates came before the Prince of Wales in a perfect daze of diamonds, 'but, at the last note of the trumpet the last tent opened and a tall commanding figure, all in white and absolutely devoid of ornament save a magnificent diamond in his turban stalked forth. All recognized the man of men, Sir Salah Jung.'

At Delhi, the Prince of Wales, who was touring India, conceived both admiration and affection for Salah Jung, as did his boon companion, the Duke of Sutherland, whose sympathies were wholly committed to the Muslim cause. The result was an invitation to Salah Jung from the Prince to visit England. When he arrived in May 1876, Salah Jung created a stir. Everywhere he went he was treated as the Prince he had no claim to be: ships saluted him and duchesses curtseyed. The Queen invited him to Windsor, the Duke of Sutherland took him about, and he dined often at Marlborough House. The newspapers were full of the pros and cons of his demand for the return of the Berars, though few M.P.s appeared impressed by this. Among those who came to his door was Laurence Oliphant. According to the Viceroy of India, the Earl of Lytton, Oliphant was part of a dangerous conspiracy mounted by Salah Jung to turn Hyderabad into an independent Muslim state in the heart of British India. Lytton told Lord Salisbury, Secretary of State for India, that he had information indicating that Oliphant had been selected 'exclusively with a view to his personal assistance in the management of a journalistic, parliamentary and social support from England to claims and assumptions by Salah Jung which are opposed to the established policy and incompatible with the continued supremacy of the Queen's Government in India'. Of course, it was something like this that Laurence Oliphant had done in Newfoundland.

It is probable that Laurence Oliphant was introduced to Salah Jung by the Prince of Wales whose intervention in the affair was roundly denounced by Lytton to the Queen. The Viceroy's account is the only one to survive for, although William Howard Russell went with the Prince to India in 1875 when he first met Salah Jung, and subsequently saw the Muslim leader with Laurence Oliphant in London, the pages of his diary for this period have been torn out. According to Lytton, the first he ever heard of the matter was when Arthur Oliphant, Laurence's cousin, who was Salah Jung's private secretary in Hyderabad, wrote to ask for the Viceroy's permission by return of post for Laurence to proceed to India, there to preside over the council of Hyderabad notabilities. On making enquiries Lytton found that Laurence Oliphant had already drawn up a constitution for this council. Lytton immediately complained to Salisbury that Laurence was a dangerous man, far abler than his cousin, Arthur, clever and unscrupulous, 'a born intriguer'. He asked that Laurence should be banned from India and Arthur Oliphant dismissed his post. Both of his requests were granted and Laurence's involvement in the affair never became public. But Arthur Oliphant's dismissal was only procured after an outcry in the English newspapers and some sharp questions from the Queen who, like many other people, felt that Lytton was exaggerating the threat in Hyderabad.

Nevertheless there were traces of a conspiracy in Hyderabad; Salah Jung was secretly manufacturing Martini Henry rifles and armed men were coming into the state from the Arabian coast. Salah Jung was deposed as Chief Minister and died shortly after. There were people who said he had been poisoned. We do not know what Laurence Oliphant's purpose was in India, but in view of his early interest in the Muslim cause and his growing respect for the Islamic religion, it is likely that he would have supported Salah Jung in an attempt to raise the status of his co-religionists. Lytton always maintained that the Hyderabad affair was the most dangerous threat to the stability of India during his time as Viceroy, not excepting the war in Afghanistan against Shere Ali. The full details would never appear on the official record, Lytton told the India Office, but India had escaped the emergence of an energetic, independent, and hostile State in her midst.

As the prospect of employment in Hyderabad vanished, so did the post of Manager of the Direct US Cable Company. Once it had been taken over, in May 1877, after a lengthy battle between its shareholders and those of Anglo-American, Laurence's days in control were at an end. So, at the age of forty-eight, he was suddenly without a job, without the prospect of one, and without a home. Alice, his wife, was long gone, far beyond his reach.

CHAPTER 9

PALESTINE

IN the autumn of 1876, before snow threatened to close the Rocky Mountain passes, Alice made the slow and arduous journey alone across the vast width of the country to California. Behind her at Brocton she left her mother-in-law in the special care of Violet Cuthbert and the Martins. Life in the Use there went on much as before, though things were better managed by young Pitt Buckner and, in the absence of Harris, there were fewer surprises. At Fountain Grove the Prophet wanted only one other person to join the inner group. He represented the choice as lying between Alice and another young woman, whose connections in the 'real' world were even more exalted than hers. This was Olive Risley Seward, adopted daughter of Lincoln's Secretary of State, the late William Seward. Olive had long been a supplicant for admission to the Brotherhood, and Harris played on her desire with skill. If Alice did not come, he promised, Olive might. But, in spite of her availability, he was by no means pleased when Laurence, as yet unaware of Lytton's move to counter Salah Jung, asked Alice to meet him at San Francisco to go with him to Hyderabad. Harris, who had nothing to do with the Indian affair, rejoiced when it fell through. For Alice there was then no alternative to the beautiful but isolated valleys of Fountain Grove, 6,000 miles from home.

She had no money and she was not allowed to write, either to Laurence or to her family. As the months went by they all began to worry, Laurence more than the rest. For to those at Brocton it soon began to appear that the Brotherhood life at Fountain Grove was conducted upon a more intense and much more questionable level that it ever had been, or would be, on the shores of Lake Erie. The Californian sun caused Harris's ideas, like the vines he planted, to push in new directions. The growth was rank. The language in which Harris now expressed his mystical beliefs (including the assertion that Christ had come to earth again in him) became increasingly sexual in a childish and perverted way. Beside his celebration of the female element in religion, personified in the Lily Queen, there now appeared a fear of women as such, expressed in the desire to humiliate them. Sick imaginings of the sexual act were poured out in poem after poem. As for the everyday life of those at Fountain Grove, it assumed a medieval and corrupt monastic flavour. Orders of knighthood were invented and conferred; they had to bow and curtsy and call each other Sir and Lady. Men and women lived apart; the men in a Commandery, the women in the Familistery; there were now over thirty newcomers to the Brotherhood. On certain special days, at Harris's behest, they were privileged to experience the coming of their counterparts. In theory, the men at Fountain Grove were as eligible for this as the women, but the papers that survive always describe this in terms of a female receiving an influx of power, whose effect, pruriently described by Harris, was to make her pregnant. What evidence there is of Alice's part in such proceedings is not trustworthy, as all of it dates from the time after the Oliphants broke with Harris, and some from many years later. But it is clear that Alice's role at Fountain Grove was supposed to be that of the Lily Queen, Harris's counterpart made manifest on earth. What is not clear is how far Alice acquiesced in this, if at all. According to Jane Lee Waring, Alice used her beauty and her brilliant intellect to usurp the position of Golden Rose (Mrs Requa), who had held the place of honour next to Father for many years. Unlike Golden Rose, Jane said, Alice claimed the honour as a right and intended to use the power Jane believed it would give her to destroy the Brotherhood. According to Thomas Lake Harris, writing after the schism, Alice was the Devil Incarnate. Rosamond Dale Owen, Laurence's second wife, said that he told her that Harris behaved most cruelly to Alice at this time.

Certainly the practical consequences of the Lily Queen affair were severe for her. In 1878 she left Fountain Grove and went to Vallejo, a small mining village an hour from San Francisco, where she proposed to earn her living by teaching. It is likely that, when she arrived there, she was destitute, Harris having expelled her without warning from Fountain Grove. This may have been as a result of her refusal to assume the role of the Lily Queen, or as a matter of routine discipline, of the sort that was applied to Cuthbert and Fowler and which threatened Lady Oliphant. Even Jane Lee Waring did not escape and the details of her exclusion have survived. She was hurried out of

Fountain Grove in the middle of the night to a nearby town. She had no money and nowhere to stay. Ultimately, she said, she had to furnish a room with articles salvaged from the town dump.

Shortly before Alice left Fountain Grove, Laurence arrived, having made a special journey from New York because of his concern. In spite of this (or, indeed, because of it) Harris turned him away without allowing him to see Alice. In despair, he appealed for help to the only people he knew in San Francisco, a wealthy merchant, J. D. Walker, and his wife. Laurence had met Mrs Walker at a dinner in New York some years previously. Finding her nervous at the prospect of crossing the Atlantic to England alone with her children, he had altered his own reservation in order to travel with and help her. The friendship he made then was to stand him in good stead, both in 1878 and later. The Walkers could do nothing while Alice remained at Fountain Grove, so Laurence was obliged to return to New York without having seen her. Once she arrived at Vallejo, Mrs Walker appeared with offers of help and hospitality. Although Vallejo was a rough and isolated place, Alice remained for some time until she was persuaded by the Walkers to move to Benicia, a town nearer San Francisco, where she joined a school run by a woman the Walkers knew. Harris's power over Alice, though not broken, now became somewhat weaker, as is indicated by the fact that she wrote to her brother, Guy Le Strange, for the first time for several years. She told Guy she would probably stay where she was for at least two years: the climate suited her and she felt better than she had since growing up. She was teaching music, drawing and oil painting, and hoped that Laurence would not oblige her to leave until she had made a financial success of the undertaking. The letter was without the exalted note that marked her earlier letters to her mother following her marriage and removal to Brocton. Reading these, Kinglake had remarked, 'I wonder if she will ever come down and touch the earth?'

Laurence was greatly shaken by Harris's refusal to let him see Alice. It drove him to retreat from the world like a wounded animal. In March 1878 he wrote to John Blackwood that he had given up all the various occupations that kept him in New York to go into retirement; 'exchanging the society of swindlers for that of sheep', was how he put it.

His isolation lasted several weeks and seems to have formed a frontier between the old life and the new. For when he emerged he went immediately to England. There he became caught up in the enterprise that was to preoccupy him for the rest of his life, and by which he left a mark on the history of his time. This was the plan to settle Jews on land in Palestine then lying derelict. His efforts almost succeeded in bringing about a Jewish presence in the land of Israel a generation before Theodor Herzl, and nearly precipitated an international disaster. They brought him fame and the trust of thousands of Jews, so that Moses Lilienblum of Odessa, one of the forerunners of Zionism, could say of Laurence Oliphant that they hoped he would be the Messiah of Israel.

In Laurence Oliphant's personal experience there came together the two strands that over the years bound British interest to Palestine; one was political and strategic, the other religious: Palmerston was the godfather of the first, Shaftesbury of the second. As far as the first aspect was concerned, in the letter that Laurence wrote to the then Foreign Secretary, Lord Salisbury, on 14 November 1878, asking for Foreign Office backing in order to get permission to enter Palestine in search of suitable land, he stressed that he was prompted by a desire to find a solution to the Eastern Question. If Palestine, an outlying province of Turkey, could be strengthened by the establishment of a thriving colony of Jews, the whole Empire would benefit by the example, and the empty Turkish treasury be considerably enriched. Such a colony would serve the vital purpose of blocking Russia's advance to the south which threatened the recently opened route to India via the Suez Canal. For, Laurence argued, though the Treaty of Berlin had erected a barrier against that advance in the Balkans by calling into being two new States, Bulgaria and Romania, Russia was now free to transfer her attentions to Asiatic Turkey, and would do so. Salisbury recognized the truth of that. Early in 1878, when the Turkish collapse in the war against Russia appeared to open the way for a Russian advance to the Mediterranean, Beaconsfield and Salisbury had looked urgently for some part of the Turkish Empire England might hold against such an advance. Crete, Cyprus, the island of Mytilene, Haifa, and Acre, were all considered. Cyprus, which they eventually got in a secret agreement at the Congress of Berlin, was really too far away from the places that mattered. Some part of Palestine would serve the purpose far better.

In the climate of opinion of the time, such Palmerstonian ideas were readily understood and, by the majority, applauded. What was not revealed was that the Oliphant plan to settle Jews in Palestine had for its chief purpose the establishment of a British protectorate over that region. Ostensibly the colonists were to become Ottoman citizens, and the Sultan was to be asked to grant a certain amount of land on which they would settle in return for a very large sum of money. But the idea of the protectorate – which would have caused an international storm had it become known – was put to the Turkish Government by Laurence Oliphant. According to him the idea was dropped when Gladstone came into office in 1880.

Equally controversial was the religious aspect of the scheme which Laurence proposed to exploit in order to raise the vast amount of money that would be necessary. Many Christians in the West believed in the prophecy which said that the Second Coming of Christ would occur, and the souls of the righteous be saved, only when the Jews were restored to Jerusalem. This prophecy was current in the Evangelical circles in which Laurence had been brought up, and its most fervent believer was the leader of the Evangelicals, the Earl of Shaftesbury.

In 1840, following the collapse of Mehemet Ali's rule in Syria (of which Palestine was a part), Lord Ashley, as Shaftesbury then was, felt it his solemn duty to urge upon Palmerston as Foreign Secretary the settlement of Jews in that part of Syria that was their Biblical home. It grieved Ashley that he could not be open with Palmerston about his apocalyptic purpose. Palmerston, he lamented, 'weeps not like his Master over Jerusalem', and had absolutely no idea that he had been chosen by God to be an instrument of good to His ancient people.

Laurence Oliphant, well aware of the continuing power of the prophecy in certain Protestant circles in England and America, foresaw that an appeal based on it might release large sums of money. But, like Shaftesbury, he felt it was essential at first to disguise this element in his scheme from all but a few. He knew very well that it was distasteful to many people, and not least to the Jews themselves. And so, like Shaftesbury, he emphasized the political, strategic, and commercial aspect of his scheme and mentioned the prophecy, if at all, only to deny his belief in it.

One of the few people to whom he made his whole purpose plain from the start was Benjamin Disraeli, Earl of Beaconsfield, the Prime Minister, who treated it seriously and gave Laurence much assistance. Others thought the plan visionary and vague and suspected the influence of Thomas Lake Harris. This was not so. Harris was much given to announcing the end of the world; it kept his disciples up to the mark, but he effectively disposed of the Apocalypse when, at Santa Rosa, he proclaimed that Christ had come again – in his own person. Laurence Oliphant's attraction for the scheme was founded on his conviction that it would lead to the solution of the Eastern Question, and upon the belief that had grown in him during the years in which he had observed at close quarters the rise of national movements. It was sad but not surprising that a man who all his adult life had been bereft of home and hearth, passionately believed that men derive a special virtue from the soil on which they are born and that the power of regeneration is given to those who fight for their homeland. But, in 1878, these ideas were not in the forefront of his mind; John Blackwood thought him more rational and 'like himself' than he had been all the years since he met Harris. It was not until Alice re-entered Laurence's life that the balance of his mind was tilted towards the mystical and, ultimately, the fantastic.

The practical application of Laurence's scheme called for him to select a suitable area of land and apply to the Sultan of Turkey for a grant of it. A limited company would then be formed with capital subscribed throughout the Western world. This company would have powers of administration, police and customs, and would build roads and a railway. Laurence foresaw that the Jews who would settle there would be rich enough to be able to employ as agricultural labourers the *fellahin* who already lived on the land. They would have to agree to become Ottoman subjects, and guarantees as to the title of the land from the Turkish Government would be essential. As the country was closed to foreigners Laurence had to have official backing both to enter the country and to approach the Sultan.

Though he had the warm approval of the Prince of Wales, it was Princess Christian who, on 11 November 1878, addressed a letter to the Prime Minister, asking him to give Laurence, whom she had known since childhood, a hearing on a subject in which she and her husband were very interested. Even then the way to the Foreign Secretary's ear was not direct. Beaconsfield spoke to Lady Salisbury, who spoke to her husband. Salisbury, who may have harboured lingering doubts about Oliphant following the Hyderabad affair, nevertheless agreed that he would be furnished with the vital letters enabling him to move freely about the Turkish Empire, and moreover, allowed him to let it be known that he had the unofficial approval of the Foreign Office. This was on condition that the French be privy to the scheme – the public aspect of it – and agreeable. This was essential since in return for France's acquiescence in the transfer of Cyprus to England at the Congress of Berlin, Salisbury had recognized that French influence in Syria would henceforth be paramount. Waddington, the French Foreign Minister, ordered his Ambassador in Constantinople, Fournier, to give Oliphant every assistance.

The initial difficulties surmounted, Laurence waxed eloquent among his friends and acquaintances about the scheme. According to Margaret Oliphant, its great possibilities almost went to his head and in the forefront of these he put the huge profit it would make. (In fact it made no money and ate up a good deal of his.) He dwelt in glowing terms upon the chance to restore a desert land to fertility and to provide a refuge for a persecuted race where the ideal of good government and wise economy might be put into practice. To Laurence himself, Mrs Oliphant thought, the scheme came as a godsend at a difficult time. He was at a loose end and much bruised by Harris's refusal to let him see Alice. The scheme about the Jews, she said, 'gave him at once the liveliest personal interest, the pleasure of a sort of amateur diplomatic negotiation involving the largest issues, and the mixture of adventure and use, which was at all times the thing he liked best in life'. He was once more at the centre of affairs. In late November, the Prince of Wales held a house party at Sandringham. The guests were the Prime Minister, Lord Beaconsfield; the Foreign Secretary, Lord Salisbury; the Duke of Sutherland; the Austrian Ambassador, Count Beust; and Laurence Oliphant.

In January 1879 Laurence left England for Beyrout, then the nearest point of entry to the largely uninhabited region he wanted to explore. A travelling companion was essential and so he engaged Captain Phibbs, an evidently stout-hearted and competent but otherwise shadowy figure. Phibbs knew the ropes and they were able to dispense with the large and expensive entourage, armed to the teeth, which was considered essential to those travellers bold enough to venture into the wilderness east of Jordan. Laurence and Phibbs took one servant as cook and general factotum, and a muleteer and his boy to carry the luggage. This was light as they dispensed with tents. For food they had a few tins of preserved meat, Liebig's Extract, tea, coffee, sugar, a ham, cheese and a bottle of olives. They also had a spirit lamp. 'A cup of hot tea coming at the right moment, saves many a headache if one is at all susceptible to the sun' – or headaches. However reassuring, Phibbs' presence was unobtrusive, and reading the book that Laurence subsequently wrote, one sees only him riding across the barren and stony country with its ancient and famous names. As he rode he noted the traces of former occupants lying about in the utmost profusion – as if waiting to be used. There were sunken chambers for storing grain, mill stones, wine presses, water channels, wells, and the marks of chariot wheels on the surface of old roads.

In 1879, the country west of Jordan was fairly well known to travellers. Officers of the Palestine Exploration Fund led by Captain Warren, and including Lieutenant Conder and the young Kitchener, had been engaged in surveying it for the past five years. Conder's book, *Tent work in Palestine*, had just been published and Laurence, who had had conversations with Conder and Warren before leaving London, carried a copy with him. But the country east of Jordan was hardly known and subject to recurring raids by Bedouin tribesmen. Laurence found the settled inhabitants 'almost tame' and quite ready to offer him hospitality. After the arid and worn out aspect of the country west of Jordan, he was charmed to discover a series of uninhabited and fertile valleys running away from the Dead Sea up into mountains covered with trees and grass. It was here that he decided to make his Promised Land, in an area roughly twenty miles by thirty, a million acres of almost empty land (there was one little town), which belonged entirely to the Turkish Government. The climate was semi-tropical and, he thought, all kinds of crops might be grown according to the height at which they were planted. At the Dead Sea level the valley of the Jordan would be a huge hothouse for the colony, providing cotton, sugar, rice, and cultivated palms. A little higher up there would be maize, tobacco, figs, and pomegranates. Higher still, on the plains, would be wheat, barley, beans, olives, and vines. Then, if proper accommodation could be built, no end of visitors would come to the hot springs of Callirhoe. A railway would take the produce of the colony to Haifa, the nearest port (in Conder's opinion, the best on the whole Syrian coast), and in time this might be extended to Akaba on the Red Sea and into Egypt. Finally, the mineral wealth of the Dead Sea, which he was sure existed, could be exploited and great profits made. In those days the place was known as the Belka, but Laurence preferred its Biblical name, the Land of Gilead.

The next requirement was to get the assent of the Turkish authorities in Palestine. That was not difficult. Laurence had only to ride over the mountains to Damascus where he was warmly greeted and lodged in the palace. The Governor General at Damascus was Midhat Pasha, an old acquaintance of Laurence Oliphant, the Prince of Wales, and the Duke of Sutherland. Midhat kept Laurence at Damascus for three weeks while he examined the colonization scheme in detail and pronounced it viable. If Oliphant could get the necessary *firman* at Constantinople, Midhat promised that he would give every help to the Jewish colonists when they got to Palestine. But, as Laurence told Beaconsfield privately, Midhat felt that his public support would hinder rather than help the scheme; 'he is in such bad odour here'. Midhat had been responsible for the accession to the throne of the reigning Sultan, Abdul Hamid, following the deposition and mysterious death of his brother. Subsequently, Midhat had been the author of the 'liberal' constitution which Abdul Hamid had welcomed but somehow failed to put into practice in 1876. Part of Midhat's exile which followed this exercise was spent in England where the Prince of Wales paid him warm attention and the Duke of Sutherland put Dunrobin Castle at his disposal. In 1878, Midhat was recalled and sent to preside over the *vilayet* which included the region east of Jordan. But Abdul Hamid was already beginning to show signs of the pathological suspicion that was to darken the long years of his reign, and he had been much shaken in his trust of England as an ally by the provisions of the Treaty of Berlin which sought to impose reform on Turkey. The consequence was that, in 1879, he had begun to suspect that Midhat, with the help of England, would take over in Syria just as Mehemet Ali had done 45 years before.

From Damascus, Laurence went straight to Constantinople, arriving there in May 1879. Almost at once he reported to Lord Beaconsfield that progress was encouraging. He had seen the Grand Vizier, Khaireddin Pasha, and the Minister for Public Works, and he had disguised nothing of his purpose from them. He said he showed them how, if they took the initiative in providing an asylum for the Jews, they would receive great moral and financial support among the Protestants of England and America. Laurence told the Prime Minister that it had been difficult to make the Turkish leaders understand that there was a certain sort of Christian who would instantly transfer their sympathies from Greek or Bulgarian Christians (whose treatment by the Turks had lately been the subject of an international outcry), to Jews, 'the moment that the Turkish Government would form their policy so as to make it appear a fulfilment of prophecy but I think they by now see it and are a good deal struck by the notion'. Indeed the Turks were struck by this notion of the fulfilment of prophecy, but not in the way Laurence supposed. Continuing in a hopeful vein, he assured Beaconsfield that all the rich Jews he had spoken to in Syria (there were very few) promised to take land in the colony if they could be guaranteed title to it. Khaireddin Pasha seemed to have no fear of a Jewish nationality springing up in Syria and saw that, 'should Romanian, Russian and Serbian Jews flock to them to escape Christian persecution and for the sake of security and good government it would be the most favourable illustration that could be furnished of the hypocrisy of neighbouring governments'. Laurence concluded by saying that he was keeping quiet about the plan as he was afraid of Russian opposition. He was glad to be supposed both vague and visionary. Khaireddin Pasha invited Laurence to draw up a measure that would guarantee the rights of the Sultan over the colonists as Ottoman subjects while allowing the development of the colony on the lines of a limited company. To the author of the Canadian Marine Telegraph Act 1874, this was not a difficulty, and the measure was duly approved by the Turkish Cabinet. All he had to do was wait for the Sultan's approval and this, Khaireddin assured him, would not take long. Knowing the Turks, Laurence felt it might, but was not disposed to grumble at a forced holiday to be spent among a profusion of summer flowers on the shores of the Bosphorus.

Constantinople was full of friends in high places. The Ambassador, Henry Layard and his wife were generous in their invitations to picnics, excursions, parties in boats, on islands and at the delightful wooden house on the water's edge at Therapia that was the summer Embassy. Laurence was, as always, a godsend to people with a stream of visitors to entertain. He saw a good deal of Baker Pasha, now in the service of the Turkish Army, and Hobart Pasha, the head of the Turkish Navy, whose house he shared. Valentine Baker, his old friend from Ceylon days, had been forced to leave England following a prison sentence for assault upon a woman in a train. He had distinguished himself commanding Turkish troops during the war of 1877, and was now in a position to furnish useful accounts of the state of the army to the authorities in England. Even so, they would not listen to pleas for his rehabilitation. Among the journalists Laurence knew was Edgar Whitaker, Editor of the *Levant Herald*, whom

Laurence persuaded to give Valentine Chirol a job. Laurence had met Chirol, then in his late twenties, wandering in Syria, and brought him with him to Constantinople. There he launched him upon a distinguished career that was to end as Foreign Editor of *The Times*.

For a time the only flaw in this pleasant existence was the absence of Alice. Then, Khaireddin Pasha, who like Midhat had tried to introduce reform, fell from power, a victim according to Laurence of Russian intrigue. But, as he was promptly assured of continuing Government support for his scheme, he remained at Constantinople, waiting for an interview with the Sultan, which Layard, who prided himself on his influence over Abdul Hamid, promised to arrange. As the autumn passed, Laurence started to write an account of the land of Gilead which he confidently expected to have a large sale and to attract investors. His other need was for colonists, and so he went up into Romania where, in spite of the Treaty of Berlin, the large Jewish population continued to be cruelly persecuted, and to be refused citizenship unless they applied for it individually.

Meanwhile, Anglo-Turkish relations deteriorated further. When he returned to Constantinople, Laurence sent home gloomy appraisals of the situation. One of his letters was addressed to Princess Christian who thought it so important she forwarded it to the Prime Minister. Another, with the name of the addressee deleted, found its way to Lytton in India. Without divulging either this name, or that of the person who sent it to him, Lytton sent it on to Layard at Constantinople with the remark, 'Oliphant is a clever fellow but he always seemed to me an intriguant'. The letter, dated 20 November 1879, reported that the Turkish Cabinet had reacted violently to England's latest move, a demonstration by the Royal Navy off Albania. The Turks were now hard at work making a treaty with Russia and preparing to counter the next demonstration England might make, Laurence warned his unknown correspondent. 'The fleet should come here in the interest of the starving army, navy and population generally. The whole country would rise in our favour if we came as the enemy of the Sultan and his advisers, and the friend of the people ... We must choose a popular issue which will force Russia to appear as the friend of the corrupt and detested Palace. I wish if you see the Duke of Sutherland, or anyone who can influence matters, you will explain.' This view could have come as no surprise to Layard. The Ambassador told Lord Salisbury that he had constant secret communications from Turks in high places that they were prepared to change the dynasty.

On 15 February 1880, Laurence wrote a long letter describing his experiences in Palestine and Turkey to Odo Russell, then British Ambassador in Berlin. Power at Constantinople was in the hands of a clique, some of whom were in Russian pay. 'The Sultan is most hostile to Britain in general and Layard in particular though the latter is under a different impression.' In spite of this, the new Turkish Cabinet had approved the scheme and all he needed was the Sultan's consent. So Laurence asked Odo Russell to arrange for him to see Bismarck to get German support. Germany could do it without incurring disapproval, except from Russia to whom it would be a serious blow. Jews from Russia, Romania and Serbia would flock to the colony, Laurence remarked, and, in a prophetic passage, added, 'the difficulty would be to keep the emigration within due limits'. As an added incentive to the Germans he held out the prospect of a 'very good' railway project for connecting Egypt and Syria, bringing Damascus within fifteen hours of Cairo. If Prince Bismarck acquiesced in the plan people would think he was the instrument in the hands of God to fulfil the prophecy and bring about the end of the world which, said Laurence, 'they all want for some reason or other'. He added a postscript; 'I have good news of my wife in California but I hate this long separation and if I can only carry this I would rather go back or bring her here.'

It was not until April 1880 that Layard contrived to bring about the invitation to dine with the Sultan for which Laurence had been waiting. In her Journal, Lady Layard described what happened. How, 'after a charming evening he was taking leave of His Majesty and plunged boldly into the grievance of having to leave Turkey after a year's stay without having obtained his concession for bringing the Jews to settle in Palestine. The Sultan said he had wished it, but all his Ministers had been against it, at which Mr Oliphant indignantly told His Majesty that the Ministers told him His Majesty alone opposed it.' As they were both 'getting hot', a courtier rushed to separate them and, in the waiting room, Laurence broke out in abuse of everyone and vowed vengeance with his pen. Attempts were made to soothe him and a snuff box was brought to him from the Sultan, which he, for some time, refused to take. At last he stuffed it in his pocket and stalked out. Privately, Layard, who acknowledged that Laurence had been infamously treated by the Turks, remarked to a friend, Augusta

Gregory; 'He didn't think that I had given him enough support, but he himself put a stopper on it by telling the Sultan's secretary that he was seeking to fulfil the Scripture that the end of the world was to come when the Jews were restored to their native land, and his Majesty had no desire to hurry that event.'

As Layard had foreseen, on his return to England, Laurence lashed out at the Porte. In an article published by the *Jewish Chronicle* on 11 June 1880, he accused the Turkish Government of corruption, all but called the Sultan a liar, and forecast the inevitable return to office of Khaireddin Pasha and Midhat Pasha, whose assistance in drawing up the colonization scheme he now publicly acknowledged. This was not only ill-judged but inaccurate, since Midhat was soon to be arrested and tried for treason.

Shortly after this Laurence read a letter in the *Jewish Chronicle* from a group of Jews in Bucharest who wanted to emigrate to Palestine. They had raised £1,600 and needed another £1,000, for which they proposed to approach the Testimonial Committee in London that bore the name of the great English Jew and philanthropist, Sir Moses Montefiore. A copy of the letter Laurence wrote to them was published in the *Athenaeum*. In it he urged the Bucharest Jews to get in touch with him: he was sure, he said, that far more than £1,000 could be raised for them in England. They should send a delegation to London where he would do all in his power to help. Almost at once Joseph Weinberg, President of the Bucharest Committee, wrote back, calling down blessings on Laurence Oliphant and the Editor of the *Jewish Chronicle*. In moving terms, he described the sufferings of the Romanian Jews. His Committee represented 100 families who had each contributed 400 francs to the great enterprise. There was little money to spare but they would use it to send Eliezer Rokeah to London; 'To him we owe the first impulse to the project we have so certainly undertaken', wrote Weinberg.

Eliezer Rokeah was almost as unusual a man as Laurence Oliphant. Born one of the few indigenous Jews in Jerusalem, he devoted his life to the idea that the only way to make the race prosperous and independent was to reform Jewish life and culture. To this end he founded a colony on land near Safed. But that ancient town was the centre of Chassidism, a fanatical Jewish sect. Not surprisingly, the Chassidim of Safed fell out with Rokeah and his followers and the colony collapsed. Rokeah then determined to prosecute his idea among the Jews of the Diaspora. After much wandering and many adventures he came to Romania in 1880 where his speaking and writing gained support for his plan. The Bucharest Committee which proposed to send him to London was almost the first group seriously to undertake a return to the Land of Israel in the hope of making a new life there, rather than retiring to die there. At the time the hope of most Jews in Europe, and even in Russia, was still of assimilation into the national society in which they happened to live. Palestine was a barren and unknown country where to survive demanded skills they did not have. This was the attitude which inhibited emigration for some time and which, for even longer, prevented wealthy Jews from contributing towards the cost of the Return.

Laurence Oliphant did his best for the Bucharest Committee; he applied to the Jewish Board of Deputies to recommend a loan from the Montefiore Fund and, in the temporary absence of approval for his own scheme, advised the Romanians to settle on land west of Jordan that Conder had surveyed. The most important result of his intervention at this stage was to make his name known to Jews all over Europe, as news of his advice was reported in all the Hebrew papers. His fame was increased when *The Land of Gilead* was published in December 1880. Reviewing it the *Jewish Chronicle* approved the scheme as practical and feasible because 'unsentimental'. Mr Oliphant, it remarked, was a follower of no sect, and a believer in no religion. He was merely a politician with a theory to prove.

Though his international reputation grew, a cloud hung over Laurence's private life. Society was less well disposed towards him than hitherto, and the number of invitations he received declined. The reason was that people were a little tired of him; not only had he fallen short of the goal he had so widely proclaimed, but there was the question of Alice, whose long absence he could not convincingly explain. Apart from some friends, including Lady Airlie, Laurence saw few people after his return from Turkey, and spent the summer in London correcting proofs. In September he went to Hunstanton where, at last, he heard that Alice was coming home.

It seems her return was in answer to an appeal from him; he was depressed and, increasingly, ill. Alice's re-appearance was heralded by a letter to her mother in which she briskly dismissed the gossip her separation from her husband had caused. The plain truth about her 'peculiarities' she insisted was that she had always made Laurence leave her free to make her own experiments as to how best she could be of service in the world. During the period of their separation she had solved to her own satisfaction the question of being a producer in the social scheme, unaided by her social connections. 'I return here for a while because I want to see you, and my friends, and because Laurence needs help that I can render him, and because I need rest – et tout est dit.'

Alice said she had not seen Harris for three years. She had not seen her family for seven. Hamon Le Strange found his sister little changed, though she was thinner and the expression of her face intensified. Her voice had acquired an American intonation – not an accent, he was obviously relieved to find – but a peculiar way of placing stress on certain words. Alice was delighted to be home, he wrote, and charmed with all the children born since she went away. She must have felt very strange at first in the huge house with its numerous staircases, courtyards and clock tower, its myriad smoking chimneys and lines of windows looking on to the wintry park. It was a far cry from California and the wooden shanty town where she had lived and worked for the past three years. It was further still from there to Sandringham House where she and Laurence, and her brother and his wife, were commanded to a ball a fortnight after her return. The talk of the evening at the ball was, naturally, the Oliphants.

Shortly after this Laurence fell ill with a fever and – the danger signal – headaches. Alice nursed him devotedly. On 19 November he was obliged to excuse himself from a meeting the Prince of Wales had arranged at Sandringham with Gladstone, now Prime Minister, and his old acquaintance, Granville, once more Foreign Secretary. What they were to have discussed, and whether they eventually met, is not known. Throughout November Laurence's illness worsened, his head being 'too weak for business', while Alice, who had suffered from weak lungs since childhood, went down with bronchitis. Finally, the doctor ordered them to spend the winter abroad. They chose to go to Egypt, not in itself an odd decision, since the winter climate was agreeable and, by 1880, there was a recognized tourist route up the Nile to Luxor. But they chose to go to Medinet el Fayoum, an oasis which was then very remote and had no accommodation for tourists, let alone invalids. But they were privileged in that, as friends of the Prince of Wales, the ruler of Egypt, the Khedive Tewfik, placed the governor's palace at Medinet at their disposal.

According to the book Laurence wrote about their time in Egypt, *The Land of Khemi*, they behaved like tourists. They rode about the oasis on the large white donkeys of Medinet, or floated for hours along the system of canals. They made excursions into the desert to visit half-buried monuments; Laurence spent hours flat on his stomach in dark and dusty passages of tombs, while Alice poked about outside, turning up beads, glass and bits of bone. The book is full of descriptions of ruins and of the religious beliefs of the Ancient Egyptians. But to find out the beliefs of the modern Egyptians, both religious and political, was the real purpose of Laurence's investigations. After some weeks at Medinet, he and Alice embarked on a series of journeys up and down the Nile, whose object was not to look at the ruins, but to converse with the headmen of the villages. Laurence's interest in their state of mind sprang, as always, from the Eastern Question. In 1880 he foresaw that a weakened Turkey would eventually lose her grip on Egypt. When that happened, he believed that Egypt would become the leader of a Pan-Arabist movement already in embryo and capable of causing havoc throughout the Middle East. If he detected signs of national and religious enthusiasm among the *fellahin* during his wanderings along the Nile, he kept it to himself. That these emotions were strong at the time is indisputable as they fuelled the Arabi revolt which broke out later in the year.

Laurence's happiness at being reunited with Alice shines through the pages of *The Land of Khemi*. His renewed life with her, however short it had been, together with his absolute determination to press on with the colonization scheme, even if he now had to finance it himself, seems to have freed him at least from his subjection to Harris. If Rosamond Dale Owen is to be believed, while they were in Egypt he went so far as to suggest to Alice that they should have a child. She refused, being still under Harris's domination and dedicated to the doctrine of counterparts. Margaret Oliphant, who saw a great deal of her shortly after this, spoke of 'vexatious restrictions' that Laurence and Alice were obliged to observe together as the price of her release from California, which Alice understood to be temporary. Whether this strain, and doubt about his wife's continued presence at his side, hindered Laurence's convalescence, one cannot say, but when they returned to England in the summer of 1881 he continued to suffer from headaches.

In spite of this he was obliged to set out for America almost at once, leaving Alice at Windsor, in a rented house conveniently close to Margaret Oliphant who lived there. The most pressing reason for his journey was to persuade Harris to surrender to him the investments he and his mother had handed to the Brotherhood over the years. Laurence wanted the money to finance his Palestine scheme. But he was also most anxious about his mother who had remained at Brocton and was rumoured to be ill. When he saw her he found that this was true; Maria Oliphant was suffering from cancer. She and the Martins and the Buckners and the other members of the community who had remained at Brocton were harrassed by constant demands for money from Santa Rosa and dismayed by rumours of questionable behaviour among the western Brotherhood. After a short rest, which he obviously needed – 'Laurence is getting *quite well* again', Alice wrote – he and Lady Oliphant set out for California, both in the hope that the journey would improve her condition.

Instead it was a disaster. When they met, Harris would not be moved on the subject of money and he and Laurence had a furious row. After that the Oliphants retreated from Fountain Grove to a nearby town where Lady Oliphant collapsed. Laurence and a hastily summoned Mrs Walker, nursed her for six days until she died. The Walkers took a badly shaken Laurence home with them to San Francisco where James Walker began proceedings to retrieve his land and money from Harris. By threatening the Prophet with exposure, presumably upon evidence that Laurence would have supplied, Walker forced him to sign a deed transferring the land at Brocton into Laurence's name.

That is the outline of a complicated and savagely fought affair, the truth of which was obscured by Laurence's refusal ever to defend his side of it. Only to William and Georgiana Cowper, now Lord and Lady Mount Temple, did he explain that he broke with Harris because, after the move to Santa Rosa, the Prophet had become arrogant and greedy. Proof of this, to Laurence, was supplied by the sight of a watch that had once belonged to Sir Antony Oliphant and which his mother had always cherished, in the possession of Golden Rose.

As far as Harris and his disciples were concerned, the breach with Laurence Oliphant was a monstrous deed of apostasy, 'the worst betrayal since Judas Iscariot'. The accusations rumbled on for years and became part of the mythology of the Brotherhood. Arthur Cuthbert, who broke with his wife Violet over it, accused Laurence of deliberately plotting to usurp Harris's position, of trying to force him and all his disciples to go with him to Palestine. Among the Harris papers is the draft of a letter to William Mount Temple in the Prophet's own hand, which is very rare since he dictated nearly all of his correspondence. It is a scream of rage and pain at the loss of his mainspring, property. 'I had letters from LO demanding *money, deeds, property* and more from Mrs Cuthbert and Mrs Fowler and that man Martin, a refugee with his dying wife and wretched child, demanding money that will leave me penniless. In 1861 I Thomas Lake Harris prophesied at table that I would be betrayed by one from Great Britain that I would treat as a son . . . They gave me the money out and out and I held the deeds in trust. When I settled the deeds with the others I sent for him to give him his deeds for his portion, he fell into a fit of weeping saying he had given the money out and out and couldn't take it back having no confidence in his internal sphere. . . . Litigation would have killed me. Forgive this long letter but it eases my heart and relieves the pain.' Only illness, Harris told the Mount Temples, forced him to abstain from a proper defence of his own in the courts. Illness did not prevent him from telegraphing Alice that Laurence was insane and asking for her help in committing him to an asylum. She did not respond.

Little trace of this enormous upheaval marked the even tone of Alice's letters at this time. To friends, she wrote that business detained her husband longer than expected. To relatives, she explained that the death of his mother had been a blow, but that she expected him back soon. In December 1881, she was sure that he would embark at San Francisco and reach Plymouth four weeks later. As he was already in San Francisco, that would have been the quickest way. But, almost as if to postpone his arrival, he chose instead to take a long and difficult route by train along a line that was not quite completed, across Arizona, New Mexico, and Texas. Eight days after leaving San Francisco, bruised and hungry, he arrived in New Orleans, the first traveller to complete the route. From there he took ship to Havana where he paused to express his nagging fear in a letter to Mrs Walker. 'I ought to be in good spirits so far as my physical condition is concerned; but I cannot help being anxious at leaving the enemy so much time to carry on machinations in England possibly during my absence. In spite of my resolution to forget all the suffering I have passed through, it keeps coming back like a nightmare, and it will be some time before my wounds are healed . . . I daresay you will have heard from my wife long before this and therefore will know what she is feeling.' For himself he could not guess, but feared that Alice was still under the influence of Thomas Lake Harris. So it was with great joy and thankfulness that he saw her waiting on the quay at Plymouth. Once again the overwhelming good sense and kindness of Georgiana Mount Temple had come to the Oliphants' rescue. On hearing of Lady Oliphant's death, she had descended on Alice at Windsor and, in Alice's words, *ordered* her off to Broadlands. It was while she was there that Harris's request for Alice to declare Laurence insane arrived. No doubt the support of the Mount Temples helped her to make a final choice. As soon as Laurence arrived at Plymouth, Lady Mount Temple insisted that they both go straight to Torquay. There, in the Mount Temple's agreeable house, Babbacombe Cliff, within sound of the sea, they stayed for a time, sheltered, warm, quiet and alone. With husband and wife together, his mother dead and the land in the Oliphant name, there were no more hostages. After seventeen years of subjection that took some time to appreciate. At Babbacombe Cliff, Laurence slowly woke to the fact that they were both free from Thomas Lake Harris. Henceforth, Alice was committed to her husband only and he to the dream of Palestine. They decided to go there at once. But the world, when they returned to it, had a much more urgent task for Laurence Oliphant.

Throughout the summer and autumn of 1881, almost unnoticed at first, a stream of Jews had fled from Russia across the Austro-Hungarian border. By the end of the year, hundreds were gathered in the Galician towns of Lemberg and Brody, destitute and starving and unable to go further. The circumstances surrounding this mass movement were singular and, in their implications, frightening. Many had fled as a direct result of savage attacks upon their lives and property – the pogroms that followed the involvement of one of their race in the assassination of the Tsar, Alexander II, earlier in the year. It was said, but not proved, that the attacks were incited by the Russian Government as a means of ridding itself of a population it did not want. More Jews were made to go by the tightening of the already severe regulations governing life in the Pale of Settlement. Others responded to letters, some purporting to be signed by Moses Montefiore, urging them to emigrate to the New World. These were thought to be faked by unscrupulous shipping agents with an eye to the profit in the cargo thus acquired.

However they came to leave, the fact that they had done so, and the speed with which the impulse spread, was alarming. What country could absorb a fraction of the millions of Jews in Russia? The obvious answer was the United States. In the autumn of 1881, representatives of the Jewish philanthropic organization based in Paris, the Alliance Israélite Universelle, went to Lemberg and Brody with funds to help send the refugees, via Hamburg and Liverpool, to New York. But, when they arrived in Galicia, the Alliance representatives found the problem almost too great for them; many of the refugees were old or sick, or young and weak, and so unfit for work. At the end of 1881, the harrassed authorities in New York called a halt to further immigration and suggested that, henceforth, only the able-bodied be allowed to travel, while their dependents be repatriated back to Russia.

By that time the plight of the Jews was becoming known in the West, following a campaign in the newspapers. On 1 February 1882, a huge and indignant meeting at the Mansion House in London, gave promise of substantial help, while castigating the Russian Government. The Committee to administer the money raised was presided over by Lord Shaftesbury, and included many of the most respected names in English Jewry. On 15 February, Laurence Oliphant wrote a letter to *The Times*, in which he argued that many of the refugees at Lemberg and Brody did not wish to go to the United States where their religion and culture would be in danger of fading away, but rather to Palestine, where it would be strengthened and renewed. He proposed a joint Council of Christians and Jews to monitor the situation and to send officials to select suitable emigrants from among the refugees. The effect of this letter was immediate. Throughout the ghettoes of eastern Europe, and in Russia, word spread that Oliphant, 'the Lord', was back, that he and his powerful friends would help the Jews: at once a great wave of hope rolled towards him. In London he was co-opted on to the Mansion House Committee and, a few days later, chosen as one of three Commissioners for Galicia. Their brief was to go to seek help in Paris, Berlin, and Vienna, and then to Brody to assess the situation.

In the middle of March 1882, Laurence, with Alice, set out ahead of the other two Commissioners on what was to be a long and very tiring journey. By the time they got to Berlin, Alice was struggling against constant headaches. Thankfully, she wrote to Georgiana Mount Temple that they only had two lots of people there to call on privately. These were the Crown Prince and Princess of Prussia, and the British Ambassador, Laurence's old friend, Odo Russell, now

Lord Ampthill. Since in the climate of anti-semitism in Berlin the Crown Princess had shown herself publicly sympathetic towards the Jews, Laurence was assured of her interest in his present purpose as well as of warm recognition of his past services. As for Lord Ampthill, ten years previously Laurence had written to him as to a fellow adept; Alice now gave him and his wife an account of affairs at Brocton and in California. She also explained the general idea of 'our method of operation in the externals of morality'. In this she was referring to the way of life which she proposed to conduct for herself, Laurence, and their entourage, according to principles of mystical belief which increasingly obsessed her. To this the Ampthills were sympathetic – more than she had supposed their duties would allow, Alice remarked.

From Berlin they travelled to Vienna where they found great concern with the plight of the refugees and a greater willingness to help than either in Paris or Berlin. There Laurence met the greatest proto-Zionist of the time, Peretz Smolenskin. To Smolenskin the idea of assimilation, which caused so many Jews to turn a blind eye to political impediments in their adopted countries in the hope of better times to come, was anathema, nothing less than a betrayal. In his widely read novels and poems of Jewish life, and in his paper published at Vienna, *Ha Shahar*, the most famous Hebrew monthly in Europe, he extolled the idea of a return to Israel as the only way to regenerate the race, to make of the Jews once more a spiritual nation. The attraction of these ideas for Laurence Oliphant can be imagined. Moreover, in September 1881, Smolenskin had undertaken to print and circulate a pamphlet at his own expense urging Jews to take advantage of Oliphant's colonization scheme as soon as it might be properly constituted. Laurence now invited Smolenskin to go with him to Palestine, where he and Alice proposed to settle, to help in setting up the first Jewish colonies there. Smolenskin hesitated, doubtful about the provision of money, and unwilling to trust his health, which was precarious. But he agreed to give support in *Ha Shahar*.

Another writer who spread news of the mission to Brody was David Gordon. His paper, *Ha Magid*, was published at Lyck in East Prussia, which was a convenient observation post for the pitiful exodus from Russia. Gordon's commitment to the Return went back at least as far as the Polish uprising of 1863. Asked which the Jews should support, Russians or Poles, Gordon replied that the quarrel was not their affair. The Jews, like other minorities, ought to be pursuing their own national revival which, he believed, could only happen on the soil of Israel. Gordon, who spent some years in England and was a correspondent of the London *Jewish Chronicle*, now emerged as one of Laurence Oliphant's chief supporters, publicizing his movements and advocating his ideas. At the end of April 1882, *Ha Magid* published a letter from Laurence himself, which had a tremendous and dangerously inflammatory influence upon the situation. For, while he declared that no contribution was to be expected from wealthy Jews in England towards the colonization of Palestine, 'as soon as your Christian sympathizers in England are convinced the Jews fleeing from Russia can settle with safety in the land of their ancestors, then they will contribute thousands, I may well say, hundreds of thousands of pounds to promote this great object'.

The result of this and other publicity was a cascade of letters to Laurence Oliphant from all parts of Russia and Eastern Europe, and the spread of 'emigration fever' throughout the Russian ghettoes. 'Lord, Providence itself has delivered the wand of our nation's leadership into your hands and with your possession of it a new era in the history of the Jews ... begins,' wrote one hundred and five would-be emigrants to Palestine from Southern Russia. To this, and expressions like it, calling him Redeemer and a second Cyrus, Laurence replied that, although not a Jew himself, as a man he was only doing his simple duty to his Jewish brethren in their time of trouble. This was too simple. Neither Laurence nor anyone else could hope to satisfy the expectations he had aroused and, in addition, he failed to take into account the particular response of those to whom his promise was directed. Y. Y. Levontin saw the false position he was in. The Jews always relied on authority, on some 'great man' he said, so that if a notable personality advised against the settlement of Palestine they would drop the idea, while if he argued in its favour they believed him. 'A great deal was expected of Oliphant and [the Jews] believed in him because all the journals said that he was indeed a great man, a wise and sensible man, an authority.' But if someone pointed out his failings, Levontin went on, their spirits fell and they were at a loss.

When they arrived at Brody in April, Laurence and Alice found 1,200 refugees gathered in the town and more expected. Laurence went about distributing funds and collecting those Jews best suited to the journey to America. Though this task was not to his liking, it was the one he had been commissioned to do by the Mansion House Committee. When, a few weeks later, his two colleagues, Dr Asher, Secretary of the United Synagogue, and Samuel Montagu, caught up with him, they reported that Oliphant and his wife were greeted affectionately wherever they appeared. By the middle of May the number of refugees had grown to 12,000; the inns about Odessa were reported to be full of Jews intent on leaving Russia, and the Austrian authorities were threatening to close the border. The Mansion House Fund, some £80,000, had been spent at the rate of £5,000 a week (it cost £10 to send one refugee to America, £2 to Palestine), so it was almost depleted. Hastily, a circular was drafted and signed by Laurence Oliphant, and the representatives of the Alliance Israélite Universelle, urging Jews not to move from home for at least four months while the numbers at Lemberg and Brody were dispersed.

After that Laurence resigned from the Committee, whose intentions, he confided to a friend, were better than their executive capacity, in order to devote himself wholly to the plan for the colonization of Palestine. This was going on apace in Romania, he told William Mount Temple; subscriptions amongst Jews there would soon amount to 50,000 francs a month. While still in Brody he received numerous deputations from colonization societies, some of which called themselves Oliphant committees. He was also the subject of careful scrutiny by certain Jewish leaders who went there for that purpose. Among the most eminent of these was Rabbi Samuel Mohilever of Bialystock. He was a leader with a flair for organization, whose name is honoured as one of the foremost proto-Zionists. He was also a scholar, with a particular knowledge of the Kabbalah. What he saw of Laurence Oliphant at Brody satisfied him that the Gentile was a suitable person on whom to rely in preparations for the Return, in which he believed most fervently. For his part, Laurence was greatly influenced by Mohilever for whom he conceived the deepest respect. According to him, it was Mohilever who convinced him that only through a return to the observance of the laws described in the Kabbalah, could man hope to achieve regeneration; a belief that he promptly wove into the multicoloured web of his own peculiar philosophy.

At Brody, Laurence also received the representative of one of the most famous groups of people in the early history of Israel, whose members were known as Biluim. BILU, the name of the group, was formed from the initial letters of a Hebrew phrase which, translated, meant, 'O house of Jacob, come ye and let us go'. They were young students of Kharkov who, in early 1882, determined to go to Palestine in order to show the way to others. They were activists and pragmatists; austere young men who believed in education by precept. They envisaged a society in Palestine based on agricultural labour that, in due course, would aspire to political independence. It would be guided by an élite whose members would be called on to make sacrifices in their private lives (including abstaining from marriage), in order to achieve their exalted purpose. Of course these ideas appealed to Laurence Oliphant. It seems that the BILU delegate returned to Kharkov heartened by his meeting with Oliphant and assured that the powerful Gentile would give them vital assistance in approaching the Porte for a grant of land.

In the middle of May, Laurence and Alice, who, between moments of acclaim, took to her bed exhausted, left Galicia and travelled into Romania. Wherever they went they were met and followed by large crowds. So it was useless to suggest, as they tried to, that the visit they paid to the Rabbi of Sodogora, near Czernowitz, was a purely private affair. This rabbi was a so-called 'miracle worker', renowned for his deeds among the Chassidim. Figures like his were a recurring manifestation of the fanatical and exalted nature of that sect. Laurence had two reasons for going to see him; in spite of the schism with Harris he believed that such people possessed unusual powers; and he had noticed that the desire to return to Palestine was more passionate and immediate among the Chassidim than in any other group of Jews. The visit to the rabbi and the article he wrote about it in *Blackwood's Magazine* did Laurence great harm among Western Jews; for instance, the *Jewish Chronicle*, until then one of his most energetic advocates, began to distance itself from him after this.

But in May 1882 his prestige rose to new heights when by special invitation he attended a conference at Jassy in Moldavia of Romanian Jews determined to go to Palestine. The atmosphere was elated; prolonged cheers greeted Laurence's appearance and when he rose to speak. In French he told his audience that his sympathies lay wholly with their desire to go to Israel. His respect for Judaism was too great to permit him to contemplate the decline that would follow emigration to America. He repeated his promise that huge sums of money would be sent from England, though not from English Jews, and he assured the Romanians that his sum would amount to ten times that in the Mansion House Fund for the Russian refugees. As a result of this speech he was proposed as President of the Central Committee now to be formed. This office he declined, preferring to be an honorary member. But he did agree to a power of attorney being vested in him to treat with the Sultan on behalf of the Committee. For this he was acclaimed again, and as he and Alice returned to their hotel they were surrounded by eager and grateful crowds who stood outside waiting for another glimpse of him. Their journey by train from Jassy to Bucharest and thence to Constantinople, the *Jewish Chronicle* reported, was in the nature of a triumphal progress.

But at Constantinople the cheering stopped, the crowds fell silent and eventually drifted away. The reason was that at the end of May 1882 the Porte issued a decree to be circulated to all its officials at the points of entry. This said that Jews would be welcome as settlers, provided they became Ottoman subjects. They might go wherever they wished, except to Jerusalem and the immediate area. There were good reasons why the Turks insisted on this. They wished to check an enthusiasm which, in the wrong hands, might well turn into mass hysteria, and they feared a renewed interference by the Western powers in the government of the Holy Places. But in an article written for the *Jewish Chronicle* from Constantinople, Laurence Oliphant advanced another cause. According to him, the Sheikh ul Islam had reminded the Sultan, as Caliph, of certain 'uncomfortable' passages in the Koran and of other prophets familiar to Muslims: these foreshadowed the doom of Islam whenever Jews were restored to Jerusalem. Laurence – who was responsible for introducing prophecy into the affair in the first place, and for raising the expectations of the Jews to fever point – now deplored their plight as a result of this 'capricious' decree.

He wrote urgent letters to the heads of the Russian and Romanian committees begging them to wait patiently until the obstacles were removed. What these obstacles were and the kind of difficulty he was in, appear very clearly in the letter he wrote to Moses Gaster at Bucharest on 9 June 1882. He said that he was overwhelmed by a daily correspondence requiring answers from all over Russia and Romania. He had a scheme whereby he hoped to persuade the Porte to make an exception from the ban on entering Palestine for the Romanian Jews. But he said, 'I have been completely paralysed by this Egyptian crisis which has absorbed the Sultan and his Ministers to the exclusion of any other topic, and some untruthful newspaper reports have been also shown to His Majesty which did great harm as

I was made to say that I was endeavouring to have a British protectorate established over Palestine, which, as you know, is entirely untrue.' On the contrary, it was true, and he had acknowledged as much in public earlier in the year. But his denial was undoubtedly due to the hostility he had encountered since arriving in Constantinople.

The loophole he hoped to use for Romanian Jews rested on an argument concerning their citizenship. Until the Treaty of Berlin, Romania had been under Turkish rule and all her inhabitants citizens of the Ottoman Empire. Because the new Romanian Government had withheld citizenship from the Jews within her borders, they remained Turkish subjects, Laurence argued. As such, they were entitled to profit under the long standing law which allowed freedom of movement within the Empire to all subjects possessed of a little capital. At the beginning of June, Laurence telegraphed for two members of the Bucharest Committee for emigration to Palestine to go to Constantinople to support this argument with their personal appeals. They were successful and the first Romanian colonists arrived in Palestine in the autumn of 1882.

But this exception could not help Russian Jews. And so those members of BILU who went to Constantinople with high hopes of Laurence Oliphant, were doomed to disappointment. They had to go back to Odessa where the rest of the group had gathered and make their way to Palestine, slowly and alone.

As the summer of 1882 advanced, the crisis over the British and French seizure of Egypt showed no sign of easing, and Laurence found it was a positive handicap to be British. The only way to avoid an abrupt rebuff when applying to the Porte, he found, was to do it through the American Minister at Constantinople, Lew Wallace (author of *Ben Hur*). But it was essential to remain on the spot, Laurence thought; he believed that the Egyptian crisis foreshadowed the imminent break up of the Ottoman Empire and a possible Muslim holy war. These were the circumstances he had already envisaged under which Palestine would be separated from the rest of the Empire, when the best chance of Jewish colonization would occur.

He and Alice took rooms in a tall house on the steep slope above the Bosphorus at Therapia. They were surrounded by gardens and hospitable friends. The English Ambassadress, their old acquaintance from Ottawa, Lady Dufferin, sent a donkey every day to carry Alice down the cobbled street to bathe in the embassy enclosure, and the Italian Ambassador, Count Corti, gave her a key to the door in the

Laurence and Alice Oliphant in Palestine

James Murray Templeton

Rosamond Dale Owen in her thirties

wall of his garden opposite their house, 'so that I have his hanging terraces to myself and a short cut down to the water's edge'. The only cloud in the summer sky were the accusations put about by Lady Strangford, a formidable figure in the world of hospital administration at home, and with a special knowledge of the Middle East. As a member of the Women's Committee of the Mansion House Fund, she was complaining that the Oliphants were living rather too well on the money Laurence had been given for the refugees. Lady Strangford was preposterously rude, Alice told her mother. 'I wish we *had* the benefits our interest in the distressed populations is supposed to bring us. With a little more money we could do much more good . . . though our travelling expenses were given by the Mansion House, individual matters of charity . . . have made us some hundreds of pounds out of pocket this spring.' They had sent fifty refugees to Brocton where all the first years' expenses would have to be borne by them until the refugees' labour could make them independent. 'Poor things, we get such grateful letters from them. We gave orders to have their Sabbaths and all food and other special observances respected, of course.' (Kosher food had to come from Buffalo.) This experiment interested Laurence particularly, Alice said, because the great fault and weakness of the Jews was their inability for handy work; 'and he says to train even a few into that, and into a co-operative manner of life will be a great gain'.

A further drain on their resources was the secretary Laurence was obliged to employ, who spoke eleven languages and wrote in five, which resulted in a 'perfectly ruinous bill for postage'. This secretary was a Jew, aged 26, Naphtali Herz Imber, who was born in Galicia and brought up in strict orthodoxy. His name was to become famous in the history of Israel for, while he lived with the Oliphants, he wrote the 'Ha Tikvah', the hymn that celebrates the Return to Israel.

As the summer ended, they moved to Prinkipo Island, within sight of the Golden Horn. There they were joined by Violet Cuthbert who had become estranged from her husband, Arthur, following the schism with Harris. To her mother, Alice described the ménage on Prinkipo as a happy and hard-working one. They had a Greek man of all work who did the cooking excellently and the rest indifferently. They were all hard at it; Imber learning English, Laurence, Hebrew, Violet, German, which Alice taught her (German was the *lingua franca* of the Eastern European Jews). Laurence wrote most of the time, and what with needlework, sketching, donkey riding, and bathing, they were a perfect ant hill of activity. To Georgiana Mount Temple she wrote in different terms. She was too weak to say much and suffered from headaches; 'I dare not give out much life'. The international situation was threatening and her sense of spiritual mission bore hard on her. 'Our internal instructions indicate that we are to watch the scene of action from a safe place near at hand.' Arabi, the Sultan, and Gladstone, said Alice, were driven by forces they could not resist. 'It is the necessary redistribution of the world's political forces in preparation for what is to be.' Her next letter to Georgiana, written in October 1882, came from Beyrout, where she and Laurence had gone on their way to Palestine. Cold weather and the charcoal heating in the cottage on Prinkipo had increased her headaches so that Laurence had been frightened into leaving. From that time on a fear was always in his mind.

CHAPTER 10

HAIFA

From Beyrout they went to Haifa, a small, white, Arab town lying in the curve of a great bay that ended at the monastery of Carmel standing on a ledge above the sea. Haifa was to be their home until they died and, though it came late and lasted only a short time, their happiness was very great. It was there that Laurence achieved the practical expression of his deepest instinct; to be of service to his fellow men, so that, for a short time, he was at peace. For Alice, their life at Haifa was also a satisfaction and a delight. On one level she found the task of organizing a household in primitive surroundings interesting and rewarding. She had already proved her ability to her own satisfaction in California, but there she had been alone. At Haifa she had husband, friends, visitors, servants and hangers-on dependent on her enterprise and eager to applaud it. On a higher level, it was she who – as perhaps always when they were together – directed their spiritual life, and brought to it a new sense of exaltation derived from her belief that now they were in Palestine, the time, the place, and the specially selected people would join to produce some wonderful event.

Others who shared her view had come to Haifa fifteen years before, and though they had suffered great hardship in the beginning were now established, a mile beyond the Arab town, in a settlement looking for all the world like a village in Würtemberg. This was the Templars' colony of some three hundred Germans who, believing that the Second Coming would occur in Palestine, took steps to ensure they would be present at it. It was there, next door to the leader of the colony, Gottlieb Schumacher, that Laurence and Alice settled down. Like the others, their house was built of stone, with a red-tiled roof and a text in German above the door. They had a garden, in front of which ran a gravel path shaded by mulberry and sycamore trees. Mount Carmel rose abruptly at the end of the street, terraced to the summit with vines and olives. The vines, which had come from Germany, suffered from mildew, so in time Laurence had them replaced with the Concord and other hardy American varieties. There was a good hotel in the Templars' colony, a schoolroom with a piano on which Alice played, a library, and a bathing shed on the beach. There were two mills, and a factory making soap from the olives of Carmel, which was exported to New York. Fifteen years before wheeled transport was unknown, now the Würtembergers had a carriage builder. Four times a day the local Arabs drove a cart to Acre, ten miles away across the smooth wide beach. Towards Jaffa, the plain of Sharon was so flat and smooth that no road was needed.

Laurence found a never ending delight in the view from the house in which they lived. To the east, they looked over the harbour, with date groves and the plain of Kishon beyond, which a wooded range of hills separated from the plain of Esdraelon. To the north east, Mount Hermon towered 9,000 feet, its summit covered with snow. Across the blue waters of the bay the white walls and minarets of Acre rose from the margin of the sea, beyond which was the white projecting cliff known as the Ladder of Tyre. Though the shadow of Carmel lay over the colony from the middle of the afternoon, they did not grudge it for even on New Year's Day the thermometer stood at 66 degrees in the shade.

How pleasantly the Biblical names rolled off the tongue, and how agreeable it was to ride about the country in the warm sunshine, exploring ruins and caves, and talking to the inhabitants of remote villages! The excuse for this was a series of articles commissioned by Laurence's acquaintance from his days in the U.S., Charles A. Dana, for the paper he edited, the *New York Sun*. But for some people who had lately been his companions in the enterprise of Palestine life was unmitigatedly grim. Those Romanian Jews who, after much hardship and frustration, managed to settle on land at Rosh Pina in Galilee, and Samarin, south of Haifa, found that their struggle had only just begun. From the beginning they were short of money, food, tools, draught animals, and seed; the land was poor and difficult to work and lacking in sufficient water. As the autumn advanced they felt cold, the unaccustomed physical labour exhausted them and soon they fell ill. Laurence did what he could, buying tools and seed with funds sent to him from England, and interceding for them with the Turkish authorities. But he and they knew that only drastic measures would save them. An approach was made on their behalf by, among others, Rabbi Mohilever to Baron Edmond de Rothschild to take control of the colonies; although Laurence was associated with the approach, in that quarter his name was not approved. Rothschild distrusted him, possibly because he disliked the use he made of the prophecy, and because he believed the rumour, current in Romania and at Constantinople, that Laurence's real purpose was to convert the Jewish migrants to Christianity at a time when their capacity to resist was weak. The consequence of Rothschild's attitude was to leave the name of Oliphant free from the criticism that came to be attached to his – he was accused of saving the colonies at the price of an irksome and petty tyranny. On the whole Laurence thought Rothschild's arrangements were fair and he was loathe to interfere with them. So he found it difficult to help those Jews who fell foul of the Baron's overseers. But he did come to the rescue in cases of real hardship. For instance when two Jews were expelled from Samarin on the grounds that they would not work in the fields, Laurence found jobs for them with the Templars. Since they were not worth wages to the Germans, he paid them himself. 'In this way I will test their sincerity as being willing to work as day labourers and have them learn agriculture,' he explained to Alice's mother.

The Jewish historian, Nahum Sokolov, absolved him of any intent to convert anyone, let alone Jews. He knew Laurence well and translated *The Land of Gilead* into Hebrew in 1885; according to Sokolov it was a huge success as it contained the first scientifically drawn map of Palestine many Jews had seen. To Sokolov Laurence was a man of loving kindness; sincere, intelligent, and thorough; 'a man of original mind, unselfishness and devotion'. His belief in the Jewish national revival was unshakeable, Sokolov wrote, and so it was fitting that he should be the only non-Jewish member of the English branch of a movement that swept through England and America, and became the nucleus on which Herzl would build. Dedicated to the idea of the Return to Israel, these groups were called the Lovers of Zion.

But in 1882 they were still in embryo. And by the end of that year, the emigration fever had largely died down, helped by the coming to power in Russia of a more conciliatory Minister of Interior. Recognising this, and driven by a renewed urge to help his suffering neighbours, Laurence tried to turn even the arch-enemy to their advantage. He wrote to the poetess, Emma Lazarus, in New York, saying that Russia would seize any opportunity of extending her influence in Palestine. Miss Lazarus was the author of the famous words which were to be engraved on the base of the Statue of Liberty, and a passionate advocate of help for her fellow Jews. Laurence suggested to her that she ask the United States Government to make an unofficial approach to St. Petersburg to have the Tsar's Government remonstrate with the Porte over the 'illegal' edict prohibiting Jews from settling in Palestine. Never mind that such a move would be to England's disadvantage, that was England's fault. 'If Russian intrigue stirred up the British Government, the Jews would be the gainers, it might then be a struggle between the two Powers who should protect them most.' This, he explained, was an idea he threw out in case she could use it. As an Englishman (especially as *that* Englishman) it would be difficult for him to put it forward in the newspapers. Perhaps understandably, nothing more was heard of this. And, in 1882, the world could be forgiven for thinking that the Oliphant scheme for a Jewish settlement in Palestine was wholly at an end. That was not at all the case, Alice told her mother, but Laurence was happy it should be thought so until things quietened down. Wherever he went in Palestine he was watched, as were the Jewish colonists, nor would the Turks relax their vigilance for many years.

In the spring of 1883, when Laurence was much away, Alice busied herself at Haifa with masons, carpenters, and upholsterers, making ready for their Brocton friends. In March, Mr Buckner, Pitt's father, arrived with James Fowler's widow and her son. Alice was happy at bringing together those she called the collaborators of her inner life; Mr Buckner and Mrs Fowler were heart and soul devoted to her scheme of things, she said. The domestic side of this delighted her almost as much as the spiritual. In April, she told her mother that the household had increased again. They had bought a horse, a cow and a pig, adopted a dog, and had a boxful of 'home made' kittens in the kitchen. Everyone was up at 6.30 at the latest, but Mr Buckner (who was seventy and had started life as a parson), sallied forth with a hoe among the maize and potatoes at half past five. Mrs Fowler superintended the housework and mended the clothes for all; Mrs Cuthbert supervised the laundry, the chickens, and the flowers. 'Alice, as you will guess, *food*. By about ten I have made the menu, prepared the bread, done the more delicate preparations such as croquettes and puddings, have cut up and distributed the different parts of fresh meat to the soup pot, roasting pan, dripping pot – the household economy depending more on this process than any other.' After lunch, they rested, then Alice taught them German, rode up and down the neat Teutonic street, played the piano and poured the tea. In the evening Laurence read to them, or neighbours called. By ten they were all in bed. She and Laurence shared a room with a view of Carmel; it was decorated with pale lavender paint above a Pompeian red dado and had dark navy blue cotton curtains.

But, however enjoyable it was to order the existence of a small community in its outward aspect, it was to the perfecting of their spiritual life that Alice was drawn. In this life Naphtali Herz Imber had a key role to play; as a Jew returned to the soil of Israel under the Oliphants' tutelage, he was to be a means to the regeneration of his race. 'Our beloved ones of the inner world', Alice explained to Georgiana Mount Temple, had already contrived a change in Naphtali. 'He travels as Laurence's Hebrew secretary to the outward world, but we are gradually educating [him] in the ways of life of Lily's children. It is wonderful to see the professional conceits ... and superficial clumsiness and ignorance of social life falling away from him and all kinds of unsuspected sweetness and docility and deep moral strength springing up in the atmosphere in which we hold him.'

That atmosphere was one of love – of a very particular kind. Its nature was described in a book published by William Blackwood in 1884. Called *Sympneumata*, its title page bore the name of Laurence Oliphant. But, apart from a lucid introduction in which he explained that he had devoted years to investigating the phenomena described in the book, it was like nothing he had ever written in his life. In very cloudy language it sought to define a power called Sympneuma. This was the faculty of superhuman vision, hearing, strength, and resistance to disease and death, given to those rare beings who were privileged to know their counterparts while on earth. It was the duty of these beings possessed of Sympneuma to impart it to their fellows through human contact. Thus, slowly, would the regeneration of the race occur, and men and women be restored to their happy condition of before the Fall. Prior to that event, male and female had been joined in one being and sexual love was pure. When lust shattered this ideal state and Evil entered the world, woman's fall was further than man's, her condition the more degraded. So it was she who now must play the greater role, whose struggle for her rightful equal place in the world was crucial, and had only just begun. And, when men and women again became biune, as the author quaintly put it; 'it will often be found that no provision is made for earth peopling after the fashion of the past'. In other words, in the ideal world of the author of *Sympneumata* sexual intercourse would not occur. This concept of the transmission of spiritual love through physical contact was close to that of Christ as Bridegroom, as practised in the early days at Brocton, and by various other American religious communities. Like their belief, it lent itself to misinterpretation.

A stunned silence greeted the appearance of the book in England: regular readers of Laurence Oliphant did not know what to make of it. Alexander Kinglake was among the first to guess the secret; Laurence had sent him a copy, he told Mrs Wynne Finch. 'I of course opined that your dear Alice was the writer.' Tactfully, he went on, 'I did not permit myself to write as one competent to have an opinion on the subject, I always, as you know, looked upon her – guided partly by her beauty – as a grandly gifted being.' Margaret Oliphant thought the philosophy of Sympneuma, 'something too tremendous'. She was making a prodigious effort to understand the book, she told William Blackwood, 'but I have to catch hold of the furniture . . . to keep myself from turning round and round, and yet the absorption of such a man of the world as he is in a religious idea has something very fine about it'. How much more surprised she would have been had she known that Alice had dictated the book to Laurence as if under the influence of a higher mind. The motive underlying the practice of imparting Sympneuma was intelligible enough, springing as it did from an innocent attempt to impart warmth, to experience natural affection in the only way that Alice's peculiar religious belief allowed. It was with an entirely joyful sense of mission that Alice wrote to Georgiana Mount Temple at this time. 'Isn't God managing His work marvellously, improving it astonishingly? Do you see how He lets people care as they never did before, how the strength and power comes to women and tenderness to men?'

Hardly anyone understood; the Oliphants were naive in supposing that they would. In the eyes of the world that was their crime, which drew down upon them ridicule and, in due course, calumny. Alice was puzzled by the silence of the London press about *Sympneumata* but supposed that the subject was 'prickly'. She was rather relieved than not since the 'independence of the common relations of the sexes in marriage' which their thought implied, was too delicate a subject for her to debate in public. Instead, she told her mother, she busied herself replying to letters – none from people they knew – asking for help with problems. One of these was from a Mrs Hankin, headmistress of a school at Malvern. Mrs Hankin had a burning desire to influence her girls rightly, Alice said; nearly all of them would be governesses. She and Mrs Hankin entered into a prolific correspondence.

In the summer of 1883 General Charles Gordon appeared at Haifa on his way to Jerusalem in pursuit of a private religious theory. He and Laurence already knew each other slightly having met in the trenches before Sebastopol and again in China in 1858. Now, according to Alice, they seemed at once like very old friends. 'They say it must be because they are each considered one of the craziest fellows alive.' Laurence read *Sympneumata* to Gordon who, as a fellow mystic, took it very seriously indeed. In a letter to William Mount Temple, Laurence described the scene in Alice's bedroom where she lay ill. The three of them argued the case, and Gordon complained that too little mention of the Bible was made in the book. Laurence said the power of Sympneuma was for people who could not find comfort in the Bible and became so heated that Alice had to hush him. A surge of love for Gordon impelled him to throw his arms around him. This, he confided to William, he afterwards found very embarrassing.

The next time Gordon stayed with the Oliphants, in December 1883, they had much conversation on the subject of the Sudan. According to Gordon, writing to his sister, Laurence was determined to go there to observe the progress of the Mahdi, who had but lately appeared, and, to many besides Laurence, seemed to come as the fulfilment of a prophecy. Gordon declared himself in favour of granting independence to the troubled Sudan, and thought the wisest course of action would be for a civil commissioner to go there to discuss with the Mahdi how this might be achieved. Yet he rejected Laurence's argument that, in view of his long experience of that country, he would be the best person for the task. Gordon said he was pledged to the King of the Belgians to lead an expedition to the Congo. Laurence, who had grown to love him, was very upset when Gordon departed on his ten mile walk to Acre for the steamer. On leaving, Gordon told him he felt he had no more work to do for God on this earth, and that he would not return from the Congo. Within a month of that he was in Upper Egypt at the head of the ill fated British expedition to Khartoum. Once in that city under siege,

Laurence was one of the people Gordon wrote to most constantly, and for whom he prayed. The last words of his last letter to his sister, Miss Augusta Gordon, were, 'I am quite happy thank you and, like Laurence I have *tried* to do my duty'.

In 1883, one of Gordon's visits to the Oliphants had been spent in a tent pitched near theirs on the summit of Mount Carmel to which they had retreated in order to escape the heat and disease the summer brought to Haifa. In 1884, as the hot weather approached, they determined to find a more permanent home on the mountain. Although Carmel was a steep four and a half hour climb by mule or, in Alice's case, in a litter, the summit was open, fertile and rolling, the view idyllic, the air dazzlingly clear and invigorating; the ills of the coast, dysentry, for instance, or headaches, disappeared as if by magic. Laurence's attempt to buy a piece of land near the Druse village of Esfia, where he had camped in 1883, met with little success as the price asked was exorbitant. Then the sheik of the neighbouring village of Dalieh, also a Druse, appealed to Laurence for help. His only son had been drawn as a conscript in the Turkish Army and no one in the family could afford the US$250 it cost to buy a substitute. Laurence rode up to the village to enquire into the matter, and, in return for the required sum, received a vineyard and a garden of fruit trees with a good title and a view of surpassing loveliness.

Dalieh was the southernmost village of the Druses, a sect that originated at Aleppo in the tenth century. Their religion which set them apart as a people, was secret, but it was known to embrace a belief in the return of a Prophet, in reincarnation, and in magic. According to Richard Burton, who had been fascinated by them, the Druses had a secret creed which, although women were admitted to the council chamber, was as mysterious as Freemasonry. In order to protect the secrets of their own religion, they were allowed to profess others, and so frequently appeared as ordinary Muslims. They had a curious belief that the Chinese and Japanese, albeit all unknowingly, belonged to their race, and they were particularly amiable towards the English. Add to this the fact that they were accused of licentious practices at their mysterious religious ceremonies, and one can see that the Druses and the Oliphants had a great deal in common.

It was at Dalieh that the reputation of Alice and Laurence Oliphant for wisdom and fair dealing and open-handedness was first established and subsequently spread throughout the Hauran. Their arrival on the mountain was sufficiently unusual to attract the attention of the other inhabitants who were scattered over a wide area and soon they began to come to them for help and advice. Alice had always delighted in the details of domestic economy and enjoyed managing people; now she could use both skills to their best advantage. She began to learn Arabic with a view to better instructing the Druse women in the care of the sick and in the ordering of their households which, to her tidy mind, left something to be desired. When Laurence was away, which was often, she assumed his role of arbiter of disputes and protector of the people against their overlords, the Turks. For in that outlying part of the Ottoman Empire the villagers were groaning under rapacious demands for taxes destined to prop up the bankrupt Porte. Because the Oliphants lent money to pay these taxes and hold off the harsh penalties that would otherwise be imposed they earned the undying gratitude and affection of their neighbours.

The house that Laurence built on the vineyard was of stone and battlemented, with a terrace sheltered by trees and a room set aside for visitors who, Alice said, liked to squat and drink coffee and talk – 'and think the highest politeness consists of asking silly questions', Laurence added. Even more thought had to go into the housekeeping at Dalieh than at Haifa, for everything had to be brought up 1800 feet on camels. Custom dictated they keep open house; at any one time, Alice told Georgiana, there would be a collection of nationalities gathered round the heap of rice on the mat under the fig tree outside the kitchen door. That particular morning she counted one Druse man, a little Egyptian Muslim boy, a German tramp, two Jewish beggars, and a Syrian Muslim horseman, the guide to travellers visiting them. 'Eggs, boiled rice, raw cucumbers and bread are supposed to be at the disposal of every hungry wretch in the country. Fortunately, if not artistic, our cook is very good natured.' The household at Dalieh had recently been increased by the advent of Dr and Mrs Martin who, following the schism with Harris, had sided with the Oliphants. While Dr Martin helped her as best he could with the treatment of the sick among the Druses, Alice found Mrs Martin a very great trial. She was an invalid, apparently needing constant support, incapable of being by herself; just to be with her, Alice complained, drained her of precious energy. According to Robert Martin, who disapproved of the apparently brisk treatment of his mother, Alice at the age of 42 showed signs of becoming a virago.

Quite a different view of her was provided by Valentine Chirol who, in those years, spent much of his time wandering in the Middle East and stayed often at Dalieh. He recalled in his memoirs that Laurence continued to write, 'but the inspiration seemed to come almost entirely from his wife, who retained much of the Madonna like beauty of her youth, with an added tinge of sadness and compassion'. In her faith, Chirol remarked, there was a strange tinge of mysticism that appeared in *Sympneumata*, published by William Blackwood, 'who confessed to me afterwards he had been quite unable to understand it'. As the years at Dalieh went by, Chirol said, both Laurence and Alice acquired great influence and reputation among the local people so that the house became a place of pilgrimage for members of many sects, mostly humble. 'The Turkish authorities themselves learnt to reckon with them for they were naturally credited with that measure of madness which is deemed throughout the East to derive from God.' Laurence was the strongest and best influence in his life, Chirol said; though it might be difficult to understand him it was impossible not to love him. He had been everything in turn and might have excelled in anything but for a curious waywardness which was not due to a lack of perseverance or earnestness, but to a deep seated faith in an inner voice that was constantly calling him to new lines of endeavour.

Alice was rather tart on the subject of Chirol. Laurence liked the young man, she told her mother; he was clever and agreeable. *She* wanted to stick pins in him since he could be much nicer if he only took the trouble. He wanted to meet Mrs Wynne Finch in London; 'We owe him nothing so don't put yourself out to entertain him,' Alice said. A similar tone informed her private comments on the Mount Temples at this time. Although she continued to address Georgiana as 'dearest Lowly', and to confide in her how great a drain their way of life was upon her limited strength, Alice was not above criticizing her friends behind their backs. She was astonished, she told her mother, when she heard that William and Georgiana had invited Mrs Anna Kingsford, a noted medium, to their Curzon Street house; they used not to recognize her in this way. It was all very well to gather all sorts and conditions about them when the charitable intent of it could be explained, but it was certainly out of place at London dinner parties. 'They have, of course, lost anything like real social touch.'

Problems of social touch, and other manifestations of civilized life like puddings and croquettes were, it seemed, with them even in the wilds. Early in 1885, a very large problem presented itself in the shape of a visit by the Duke of Sutherland. Long before the Duke and his party arrived in Palestine, Alice was taking care not to be drawn into arrangements she might afterwards want to cancel. She told Georgiana that Laurence was very anxious to avoid hurting the Duke's feelings and so, in order to be on the safe side, it was decided that he should go to Jerusalem alone to meet him, while Alice stayed at home. When the Duke's party returned to Haifa, Alice kept to her room. The reason for this was that, as a respectable married woman, Alice had to be spared the dreadful task of acknowledging the Duke's mistress, Mrs Blair, who was travelling with him.

Laurence's anxiety for the Duke's peace of mind sprang from his interest in one of the Duke's other passions, railways. The idea of a railway linking Turkey, Syria, and Egypt, which had formed part of the scheme of 1879, was still in the forefront of Laurence's mind. Indeed, some people thought that this, and the prospect of acquiring cheap land, was the real reason why he had come to Palestine. The first journey he made after settling at Haifa was to Cairo to drum up English capital for it. Apparently he did not succeed, for in the course of 1884 he made a determined attempt to involve the Duke of Sutherland in the scheme. As he explained in an article for the *New York Sun,* the first part of the line, to be called the Hamidiye railway after the Sultan, had already been surveyed. It was to run from the Jordan Valley to Acre and would bring the grain of the fertile Hauran out to the sea. According to him, the concession was held by a group of Christians and Muslims living at Beyrout, of whom the most prominent were bankers, the Messrs. Sursocks, who owned most of the Plain of Esdraelon over which the line would run. That much was public knowledge, since Laurence chose to make it so in the columns of the *New York Sun.* What was not made public was that he had an interest in it, possibly through the Messrs. Sursocks, with whom he was friendly, and that he had paid for the survey so far. In 1884 the concessionaires were in urgent need of money to pay baksheesh for the *firman* for the second phase, though if it were known how keen they were to go ahead the price would rise. This phase was planned to extend the line to Damascus and beyond, via Homs to Aleppo. It was vital that English money should be at least partly involved in this, Laurence told Sutherland; 'whoever gets hold of the Railway will practically control Syria and the Euphrates Valley'. The Duke was no stranger to the strategic argument; he had already tried to get the

British Government involved in financing a railway from Turkey to Baghdad by the same route, without success.

Laurence told him that the Sultan's special favour might be got for the Damascus line for the price of shares in it, 'which will have to be disguised in the prospectus'. He, together with Gottlieb Schumacher, the leader of the Temple colony, who was a civil engineer, and another German, Georg Eggar, had mapped out the course of the new survey. But, such was their urgent need for money before the concession ran out that other sources would have to be tapped. So, 'Prince Hohenlohe has taken the matter up warmly and is off to Berlin with Eggar to see Gerson Bleichröder, Bismarck's banker and financial man'. Laurence hoped the Duke would receive Eggar if he came to London. The Duke did so, but complained that Eggar was incompetent and could not raise money in England or anywhere else. In the event the Germans subscribed £10,000 for the preliminary expenses of the line and the Duke nothing. Undaunted, Laurence tried again. In the summer of 1884, he approached the Duke for money, not only for the railway, but to develop all sorts of enterprises at and around Haifa, and it was these that Sutherland came out to inspect in 1885. The letter casts a radically different light upon Laurence from that of the benefactor of the Jews and the protector of the Arabs. As entrepreneur he appears self interested, not to say greedy, but the country in question had no hope of development without the sort of capital he was trying to obtain. He told the Duke that the confidential adviser of the Governor General of Syria was a friend. 'He knows that now is the time to feather his nest and tells me he can get any concession or privilege he wants and has already proposed to me to go in with him in several things but I don't feel strong enough financially.' He would be very glad if the Duke and Earl of Dunraven, (the erstwhile Lord Adare, spiritualist and war correspondent) would come out to look into the matter, Laurence said, as there would never be such a chance again of getting what they wanted. There were tracts of land to be got for almost nothing but they could not be bought in the name of an Englishman. This confirmed what Alice told Mrs Walker, that they were holding on to their Brocton land for the time being as the Turkish Government's fear of Laurence being charged with some political mission for England made it impossible for him to buy much land. Nevertheless, Laurence told the Duke and the Earl that he was negotiating for 2,000 acres of well watered arable land which would be on the railway when it was made. He was also paying for another storey to be built on the hotel and newly furnishing it so, *pace* Alice, 'If Mrs Blair comes she will have good accommodation'. And he was contemplating a little quay at Haifa on land to be reclaimed from the sea, but it was too big a job for him alone. One does not know how far, if at all, Sutherland was tempted to invest in these projects. Circumstances intervened to make them irrelevant.

The source of the Oliphants' money for these schemes is obscure. As far as regular income was concerned, it may be that they received a reasonable amount from Brocton, where the various enterprises were now being well managed by young Pitt Buckner. But Laurence also made a considerable sum from the continuing sale of a novel, published in 1883. Both the book and its heroine took their name from the motto of the Oliphants of Condie, 'Altiora Peto'. When this was finished, it was decided that it should come out in parts – a risky business for all but the most popular authors. To William Blackwood's enormous relief it was a great success and, in some people's estimation, remained Laurence Oliphant's best book. Written in the light sardonic vein of *Piccadilly* (at the same time as Alice was dictating *Sympneumata* to him), it described the impact on English society of a delightful young American girl, Altiora, who, in the best romantic tradition, as also in real life at the time, survived a series of adventures to match her transatlantic money to the noble lineage of an English house. *Masollam*, the novel that followed in 1885 was quite different; a long, solemn, curious, and depressing account of the career of a strange man possessed of compelling power, whose beautiful daughter, again after many adventures, escaped from his tutelage to reign as Queen over an amiable and deserving Eastern tribe. As well as a detailed explanation of the prophet's philosophy, the book contained some rather turgid passages on the history of religion, and traces of Alice's mystical ideas. Needless to say, the Masollam of the title was a portrait of Thomas Lake Harris and, as such, the book was sought after by those who knew Laurence's history. 'A story that is not story', Alice called it, and remarked that Laurence was using it to say many things. Isabel Burton thought it went far to explain the riddle of his life. In fact it did not. Even though the book ended with a denial of Masollam's power, it was silent on the crucial point of how Laurence had become subject to Harris in the first place, or why his delusion eventually came to an end. Margaret Oliphant said she wished it had not been written. Although it might be taken as a warning to those who believed too much in prophets, she felt it was a waste of time. 'He had a hundred things to teach as well as one deceiver to expose,' Mrs Oliphant thought.

Though it had been happy, interesting, and rewarding, the Oliphants' retirement from the world was not intended to be permanent. After five years away they began to prepare for a visit to England. Their intention was to arrive in London in time for the season of 1886, then to make a series of visits in Scotland. For this to be possible, Alice told her mother in August 1885, she needed to be quite as well as she was then, or even a little better. The thing she must avoid was a rough sea journey and a cold Northern winter. But before her return home, she was to have the pleasure of a visit from her sister, Jamesina, and her husband, Adolphus Waller, Vicar of Hunstanton, another refugee from the cold English climate. Many excursions were planned for the Wallers, who arrived at Haifa in November 1885; among the longest was a ride of several days round Lake Tiberias. The country there was wild and largely uninhabited so they would have to take tents and provisions with them. Since Alice, as always, risked headaches as the price of too much exertion, it was agreed that the Wallers should ride on ahead while she and Laurence followed slowly behind. Alice's journal of the expedition was sent to Hamon Le Strange; although she gave a good account of her resistance to fatigue in it, in retrospect the danger signs were already clear.

The first day's journey, though it was from Haifa to Nazareth in a cart, was so long and rough that Alice had to spend the next day in bed in the Nazareth convent. She comforted herself that the camels could not go on in the rain as they were useless in mud. In the afternoon of the following day they went quietly on, but only for an hour and a half as Alice was 'limp'. When they arrived at Cana, she was glad they did not have to unfold their tent but could sleep in the parlour of the convent there and cook in its corridor. The next day's ride to Tiberias went very well; the Wallers had ordered lunch for them there, but 'as soon as our tents arrived we pitched them and slept in them'. Then for a day or two things improved; they joined the Wallers on the far side of the lake to explore Wady Hamman and lunched, sketched and 'photoed' under a fortress built in the massive rock where soldiers were let down in cages to dislodge the Jews by order of Herod. Alice carried a 'photo apparatus' which she complained she did not know how to use properly but which she found a great aid to sketching. Back at the lake heavy rain obliged them to spend two days in the tents. When it cleared they rode to Caperneum and then up some valleys in search of ruins. They came back, cold and hungry, to find their tent blown down. It was nearly dark and there was nothing but sand to hold the pegs. Fortunately 'a providential wheat magazine belonging to a rich Damascene Pacha was there, and they let us sleep in the wheat and cook in the entrance'. The next day; 'L.O. excursed, A.O. headache and fever; still in the wheat vault, marshes all round'. The day after; 'better after quinine; rode off early to get away from the marshes – buffalo in them – pitched our tent in the heart of a great Bedouin camp at the entrance of Wady Samak, east side of the lake'. Four days later at the beginning of December, they were home, and Alice ended her journal on a cheerful note. 'Thus it is established that I can manage such work if the moves do not entail more than . . . five hours in the saddle; so we may later make such journeys again.'

What happened next was described in a letter from Jamesina Waller to their mother, written in the purple indelible pencil used at Dalieh. On 16 December, Alice and Laurence went up to Dalieh to get the house ready for Christmas. On 18 December, Alice complained of a chill and suggested that it was a touch of rheumatic fever. When word of this reached Haifa, Jamesina tried to go to her, but rain made the mountain path impassable. It was not until 26 December, that she and Dr Martin reached Dalieh. They found Alice delirious and in the grip of a very high fever, and Laurence so ill from the same complaint as to be unable to nurse her. Dr Martin did what he could with homeopathic remedies, and Dr Schmidt of the Temple colony was sent for. He did not practise homeopathy but, as Laurence said later, for love he followed their discipline. The fever would not break so he was compelled to give the patient laudanum to quell the delirium and black coffee to counter the effect of the laudanum. To make Alice warm, Jamesina rubbed her with a solution of mustard and water so strong that the skin peeled off her hands. Suddenly the fever left her and, though weak, she was conscious. Laurence thought she was getting better and Alice assured him that she was, only complaining of 'fearful spiritual pressure'. That was on New Year's Day; in the evening of the following day, she died.

After he had helped Jamesina lay her out Dr Schmidt rode down through the night with a lantern to break the news to Adolphus Waller. The Germans of the colony were swift with offers of help and so, as Jamesina told Mrs Wynne Finch, 'loving hands worked both at carpentering and sewing, and in the short space of five hours everything was ready and [the coffin] dispatched to Dalieh'. Grief among the Druses was intense; as one of them put it, 'if five of best sheiks die, village not so sorry'. Asked for eight men from among them to carry the coffin down to the plain, fifty offered and vied with each other for the honour of lifting her.

Two miles from the Temple colony the small procession was met by Adolphus Waller with a large group of Germans, all the foreign consuls, their dragomen and guards. 'At the entrance to the colony and right up to Laurence's house we passed through a lane of people – almost every man, woman and child in the colony and many Arabs from the town, and a guard of honour sent by the Muslim Governor of Haifa. Had she been a Queen she could not have been received with more respectful homage.' They found the grave in view of Mount Carmel, the sea and the hills of Galilee, lovingly lined with leaves. 'An immense concourse of people accompanied us, of all ranks and classes and religions; and when the last words were spoken, the grave was nearly filled by the heaps of flowers, wreaths and garlands that were laid upon her.' So Jamesina wrote to her mother, as soon as she came from the grave, in desperate haste to catch the boat that was about to sail. Had she not, the news would have been delayed another fortnight. Laurence had been persuaded not to go to Alice's funeral; he was still unsteady from fever, hardly fit to sit the horse that brought him down the mountain, unable to comprehend the magnitude of the tragedy that had befallen him.

CHAPTER 11

COUNTERPARTS

FOR a time after Alice's death it seemed impossible to Laurence that he should go on living. Indeed, he did not think he could, he told her mother, if things had gone on as they did during the first week after the event when he seemed surrounded by darkness and despair. Then suddenly one night, 'the light seemed to burst through and she came to me so radiant, and at the same time, so sad at seeing me unhappy, that my own grief seemed to me to be lifted by the effort she made to dispel it'. In other words self-pity was not in his nature, he did not feel remorse, instinct told him that salvation lay in looking forward. There was much consolation in the hope of doing what Alice would approve; in that he was no different from others of a similar temperament. But his interpretation of the course he had to take was strongly influenced by the mystical belief that Alice had proclaimed during her lifetime. So in the empty and aching time after she died he struggled to be cheerful, to dispel the morbid condition that was creeping over him. From then on, he said, he began to feel Alice more and more and to regain his own health and spirits. 'She seems sensationally to invade my frame, thrilling my nerves when the sad fit is coming on and shaking me out of it, flooding my brain occasionally with her thoughts so that I can feel her thinking in me, inspiring me.' There was no analogy with mediumship or spiritualism in this, Laurence insisted, he was never more conscious of her than when all his faculties were alert. The sensation of Alice visiting him, as all who saw him at this time confirmed, produced a physical reaction; his body was convulsed and a shuddering motion passed through all his limbs. It was while he was in this condition that he believed he could pass on to others the love that Alice sent to him which was divine; for which there was already a name, the Sympneuma. To Mrs Wynne Finch, Laurence explained that he and Alice were now indissolubly bound, more firmly wedded than they had been while she was on earth; she was his counterpart at last; in the language of *Sympneumata*, together they would rise to new powers of use.

To those who knew him well he spoke of her presence in him so naturally that they grew used to hearing what Alice thought or intended him to do. For instance, it was at her bidding that the houses at Dalieh and Haifa were kept on, only the animals being sold, and caretakers left in charge until Laurence should return. For at her prompting he was to carry out the planned visit to England as if things were still the same. To those who saw him in England in the summer of 1886, he did not appear much changed, thinner perhaps, more elongated and stooping, the iron grey hairs more sparsely scattered on the great domed head, but still wonderfully amusing in conversation, gentle, and smiling in response to sympathy. This grace in desolation which sprang from a desire to spare others from his pain, was immensely touching and further endeared him to those who knew him. Many of them had the chance to renew their acquaintance with him, for whenever he was in London he was always to be found at the Athenaeum at the same table whose other regular occupants were his professional colleagues; Kinglake, Gallenga, and the Orientalist, Thomas Chenery. Chenery was Delane's successor at *The Times*, but his tenure as Editor was brief owing to the sudden advance of cancer from which he had suffered for years. A forlorn man, the writer Wilfrid Blunt thought him, being without intimate friends though knowing everyone.

In June while staying with Princess Christian at Cumberland Lodge in Windsor Great Park, Laurence fell ill with a recurrence of fever. The Princess had him nursed with a kindness and continuing concern that marked those members of the Royal Family who knew him as among his truest friends. Chief of these was, of course, the Prince of Wales, who saw a great deal of Laurence in 1886, both at Bad Homburg in August, then as his host for a month at Abergeldie. It was in a letter written from Abergeldie that Laurence sought to advise Pitt Buckner who, rather late in life, was contemplating marriage. Addressing him by his Use name of Earnest, Laurence tried to dissuade him but said, if he must marry, he and his bride must live in continence. Sexual love was a force that must not be dissipated while human beings were in their present corrupt state. Once they achieved a state of grace it would be permitted for 'higher beings' to conceive children on a 'higher plane'. On 4 October Queen Victoria noted in her Journal that a party from Abergeldie including Laurence

Oliphant had dined with her at Balmoral. Not for the first time the Queen reminded herself how clever Mr Oliphant was and what a lot he knew about Russia, adding, 'He has very peculiar religious views'. Although they were certainly acquainted with the idea of Sympneuma, one does not know if the Royal Family ever witnessed its appearance. Margaret Oliphant, who saw a lot of Laurence that summer, and was very worried about his health, said that she had no inkling of it at the time, nor had many other people. But in her biography of him she quoted a letter from Mrs Hankin describing how Laurence attempted to use it to help a sick woman who was staying with her at Malvern, where he had also gone. Though he declared that his 'work' was not that of healing illness, Laurence said he thought he might do her some good. According to the invalid 'I held his hand for some time, finding that a strong current poured through him, shaking my hand and arm with a powerful vibration, a motion like that produced by the current from a galvanic battery'. The result was a warm and pleasant tingling in her arm and an exhilaration of spirit, while her bodily symptoms were alleviated for several days.

After he left Cumberland Lodge and before he went to Homburg, Laurence stayed with the Mount Temples. In the company of his old friends Laurence proposed to impart Alice's love from beyond the grave to Georgiana, her 'dearest Lowly'. Present at the occasion, and included in the invitation, was another woman friend of Georgiana's who was convinced that Laurence's true purpose was to get those he approached in this way to share his bed. Her intervention caused Georgiana to hesitate so that Laurence had to protest. 'Dear Mrs Pearsall Smith, who is a most excellent, good woman,' he wrote to Georgiana, 'has got such a scare that she has frightened you ... Christ wants to commit Himself with you both as the Divine Bridegroom, but you are afraid of Him.' And he added reasonably, if somewhat testily, 'how can you possibly know without trying?' This argument was evidently successful, for later in the month Georgiana told her other close friend, Emilia Gurney, of her joy at holding Alice once more in her arms. Mrs Gurney, who had first encountered the practice at Brocton in 1872, welcomed the news. Mrs Pearsall Smith's reaction was different; it was hostile and very bitter.

That was not surprising. This doctrine of Christ the Bridegroom was the same that Hannah Pearsall Smith's husband, Robert, a famous evangelical preacher, had practised, and which, in 1875, had betrayed him into scandal and public humiliation. In 1886, after eleven years of frustration, Hannah had just about succeeded in re-establishing herself – if not Robert – in the place in the world to which she felt she was entitled. Now, by her account, Laurence Oliphant, not content with approaching her, proposed that Robert Pearsall Smith join him and propagate his views. That was anathema to Hannah. Though it was the first and only time she met Laurence, she became wholly prejudiced against him. The result was that she recorded a series of very damaging and, in my view, inaccurate charges against both Laurence and Alice Oliphant in a book, *Religious Fanaticism*, published in 1928.

In this book Hannah remarked, reasonably enough, that Laurence equated spirituality with sexuality. But, though it was quite clear that he intended the imparting of the Sympneuma to stop well short of the sexual act, Hannah believed that it did not. Since to her mind sex was undesirable – degrading even – she condemned the practice as corrupt. In *Religious Fanaticism* Hannah further charged that Laurence was incapable of writing anything unless sexually aroused. This seems unlikely and if we cannot know the truth, neither could she. Hannah also said that the Haifa community contained many 'refined' people from England and had to be closed at the instigation of the National Vigilance Association, a body of feverishly public spirited people that will occur in this story again. Neither of these statements was true; with the exception of Imber all the members of the Oliphant household at Haifa while Alice was alive came from Brocton; nor was it closed, by the National Vigilance Association or anyone else. But Hannah's most damaging accusation in *Religious Fanaticism* was reserved for Alice Oliphant whom she had never met. She said that in France she met a Madame C, a disciple of the Oliphants, who told her that Alice was doing wonderful missionary work among the Arabs by getting into bed with them, no matter how dirty or degraded, to bring about the coming of the counterpart. Privately, Hannah also charged that Laurence forced Alice to do this at great risk to her health. Hannah's daughter, Mary Berenson, later identified Madame C as the wife of the Emperor Napoleon's former commander in the Crimea, Madame la Maréchale Canrobert. (She was born Leila Flora Macdonald, married Canrobert in 1863 and became a close friend of the Empress Eugénie.) It is difficult to believe this story. There is no evidence outside Hannah's papers to support the story that Alice imparted the Sympneuma to Arabs.

There is much to suggest why she would not do so. As Alice's letters to her mother show, she was at pains to conceal her role as author of *Sympneumata* and shrank from discussing the ideas expressed in it. Her precarious health and Laurence's obvious concern for it seem to rule out the sort of obligatory nocturnal adventures Hannah envisaged. There were no Arabs in the Temple colony at Haifa. Could two strangers who hardly spoke the language introduce such practices into the small community of Dalieh without arousing suspicion, ridicule, and hostility? Jamesina Waller's account of her sister's death stresses the respect the Druse and Arabs showed her. Was that compatible with so personal and, to say the least, unusual an approach?

Though they were not published for many years Hannah's strictures against the Oliphants were known at the time. Hers was one of the voices raised against them after Alice's death which caused Laurence to be isolated when he was most in need of friends, and the reason why Edith Sitwell, who wrote about them in a book in 1933, labelled the Oliphants as 'this unpleasing pair'. The impulse that drove Hannah to wish to destroy them was prompted by her own experience and arose from events occurring in 1875. In that year the Pearsall Smiths were much courted in certain religious circles in England, were close friends with the Cowper-Temples (as they then were), and were often at Broadlands. Though Laurence and Alice were abroad, living at Brocton, they were closely concerned with what happened for it was still the time of Thomas Lake Harris's greatest influence over the Cowper-Temples and there was much correspondence and visiting between the community on Lake Erie and the great house in Hampshire.

Both the Pearsall Smiths were birthright Quakers from Philadelphia. Hannah, who was born in 1832, was a woman of relentless ambition, ability, and abundant energy, married to a man gentler than herself, of unstable temperament, in whose family there was a history of nervous depression. Hannah did not disguise her resentment at the way in which, after her marriage to Robert in 1851, childbirth prevented her from advancing herself, as she fancied she would, through study. In the late 1850s they became caught up in the evangelical fervour sweeping America which also served the ambition of Thomas Lake Harris. From the muted and sober Quaker way of life they broke into the circus swirl of frontier religion with its crowded and rowdy camp meetings, frantic hymns and hell-fire shouting preachers, all of which the Friends abhorred. But in that atmosphere Robert and Hannah thrived. In the course of the next ten years he became famous as a preacher for his ability to sway crowds and she for her undoubted talent as a writer of religious tracts. Her exposition of Robert's philosophy, *The Christian's Secret of a Happy Life*, sold in vast numbers all over the world. And so, while in the process of adding Mary, Alys, and Logan to the Pearsall Smith family, Hannah did begin to achieve her ambition. She was often consulted by persons as to whether they should commit themselves to one or another of the forms of religious enthusiasm then so common. Hannah referred to these as 'fanaticisms' and began to collect information about them. Though she represented this task as one performed in a spirit of enquiry, and her approach as, above all, that of common sense, she was actively interested on her own account for she longed to achieve some mystical experience; as she later explained to William Cowper-Temple, she suspected that she was herself the stuff of which fanatics were made. It was these collected papers, edited by her granddaughter, Ray Strachey, that were published as *Religious Fanaticism* in 1928.

In 1873 a nervous breakdown obliged Robert to spend some months in a sanatorium. While there he came under the influence of a Dr Foster who, according to *Religious Fanaticism*, taught him the doctrine of the so-called Baptism of the Holy Spirit which produced a sensation of thrills from head to foot. Though Hannah declared in the book that she had never experienced this sensation, in a letter to Georgiana Cowper-Temple she said that on hearing Dr Foster preach she 'shook with ecstasy for five minutes'. When Robert was well again they went to England. There they were taken up by the Cowper-Temples. Broadlands, which William inherited at Lady Palmerston's death in 1869, was then the headquarters of a very lively evangelical movement given a special flavour by William's passionate ecumenicalism. Just as Moody and Sankey were the heroes of the crowds filling the chapels and church halls, so their compatriot, Robert Pearsall Smith, filled the same role at the meetings in the great houses. Hannah could not have been more pleased by the circles in which they moved. 'I confess I do enjoy them exceedingly . . . For one thing they are far more like Americans than the classes below them . . . it delights me to see how they appreciate us.' In the summer of 1874 a great religious picnic was held at Broadlands to which all manner of spiritual writers, thinkers and performers were invited, but at which Robert was the undoubted star, and next to him Hannah, conspicuous in her Quaker dress, reading the bible to rapt audiences under the spreading trees, theeing and thouing lords, bishops and clergymen. In the spring of 1875 Robert made a brilliantly successful tour of fashionable churches on the Continent. On his return Brighton was given up to more religious deliberation led by him. The Dome where he preached was filled to overflowing and Hannah, the 'Angel of the Churches', had to repeat her Bible readings by popular request.

Disaster then occurred. While he was engaged in discussions with the organizers of yet another meeting to be held at Keswick in the Lake District, Robert was accused of practising the doctrine of the Baptism of the Holy Spirit with a young woman disciple who complained. That Robert's conduct was chaste is clear from the letter he sent William Cowper-Temple, but as he said, her head was on his shoulder, his arm round her waist and the door *was* locked. The sensation resulting from his forced and hasty withdrawal from the Keswick conference was all the greater for the organizing committee's clumsy attempts to disguise the cause. Rumours that something ugly had been suppressed circulated for years and clouded the first of the series of Keswick conferences that continue to the present day. Hannah, her world in pieces, was obliged to take Robert home at once. Politely but firmly all their English acquaintances turned their backs. All that is but the Cowper-Temples. True to form, Georgiana could not see why these good people should not kiss each other if they were so inclined, and William, as always was a law unto himself. Nevertheless the subject *was* awkward, not least because it coincided with the public uproar over Valentine Baker's alleged assault upon a woman in a train.

In her letters to the Cowper-Temples after the event, Hannah laid the blame for Robert's downfall, not as stated in *Religious Fanaticism* on the doctrine taught by Dr Foster, but upon practices introduced at Broadlands from Brocton. Her reaction to their public humiliation was bitter. Though the outward conventions of married life were preserved, henceforth Hannah looked upon her husband, as upon all men, with condescension bordering on contempt. And, except as a means to beget children – girls preferably – she rejected sex. In the circumstances it was not surprising that in 1875 she declined William's suggestion that she visit Thomas Lake Harris in California. It was not until 1880, when careful soundings revealed the disappointing fact that she and Robert would not yet be welcome back in England, that she went to Santa Rosa. Her account of Harris was cautiously favourable, though she told the Cowper-Temples she did not understand his doctrine. Her second visit in 1882 came when the schism between Harris and Laurence Oliphant had newly poisoned the air of Fountain Grove. Hannah took Harris's side. In a letter to Georgiana Cowper-Temple she said that Father was deeply concerned that Oliphant might harm those who did not know his true attitude, especially those at Broadlands. 'Harris took Mr Oliphant into his home and into his heart and when he was almost lost through dissipation and by tender loving care lifted him up into a restored manhood,' said Hannah. And she reported Harris's description of Alice as the Devil Incarnate. In 1886 when she at last met Laurence, Hannah was in the process of settling in England for good. She had renewed her friendship with Georgiana – who, in the fashion of Fountain Grove, she now called the Ladye – and was about to begin a new career in England furthering the cause of temperance. No wonder Laurence's invitation to impart the Sympneuma as addressed to Robert upset her; was she to see her husband disgraced for a second time and for the same reason?

Oblivious to the sensation he had caused, Laurence went home to Palestine at the end of 1886. He was warmly greeted both by the German Templars and the members of his own household. To this was now added a Lincolnshire parson, Haskett Smith, a convert to Laurence's faith, who was to become his right hand man. At Haifa Laurence found Alice's photograph hanging up framed in almost every German cottage, while the Druses venerated the monument he had set up to her on Carmel, 'for they say that, although she was not conscious of it, she was a Druse all the time', he told Mrs Hankin. His outward life continued much as it had while Alice was alive. In 1887 he became actively concerned in the attempt by native Jews to farm land below the hill town of Safed instead of living as they had done for generations on the Haluka, the charitable sum levied from Jews of the Diaspora. Laurence canvassed for funds for this colony, Benei Yehuda, in England, saying that it was the most deserving and the one most likely to succeed since the Turks were not so jealous of native-born Jews as they were of foreign immigrants.

The founders of the colony sent Laurence an account of their enterprise cast in the form of question and answers. This revealed the extreme poverty and vulnerability of the place, the lack of shelter and of tools. Its spelling might be quaint but its spirit was one of determination to get to grips with reality, something their critics had claimed the Jews would never do; as such Laurence welcomed it.

REPORT of the New Setelment Colonie of Julam
of Soctie Benei-Jehuda.

In wich place?	From Tel-ei-Fares, Sout east, tow hours; from Tel-abu-Nida, Nord west, tow hours.
Woth was the name before?	At present called Chirbet-belled el Romsanie; in Olden timed colled Romy.
Omeny springs?	3 Springs largeoons; 13 Sometimes flood in difret directions.
Wath kind of catel?	Wolle kind. Kaus, 8; Oksens, 10; Orshes, 4; Donkes, 2; Gouts, 30.
Plouing Tooles?	Komen Arabien plous, 5.
Omeny buildings?	One big Bilding, 38 jards long, 18 wide; 6 stables for catel; plenti of stons wolle redy to beld from the pondations.

Equally touching in its dignified appeal for help was the petition translated from Hebrew that Margaret Oliphant also found among Laurence's papers after his death, evidence of the colonists' faith in him and warm regard for him.

'To the honourable and benevolent Sir Oliphant, unceasing in his good deeds, we come today before he sets out on his intended journey. We do bless him with all our hearts and pray that he may arrive at his destination safely ... Up to the present time we have done all in our power not to become the objects of charity, and are truly grateful to his honour for the former many kindnesses which he has voluntarily shown us. And his past kindness makes us bold enough to ask him to afford us some relief in this time of our great need.'

It was at Haifa, in the spring of 1887, that Laurence embarked upon the writing of a pamphlet to contain the clearest statement yet of his philosophy. It was to be directed at the followers of different religions, Muslim, Jewish and Hindu and each version was to draw upon the appropriate sacred text. Margaret Oliphant who saw the version to be translated into Arabic for Muslims, did not conceal her surprise at its many quotations from the Koran which, she said, were treated with 'perfect equality' beside those from the Gospels. But, she explained, Laurence was of the opinion not only that the sacred books of religion were, in their hidden meaning, equally inspired, he also considered as inspired all those men who influenced the human race, whether Moses, Muhammed, or Buddha, though, she hastened to add, 'Our Lord always held with him the highest place'. The pamphlet states with exactitude Laurence's belief in the original creation of man in a semi-spiritual body, containing both sexes in one, and in the change of nature produced at the Fall when the two were divided into male and female. By His miraculous birth, Laurence explained, Christ was restored to this dual being and capable of communicating His love to the world by which, gradually, the original nature was to be restored, 'so now many men begin to feel they have the feminine half enclosed within them and many women feel they have the male half enclosed within them'.

For Christians the message took a longer form, that of a book. It was abstruse; it ranged over the spectrum of religious writing from the Kabbalah to the Epistles of St Paul. In order to write it Laurence withdrew to Dalieh, to the room in which Alice died, where he placed her portrait on an easel beside his writing table. He took the view that she inspired what he wrote. 'It will be altogether an extraordinary book,' he told William Blackwood who, following the death of his uncle John in 1879, was now head of the publishing firm. 'I can't help thinking I shall explode rather noisily on the sleeping conscience of the public.' Explode he did, but on the editorial judgement of the long suffering William. Blackwood told him he must not call the book the *Divine Feminine*, it would put people off. Then, as he said, 'there are those who would say a publisher had no right to give his *imprimatur* to such a work unless he can to some extent share the view he advances'. Laurence brushed this aside but agreed to change the title to *Scientific Religion*. For that his friend was grateful. But to Alexander Innes Shand, Blackwood confided that it was a terrible book: it would unsettle men's minds without supplying them with any surer foundation of belief. It professed to be a revelation and Laurence assumed the position of leader of a new religion, a religion only recognizable to those who raised themselves above the level of ordinary mortals. 'If it was not the work of a man like Oliphant,' Blackwood lamented, 'you would say it was all bosh.'

According to Margaret Oliphant, with the publication of *Scientific Religion* Laurence might be said to disappear from that place in the world he had hitherto held. By that she indicated that she was not prepared to recount what happened next. Indeed she felt that she had gone to the limit in setting down the course of his life after Alice died, for she found his conduct concerning the Sympneuma bizarre and disconcerting. But in the interest of truth she had recorded it, while making no mention of the Mount Temples or Hannah Pearsall Smith. In 1887 she represented Laurence as lost among a crowd of enquirers, of sympathizers, of people anxious to share his faith in his mystical experiences, none of whom she cared to name. But, with a certain satisfaction that she thought many spectators of the last acts of his life would share, she said that, by the end of 1887 the first wave of inspiration breathed into him by the spirit of Alice had begun to fail and he was no longer so strongly moved by the 'influx' as he had been when he was in England in 1886. To remedy this, she said, he had recourse to Mrs Hankin, who she described as moderate and full of sense though strongly believing in his faith. Through her Laurence transmitted the vibration that was the sign of Alice's spiritual presence; although it appeared more rarely he remained convinced that he must pass on its healing power. The risk he ran in this was naturally acute. Hannah apart, for a man with the reputation he had acquired in his youth, of reckless promiscuity and instability of mind, to propagate an unorthodox belief which involved physical contact between the sexes, was bound to meet with misrepresentation however well intentioned people might be towards him. Laurence was not unaware of the difficulty of his position; he said he felt the lack of a woman assistant to do Alice's work. Now he who, all his life, had been subject to the influence of women – as mother, mistress or wife – could no longer support living by himself. To remedy this isolation was the motive for the next course he took, one so hasty as to suggest an impulse he might one day bitterly regret.

In the early summer of 1888 Laurence returned to Paris where Mrs Wynne Finch was shocked by his haggard appearance. She put it down to the fact that while writing *Scientific Religion* (which William Blackwood published as 'for the author') he told her he had lived entirely on boiled rice, 'while wound up to the utmost possible spiritual excitement and strain of physical work'. And yet his letters to Blackwood show that, during this period of apparent asceticism, he found time to give a huge party in honour of the Queen's Jubilee which was remembered for years for the tents, the flags, the bands, and the speeches he arranged and for the invitation he sent to Christian Arab women who, unusually, accepted it. The real reason for his worn appearance was not work but illness, as would soon be discovered.

While in Paris Laurence renewed his friendship with a young art student he had known for some years. This was James Murray Templeton, son of a Glasgow carpet manufacturer, whose desire to paint was not matched by his ability. Templeton's father, not unsympathetic to his ambition, paid for him to study in London during the 1870s, during which time, frustrated by his lack of talent, neurotic and lonely, he turned to spiritualism for comfort. That was how he met an American woman, Rosamond Dale Owen, whose ancestry conferred on her a high place in that world and who was eager to make her own mark on it by lecturing about spiritualism and socialism. But she suffered from poor health and nerves which put her at odds with her audience, so that her appearances became a penance, both for herself and her hearers. Increasingly her subject matter came to be devoted to an hysterical denunciation of sex and this led her to exhort her startled and uncomfortable audience to choose 'purity' in marriage. Eventually the strain of such appearances became too much for everyone concerned and Miss Dale Owen withdrew to her home in the Middle West. Templeton was one of the few reminders of her time in London: they corresponded. When he met Laurence Oliphant again in 1888, Templeton showed him Rosamond's letters. On reading them, the story went, he exclaimed, 'I must see the woman who wrote that' – and dashed at once to America.

That his journey was not, as it seemed, wholly unpremeditated, appears from the fact that, on arrival, he was met by a deputation of the New York branch of the 'lovers of Zion'. Its members included Abraham Goldfaden, founder of Yiddish drama, Joseph Bluestone, who was to become famous as a doctor on the Lower East Side, and Adam Rosenberg who, though still very young, had already begun a distinguished career in trade union organization. To them Laurence reaffirmed that his involvement with Jewish immigration to Palestine was for humanitarian reasons only and had nothing to do with a desire to convert anyone. After that he did indeed make the long train journey through the Middle West to a small town with an historic name – New Harmony, Indiana. There he found Rosamond Dale Owen.

In 1888 Rosamond was forty-two. She was the grand-daughter of a very famous man, Robert Owen, the social reformer, who had left the mills of New Lanark in 1825 to found an ideal community at New

Harmony. But in her lifetime, Rosamond's father, Robert Owen's eldest son, Robert Dale Owen, was even more celebrated. He was ardent in every liberal cause, instrumental in advancing married women's rights. He and his colleague, Frances Wright, had been among the first to advocate birth control in the United States. As a Congressman he was largely responsible for founding the Smithsonian Institution and was credited with inspiring Abraham Lincoln to issue the Emancipation Proclamation. In 1853 he was appointed US Minister to the court of Naples where he took his family, including Rosamond, aged seven. While he was there, and in the aftermath of the death of a beloved son, he developed an interest in spiritualism and, during the course of his investigations, played host to D. D. Home. But the book that he wrote on his return, *Footfalls on the boundary of another World*, was informed by a cool and analytical approach, so that he became known as a student of the subject rather than a convert to the belief – a belief which his distinguished father wholeheartedly embraced.

New Harmony, where Rosamond grew up after her family's return from Naples, was a neat and proper town with brick houses, peaked roofs and tree-lined streets when other Indiana settlements were no more than log cabins fronting dirt roads. New Harmony was a centre of intellectual effort with access to music, history and science, and the site of the US Geological Survey under David Dale Owen, Rosamond's uncle. All the Owens lived together in a large and rambling house which was organized as a commune with rotas for housework and a special school for the numerous children. Rosamond ought to have been happy but something went disastrously wrong. As she grew up fear betrayed her into a lack of charity towards other people, jealousy, self-pity, and a certain meanness in financial affairs. When she was twenty-four she began to suffer from the dread of going blind and of being paralysed, a fear which condemned her to seven years of seclusion, idleness and frustration.

In her autobiography, *My Perilous Life in Palestine*, which, one must remember, was written when she was over eighty, Rosamond said this illness was caused by an accident she had suffered while doing housework that had been neglected by her cousins. But it is obvious that it was hysterical in origin, the result of her fear of sex. At the time of the accident she was engaged to be married to a young man who, in spite of her strenuous efforts to release him, persisted in honouring the agreement. 'The thought of our union was coming to be a dread, which darkened all my life,' Rosamond wrote. 'Had he been a bad man the matter would have been simple, but he was a man of whom many women would have been justly proud.' Eventually, as Rosamond grew more ill, the engagement was broken off.

Her disturbance seems to have originated in an incident at an hotel in Cincinatti when she was seventeen and on her way from New Harmony to New York to finish her education. She said that a drunken man had forced his way into her bedroom and was only deterred from assaulting her by the remarkable dignity and courage she displayed. From then on Rosamond was suspicious of men, of their coarse emotions and their habit of eyeing her wherever she went, which, she complained, deprived her of what little peace she, as an invalid, could enjoy. When she was thirty-one her family found a doctor who, unlike all the others, succeeded in persuading her that she was not going blind and that all her muscles needed was exercise. Once she had recovered from her illness her family encouraged her to go to England where, in the 1870s, she embarked on a series of lectures about her grandfather, Robert Owen, spiritualism, and socialism. While in England she became one of the earliest members of the Fellowship of the New Life (nothing to do with Harris), the precursor of the Fabian Society. But, as time went on her lectures became devoted to preaching the need for 'purity' in marriage, which subject, as we have seen, did not commend itself to more than a handful of her audience. Soon she resolved not to waste further time 'slumming' as she called it, and returned to New Harmony where she charged herself with the upbringing of two nieces.

When he found her at New Harmony, Laurence lost no time in proposing to Rosamond that she accompany him back to Palestine. She accepted at once in the knowledge that she was to become the means of transmitting Alice's message to the world – through her would flow the Sympneuma which she would impart to Laurence's male disciples. In spite of opposition from certain members of her family who had heard rumours of Hannah Pearsall Smith's denunciation of this doctrine, Rosamond joined Laurence on board ship at New York, bound for England and thence to Haifa. In her autobiography, Rosamond left no doubt as to why she went. She depicted Laurence as a man of enormous charm, of worldly habits and taste, elegant (which would have surprised his friends who thought him careless in matters of dress), and masterful. But she also stressed his kindness, warmth, and, when he was not feeling ill, immense capacity for fun. In short, she fell in love with him. As for him, though they began the voyage as colleagues in a common enterprise, he said that during it something impelled him to propose to Rosamond. She accepted at once. Writing to Alice's mother to break the news that he knew would distress her deeply, Laurence defended it as the only course society would accept and one that Alice approved. Rosamond would make an awkward wife and a difficult companion; there is no reason to suppose that Laurence deceived himself as to that. But he was ill and exhausted, having borne the burden of Alice's death for more than two years; perhaps he hoped that the sun of Palestine would smooth away Rosamond's angularities.

On landing at Southampton he intended to take his fiancée to Broadlands where they could be married without publicity. But William Mount Temple had been ill for many months; he and Georgiana were abroad in search of a warm climate in which he might recover – to no avail. So Laurence and Rosamond went to Malvern where Mrs Hankin took them in, but without a welcome and in a spirit of implacable hostility to Rosamond. The marriage took place there on 8 August and, after it, they went to London, intending to proceed to Haifa almost at once. Their sojourn there in temporary lodgings was most unhappy.

Whatever the apprehension about the effect of his marriage upon his friends, Laurence had not bargained for the sensation it caused. Margaret Oliphant voiced the general view in a letter to William Blackwood. 'But oh what is this dreadful business about Laurence Oliphant? *Married* after publishing a book to convince the world if possible that marriage should not be and with such a wife lately buried.' She supposed that he had gone through the form merely to make it possible to have a companion and a 'caretaker', as she could not suppose he would contradict the tenor of so many years at his age – 'but he ought not to have done it anyhow'. Those who shared her view were influenced in it by a particular dislike of Rosamond. She suffered in comparison with Alice. She acknowledged that she was not beautiful; she had the Owen nose which was prominent and a receding chin, nor was her readiness to make light of these faults much appreciated. She was gauche and badly dressed; she flinched from the thought of the low cut dresses obligatory at Marlborough House, she did not want to show her 'peaks and hollows' she complained to Laurence. She was ignorant of English etiquette – she rather rejoiced at this, and caused offence through clumsiness. Her religious views were not condoned as Alice's had been as the product of an exalted imagination, but condemned as odd, boring, and positively undesirable.

But she was brave and steadfast and these qualities were to sustain her in the difficulties that now beset her. She and Laurence were no sooner married than he collapsed with an illness diagnosed as pleurisy. On closer examination the doctor found him to be suffering from cancer of the lung which was far advanced. It was an evil time to be without a place to go and unusual for one who had once had so many friends, yet that was the case. The Walkers, Laurence's old friends from San Francisco who were in England for an extended visit, asked them to stay in the house they were renting at Surbiton. That did not serve, the house was small and friction developed between the Walkers and Rosamond. Soon it became all too clear that the Walkers wanted them to go. So, when at the end of September, Sir Mountstuart Grant Duff came to the rescue and had Laurence removed to York House at Twickenham, it was almost like coming home.

Grant Duff belonged to the world in which Laurence had grown up, in which he had once been popular and successful. He was an old confidant – he knew all about Harris – and had rented the house at Dalieh when Laurence was away after Alice's death. He was a member of the same clubs and had the same friends. He had been a Member of Parliament, held office as Under Secretary for the Colonies, and governed Madras. He was a small, red haired, bustling, gregarious man, one of whose passions was for lavish entertaining in large houses. In 1877, he bought York House from the Comte de Paris. It was Jacobean and very grand, built on the site of the palace in which the Stuart Queens had been born. Grant Duff transformed it with Morris wallpapers and Indian furniture; it was comfortable, warm and, at last, welcoming. Laurence was put to bed in Lady Grant Duff's own room overlooking the garden with its Italian statues, fountains, cypresses and view of the River Thames. His religious faith now assumed the form of hope that he would recover, of a refusal to countenance the possibility of death. Both he and Rosamond spoke of the journey to Palestine as one they would resume in a matter of weeks. But to those who visited him, William Blackwood, Arthur Oliphant, Shand, and Kinglake, it was clear that he could not recover and that he was in dreadful pain. News of this spread quickly and a daily bulletin was posted at the Athenaeum. But it did not draw many to York House where few of Laurence's old friends appeared. William Mount Temple had died in October. Though Margaret Oliphant was living close by at Windsor she did not go; her absence William Blackwood told her afterwards was among those that hurt Laurence most. Blackwood himself made the journey south from Edinburgh several times that autumn and tried his best to ease the burden on Rosamond. Laurence had been associated with his family firm for 36 years, had introduced to it writers like Speke, Kinglake, Grant, and Henry Stanley and had been a close friend of his uncle John. After his death in 1879 William Blackwood had turned to Laurence for advice which had not been refused; it was a debt he intended to repay. So he was greatly distressed to have to leave him to a lonely end. It was Christmas when Laurence died and Blackwood could not leave his family. Few people attended the funeral; the list of mourners was very small. The Grant Duffs went – Lady Grant Duff was the only woman – Arthur Oliphant and Hamon Le Strange. From Palestine there was Haskett Smith whose touch Laurence had hoped would heal him, and Naphtali Herz Imber. Princess Christian sent a wreath, the Prince of Wales and the Empress Frederick, telegrams. It was calm only until the end of the year when the wind of comment began to rise, scattering as it went the seeds of calumny.

AFTERMATH

It was the age of long obituaries and those of Laurence Oliphant occupied more space than most in the newspapers and magazines. Merely to chronicle his romantic life was a task requiring thousands of words, to seek to explain it was much more daunting. As Grant Duff put it, when with Laurence you stepped off perfectly solid ground into mere chaos. *The Times* remarked that Laurence was two men in one and kept each of them carefully apart. It preferred to let the reader draw his own conclusions about his spiritual life, though it made a point of calling Thomas Lake Harris a fanatical imposter. The *Spectator* was irritated by the generally baffled air. 'Mr Oliphant was no maniac nor was his attitude of mind so surprising as English clubmen fancy', it began. 'It has been noticed for a century at least that Englishmen thrown into close contact with Orientals grow either indifferent or religious and that if religious they are apt to become singularly detached and, in some way or other, mystical.' The last time the *Spectator*'s writer saw Laurence, he said, he was writing *Scientific Religion*, 'a wildly visionary book, yet he discussed the changes he had noticed when visiting London like a keen, highly travelled and minutely observant man of the world'. *The Times* concurred; it judged Laurence sound and shrewd on matters of politics and finance. As many other papers did it paid a warm tribute to his charm, enthusiasm and wit, his lofty and unselfish aims and broadminded philanthropy. Eccentric he might have been, 'yet no one ever sneered at Oliphant to his face and no one would have done more than smile at his doings behind his back'. In that *The Times* was wrong. Laurence's attempts to impart the Sympneuma had so enraged certain people, the story went, that a case was prepared against him involving criminal charges. Only his death, it was said, prevented the case from coming to court and the evidence collected was destroyed. That may have been so, though one may take leave to doubt there was a case at all. The tragedy was that, although the accused was dead and the precise charge unspecified, the intention to prosecute was, in the end, made public. Laurence stood condemned without trial, sentenced to perpetual suspicion.

Some facts are known. Both the sources that speak of a case agree that the charge concerned Laurence's imparting of the Sympneuma. Both agree that the purpose of prosecution was to punish him for alleged harm done to a particular young man – James Murray Templeton. One source, that which stems from Hannah Pearsall Smith, held that the case to be brought was for corrupting the morals of two young people, a brother and sister. In her preface to her grandmother's book, *Religious Fanaticism*, Ray Strachey said that friends of these two had lodged a complaint against Laurence with the National Vigilance Association, and that an action brought by the Association for '*détournement des mineurs*' was pending in 1888 when he died. In 1930, Hannah's eldest daughter, Mary Berenson, confirmed this to Dr Herbert Schneider, Professor of Religion at Columbia University, New York, who was collecting material for a book about Harris and Oliphant. Mrs Berenson further remarked that the case had been prepared by her first husband, Frank Costelloe. Though *Religious Fanaticism* does not say so, in 1888 both she and her husband were members of the Executive Committee of the National Vigilance Association and he was its most active lawyer. It came into being in 1885 on the great wave of public indignation that followed sensational disclosures about child prostitution, 'The Maiden Tribute of Modern Babylon', that appeared in the *Pall Mall Gazette* edited by W. T. Stead. Among the public figures rumoured to have been involved in the matter was the Prince of Wales. A vast and excited public meeting in Hyde Park made Stead President of the new Association which was to keep a close watch over public decency. One of its first aims was to remove from positions of authority in the political parties any men of 'known immoral life'. Apart from the Costelloes the other members of the Association included two women prominent in the suffragist movement, Millicent Fawcett and Ellice Hopkins, and G. W. E. Russell M.P. William Mount Temple was invited to join but did not. Though the Preventive subcommittee of the Association keenly sought out cases of moral offence, the police frequently refused to prosecute. Often when the Association brought a case itself the result was a dismissal incurring costs. The number of successful prosecutions was very small, perhaps the most famous being that conducted by Frank Costelloe against

Henri Vizetelly in 1889 for selling Zola's novels in England: he was sentenced to three months in prison. Though the Association did valuable work combating the white slave trade abroad, its efforts to curb prostitution at home bordered on the ridiculous. Its members patrolled nightly outside brothels, notebook and pencil in hand, but few callers were persuaded to give their names and addresses and fewer still to stay away.

Nevertheless, in 1888 the Vigilance Association was an active force. But Ray Strachey's account of the charge it meant to bring against Laurence is curious. In the first place why did she express it in French? Presumably by *détournement des mineurs* she meant the abduction of persons under age. This offence was newly defined by the Criminal Law Amendment Act passed in 1885 as a result of the uproar over Stead's revelations. The Act imposed penalties for abducting children of both sexes under 14, of girls under 16, and for marrying girls under 18 without their parents' consent. But in 1888 James Murray Templeton was over thirty and had lived apart from his family for several years. And his diary shows that his sister Alice was even more unsympathetic to him than his father. She can hardly have been at risk from Laurence Oliphant, nor was she a minor. If Ray Strachey's phrase is taken to mean the corrupting of the morals of the young, as other writers have interpreted it, that makes even less sense as there was no such offence in English law. Then, if its purpose was to prevent *Laurence* from further corrupting Murray Templeton, the timing of the Vigilance Association's activities are hard to understand. Mary Berenson said the case was dropped when Laurence died. Yet a month after his death Hannah Pearsall Smith revealed herself most anxious to know if the 'practices' continued. According to information she gathered from letters written by Rosamond Oliphant to an unidentified third party, the imparting of the Sympneuma was still going on. Later in February 1889 Hannah wrote to Emilia Gurney urging her to find out all she could about *Rosamond*'s behaviour. In fact it was Rosamond's relations with Murray Templeton after Laurence's death that caused the greatest uproar and led to her harassment by the Vigilance Association, one result being the disinheriting of Murray Templeton by his father. But this is not mentioned in *Religious Fanaticism*.

In the book Hannah recounted how a young American woman called on her in London. 'She told me the following sorrowful story,' said Hannah. She had been an art student in Paris and become engaged to a fellow student, a young Scot of wealthy family (Murray Templeton), a disciple of Laurence Oliphant. She too became Laurence's follower and in due course was invited to share his bed, 'with the idea that the personal touch would bring about the sympneumata for which she so longed', explained Hannah. She grew more and more uneasy, feeling this could not be the Divine method of propagating the truth, and when Laurence urged her to spread it by indulging in the practice with other young men, went home to America to lay the matter before her brother. He was a clergyman who, Hannah said, assured her it was all of the flesh and a species of free love. Back in Paris she found it impossible to extricate her fiancé from Oliphant's snare and was reluctantly obliged to break off the engagement and return to Boston 'to escape the malign influences that surrounded her'. This story omitted some important detail. The young woman was a widow; her name was Jennie Tuttle. Her objection to Laurence's teaching was not the recognition (in the circumstances somewhat belated) that the practice of Sympneuma might lead to free love, but that it would not. If she married Murray Templeton – supposing that his belief in Laurence's teaching allowed such a course – Jennie Tuttle knew that she would have to live in continence with him.

Far from returning to the calm of Boston Mrs Tuttle girded herself for a bitter contest. She went to Glasgow whence came disturbing rumours of her open accusation against Laurence Oliphant and of her importuning the Templeton family. In March 1889 – three months after Laurence's death – Murray Templeton's father and a man named Allen jointly wrote to Arthur Oliphant. What they had to say so upset Arthur – who had loved Laurence and missed him greatly – that he telegraphed at once to William Blackwood for advice. Blackwood was also deeply shocked and advised instant recourse to Laurence's solicitors while expressing himself astonished that a man like Templeton could lend his name to such a document, 'a monstrous and disgusting attempt to blacken Laurence's character'. Blackwood agreed with Arthur Oliphant's theory that Thomas Lake Harris was at the bottom of the affair.

Laurence's solicitors advised that no move should be made. The matter was left to rest by those who held his memory dear. But in 1897 a book was published containing an accusation that strengthened the probability that Harris was involved in the attack. Dr

C. M. Berridge, a long standing and ardent disciple of Harris, appointed himself chronicler of the deeds and pronouncements of the Prophet. He conceived a history of the Brotherhood of the New Life to appear in twelve parts – the last of which was to recount the truth about the schism with Oliphant. As author Berridge assumed the name Respiro. He did not complete the work but, in passing, he remarked that Laurence Oliphant was to have been charged with an offence under the Criminal Law Amendment Act; 'he was only saved by death from sharing the fate of a well known dramatist of the present day', said Respiro. The conclusion one draws from this reference to Oscar Wilde is that the charge against Laurence was to have been that of homosexuality, which, following the introduction of the Act in 1885, was a new offence. The Act was so framed as to make proof of innocence by those accused extremely difficult. If Laurence had indeed been so charged – as the first offender under the Act (whose relevant clause was framed by Laurence's former colleague in the Direct US Cable Company, Henry Labouchère), and with the exalted friends he possessed – the sensation would have been enormous.

But was such a case ever seriously considered? Were the accusations true? I think not. From the evidence available in Laurence and Alice Oliphant's writings, in their letters and in the accounts of those who witnessed the imparting of the Sympneuma two facts emerge. One is that it did not involve the sexual act. The other that it was always imparted from man to woman and vice versa, and not between members of the same sex – that was, after all, the whole point of the doctrine of counterparts. If guilt is a word that must be used, then Laurence was guilty of embracing women to whom he was not married, and not of homosexuality. But, given the general incomprehension of the motive for his action, which sprang from deep need and the conviction of its religious significance, Laurence was desperately vulnerable to gossip and malice. It was malice that drove Thomas Lake Harris. As his papers show, he spent hours boasting that he, Father, had been the direct cause of Laurence Oliphant's death. From that it was only a step to destroying all that was left, Laurence's reputation. Whatever the motive that inspired the alleged prosecution of Oliphant by the National Vigilance Association, there was another link between it and Thomas Lake Harris. In 1893, on his first visit to America, W. T. Stead, President of the Association, dined with Harris (now married to Jane Lee Waring and living in New York). On that occasion Stead called Harris one of the most influential figures in spiritualism.

Finally, there is something else which, though it may have no direct bearing on the posthumous reputation of Laurence Oliphant, ought to be recorded. The evidence for Oliphant's adverse effect upon relations between Richard Burton and John Hanning Speke rests upon the comments made in Isabel Burton's life of her husband, in which she portrayed Oliphant as a capricious man, driven to break up friendships. This conflicts with the testimony of men like Wade, Shand, Kinglake and both Blackwoods, and of many women who were his friends. They found Laurence steadfast and loyal throughout his life. Moreover, Hamon Le Strange and Mrs Wynne Finch, having started off on the worst possible terms with Laurence over Alice's marriage, were not only reconciled to him fairly soon, but came to love him dearly in the end.

Isabel Burton wrote her account of her husband's life, which contains the criticism of Oliphant, after Burton's death in 1891; the book was published in 1893. In September 1896, after she died, the world was startled to learn that as her literary executor she had appointed a certain William Alexander Coote, sometime compositor on the *Evening Standard*. For the past eleven years he had been, as he remained for many more, the devoted secretary of the National Vigilance Association.

After Laurence's funeral Rosamond stayed in London just long enough to attend an interview at Buckingham Palace with a sympathetic Princess Christian, in a dress, and with advice on how to curtsy, provided by Georgiana Mount Temple. Then she departed to claim her inheritance at Haifa and Dalieh. From Palestine Rosamond wrote to William Blackwood asking for money; there was difficulty in settling Laurence's estate, she said, because he had helped so many people. She found the Buckners and Violet Cuthbert shaken by rumours from England and so, when she received an abusive letter from Jennie Tuttle, she decided to go back to defend herself and Laurence. The second letter she opened after her arrival contained a threat from Mrs Tuttle that she was to be arrested. So it was with extreme apprehension that she heard she was to have a visit from an official of the National Vigilance Association. Rosamond thought he had come to arrest her.

But he began by offering himself as a novice in the esoteric arts he said he knew she practised. This trick did not work and he was floored by the strength of her indignation. Though she said she thought Laurence had been wrong in advocating the imparting of the Sympneuma through physical contact, she defended his life and intentions as wholly pure. The official then asked to be allowed to take her hand as he had been told she possessed some strange force of magnetism. What he got was a further impassioned defence of Laurence. With apologies he departed and was heard of no more. Then Jennie Tuttle demanded an interview which took place in the consulting room of a doctor. According to Rosamond, Mrs Tuttle was hysterical and abusive, objecting to the fact that Murray Templeton had been much with Rosamond during Laurence's illness. She accused Laurence and Rosamond of all kinds of perversion. The doctor remarked that it was time the facts were supplied to support such accusations and, when none were forthcoming, ended the encounter.

Though she was alone in a foreign country and the victim of a vicious attack, Rosamond behaved throughout with dignity and courage. She had known her husband for five months only, during which time he had been very ill. Yet she cherished his memory and defended his reputation until the end of her life. It was very long, the part that remained to her after Laurence's death being even stranger than the years that went before. She established herself at Haifa with her nieces and Murray Templeton, hoping to continue things just as they had been. But the reduction in scale of household expenses which she decreed in the pursuit of what she called 'socialistic living' was so drastic as to drive the older members of the community away. And, as much as they had respected Alice, the Druses of Carmel hated her. So did Pitt Buckner who as Laurence's trustee was a target for her demands for money.

In 1890 she married Murray Templeton who, as she told William Blackwood, 'has suffered much, losing his property because of his adherence to *Scientific Religion*, Laurence Oliphant and me'. With him she wandered from Haifa to London to Paris and back, he painting as he went. He grew no better at it and no happier and, in 1892 while at sea between Beyrout and Haifa, jumped overboard. Rosamond lived on at Haifa after his death, locked in combat with the Turkish authorities over the land on the plain of Esdraelon which she wanted to sell but could not as the title was not clear. It became an obsession with her, as did the urge to convert Jews to Christianity, a cause in which, unblushingly and quite improperly, she enlisted

Laurence Oliphant's name. To the scandal of the inhabitants of Haifa she adopted a young man, part Italian, part Spanish, called Carlos Ronzevalle to whom she taught her belief in the need for purity in sex. In 1930 she was at last able to sell the land, some of which formed the site of the railway station at Haifa. With the money from the land Rosamond and Ronzevalle were able to retire from Palestine. Their new address was rather more sedate than Mount Carmel though hardly less bracing. It was The Laurels, Brighton Road, Worthing, and there, on the South Coast of England, they lived until Rosamond died, aged 92, in 1937. Ronzevalle, who was devoted to her, wrote a pamphlet describing her last hours, and had her buried at Newtown, Montgomeryshire, beside her grandfather, Robert Owen.

Rosamond's memoir of Laurence Oliphant was not published until 1928, a lapse of time that was not altogether her fault. In January 1889, barely a month after he died, she had proposed to William Blackwood that he advertise for material for a life of Laurence that she would write in order to prevent anyone else from doing so. Blackwood was not at all anxious for such a book; he was already aware that there was friction between her and Mrs Wynne Finch and apprehensive about her religious views. So he was all the more pleased when Margaret Oliphant, who had first offered him an article about Laurence for the *Magazine*, became so fired with enthusiasm that she proposed to expand it into a full length book. Blackwood gave her access to the correspondence extending over thirty years between Laurence and his uncle, John Blackwood. And once they were reassured that it was Mrs Oliphant the celebrated novelist who was involved and not, as they called her, 'Mrs Rosamond,' Alice's family sighed with relief. Blackwood explained that they did not seem to be getting on well with Rosamond and did not wish her to write about Laurence's life as she knew nothing of it. According to Jamesina Waller, however, there was a great mass of letters at Haifa that could throw useful light on Laurence's career if Rosamond could be got to release them. They included Laurence's early letters to his mother, 'and also a great deal of what they call the Foreign Office correspondence in which, no doubt, there will be much of the most interesting character which might be used without indiscretion' Margaret Oliphant wrote. In the event Rosamond did lend her the letters and she made use of some of them in the biography. As for the Foreign Office letters she was discretion itself, if in fact she saw them, for the traces of his career as a secret agent were very well covered and appeared only in the slightest hint that his purpose in going to such countries as Italy, Austro-Hungary, Poland and Russia was not altogether as he said it was.

Though she had not known him well – she was not a relation – Margaret Oliphant had by chance been present at some of the most important moments of his life. She had been in the gallery of the House of Commons on the night his impatience at the manoeuvres over the Reform Bill had come to a head. She saw him in the full flush of his enthusiasm for Harris in 1865, and on his return from Brocton in 1869. Her last sight of Alice had been one foggy afternoon in lodgings in London the day before they set off for Brody on the mission to the Jews. Mrs Oliphant was diligent in collecting information about both Laurence and Alice from those who had known them though, she complained, they all began by talking at length about themselves. She went to Haifa and was charmed by the 'nice airy rooms' in the house in the Templar colony and fancied she saw Alice flitting in and out – 'you know what a taste she had for cooking and managing', she wrote. Not without difficulty, for she was very stout, she had herself carried up to Dalieh where Haskett Smith gave a party for her. On learning that she was a friend of Laurence Oliphant, the Druse attending him 'kissed my hands and put his to his forehead, lips and chest to express devotion'.

Her book was published in 1891, an immediate and huge success. Its undisguised hostility to Thomas Lake Harris provoked a bitter attack from his disciples which rose to a crescendo when Mrs Oliphant publicly revealed that Harris had claimed to be the direct cause of Laurence's death. Respiro's lengthy work was a response to what he saw as a wicked distortion of the truth. Hannah Pearsall Smith was not pleased either. 'I felt as if it was not right to have such a eulogy set forth of him when all these things were behind the scenes but I concluded that it was not my business to enlighten her, and I felt sure she would never have believed it if I had told her,' she wrote. But in the main those who knew Laurence and Alice, including Mrs Wynne Finch who approved the book in draft, had nothing but praise for it and sympathy coloured with admiration for its subject. Those who knew Laurence best gave him credit for a battle bravely fought against overwhelming odds. As Emily Lawless, who knew both Laurence and Alice well, said to Margaret Oliphant, she read the book through at one sitting marvelling at the tact with which she had contrived to tell the whole truth about him and yet never to cross the line where his 'divagations' plunged him into absurdity. 'You care about your two friends' name and fame,' said Miss Lawless, 'and you have brought that out gallantly at moments, as it were, almost in spite of themselves.'

It was sad that those who cared about Laurence and Alice did not bring the scandal out into the open after his death. The result was that his detractors might be said to have won the day. Hannah's revenge was the more complete for being long delayed, for when her papers were published in 1928 there was no one to ask if what they said was true. And while he lived Harris was strident in his abuse of Laurence and Alice; though Margaret Oliphant had not flinched from calling him a charlatan, he did not lack disciples who marched to his defence in the newspapers.

Harris maintained his empire over the minds of certain people until his death, which occurred in New York in 1906. There were some who could not bring themselves to believe that Harris could die, who watched the body until signs of decomposition forced them to admit that their vigil was in vain. Among them was Jane Lee Waring. In 1895, after the death of poor mad Emily, she had become the Prophet's third wife, a marriage which, after all Harris had preached against it over the years, brought a storm of criticism in the San Francisco newspapers. Harris found it prudent to withdraw from California. Fountain Grove and its vineyards were left in the care of Kanaye Nagasawa; after Harris died he inherited them. He spent the Prohibition years storing up sherry in the hope of better times to come. At his death the property passed to his heir, a Japanese American.

There is one more thing to be said, which I believe was in Margaret Oliphant's mind as she wrote her biography of Laurence Oliphant, and which, if it were true, would explain much that is puzzling about his life, not least his submission to Thomas Lake Harris. It is that he was infected by syphilis, one of the scourges of the time, and that Harris promised him a cure. That could have been the cause of the mysterious recurring illnesses, the blinding headaches, and the symptoms of 'softening of the brain'. It could account for the sudden withdrawals from the world, the isolation at Amenia, the remedies Laurence was forced to take there, and the ban upon sexual intercourse.

Similarly, the belief that he had been cured could have prompted his equally sudden return to England in 1869 – in a state of 'holiday happiness' – and the fact that Jane Waring referred to in her first letter to Alice; 'Father left word that Woodbine was no longer to hold himself from seeking a wife'. That the disease recurred in 1873 might be supposed from the letter of resignation from *The Times* that he addressed to Delane with its mention of headaches, his second withdrawal to Brocton, and the terms of his submission to Harris which obliged him and Alice not to live together as man and wife. It may also have been the cause of their long separation.

To go further. It is even possible that the shadow of the disease lay over Laurence at his birth, darkening the lives of his parents, who in their attitude towards the child as reported by Mrs Oliphant, betrayed a fear that can hardly be explained as arising from a reasonable cause. If that were true, though Antony Oliphant might have suffered guilt, the chief victim was Maria. She was condemned to years of frustration, anxiety and nervous illness. It is perhaps significant that her symptoms disappeared when she arrived at Amenia, partly, no doubt, because Harris forced her to occupy herself with manual labour, but also, perhaps, because she believed Laurence would be cured.

Where Alice was concerned we do not know enough about her to say whether her acquiescence in Harris's control over her married life came as a result of her knowledge of Laurence's disease, or sprang from some inclination already present in her when they met. But there can be no doubt that she loved Laurence dearly in her own particular way, and honoured him as the exponent of religious views which she profoundly shared. And, contrary to the opinion of many people who knew and marvelled at the history of her life with Laurence Oliphant, Alice would have been the last person to consider it as wasted.

As for Laurence, it was a tragedy that this good and gentle man was, for whatever reason, deprived of the normal means of experiencing human love. Although in his despair he fell into the hands of an evil charlatan, he was not corrupted by Thomas Lake Harris. Laurence passionately believed what Harris preached but did not practise – that sexual love was holy. As his Evangelical parents unconsciously may have done, he sought to express that passion in the only way open to him – as a religious creed. This was the inspiration that sustained both him and Alice in the last years of their life together. And, in the bruised and wandering time after she died, he set out to prove the literal truth of their belief, defying convention and thereby inviting disaster. Recognizing the strength of his conviction and the honesty of his motive, his true friends never ceased to hold him in affection and esteem.

NOTES

1. *Sentenced to Life.*

Page 1. *A difference in age.* Louis Liesching, *Personal Reminiscences of Laurence Oliphant*, p. 7. (Marshall Bros., 1891.)

Page 2. *Mrs Oliphant . . . drew upon papers.* Margaret Oliphant, *Memoir of Laurence Oliphant and of Alice Oliphant, his Wife.* (William Blackwood & Sons, 1891.)

Page 3. *Edward Irving.* Liesching, op. cit., p. 12.

Page 4. *Seventeenth century MS,* M. Oliphant, op. cit., i, p. 2.

Page 4. *A story was told of him.* Ibid., i, p. 3.

Page 4. *'You asked me to speak.'* Ibid., p. 14.

Page 5. *'Mr B'.* Ibid., p. 11.

Page 5. *Liesching objected.* Liesching, op. cit., p. 12.

Page 5. *'. . . the East burst for the first time'.* Laurence Oliphant, *Episodes in a Life of Adventure*, p. 13. (William Blackwood & Sons. 1887.)

Page 7. *She forbade it.* M. Oliphant, op. cit., i, p. 233.

Page 7. *'I shall never forget'.* L. Oliphant, *Episodes.* p. 24.

Page 8. *as someone observed. The Times*, 24 December 1888.

Page 9. *his old straw hat.* L. Oliphant, *Episodes.* p. 35.

Page 9. *speculation among their fellow passengers.* Liesching, op. cit., p. 7.

Page 9. *the centre of everything.* M. Oliphant, op. cit., i, p. 30.

Page 9. *the Baker brothers.* Samuel Baker. *Eight Years in Ceylon*, p. 16. (Longmans, Green and Co. 1874.)

Page 10. *Ceylon . . . a raffish place. Blackwood's Magazine.* July 1891.

Page 11. *a personal affront.* Oswald Smith, *Time*, January–June 1889.

Page 11. *Laura Bell.* S. M. Ellis, *A Mid-Victorian Pepys*, i, p. 193. (Palmer, 1923.)

Page 11. *My approval . . . never meant.'* M. Oliphant, op. cit., i, p. 33.

Page 11. *'. . . a pleasant enough fellow . . .'* Ibid., p. 34.

Page 12. *Laurence was so facile.* Liesching, op. cit., p. 16.

Page 13. *'How would you like a Roman Catholic daughter-in-law?'* M. Oliphant, op. cit., i, p. 43.

Page 14. *description of Nepal.* L. Oliphant, *Journey to Katmandu.* (John Murray, 1852.)

Page 14. *self examination.* M. Oliphant, op. cit., i, p. 49.

Page 15. some question of illness. Ibid., p. 55.

Page 16. Lady Troubridge. J. Hope-Nicholson, ed. *Life amongst the Troubridges,* p. 34. (John Murray, 1966.)

Page 16. 'a friend of the people'. M. Oliphant. op. cit., i, p. 64.

Page 17. skating in Kent. O. Smith. op. cit.

Page 18. Maga on Katmandu. Blackwood's Magazine. July, 1852.

Page 18. the book he wrote. L. Oliphant. *The Russian Shores of the Black Sea.* (William Blackwood & Sons. 1853.)

Page 19. Sir Hamilton Seymour. O. Smith. op. cit.

Page 19. at Novgorod. L. Oliphant. *Russian Shores.* p. 105.

Page 20. St. Petersburg, Moscow, and Odessa connected. Ibid., p. 8.

Page 20. Nothing ... bore looking into. Ibid., p. 61.

Page 21. 'The country was like the sea ...' M. Oliphant, op. cit., i, p. 96.

Page 21. heard about Schamyl. L. Oliphant. *Russian Shores,* p. 319.

Page 21. description of the Crimea. A. Kinglake. *The Invasion of the Crimea,* i, p. 1. (William Blackwood & Sons, 1863.)

Page 22. Sebastopol undefended to the south. L. Oliphant, *Russian Shores,* p. 260.

2. 'This restless, sagacious traveller'

Page 24. 'A mighty handsome spec.' Blackwood Archive. D. 1. John Blackwood to Laurence Oliphant, 3 May 1854.

Page 24. The Rifle and Hound in Ceylon. S. Baker, *The Rifle and Hound in Ceylon.* (Longman, Brown, Green & Longmans, 1854.)

Page 24. the loose box. Blackwood Archive. D. 6. John Blackwood to Alexander Kinglake, 5 June 1866.

Page 25. 'confoundedly fidgety'. Ibid., D. 20. William Blackwood to A. I. Shand, 28 May 1889.

Page 25. philanthropic field. M. Oliphant, op. cit., i, p. 105.

Page 26. Oliphant's book evoked the desire. A. Kinglake, op. cit., iii, p. 382.

Page 26. he gave Lord Raglan. Ibid.

Page 26. 'I recommend their landing.' M. Oliphant, op. cit., i, p. 103.

Page 26. Identified the Malakoff Tower. The Times, 30 June 1855. F. Head. F. M. *Sir John Burgoyne,* p. 33. (John Murray, 1872.)

Page 27. 'Progress and Policy ...'. Blackwood's Magazine, May, 1854.

Page 27. letters to his father. M. Oliphant, op. cit., i, p. 103.

Page 27. Delane ... favourably impressed. Ibid., p. 106.

Page 28. 'Allah is great.' F. Wagner, *Schamyl, the Sultan, Warrior, and Prophet,* p. 12. (Travellers Library, 1854.)

2 · 'THIS RESTLESS, SAGACIOUS TRAVELLER' 263

Page 28. *inspecting . . . even the Mormons.* W. Pollock, *Personal Remembrances*, ii, p. 2. (Macmillan, 1887.)

Page 28. *Clarendon told Stratford.* PRO. FO 352/37a. Clarendon to Stratford. 7 March 1854.

Page 28. *Colonel Lloyd. Report of the Select Committee on the Army before Sebastopol. Third Report.* 15032.

Page 29. *Elgin's career.* G. Wrong, *The Earl of Elgin*. (Methuen, 1905.)

Page 29. *'all my . . . friends'.* L. Oliphant, *Episodes*, p. 49.

Page 30. *'Elgin is a short, stout, gentleman'.* Wrong, op. cit., p. 65.

Page 30. *Letters to his mother.* M. Oliphant, op. cit., i, pp. 122, 154.

Page 31. *the prevailing preacher.* Ibid., i, p. 141.

Page 31. *'the . . . Melbourne school'. Blackwood's Magazine*, Shand memoir, July 1891.

Page 33. *Journey to the West.* L. Oliphant, *Minnesota and the Far West*. (William Blackwood & Sons, 1855.)

Page 34. *Laurence 'down to the heels.' Blackwood's Magazine*, July, 1891.

Page 34. *life like a Cabinet Minister.* M. Oliphant, op. cit., i, p. 147.

Page 35. *'the wife is buttoned'.* Ibid, i, p. 107.

Page 35. *The Coming Campaign.* L. Oliphant, *The Coming Campaign*. (William Blackwood & Sons, 1855.)

Page 35. *Stratford sent Longworth.* PRO FO 78/1243. Clarendon to Longworth, 13 April 1855.

Page 36. *Longworth failed.* Ibid. Longworth to Stratford, 20 July 1855.

Page 36. *Stratford's career. Dictionary of National Biography*.

Page 37. *Russell's interest in alternative religion.* PRO FO 918/78, 83.

Page 37. *'the flower of the Embassy'.* PRO FO 352/42B. Stratford to Clarendon, 23 August 1855.

Page 37. *Stratford favours expedition.* PRO FO 78/1082. Stratford to Longworth, 23 July 1855.

Page 37. *Siege of Sebastopol. The Army before Sebastopol. Third Report.* 17628.

Page 38. *Burgoyne regretted the delay.* Ibid., 17217. L. Oliphant, *Episodes*, p. 87.

Page 39. *Russian pact with Schamyl.* PRO FO 352/42B. Clarendon to Stratford, 15 October 1855.

Page 39. *Stratford had suggested a visit.* I. Burton, *Life of Sir Richard Burton*, i, p. 243. (Chapman & Hall, 1893.)

Page 39. *Burton on the Caucasus. The Times*, 19 February 1856.

Page 40. *'My religion . . . is not . . . happy.'* M. Oliphant, op. cit., i, p. 185.

Page 41. William Walker. L. Oliphant, *Patriots & Filibusters*, p. 170 et seq. (William Blackwood & Sons, 1860.)

Page 42. Palmerston determined to keep Mosquito. J. Ridley, *Palmerston*, p. 616. (Panther, 1972.)

Page 42. of this project Laurence remarked. L. Oliphant, *Episodes*, p. 113.

Page 43. The Admiral was his cousin. Ibid., p. 116.

Page 43. Panama. L. Oliphant, *Patriots*, p. 210.

Page 44. he warned Maximilian. Ibid., p. 121.

Page 45. 'I thought you were hung.' P. Henderson, *Laurence Oliphant*, p. 60. (Hale, 1956.)

3. Mission to China

Page 46. He told Mrs Ashley. BM. Add. 39168. Laurence Oliphant to Mrs William Ashley, April 1857.

Page 47. Thirty dollars a head. Ridley, op. cit., p. 627.

Page 48. uncomfortable journey. James Bruce. *Extracts from the letters of James, Earl of Elgin to Mary Louise, Countess of Elgin. 1847–62*, p. 25. (Privately printed.)

Page 48. a belief encountered in America. M. Oliphant, op. cit., i, p. 196.

Page 49. Shannon's voyage. L. Oliphant. *Elgin's Mission to China and Japan*, i, p. 54. (Oxford University Press, 1970.)

Page 49. the China force saved Calcutta. BM. Add 39168. L. Oliphant to Mrs Ashley, 22 August 1857.

Page 50. 'a terrible business'. Bruce, op. cit., p. 23.

Page 50. Laurence met a clergyman. Ibid., p. 25.

Page 51. 'Pity me.' The Times Archives. L. Oliphant to Delane, 5 October 1857.

Page 51. he longed for a creed. M. Oliphant, op. cit., i, p. 212.

Page 51. a place in the Litany. Bruce, op. cit., p. 48.

Page 51. Chinese warfare. M. Oliphant, op. cit., i, p. 226.

Page 52. Seymour disapproved. Bruce, op. cit., p. 50.

Page 52. Soochow. BM. Add. 39168. L. Oliphant to Mrs Ashley, 14 April 1858.

Page 53. 'Cutting north-east gales'. L. Oliphant, *Elgin's Mission*, i, p. 263.

Page 53. at his wits' end. Bruce, op. cit., p. 97.

Page 53. Wingrove Cooke and Oliphant. Prof. J. Gerson, Letter to author.

Page 54. Tientsin. L. Oliphant, *Elgin's Mission*, i, p. 325 et seq.

Page 55. Hot weather at Shanghai. The Times Archive, L. Oliphant to Delane, July 1858.

Page 55. Japan. G. Fox, *Britain and Japan, 1858–1883.* (Oxford University Press, 1969.)

Page 56. first landfall. L. Oliphant, *Elgin's Mission,* ii, p.2.

Page 56. looking 'with large hollow eyes'. R. Alcock, *The Capital of the Tycoon,* i, p. 74. (Greenwood Press, 1969.)

Page 57. could not account for such a proceeding. M. Costenza, ed. *The Complete Journal of Townsend Harris,* p. 252. (Japan Society, New York, 1930.)

Page 57. Vice-Governor of Nagasaki. L. Oliphant, *Elgin's Mission,* ii, p. 56.

Page 58. Higo no Kami. Ibid., p. 106. S. Okuma, *Fifty Years of New Japan,* i, p. 81. (Smith, Elder, 1909.)

Page 60. Elgin watched by Kincardine. L. Oliphant, *Elgin's Mission,* ii, p. 98.

Page 62. Tariff negotiations. Ibid., p. 272.

Page 62. Laurence knew this would be opposed. BM. Add. 39168. L. Oliphant to Mrs Ashley, September, 1858.

Page 63. Yangtse journey. L. Oliphant, *Elgin's Mission,* ii, p. 289 et seq.

Page 64. Death of his father. M. Oliphant, op. cit., i, p. 240.

4. Private Diplomacy

Page 65. Furious anchored. PRO ADM 53/6944. *Furious* log.

Page 65. 'I shall hurry up.' Isabel Burton, op. cit., i, p. 327.

Page 66. Homosexuality charge. F. Brodie, *The Devil Drives,* p. 167. (Eyre & Spottiswoode, 1967.)

Page 66. Mission to Schamyl. I. Burton, op. cit., i, pp. 242–43.

Page 66. Speke's distress. Richard Burton, *Lake Regions of Central Africa,* ii, p. 209. (Longman, 1861.) A. Maitland, *Speke,* p. 88. (Constable, 1971.)

Page 67. Speke's plan. National Library of Scotland, 17910. Speke to Grant, 24 February 1864.

Page 67. Oliphant in Central America. L. Oliphant, *Patriots & Filibusters,* p. 221.

Page 67. First to breakfast. L. Oliphant, *Elgin's Mission,* ii, p. 480.

Page 68. Yangtse voyage. Royal Geographical Society, *Proceedings,* 28 March 1859.

Page 68. 'We must send you there again.' J. H. Speke, *Journal of the Discovery of the Source of the Nile,* p. 2. (William Blackwood & Sons, 1863.)

Page 68. ad hoc sub-committee. R.G.S. Minutes, 21 June 1859.

Page 68. Speke accused Burton. National Library of Scotland, 17910. Speke to Rigby, 3 September 1859.

Page 68. Speke and Burton's plans. R.G.S. Minutes, 21 June 1859.

NOTES

Page 69. Oliphant approached Blackwood. Blackwood Archive, 4143. Speke to John Blackwood, 10 July 1859.

Page 69. 'Unpretending, simple hearted.' Ibid., D.3. John Blackwood to L. Oliphant, 7 May 1860.

Page 70. 'Charming women at hand.' M. Oliphant, op. cit., i, p. 296.

Page 71. Queen Victoria noted. Royal Archives. Queen Victoria's Journal, 24 September 1859.

Page 71. Princess Helena. Ibid., S 31/81. Princess Christian to Lord Beaconsfield, 3 February 1880.

Page 71. At Cortachy and Alderley. Blackwood Archive, 4141, L. Oliphant to John Blackwood. Various dates in 1859.

Page 72. 'A very pretty quarrel'. The Times, 27 February 1860.

Page 72. letter to The Times. Ibid., 28 February 1860.

Page 72. 'He is like a monkey.' Blackwood Archive, 4152, L. Oliphant to John Blackwood, 27 February 1860.

Page 72. 'imposed high conditions'. Ibid., L. Oliphant to John Blackwood, 18 February 1860.

Page 73. to save Nice and Savoy. L. Oliphant, *Episodes*, p. 166.

Page 73. France down to the Simplon. Broadlands Archive, Russell to Palmerston, 12 March 1860.

Page 73. 'He will make a great mistake'. PRO 30/22/21, Palmerston to Russell, 5 February 1860.

Page 74. 'Imagine my coming from Paris'. A. Hayward, *Collected letters*, ii, p. 243. L. Oliphant to Hayward, 30 March 1860. (John Murray.)

Page 74. Lady Palmerston's 'chief of staff'. M. St. Helier, *Memories of fifty years*, p. 80. (Arnold, 1909.)

Page 75. Letter to de Grey. BM Add. 43621, L. Oliphant to Lord de Grey and Ripon, 3 April 1860.

Page 75. Cavour, 'a thick set solid man'. M. Oliphant, op. cit., i, p. 249.

Page 75. He would have been pleased. L. Oliphant, *Episodes*, p. 170.

Page 75. Hudson on Garibaldi. PRO 30/22/14a, Hudson to Russell, 20 April 1860.

Page 76. motion for the Chamber. L. Oliphant, *Episodes*, p. 168.

Page 76. Laurence coached Garibaldi. Ibid., p. 171.

Page 77. Laurence's instructions. Ibid., p. 174.

Page 77. President of an independent state. Blackwood Archive, 4152, L. Oliphant to John Blackwood, 8 May 1860.

Page 77. Clanricarde told the Lords. Hansard, Lords, 23 March 1860.

Page 77. Cavour had agreed. PRO 30/22/14a, Clanricarde to Russell, 20 March 1860.

4 · PRIVATE DIPLOMACY

Page 78. Garibaldi invited Laurence. L. Oliphant, *Episodes*, p. 177.

Page 78. 'not at Cayenne'. Blackwood Archive, D 4, John Blackwood to L. Oliphant, 7 May 1860.

Page 78. 'pitch in to the hound'. Ibid., John Blackwood to L. Oliphant, 29 June 1860.

Page 79. Invited to Gotha. Ibid., 4152, L. Oliphant to John Blackwood, 22 August 1860.

Page 80. Letter to Hayward. National Library of Scotland, 966, L. Oliphant to A. Hayward, 27 September 1860.

Page 80. Bosnia and Herzgovina. L. Oliphant, *Episodes*, p. 180.

Page 80. His friend Eber. Ibid., p. 183.

Page 81. Discoursing on spirits. Bertrand Russell, ed., *The Amberley Papers*, i, p. 80. (Hogarth, 1937.)

Page 81. '. . . go and see Miss Fawcett.' M. Oliphant, op. cit., ii, p. 2.

Page 82. Russell told the Queen. Royal Archives, B 18/157, Russell to the Queen, 29 December 1860.

Page 82. 'An exceptional appointment'. The Times, 24 August 1887.

Page 82. he disliked going. B. Russell, op. cit., i, p. 114.

Page 82. 'Maude . . . going to marry.' Ibid., i, p. 133.

Page 83. polite wrangle. PRO FO 46/16, 12 February 1861.

Page 83. Japanese hostility. G. Fox, op. cit.

Page 83. Heusken's contribution to Oliphant's book. L. Oliphant, *Elgin's Mission*, ii, p. 90.

Page 84. 'You little know.' PRO FO 391/1, Alcock to E. Hammond, 18 October 1861.

Page 84. a vast and scrambling place. R. Alcock, op. cit., ii, p. 153.

Page 84. Letter to the Duchess. M. Oliphant, op. cit., i, p. 254.

Page 85. Assassination attempt. L. Oliphant, *Episodes*, pp. 187–202.

Page 86. 'Whatever is, is best'. M. Oliphant, op. cit., i, p. 262.

Page 87. 'I, though I am a person of low standing'. L. Oliphant, *Episodes*, p. 198.

Page 87. Prince of Tsushima planned attack. PRO FO 46/12, Alcock to Russell, 26 July 1861.

Page 87. secret work. Ibid., Alcock to [Hammond], 27 August 1861.

Page 88. Meeting with Japanese Foreign Ministers. PRO FO 46/16. Oliphant's *Compte rendu*, 3 September 1861.

Page 89. Possadnik at Tsushima. L. Oliphant, *Episodes*, pp. 212–227.

Page 90. Oliphant suggests Chusan. PRO FO 46/16, 2 September 1861.

Page 90. Went to Broadlands. Broadlands Archive, Palmerston's Diary, 4 November 1861.

268   NOTES

Page 90. 'he is very able'. S. Lane-Poole, *Life of Sir Harry Parkes*, i, p. 450. (Macmillan, 1894.)

5. Secret Agent

Page 91. At Russell's bidding. PRO 30/22/110, Russell to Oliphant, 3 February 1862.

Page 91. Russell told Layard. BM Add. 38988, Russell to Layard, 21 January 1862.

Page 92. Prince's invitation. PRO 30/22/73, Oliphant to Russell, 27 February 1862.

Page 92. Letter to Madame de Bury. P. Henderson, op. cit., p. 109n.

Page 92. Russell hoped the Queen would not insist. Broadlands Archive, Russell to Palmerston, 1 January 1862.

Page 92. Oliphant on Prince. M. Oliphant, op. cit., i, p. 269.

Page 93. Visit to Venice. PRO 30/22/73, Oliphant to Russell, 27 February 1862.

Page 93. 'What a curious tangle.' BM Add. 39102. Oliphant to Layard, 18 March 1862.

Page 93. Wandered through Italy. L. Oliphant, *Episodes*, p. 231 et seq.

Page 94. La Marmora's assistance. PRO 30/22/73, Oliphant to Russell, 20 May 1862.

Page 95. Russell's minute. Ibid.

Page 95. His pen at the disposal of his masters. Blackwood Archive, 4172, Oliphant to John Blackwood, June 1862.

Page 95. 'There can be no Harm.' PRO 30/22/22, Palmerston to Russell, 13 July 1862.

Page 95. Russell told the Queen. Royal Archives, B 19/119, Russell to the Queen, 19 July 1862.

Page 95. letter to King Leopold. PRO 30/22/46, ? to Russell, 25 July 1862.

Page 96. letter to Fane. PRO 30/22/98, Russell to Fane, 30 July 1862.

Page 96. 'lavender kid gloves'. A. Redesdale, *Memories*, i, p. 125. (Hutchinson, 1915.)

Page 96. party at Fryston. Henry Adams, *The Education of Henry Adams*, p. 139. (Constable, 1919)

Page 97. rode to Stonehenge. Broadlands Archive, Palmerston's diary, 12 December 1862.

Page 98. 'Why confine exploration ...?'. L. Oliphant, *Episodes*, p. 265.

Page 98. ordered to Poland. Royal Archives, Queen Victoria's Journal, 28 February 1864.

Page 98. an account of the situation. Henderson, op. cit., p. 114.

5 · SECRET AGENT

Page 98. wrote to Layard. BM Add. 39105, Oliphant to Layard, 31 March 1863.

Page 98. bands of partisans. L. Oliphant, *Episodes*, p. 302 et seq.

Page 100. plea for help. BM Add. 39105, Oliphant to Layard, 31 March 1863.

Page 100. with Ashley to Ruthenia. L. Oliphant, *Episodes*, p. 333.

Page 100. Ashley wrote to Palmerston. Broadlands Archive, Ashley to Palmerston, 14 September 1863.

Page 103. visits to the convents. L. Oliphant, *Episodes*, p. 355 et seq.

Page 103. At Primkenau. Ibid., p. 381.

Page 104. The Queen and Paget 'at Cross Purposes'. PRO 30/22/21, Palmerston to Russell, 5 April 1860.

Page 105. Oliphant at Gotha. Blackwood Archive, 4184, Oliphant to John Blackwood, 16 December 1863.

Page 105. 'Dearest Victoria.' Royal Archives, I 92/69, Duchess of Coburg to Queen Victoria, 16 December 1863.

Page 106. 'put on too much steam'. Blackwood Archive, 4184, Oliphant to John Blackwood, n.d. but December 1863.

Page 106. Three men at Gluckstadt. L. Oliphant, *Episodes*, p. 383.

Page 107. The Times *correspondent found him.* A. Gallenga, *The Invasion of Denmark*, p. 22. (R. Bentley, 1864.)

Page 107. Inspected the Dannewirke. Blackwood's Magazine, March 1864.

Page 107. Saw the Crown Prince and Bismarck. Mrs G. Porter, *Annals of a Publishing House*, iii, p. 125. (Blackwood & Sons, 1898.)

Page 108. Queen following independent policy. Count von Beust, *Memoirs*, i, p. 251. (Remington, 1887.)

Page 108. attack on Palmerston. Blackwood's Magazine, March 1864.

Page 108. 'in tremendous hot water'. Porter, op. cit., iii, p. 122.

Page 109. 'They must be in a funk.' Blackwood Archive, D 5, John Blackwood to L. Oliphant, 10 March 1864.

Page 109. audience with the Queen. Royal Archives, Queen Victoria's Journal, 28 February 1864.

Page 109. Queen Victoria's letter to Crown Princess. R. Fulford, Ed. *Dearest Mama*, pp. 304, 305. (Evans, 1968.)

Page 110. The Owl. Fremantle, *Lord Glenesk and the Morning Post*, p. 195 et seq. (Alston Rives, 1910.)

Page 110. 'Oliphant is a good fellow.' Blackwood Archive, D 5, John Blackwood to Charles Lever, 27 April 1864.

Page 110. told the French geographers. Société de Géographie de Paris, *Bulletin*, 8 May 1864.

Page 111. *Speke's letters showed.* National Library of Scotland, 17910, 17931, 17933, Speke to Rigby, Blackwood, (various dates.)

Page 111. *'The tail'.* Blackwood Archive, 4872.

Page 111. *'Pray speak to him.'* Ibid., D 5. John Blackwood to Oliphant, 30 June 1864.

Page 111. *Burton goaded into accepting.* I. Burton, op. cit., ii, p. 426.

Page 111. *'Poor fellow.'* Blackwood Archive, 4925. L. Oliphant to John Blackwood, 22 September 1864.

6. The Brotherhood of the New Life

Page 113. *He told Blackwood.* Porter, op. cit., iii, p. 124.

Page 113. *Royal Geographical Society.* RGS Archives, Oliphant file. Committee Minute Book.

Page 113. *Piccadilly.* L. Oliphant, *Piccadilly.* (William Blackwood & Sons, 1865.)

Page 114. *Lady Palmerston's party.* Ibid., p. 3.

Page 114. *a grate without fire.* Ibid., p. 35.

Page 115. *letter to his mother.* M. Oliphant, op. cit., ii, p. 2.

Page 115. *doctrine revealed in the sermons.* T. L. Harris, *The Millenial Age.* (Ratcliffe, 1860.)

Page 116. *'live the Life'.* L. Oliphant, *Piccadilly*, pp. 239, 268.

Page 116. *Harris studied the Shakers.* W. P. Swainson, *Thomas Lake Harris. Mad or Inspired?*, p. 5. (Brotherhood Publishing Co., 1895.)

Page 116. *'burned over' districts.* W. R. Cross, *The Burned Over District*, pp. 257, 258. (Cornell University Press, 1950.)

Page 117. *Harris, origins and career.* R. M'Cully, *The Brotherhood of the New Life.* (Glasgow, 1893.)

Page 117. *Hydesville rappings.* S. E. Ahlstrom. *A Religious History of the American People*, p. 488. (Yale University Press, 1972.)

Page 118. *Andrew Jackson Davis.* F. Podmore, *Modern Spiritualism*, p. 170. (Methuen, 1902.)

Page 118. *Mountain Cove.* E. H. Britten, *Modern American Spiritualism*, p. 208. (New York, 1870.)

Page 119. *Swedenborg's influence.* Ahlstrom, op. cit., pp. 484–8.

Page 119. *doctrine of counterparts.* T. L. Harris, *The Arcana of Christianity.* (New York, 1858.)

Page 120. *'Here find thy mate.'* T. L. Harris, *An Epic of the Starry Heaven.* (Partridge & Brittan, 1854.)

Page 120. *Horace Greeley. Appleton's Cyclopedia of American Biography.*

6 · THE BROTHERHOOD OF THE NEW LIFE

Page 121. *Garth Wilkinson.* Clement Wilkinson, *John James Garth Wilkinson*, pp. 102, 105. (Kegan Paul, 1911.)

Page 121. *'How heart sinking.'* Robert Dale Owen, *The Debatable Land between this World and the Next*, p. 46. 1872.

Page 121. *Harris's sermons.* T. L. Harris, *The Millenial Age.*

Page 122. *florid in phraseology.* M. Oliphant, op. cit., ii, p. 4.

Page 122. *Apocalypse of St. John.* H. Schneider & G. Lawton. *A Prophet and a Pilgrim*, p. 44. (Columbia University Press, 1942.)

Page 123. *Wilkinson an enemy.* C. Wilkinson, op. cit., p. 103.

Page 123. *the new inspiration. Herald of Light.* (June 1861.)

Page 124. *About sixty people joined him.* Columbia University Archive. Harris/Oliphant papers. Box 13, file 4.

Page 124. *First National Bank of Amenia.* Wilkinson, op. cit., p. 103.

Page 124. *Fawcett/Cuthbert marriage.* M'Cully, op. cit., p. 78.

Page 124. *work as a lumberjack.* Columbia University Archive. Box B, file 11.

Page 124. *Pitt Buckner.* Ibid. Box 13, file 4.

Page 125. *Casting out infernals.* M. Oliphant, op. cit., ii, p. 25.

Page 125. *Jane Lee Waring.* Columbia University Archive. Box 13, file 2.

Page 125. *Mr Masollam.* L. Oliphant, *Masollam*, pp. 29–33. (William Blackwood & Sons, 1886.)

Page 126. *'My heart leapt.'* L. Oliphant, *Piccadilly*, p. 237.

Page 126. *'People call me odd.'* Ibid., p. 64.

Page 126. *'the law of my members'.* M. Oliphant, op. cit., i, p. 244.

Page 126. *attacked by syphilis.* Broadlands Archive. Letters to Lord and Lady Mount Temple. Jane Waring to Georgiana Mount Temple. June 1882. Columbia University Archive. Box 13, file 1.

Page 127. *blinding headaches.* Blackwood Archive, 4213. Lady Oliphant to John Blackwood. 11 December 1865.

Page 127. *John Bright's speech. Hansard.* Third Series. Vol. 181. Col. 685.

Page 127. *shouts of 'Oliphant'. The Times*, 24 February 1866.

Page 128. *Laurence's maiden speech. Hansard.* Third Series. Vol. 181. Col. 1046.

Page 128. *Gladstone dragged his feet.* M. Cowling, *1867, Disraeli, Gladstone and Revolution*, p. 90. (Cambridge University Press, 1967.)

Page 128. *motion for debate. Hansard.* Third Series. Vol. 182. Cols. 854, 1072.

Page 128. *'Obnoxious motion.' Illustrated London News*, 24 March 1866.

Page 128. *leader of the Tea Room Party.* M. Oliphant, op. cit., ii, p. 16.

Page 129. *Bright did not approve. John Bright's Diaries*, p. 301. (Cassell, 1930.)

Page 129. *envoys from Satsuma.* G. Fox, op. cit., p. 174.

Page 129. *Matsuki Koan.* Author's note. Matsuki Koan changed his name to Terashima Munenori in 1867/68. See M. Jansen. *Sakamoto Ryoma and the Meiji Restoration.* Princeton 1961. 'Matsuki Koan'.

Page 129. *Letter to Layard.* BM Add. 39116. Oliphant to Layard, 28 July 1865.

Page 129. *Oliphant memo to Clarendon.* PRO FO 46/63. Clarendon to Parkes, 25 March 1866.

Page 130. *Kanaye Nagasawa.* Mr Arthur McCombie to the author.

Page 130. *Lloyd in charge of Japanese.* Columbia University Archive. Box B, file 11. Oliphant to Cowper, 1 December 1866. Fox, op. cit., p. 460.

Page 130. *William Cowper. Dictionary of National Biography.* G. Mount Temple, *Memorial.* (Private circulation, 1890.)

Page 130. *invited Harris to Broadlands.* Wagner College Archive. Box 2. J. L. Bradley. Ed. *Letters of John Ruskin to Lord and Lady Mount Temple*, p. 289. (Ohio University Press, 1964.)

Page 130. *Introduced him to Ruskin.* Ibid.

Page 130. *gave him money.* Broadlands Archive. Harris to W. Cowper Temple, 20 January 1875. 1 September 1875.

Page 131. *Georgiana turned to spiritualism.* G. Mount Temple, op. cit., p. 107.

Page 131. *William's ecumenicalism.* Ibid., p. 34.

Page 132. *William on Harris.* Broadlands Archive. W. Cowper-Temple to Oliphant, 9 August 1868.

Page 133. *Georgiana's upbringing.* G. Mount Temple, op. cit., *Some Reminiscences of Lady Mount Temple by her surviving brother.* (Private circulation.)

Page 133. *'just the sort of person'.*.. Mount Temple, op. cit., p. 68.

Page 133. *'where no cruelty existed'.* Logan Pearsall Smith, *Unforgotten Years*, p. 41. (Constable, 1938.)

Page 133. *Georgiana and Rose La Touche.* Bradley, op. cit., pp. 85, 87.

Page 133. *'statuesque severity'.* John Ruskin. *Praeterita*, ii, p. 66. (George Allen, 1887.)

Page 133. *Archbishop Benson.* B. Askwith, *Two Victorian Families*, p. 167. (Chatto & Windus, 1971.)

Page 133. *'Green was her colour.'* E. Clifford, *Broadlands as it was.* (Private circulation, 1890.)

Page 134. *Negotiations for Brocton.* Columbia University Archive. Box 13, file 4.

6 · THE BROTHERHOOD OF THE NEW LIFE

Page 134. Laurence's discarded mistress. San Francisco Chronicle, 21 June 1891.

Page 134. Harris imposed silence. Schneider & Lawton, op. cit., p. 108.

Page 135. 'I find the greatest benefit.' Broadlands Archive. Oliphant to Georgiana Cowper, 13 June 1867.

Page 135. Maria appealed to The Times. Times Archive. Delane to Jennings. 1867.

Page 135. 'softening of the brain'. Columbia University Archive. Box B. Misc. file. Oliphant to W. Cowper, 17 February 1868.

Page 135. 'the sight of the abject human being'. Columbia University Archive. Box 13, file 4.

Page 135. Harris was able to bully Laurence. Rosamond Dale Owen, *My Perilous Life in Palestine*, p. 28. (Allen & Unwin, 1928.)

Page 135. Conversation with Bright. Bright, op. cit., p. 304.

Page 137. Ruskin on Harris. Bradley, op. cit., p. 213.

Page 137. Laurence at Denmark Hill. Ibid., pp. 224, 229.

Page 137. 'that sense of the humorous'. M. Oliphant, op. cit., ii, p. 22.

Page 137. Kinglake hoped. Porter, op. cit., iii, p. 137.

Page 137. Laurence's instructions. Columbia University Archive. Box B. Misc. file.

Page 137. arrival at Amenia. Ibid. Box 13, file 4.

Page 138. remedy for syphilis. Ibid.

Page 138. religion aroused him sexually. M. Oliphant, op. cit., i, p. 244.

Page 138. depravity was sexual intercourse. M'Cully, op. cit., pp. 131, 147. Broadlands Archive. Jane Waring to Georgiana Mount Temple, 13 June 1882.

Page 138. a celibate existence. Rosamond Dale Owen, op. cit., p. 23. Broadlands Archive. Jane Waring to Georgiana Mount Temple, 13 June 1882.

Page 139. Jane Waring's story. Columbia University Archive. Box 13, files 1/14.

Page 139. James Requa's death. Mayville Sentinel, 8 April 1868.

Page 140. 'Mrs Harris is very quiet.' Colombia University Archive. Box 13, file 4.

Page 140. 'to get up at half past four'. Broadlands Archive. Oliphant to W. Cowper, December 1867.

Page 140. Brocton view of Laurence. Columbia University Archive. Box 13, file 4.

Page 141. the Ruxtons depart. Broadlands Archive. Oliphant to W. Cowper, 9 August 1868.

Page 142. *Cowpers' offer of a home.* Columbia University archive. Box B, file 11. Oliphant to W. Cowper, 17 February 1868.

Page 142. *applied for Chiltern Hundreds.* Hansard. Third Series. Vol. 182, April 1868.

Page 142. *'voters are like cards'.* L. Oliphant, *Episodes*, p. 418.

Page 143. *Asks the Cowpers to come to Brocton.* Columbia University Archive. Box B, file 12. Oliphant to W. Cowper, 6 August 1868.

Page 143. *Georgiana tempted.* Bradley, op. cit., p. 212.

Page 143. *Melbourne's maxim.* Broadlands Archive. W. Cowper to Oliphant, 9 August 1868.

Page 143. *Cowper to help Japanese.* Columbia University Archive. Box B, file 12. Oliphant to W. Cowper, 1 December 1867.

Page 143. *Japanese at Brocton.* Columbia University Archive. Box 13, file 4. Wagner College Archive. Box 4. Prof. Hayashi's note.

Page 143. *Matsuki Koan, Mori Arinori, Hisanobu Sameshima.* Wagner College Archive. Prof. Hayashi's note.

Page 143. *Fukusawa anxious to join Harris.* Columbia University Archive. Box B, file 12.

Page 144. *'Mr Harris talks too many wonders.'* Wagner College Archive. Box 4. Mori Arinori to ?, 1870.

Page 144. *Menial work at Brocton.* Columbia University Archive. Box 13, file 2.

Page 144. *Editorial in London paper.* Daily News, 16 October 1869.

Page 145. *confused with Townsend Harris.* M. Oliphant, op. cit., ii, p. 1, n. Columbia University Archive. Box 13, file 19.

7. War Correspondent

Page 146. *'Dollie and the Two Smiths.'* L. Oliphant. *Traits and Travesties.* p. 203. (William Blackwood & Sons, 1882.)

Page 147 *'Sugar doodling.'* Liesching. op. cit., p. 16.

Page 147. *Return to London.* M. Oliphant. op. cit., ii, p. 60.

Page 147. *Laurence paid a tailor.* Columbia University Archive. Box 4.

Page 148. *'laugh, a jest'.* M. Oliphant. op. cit., ii, p. 66.

Page 148. *some people's questions.* Valentine Chirol. *Fifty Years in a changing world.* p. 84. (Cape, 1927.)

Page 149. *Invited to Walmer.* M. Oliphant. op. cit., ii, p. 71.

Page 150. *Bakunin at Lyons.* Alistair Horne. *The Fall of Paris.* p. 206. (Macmillan, 1965.)

Page 150. *Cluseret's claim to fame.* The Times. 4 October 1870.

7 · WAR CORRESPONDENT

Page 150. *Directed Fenians in America.* Horne, op. cit., p. 316.

Page 150. *Leroy Beaulieu.* Alexander Innes Shand. *Days of the Past.* p. 187. (Constable, 1905.)

Page 150. *'a yelling crowd.'* The Times. 7 October 1870.

Page 151. *on terms with Prussian King.* Times Archive, Morris to W. H. Russell. 29 September 1870.

Page 151. *'this silly resolution'.* Ibid., Delane to Morris. 5 October 1870.

Page 151. *telegraphed to Bismarck.* Ibid., Morris to Oliphant. 21 October 1870.

Page 152. *thundered in vain.* The Times. 27 July 1870.

Page 152. *Laurence at Frankfurt.* PRO FO 918/78. Oliphant to Odo Russell. 22 October 1870.

Page 152. *Lindau, Bismarck's mouthpiece.* Paul Knaplund. *Letters from the Berlin Embassy.* American Historical Association. 1944. ii, p. 395.

Page 152. *'he is* mal vu *here'.* Times Archive. W. H. Russell to Morris. 9 November 1870.

Page 153. *Crown Prince* persona non grata. Ibid., W. H. Russell to Morris. 25 October 1870.

Page 153. *articles about Loire campaign.* The Times 26 and 28 November, 1870.

Page 154. *'Was it not strange.'* Times Archive. W. H. Russell to Morris. 13 November 1870.

Page 155. *'not an ideal war correspondent'.* Shand. op. cit., p. 187.

Page 155. *'something awful about getting up'.* The Times. 17 December 1870.

Page 155. *Destruction of Châteaudun.* Ibid. 8 December 1870.

Page 156. *entry into Orleans.* Ibid., 14 December 1870.

Page 156. *W. H. Russell's irritation.* Times Archive. W. H. Russell to Morris. 14 January 1871.

Page 156. *Laurence with Duke of Coburg.* Ibid., W. H. Russell's diary. 1 January 1871.

Page 157. *Mr Sludge the medium.* Frederick III. *War Diary of Emperor Frederick III.* pp. 55, 69. (Stanley Paul, 1927.)

Page 157. *'New Life is a nuisance.'* Times Archive. W. H. Russell's diary. 25 December 1870.

Page 157. *guns of Mont Valérien.* The Times. 5 January 1871.

Page 158. *'does the bombardment turn your stomach?'* Times Archive. Morris to W. H. Russell. 27 January 1871.

Page 158. *'moony melancholy'.* Ibid., W. H. Russell's diary. 2 January 1871.

Page 158. *preparations for new campaign.* Ibid.

Page 158. *entry into Paris.* The Times. 10 February 1871.

Page 159. *'Highly as we esteem your opinion.'* Times Archive. Morris to Oliphant. 13 February 1871.

Page 160. *Russell to return.* Ibid., Morris to Russell. March 1871.

Page 160. *a flexible felt.* Shand. op. cit., p. 189.

Page 160. *'when this movement begins.'* The Times. 15 February 1871.

Page 161. *Germans at Arc de Triomphe.* The Times. 4 March 1871.

Page 162. *the Parti de l'Ordre.* The Times. 24 March 1871.

Page 163. *why Laurence left Paris.* Times Archive. W. H. Russell to Morris. 22 March 1871.

Page 163. *arrangements for return.* Ibid. Morris to Calonne. 23 March 1871.

Page 163. *she, who broke her heart.* M. Oliphant. op. cit., ii, p. 31.

Page 164. *death of Fowler.* Columbia University Archive. Box 4.

Page 164. *Harris surprised Laurence.* Wagner College Archive. Box 4.

Page 164. *Colonne Vendôme.* Chirol. op. cit., p. 19.

Page 165. *Chief correspondent in Paris.* Times Archive. Morris to Oliphant. 25 April 1871.

Page 165. *'everyone consults him'.* Blackwood Archive. D8. John Blackwood to his wife. 6 December 1871.

Page 165. *Sameshima a Harrisite.* Ibid., D8. John Blackwood to Kinglake. 4 September 1871.

Page 166. *Blowitz and Thiers.* Henri Blowitz. *My Memoirs.* Arnold. 1903. pp. 32, 48.

Page 166. *Goncourt's story.* Edmond de Goncourt. *Journal.* viii, p. 116.

Page 167. *Blowitz view of Harris.* Blowitz. op. cit., p. 54.

Page 167. *sobered out of his first elation.* M. Oliphant. op. cit., ii, p. 83.

8. Alice

Page 168. *'She is twenty six.'* Guy Le Strange Bequest. Oliphant to Lady Pollock. March 1872.

Page 168. *Robert Browning.* M. Oliphant. op. cit., ii, p. 86.

Page 168. *Alice's family.* Le Strange family records.

Page 169. *Madame Mohl.* M. C. M. Simpson. *Letters and Recollections of Julius and Mary Mohl.* Kegan Paul. 1887.

Page 170. *Kinglake on Alice.* Guy Le Strange Bequest. Kinglake to Mrs Wynne Finch. 20 January 1886.

Page 170. *Alice's love for Laurence.* M. Oliphant. op. cit., ii, p. 111.

Page 171. *'the great dual principle'.* Ibid., ii, p. 108.

Page 171. *'when Father left word'.* Ibid., ii, p. 93.

Page 171. *Laurence excuses Harris.* Ibid., ii, p. 117.

Page 172. *Laurence to Odo Russell.* PRO FO 918/78. Oliphant to Odo Russell. 5 April 1872.

Page 172. *no marriage in America.* Locker Lampson Papers. Oliphant to F. Locker. 2 April 1872.

Page 172. *Alice's money.* M. Oliphant. op. cit., ii, p. 115.

Page 172. *Laurence asked for leave.* Times Archive. Oliphant to Morris. 28 May 1872.

Page 172. *Georgiana to the rescue.* Broadlands Archive. Lady Oliphant to G. Mount Temple. no date.

Page 173. *Blowitz on their menage.* Blowitz. op. cit., p. 73.

Page 173. *Coincidence at Bilbao.* Blackwood Archive. D8. John Blackwood to Kinglake. 4 September 1872.

Page 174. *Not his business.* Sydney Lee. *Edward VII.* i, p. 410. (Macmillan. 1925).

Page 174. *What design Providence may have.* Broadlands Archive. Oliphant to G. Cowper-Temple. September 1872.

Page 174. *Alice on her mother.* Ibid., Alice to G. Cowper-Temple. No date.

Page 175. *'threw the bridle on my neck'.* Blowitz. op. cit., p. 75.

Page 175. *resignation letter.* Times Archive. Oliphant to Delane. 5 March 1873.

Page 176. *Blackwood's regret at his departure.* Blackwood Archive. D8, John Blackwood to F. Marshall. 17 May 1873.

Page 176. *Alice's letter to Harris.* M. Oliphant. op. cit., ii, p. 109.

Page 176. *Alice at Brocton.* Guy Le Strange Bequest. Alice to Mrs Wynne Finch. 2 July 1875.

Page 177. *not counterparts.* Broadlands Archive, Jane Waring to G. Cowper-Temple. March 1875.

Page 177. *Laurence told Rosamond.* R. D. Owen. op. cit., p. 23.

Page 178. *The Direct United States Cable Company.* F. W. Chesson. *The Atlantic Cable.* Royal Exchange. 1875. *Canadian Sessional Papers.* 1875. number 20.

Page 179. *'a paid servant of the G'.* Guy Le Strange Bequest. Alice to Guy. 12 Nov. 1873.

Page 179. *Newfoundland view of cable war.* D. W. Prowse. *History of Newfoundland.* p. 497. (Macmillan, 1895.)

Page 180. *Lady Dufferin's diary.* Hariot, Marchioness of Dufferin and Ava. *My Canadian Journal.* p. 238. (John Murray, 1981.)

Page 181. *Blake took up the bill. Canadian Sessional Papers.* number 20.

Page 181. *Anglo-American control undesirable.* De Kewiet, ed. *Dufferin/Carnarvon Correspondence.* Champlain Society. 1955. Dufferin to Carnarvon. 17 September 1874.

Page 182. *Laurence on Jay Gould.* M. Oliphant. op. cit., ii, p. 141.

Page 183. *Harris to California.* Columbia University Archive. Box 14.

Page 183. *'If dearest William.'* Broadlands Archive. Harris to William Cowper-Temple. 1 September 1875.

Page 183. *Alice and Lady Oliphant at Brocton.* Columbia University Archive. Box 13, file 4.

Page 184. *Laurence friendly with Hamon Le Strange.* Hamon Le Strange diary. 4 February 1876.

Page 184. *Hyderabad Council.* India Office Library. EUR E218/518.

Page 185. *Salah Jung in London.* T. H. Thornton. *Sir Richard Meade.* p. 292 (Longmans, Green. 1898.)

Page 185. *chosen for his journalistic abilities.* India Office Library. EUR E218/518.

Page 185. *Laurence seen with Salah Jung.* Times Archive. W. H. Russell's diary. 31 July 1876.

Page 186. *Laurence had devised a constitution.* India Office Library. EUR E218/518.

Page 186. *Situation in Hyderabad.* Ibid.

Page 186. *the most dangerous threat.* Ibid.

9. Palestine

Page 187. *Olive Seward.* Columbia University Archive. Microfilm. Reel 9/236. Harris to O. Seward. 25 September 1876.

Page 187. *Alice at Fountain Grove.* Ibid. Box 4.

Page 189. *Alice's letter.* Guy Le Strange Bequest. Alice to Guy. December 1878.

Page 189. *Kinglake remarked.* Ibid. Kinglake to Mrs Wynne Finch. 9 April 1878.

Page 189. *the society of sheep.* M. Oliphant. op. cit., ii, p. 157.

Page 190. *Moses Lilienblum.* Mark Wischnitzer. *To Dwell in Safety.* p. 57. Jewish Publication Society of America. 1948.

Page 190. *Laurence's plan for Palestine.* Royal Archives. T7/52. Oliphant to Salisbury. 14 November 1878.

Page 190. *Cyprus, Mytilene, Haifa.* R. W. Seton-Watson. *Disraeli, Gladstone and the Eastern Question.* p. 324. (Frank Cass, 1962.)

Page 190. *British protectorate.* Wischnitzer. op. cit. p. 58. Gaster papers. Oliphant to Gaster. 9 June 1882.

Page 191. *'weeps not like his Master'.* Edwin Hodder. *The Life and Work of The Seventh Earl of Shaftesbury.* p. 167. (Cassell, 1887.)

Page 192. *'like himself.'* Blackwood Archive. D10. John Blackwood to Kinglake. 25 November 1878.

Page 192. *Practical application of the plan.* Royal Archives. T7/52. Oliphant to Salisbury. 14 November 1878. *Nineteenth Century.* August 1882.

Page 192. *Princess Christian's letter.* Ibid., S31/69. Princess Christian to Beaconsfield. 11 November 1878.

Page 192. *Beaconsfield to Lady Salisbury.* Ibid. H50/145. no date.

Page 193. *Mrs Oliphant's opinion.* M. Oliphant. op. cit., ii, p. 171.

Page 193. *Sandringham house party.* Monypenny and Buckle. *The Life of Benjamin Disraeli, Earl of Beaconsfield.* ii, p. 1265. (John Murray, 1910).

Page 193. *Travels in Palestine.* L. Oliphant. *The Land of Gilead.* (William Blackwood & Sons, 1880.)

Page 195. *Midhat Pasha in bad odour.* Hughenden Papers. Box XXI. Oliphant to Corry. 29 May 1879.

Page 195. *Abdul Hamid suspicious.* BM. Add. 38962. Layard to Hammond. 3 November 1879.

Page 195. *progress encouraging.* Hughenden Papers. Oliphant to Corry. 29 May 1879.

Page 197. *letter to Princess Christian.* Royal Archives. S 31/81. Princess Christian to Beaconsfield. 3 February 1880.

Page 197. *Letter received by Lytton.* BM. Add. 38969. Lytton to Layard. 26 December 1879.

Page 198. *Oliphant appealed to Odo Russell.* PRO FO 918/78. Oliphant to Russell. 17 February 1880.

Page 198. *Enid Layard's journal.* BM. Add. 46157. p. 89.

Page 198. *Layard told Augusta Gregory.* A. Gregory. *Seventy Years.* p. 110. (Colin Smythe, 1974.)

Page 199. *letter to the Athenaeum. Athenaeum.* 20 September 1880.

Page 199. *Weinberg reply. Jewish Chronicle.* 22 October 1880.

Page 199. *Eliezer Rokeah.* Nahum Sokolov. *Hibbath Zion.* p. 272. (Rubin Mass. 1934) David Vital. *The Origins of Zionism.* p. 93. (Oxford, 1975.)

Page 200. *Oliphant and Board of Deputies. Jewish Chronicle.* 29 October 1880.

Page 200. *Jewish Chronicle approved his scheme.* Ibid., 17 December 1880. 31 December 1880.

Page 200. *Alice to her mother.* M. Oliphant, op. cit., ii, p. 193.

Page 201. *Hamon found his sister little changed.* Hamon Le Strange diary. 6 November 1880.

Page 201. *Sandringham ball.* Ibid., 12 November 1880.

Page 201. *meeting with Gladstone and Granville.* Ibid., 19 November 1880.

Page 201. *Medinet el Fayoum.* Guy Le Strange Bequest. Alice to Guy. 29 January 1881.

Page 202. *Laurence foresaw a pan-Arabist revolt.* L. Oliphant. 'The Jew and the Eastern Question'. *Nineteenth Century.* (August, 1882.)

Page 202. *Rosamond on Laurence and Alice.* Rosamond Dale Owen, op. cit., p. 26.

Page 203. *Harris became greedy.* Broadlands Archive. Oliphant to William Mount Temple. 13 April 1883.

Page 203. *Oliphant's apostasy.* Columbia University Archive. Jane Waring's diary. 19 August 1899.

Page 204. *Harris's lament.* Wagner College Archive. Box 4. 'Declaration 33'. no date.

Page 204. *Alice's letters.* Blackwood Archive. 4424. Alice to William Blackwood. November 1881.

Page 204. *Laurence wrote to Mrs Walker.* M. Oliphant. op. cit., ii, p. 209.

Page 205. *Georgiana* ordered *Alice to Broadlands.* Blackwood Archive. 4424. Alice to William Blackwood. 2 December 1881.

Page 205. *Jewish flight from Russia.* Wischnitzer. op. cit., p. 37 et seq.

Page 205. *Montefiore letters. Jewish Chronicle.* 2 December 1881.

Page 206. *Mansion House committee. The Times.* 2 February 1882.

Page 206. *Oliphant's letter.* Ibid., 15 February 1882.

Page 206. *'Oliphant, the Lord.'* Vital. op. cit., p. 96.

Page 206. *Alice at Berlin.* Broadlands Archive. Alice to G. Mount Temple. 23 March 1882.

Page 207. *Peretz Smolenskin. Jewish Chronicle.* 5 May 1882.

Page 207. *Smolenskin's pamphlet.* Ibid., 30 September 1881.

Page 207. *David Gordon. Jewish Encyclopedia.* David Gordon. *Jewish Chronicle.* 17 March 1882.

Page 207. Ha Magid *letter.* Ibid., 28 April 1882.

Page 208. *'Lord, Providence has delivered.'* Vital. op. cit., p. 96.

Page 208. *Y. Y. Levontin.* Ibid., p. 103.

Page 209. *Asher/Montagu at Brody. Jewish Chronicle.* 2 June 1882.

Page 209. *number of refugees at Brody.* Wischnitzer. op. cit., p. 47.

Page 209. *a circular drafted.* M. Oliphant. op. cit., ii, p. 220.

Page 209. *Rabbi Mohilever.* Sokolov. *Hibbath Zion.* p. 221.

Page 209. *BILU.* Ibid., p. 170. Vital. op. cit., p. 96.

Page 210. *Rabbi of Sodogora. Blackwood's Magazine.* November, 1882. *Jewish Chronicle.* 2 June 1882.

Page 210. Jewish Chronicle *displeasure.* Ibid., 28 December 1888.

Page 210. *Jassy meeting.* Ibid., 2 June 1882.
Page 211. *Porte's decree.* Ibid. Vital. op. cit., p. 104.
Page 211. *'uncomfortable passages.' Jewish Chronicle.* 2 June 1882.
Page 211. *scheme for Romanian Jews.* Gaster papers. Oliphant to Gaster. 9 June 1882.
Page 212. *US Minister at Constantinople.* M. Oliphant. op. cit., ii, p. 224.
Page 212. *Count Corti and Lady Strangford.* Ibid., pp. 228, 230.
Page 213. *Naphtali Herz Imber.* Columbia University Archive. Box I.
Page 213. *Prinkipo. Alice to her mother.* M. Oliphant. op. cit., ii, p. 233.
Page 213. *Prinkipo. Alice to Georgiana.* Broadlands Archive. Alice to G. Mount Temple. 1 August 1882. 17 September 1882.

10. *Haifa*

Page 215. *Templar colony.* L. Oliphant. *Haifa.* p. 17. (William Blackwood & Sons. 1887.)
Page 216. *Plight of Jews. Jewish Chronicle.* 2 March 1883.
Page 216. *Mohilever approaches Rothschild.* S. Schama. *Two Rothschilds and the Land of Israel.* p. 41. (Collins, 1978.)
Page 217. *Rothschild suspected.* Ibid., p. 277n.
Page 217. *Laurence did not interfere.* M. Oliphant. op. cit., ii, p. 239.
Page 217. *Sokolov on Laurence.* N. Sokolov. *Hibbath Zion.* p. 278.
Page 217. *letter to Emma Lazarus.* Columbia University. Department of MSS. x812L45.
Page 218. *Scheme not finished.* Guy Le Strange Bequest. Alice to Mrs Wynne Finch. 15 July 1883.
Page 218. *Life at Haifa.* Ibid., 6 April 1883.
Page 219. *Naphtali Herz Imber.* Broadlands Archive. Alice to G. Mount Temple. 10 October 1882.
Page 219. *Sympneumata.* Guy Le Strange Bequest. Kinglake to Mrs Wynne Finch. 2 March 1885.
Page 220. *'something too tremendous.'* Mrs H. Coghill. *The Autobiography and Letters of Mrs Margaret Oliphant.* p. 324. (William Blackwood & Sons, 1899.)
Page 220. *'Isn't God?'* Broadlands Archive. Alice to G. Mount Temple. 22 August 1885.
Page 220. *too delicate to debate.* Guy Le Strange Bequest. Alice to Mrs Wynne Finch. 29 September 1885.
Page 221. *Mrs Hankin.* Ibid.
Page 221. *Gordon at Haifa.* Ibid., Alice to Mrs Wynne Finch. 15 July 1883.

NOTES

Page 221. Laurence embraces Gordon. Broadlands Archive. Laurence to Mount Temple. 30 January 1886.

Page 221. Conversation about the Sudan. Charles Gordon. *Letters to his sister.* p. 276. (Macmillan, 1888.)

Page 222. Gordon's last letter. National Library of Scotland. 5793. Augusta Gordon to M. Oliphant. 5 October 1885. Facsimile enclosed.

Page 222. Dalieh. L. Oliphant. *Haifa.* p. 162.

Page 222. Burton on Druses. Isabel Burton. op. cit., i, p. 503.

Page 222. Chinese members of Druse sect. L. Oliphant. *Land of Gilead.* p. 385.

Page 222. Alice's position at Dalieh. M. Oliphant. op. cit., ii, p. 253.

Page 223. Visitors at Dalieh. Broadlands Archive. Alice to G. Mount Temple. 25 August 1883.

Page 223. Alice a virago. Columbia University Archive. Box B.

Page 223. Chirol on Alice. V. Chirol. op. cit., p. 86.

Page 224. Alice on Chirol. Guy Le Strange Bequest. Alice to Mrs Wynne Finch. 13 May 1883.

Page 224. Alice on the Mount Temples. Ibid., 28 August 1885.

Page 225. Alice and the Duke. Broadlands Archive. Alice to G. Mount Temple. 2 March 1885.

Page 225. Hamidiye railway. L. Oliphant. *Haifa.* p. 63.

Page 225. Laurence proposed to the Duke. Sutherland Archive. D593/P/27/6/1. Oliphant to Sutherland. 14 May 1884. 22 June 1884.

Page 226. Alice told Mrs Walker. M. Oliphant. op. cit., ii, p. 265.

Page 227. Altiora Peto. L. Oliphant. *Altiora Peto.* (William Blackwood & Sons, 1883.)

Page 227. Masollam. L. Oliphant. *Masollam, a problem of the period.* William Blackwood & Sons, 1886.

Page 227. Isabel Burton thought. I. Burton. op. cit., ii, p. 393.

Page 228. 'A hundred things to teach.' M. Oliphant. op. cit., ii, p. 296.

Page 228. Alice needed to be well. Guy Le Strange Bequest. Alice to Mrs Wynne Finch. 28 August 1885.

Page 228. Alice's journal. M. Oliphant. op. cit., ii, p. 300.

Page 229. Jamesina's account of Alice's illness and death. Guy Le Strange Bequest. Jamesina Waller to Mrs Wynne Finch. 5 January 1886.

11. *Counterparts*

Page 231. he told her mother. M. Oliphant. op. cit., ii, p. 316.

Page 232. table at the Athenaeum. T. H. S. Escott. *Masters of English Journalism.* p. 327. (Fisher Unwin, 1911.)

Page 232. Chenery. W. Blunt. *Gordon at Khartoum.* p. 210. (Stephen Swift, 1911).

Page 232. Princess Christian. M. Oliphant. op. cit., ii, p. 321.

Page 232. Abergeldie letter. Columbia University Archive. Box B, file 4.

Page 233. 'very peculiar religious views.' Royal Archives. Queen Victoria's Journal. 4 October 1886.

Page 233. Mrs Hankin. M. Oliphant. op. cit., ii, p. 325.

Page 233. Laurence to impart the Sympneuma. Broadlands Archive. Oliphant to G. Mount Temple. June 1886. H. Pearsall Smith. *Religious Fanaticism.* p. 225. (Faber & Gwyer. 1928.) Columbia University Archive. Box 13, Memo by Mary Berenson.

Page 233. Emilia welcomed it. Broadlands Archive, E. Gurney to G. Mount Temple, 20 June 1886.

Page 234. Laurence suggested Robert join him. H. Pearsall Smith. op. cit., pp. 225, 228.

Page 234. equated spirituality with sexuality. Ibid., p. 223.

Page 234. community had to be closed. Ibid., p. 220.

Page 234. Madame C. Ibid., p. 221.

Page 234. Mary Berenson identified her. Columbia University Archive. Box 13. Memo by Mrs Berenson.

Page 235. 'this unpleasing pair.' Edith Sitwell. *English Eccentrics.* p. 97. (Penguin, 1971.)

Page 235. much correspondence and visiting. Broadlands Archive, Jane Waring to G. Cowper-Temple, June 1874, September 1874. T. L. Harris to W. Cowper-Temple. 1 September 1874.

Page 235. Hannah's character. Barbara Strachey. *Remarkable Relations.* pp. 21 et seq. (Gollancz, 1980).

Page 236. She explained to William. Broadlands Archive. H. Pearsall Smith to W. Cowper-Temple. 21 August 1875.

Page 236. Doctor Foster. H. Pearsall Smith. op. cit., p. 167.

Page 236. shook with ecstasy. Broadlands Archive. H. Pearsall Smith to G. Cowper-Temple. 29 December 1878.

Page 236. I confess I do enjoy. K. Fitzpatrick. *Lady Henry Somerset.* p. 141. (Cape, 1923).

Page 236. great religious picnic. E. Clifford, op. cit., p. 55.

Page 237. Robert's conduct chaste. Broadlands Archive. Robert Pearsall Smith to W. Cowper-Temple. 18 January 1876.

Page 237. Georgiana could not see why. Logan Pearsall Smith. op. cit., p. 56.

Page 237. Hannah blamed Brocton. Broadlands Archive. H. Pearsall Smith to G. Cowper-Temple. 26 September 1876.

Page 237. Hannah rejected William's suggestion. Ibid., H. Pearsall Smith to W. Cowper-Temple. 21 August 1875.

Page 237. careful soundings. Ibid., H. Pearsall Smith to Sarah Beck. 23 April 1880.

Page 238. Hannah's first account of Harris. Ibid., H. Pearsall Smith to G. Mount Temple. 1 August 1880.

Page 238. Hannah's second account of Harris. Ibid., H. Pearsall Smith to G. Mount Temple. 25 August 1882. cont. on 12 Oct. 1882.

Page 238. called her the Ladye. Ibid., E. Gurney to G. Mount Temple. 20 June 1886. H. Pearsall Smith to G. Mount Temple. 13 November 1882.

Page 238. Alice a Druse. M. Oliphant. op. cit., ii, p. 350.

Page 238. Benei Yehuda. Ibid., ii, p. 347.

Page 239. the Jews' petition. Ibid., ii, p. 347.

Page 239. the pamphlet. Ibid., ii, p. 343.

Page 240. Blackwood told Shand. Blackwood Archive. D18. William Blackwood to Shand. 28 November 1887.

Page 241. Laurence lost among enquirers. M. Oliphant. op. cit., ii, p. 356.

Page 241. spiritual exaltation. Ibid., ii, p. 355.

Page 241. Jubilee party. Blackwood Archive. D17. Oliphant to William Blackwood. 21 July 1887.

Page 242. a young art student. Columbia University Archive. Box 14. J. M. Templeton's MS diary.

Page 242. 'I must see the woman who wrote that'. R. D. Owen. op. cit., p. 41.

Page 242. New York Lovers of Zion. N. Sokolov. *Hibbath Zion.* p. 289.

Page 243. Robert Dale Owen. E. Pancoast. *The Incorrigible Idealist.* Principia Press. 1940.

Page 243. Rosamond's youth. R. D. Owen. op. cit.

Page 244. Not to waste time slumming. Columbia University Archive. R. D. Owen file.

Page 245. Wrote to Alice's mother. Guy Le Strange Bequest. Oliphant to Mrs Wynne Finch. 4 August 1888.

Page 245. what is this dreadful business? Mrs H. Coghill. op. cit., p. 357.

Page 245. Rosamond not good looking. R. D. Owen. op. cit., p. 21.

Page 246. cancer of the lung. Blackwood Archive. D19. William Blackwood to Shand. 13 September 1888.

Page 246. Grant Duff and York House. Anne Fremantle. *Three cornered Heart.* pp. 19, 111, 112. (Collins, 1971.)

Page 246. refusal to believe in death. Augusta Gregory. op. cit., p. 234.

Page 246. Daily bulletins at the Athenaeum. The Times obituary. 24 December 1888.

Page 247. Blackwood helped Rosamond. Blackwood Archive. D19. William Blackwood to Rosamond Oliphant. 2 November 1888. 26 December 1888.

Page 247. Laurence's funeral. The Times. 28 December 1888.

Aftermath

Page 248. The Times obituary. The Times, 24 December 1888.

Page 248. Spectator obituary. The *Spectator.* 29 December 1888.

Page 249. Ray Strachey said. H. Pearsall Smith. op. cit., p. 139.

Page 249. Mrs Berenson confirmed. Columbia University Archive. Box 13.

Page 249. National Vigilance Association. Nat. Vigilance Assoc. Annual Report. 30 September 1887. W. A. Coote, *A Romance of Philanthropy.* Montefiore 469.

Page 250. Criminal Law Amendment Act. 48 & 49 Victoria. C69.

Page 250. Murray Templeton's diary. Columbia University Archive, Box 14. MS diary.

Page 250. Hannah anxious to know about 'practices'. Pearsall Smith papers Hannah to? 3 February 1889. Hannah to E. Gurney. 20 February 1889.

Page 250. young American woman. H. Pearsall Smith. op. cit., p. 221.

Page 251. her name was Tuttle. Schneider & Lawton. op. cit., p. 404.

Page 251. Templeton wrote to Arthur Oliphant. Blackwood Archive. D20. William Blackwood to Arthur Oliphant. 12 March 1889.

Page 252. a well known dramatist. Respiro. *The Brotherhood of the New Life.* p. 172n. (E. W. Allen, 1897.)

Page 252. Harris boasted. Columbia University Archive. Box 13, file 4.

Page 252. Stead dined with Harris. Ibid., Box 13, file 4.

Page 253. Isabel Burton's literary executor. Coote. op. cit., p. 111.

Page 253. Saw Princess Christian. R. D. Owen. op. cit., p. 67.

Page 253. Vigilance official called. Ibid., p. 104.

Page 254. Saw Jennie Tuttle. Ibid., p. 105.

Page 254. He 'suffered much'. Blackwood Archive. 4570. Rosamond Templeton to William Blackwood. 5 February 1890.

Page 254. Templeton jumped overboard. R. D. Owen. op. cit., p. 259.

Page 255. Carlos Ronzevalle. Ibid., p. 301.

Page 255. Foreign Office correspondence. Blackwood Archive. 4570. M. Oliphant to William Blackwood. 31 May 1889.

Page 256. the Druse 'kissed my hands.' National Library of Scotland, 5793. M. Oliphant to D. Oliphant. 1890.

Page 256. '*I felt as if it were not right.*' H. Pearsall Smith. op. cit., p. 226.

Page 257. '*you care about your two friends*'. National Library of Scotland. 5793. Emily Lawless to M. Oliphant. 25 May 1891.

Page 257. *Harris's death.* Columbia University Archive. Box 13, file 8. Jane Waring's diary.

Page 257. '*softening of the brain*'. Ibid., Box B, Misc. file.

Page 257. *holiday happiness.* M. Oliphant. op. cit., ii, p. 60.

Page 258. '*Father left word.*' Ibid., ii, p. 93.

Page 258. *Resignation letter. The Times* Archive. Oliphant to Delane. 5 March 1873.

Page 258. *Maria's symptoms disappeared.* Blackwood Archive, 4213. Maria Oliphant to John Blackwood. 11 December 1865.

BIBLIOGRAPHY

A. List of Works by Laurence Oliphant

Journey to Katmandu. John Murray, London. 1852.
The Russian Shores of the Black Sea in the autumn of 1852, with a voyage down the Volga, and a tour through the country of the Don Cossacks. William Blackwood & Sons, Edinburgh and London. 1853.
The Coming Campaign. ibid. 1855.
Minnesota and the Far West. ibid. 1885.
The Trans-Caucasian Campaign of the Turkish Army under Omar Pasha. ibid. 1856.
Narrative of Elgin's Mission to China and Japan. ibid. 1859.
Universal Suffrage and Napoleon the Third. ibid. 1860.
Patriots and Filibusters, or incidents of political and exploratory travel. ibid. 1860.
Piccadilly. ibid. 1865.
The Land of Gilead, with excursions in the Lebanon. ibid. 1880.
The Land of Khemi: up and down the Middle Nile. ibid. 1882.
Traits and Travesties, social and political. ibid. 1882.
Altiora Peto. ibid. 1883.
Sympneumata, or, evolutionary forces now active in man. ibid. 1885.
Masollam, a problem of the period. ibid. 1886.
Fashionable Philosophy and other sketches. ibid. 1887.
Haifa, or life in modern Palestine. ibid. 1887.
Episodes in a Life of Adventure; or Moss from a Rolling Stone. ibid. 1887.
Scientific Religion, or the higher possibilities of life. ibid. 1888.

In addition, articles too numerous to count, in *Blackwood's Magazine,* the *London Review, The Fortnightly, The Athenaeum* etc.

B. Unpublished Sources

Ampthill Papers. Public Record Office.
Blackwood Papers. National Library of Scotland.
Broadlands Papers. Letters to Lord and Lady Mount Temple. Hampshire County Record Office.
Broadlands Papers. Historical Manuscripts Commission.
Foreign Office papers. Public Record Office.
Hammond Papers. Public Record Office.
Hughenden Papers. London School of Economics. (microfilm.)
Gaster Papers. Mocatta Library, University College, London.
Hamon Le Strange diary. In private hands.

Guy Le Strange Bequest. Fitzwilliam Museum, Cambridge.
Harris/Oliphant Papers. Rare Book and Manuscript Library, Columbia University in the City of New York.
Layard Papers. British Museum. Department of Manuscripts.
Locker Lampson Papers. East Sussex County Record Office.
Lytton Papers. India Office Library.
Markham Papers. Horrmann Library, Wagner College, Staten Island, New York.
Pearsall Smith papers. In private hands.
Russell Papers. Public Record Office.
Royal Geographical Society. Minute Book and Oliphant file.
Royal Archives, Windsor Castle.
Sutherland Papers. Stafford County Record Office.
Times correspondence. Times Newspapers Limited.
Stratford Canning papers. Public Record Office.

C. *Secondary Sources*

Adams, Henry, *The Education of Henry Adams*. Constable 1919.
Ahlstrom, S. E., *A Religious History of the American People*. Yale University Press. 1972.
Alcock, Rutherford, *The Capital of the Tycoon*. Greenwood Press. 1969.
Askwith, B., *Two Victorian Families*. Chatto & Windus. 1971.
Baker, Samuel, *The Rifle and Hound in Ceylon*. Longman, Brown, Green & Longmans. 1854.
Baker, Samuel, *Eight Years in Ceylon*. Longmans, Green & Co. 1874.
Beust, Count von, *Memoirs*. Remington. 1887.
Blake, Robert, *Disraeli*. Eyre & Spottiswoode. 1966.
Blowitz, Henri de, *My memoirs*. Arnold. 1903.
Blunt, W. S., *Gordon at Khartoum*. Stephen Swift, 1911.
Bradley, J. L., ed. *Letters of John Ruskin to Lord and Lady Mount Temple*. Ohio University Press. 1964.
Bright, John, *Diaries*. Cassell. 1930.
Brodie, F., *The Devil Drives*. Eyre & Spottiswoode. 1967.
Bruce, James, *Extracts from the letters of James, Earl of Elgin to Mary Louise, Countess of Elgin. 1847–62*. Privately printed.
Burton, Isabel, *Life of Sir Richard Burton*. Chapman & Hall. 1893.
Burton, Richard, *Lake Regions of Central Africa*. Longman, Green, Longman & Roberts. 1861.
Burton, Richard, *Zanzibar*. Tinsley Brothers. 1871.
Chesson, F. W., *The Atlantic Cable*. Royal Exchange. 1875.
Chirol, Valentine, *Fifty Years in a Changing World*. Cape. 1927.
Clifford, E., *Broadlands as it was*. Private circulation. 1890.
Coghill, Mrs H., *The Autobiography and Letters of Mrs Margaret Oliphant*. William Blackwood & Sons. 1899.
Coote, W. A., *A Romance of Philanthropy*. Montefiore. 469.

BIBLIOGRAPHY

Costenza, M., ed. *The Complete Journal of Townsend Harris.* Japan Society of New York. 1930.
Cowling, M., *1867: Disraeli, Gladstone and Revolution.* Cambridge University Press. 1967.
Cross, W. R., *The Burned Over District.* Cornell University Press. 1950.
Cuthbert, A., *The Life and World Work of Thomas Lake Harris.* Pearce. 1908.
de Goncourt, E., *Journal.* Charpentier. 1887.
de Kewiet, *Dufferin/Carnarvon Correspondence.* Champlain Society. 1955.
Duff, Mountsteuart Grant, *Notes from a Diary.* John Murray. 1905.
Ellis. S. M. ed. *A Mid Victorian Pepys.* Palmer. 1923.
Escott, T. H. S., *Masters of English Journalism.* Fisher Unwin. 1911.
Fitzpatrick, K., *Lady Henry Somerset.* Cape. 1923.
Fox, Grace, *Britain and Japan. 1858–1883.* Oxford University Press. 1969.
Frederick III, *The War Diary of Emperor Frederick III.* Stanley Paul. 1927.
Fremantle, A., *Three Cornered Heart.* Collins. 1971.
Fremantle, R., *Lord Glenesk and the Morning Post.* Alston Rives. 1910.
Fulford, R., *Dearest Mama. Letters of Queen Victoria to the Crown Princess of Prussia. 1861–1864.* Evans. 1968.
Gallenga, A., *The Invasion of Denmark.* Bentley. 1864.
Gordon, Charles, *Letters to his sister.* Macmillan. 1888.
Gregory, A., *Seventy Years.* Colin Smythe. 1974.
Greenberg, L., *Jews in Russia.* Yale University Press. 1951.
Hariot, Marchioness of Dufferin and Ava, *My Canadian Journal.* John Murray. 1891.
Harris, Thomas Lake, *The Millenial Age.* Ratcliffe. 1860.
Harris, Thomas Lake, *The Arcana of Christianity.* New York. 1858.
Harris, Thomas Lake, *An Epic of the Starry Heaven.* Partridge & Brittan. 1854.
Hayward, A., *Collected Letters.* John Murray. 1886.
Head, F., *Field Marshall Sir John Burgoyne.* John Murray. 1872.
Heasman, K., *Evangelicals in Action.* Bles. 1962.
Henderson, P., *Laurence Oliphant.* Hale. 1956.
Hope-Nicholson, J. ed., *Life amongst the Troubridges.* John Murray. 1966.
Hodder, E., *The Life and Work of the Seventh Earl of Shaftesbury.* Cassell. 1887.
Horne, A., *The Fall of Paris.* Macmillan. 1965.
Jansen, M., *Sakamoto Ryoma and the Meiji Restoration.* Princeton University Press. 1961.
Kinglake, A., *The Invasion of the Crimea.* William Blackwood & Sons. 1863.
Knaplund, P., *Letters from the Berlin Embassy.* American Historical Association. 1944.
Lane-Poole, S., *Life of Sir Harry Parkes.* Macmillan. 1894.
Lanman, C., *Leading Men of Japan.* Lothrop. 1883.
Lee, Sir S., *Edward VII.* Macmillan. 1925.
Liesching, Louis, *Personal Reminiscences of Laurence Oliphant.* Marshall Bros. 1891.

BIBLIOGRAPHY

M'Cully, R., *The Brotherhood of the New Life*. Glasgow. 1893.
Monypenny W. F. and Buckle, G. E., *The Life of Benjamin Disraeli, Earl of Beaconsfield*. John Murray. 1910.
Mount Temple, G., *Memorial of Lord Mount Temple*. Private circulation. 1890.
National Vigilance Association, *Annual Report 1887*.
Okuma, S., *Fifty Years of New Japan*. Smith, Elder. 1909.
Oliphant, Mrs Margaret, *Memoir of Laurence Oliphant and of Alice Oliphant, his wife*. William Blackwood & Sons. 1891.
Owen, Robert Dale, *The Debatable Land Between this World and the Next*. 1872.
Owen, Rosamond Dale, *My Perilous Life in Palestine*. Allen & Unwin. 1928.
Pearsall, R., *The Table Rappers*. Michael Joseph. 1972.
Pearsall Smith, Hannah, *Religious Fanaticism*. Faber & Gwyer. 1928.
Pearsall Smith, Logan, *Unforgotten Years*. Constable. 1938.
Podmore, F., *Modern Spiritualism*. New York. 1870.
Pollock, W., *Personal Remembrances*. Macmillan. 1887.
Porter, Mrs B., *Annals of a Publishing House*. William Blackwood & Sons. 1898.
Prowse, D. W., *History of Newfoundland*. Macmillan. 1895.
Redesdale, A., *Memories*. Hutchinson. 1915.
'Respiro', *The Brotherhood of the New Life*. E. W. Allen. 1897.
Ridley, J., *Palmerston*. Panther. 1972.
Ruskin, John, *Praeterita*. George Allen. 1887.
Russell, B. ed., *The Amberley Papers*. Hogarth. 1937.
Schama, S., *Two Rothschilds and the Land of Israel*. Collins. 1978.
Schneider, H. & Lawton, G., *A Prophet and a Pilgrim, Being the Incredible History of Thomas Lake Harris and Laurence Oliphant*. Columbia University Press. 1942.
Seton-Watson, R. W., *Disraeli, Gladstone and the Eastern Question*. Frank Cass. 1962.
Shand, A. I., *Days of the Past*. Constable. 1905.
Simpson, M. C. M., *Letters and Recollections of Julius and Mary Mohl*. Kegan Paul. 1887.
Sitwell, Edith. *English Eccentrics*. Penguin. 1970.
Sokolov, Nahum, *Hibbath Zion*. Rubin Mass. 1934.
Sokolov, Nahum, *A History of Zionism*. Longman. 1919.
Speke, John Hanning, *Journal of the Discovery of the Source of the Nile*. William Blackwood & Sons. 1863.
St. Helier, E., *Memories of fifty years*. Arnold. 1909.
Strachey, B., *Remarkable Relations*. Gollancz. 1980.
Strachey, Ray, *A Quaker Grandmother*. New York. 1914.
Swainson, W. P., *Thomas Lake Harris. Mad or Inspired?* Brotherhood Publishing Company. 1895.
Thornton, T. H., *Sir Richard Meade*. Longman. 1898.
Tollemache, ?, *Some Reminiscences of Lady Mount Temple by her surviving brother*. Private circulation. n.d.

Vital, David, *The Origins of Zionism*. Oxford University Press. 1975.
Wagner, F., *Schamyl, the Sultan, Warrior and Prophet*. Travellers Library. 1854.
Warfield, B., *Perfectionism*. Oxford University Press. 1931.
Wilkinson, Clement, *John James Garth Wilkinson*. Kegan Paul. 1911.
Wischnitzer, M., *To Dwell in Safety*. Jewish Publication Society of America. 1948.
Wrong, G., *The Earl of Elgin*. Methuen. 1905.

INDEX

Abdul Hamid II, Sultan of Turkey, 192, 195, 196, 197, 198–9, 211, 214, 225
Abdul Mejid I, Sultan of Turkey, 35, 36
Adams, Henry, American writer, 96–7
Adare, Lord, see Dunraven
Airlie, Blanche, Countess of, 71, 79, 81, 82, 144, 151, 200
Airlie, Earl of, 71, 79
Albert, the Prince Consort, 71, 79, 92, 104, 109, 121
Alcock, Sir Rutherford, Minister to Japan, 82, 83, 86, 88–9, 129
Alexander II, Tsar of Russia, 40, 97, 205
Allen, Mr, 251
Alison, Charles, diplomatist, 37, 38
Alliance Israélite Universelle, the, 206, 209
Altiora Peto, 227
Amadeo, King of Spain, 173–4
Anglo-American Telegraph Company, the, 178–9, 184, 186
Arabi, Ahmed, Egyptian rebel leader, 202, 214
Arnim, Count von, Prussian Ambassador in Paris, 165, 166
Arrow incident, the, 47
Ashburnham, General, Army commander in India, 47
Asher, Dr, 209
Ashley, Evelyn, Palmerston's private secretary, 17, 80, 94, 100, 101–3, 110
Ashley, Mrs William, Shaftesbury's sister-in-law, 46, 49, 52, 55, 62
Athenaeum, the, 199
Athenaeum Club, the, 34, 135, 232
Augustenburg, Duke of, 103, 104, 106, 110, 111
Augustenburg, Prince Frederick of, 104, 105–6, 107, 110, 111

Aumale, Duc d', Orleanist leader, 165
Aurelle de Paladines, General d', French army commander, 153
Austin, Alfred, war correspondent, later Poet Laureate, 158
Azeglio, Marquis d', Sardinian Minister in London, 107

Baker, John, 9
Baker, Samuel, African explorer, 9–10, 24
Baker, Valentine, soldier, 9, 38, 196, 237
Bakufu, the, government of the Shogun, 55, 56, 57, 58, 59, 83, 84, 87, 129
Bakunin, Mikhail, Russian anarchist, 150
Balmoral, 70, 233
Barileff, Captain, of the *Possadnik*, 89–90
Barnum, P. T. impresario, 118, 121
Beamish, the Rev., Evangelical preacher, 132
Beatson's Horse, 39
Beaulieu, Leroy, 150
Bede, the Venerable, 106
Bell, Laura, courtesan, 11
Benson, Archbishop, 133
Berenson, Mary, see Smith, Mary Pearsall
Berridge, Dr C. M., 'Respiro', Harrisite, 251–2, 256
Beust, Count, Austrian Ambassador in London, 193
BILU, Jewish emigrant group, 209–10, 212
Birkhall, 70–1
Bismarck, Prince, 17, 107–8, 109, 150, 151, 152, 157, 158, 173, 198
Blackwood, John, character, 24–5

Blackwood, John (cont.):
  and L.O., 24, 71, 73, 77, 82, 95, 109, 110, 113, 176, 192
  and L.O.'s mother, 127
  L.O.'s letters to, 40, 79, 106, 146, 159, 182–3, 189
  and Speke/Burton affair, 69, 111
  in Paris (1872), 165
  death, 240
Blackwood's Magazine, 18, 24, 27, 69, 78, 106, 107, 111, 113, 146, 178, 210
  as cover for espionage, 79, 95
  L.O.'s attack on Palmerston and Russell, 108, 128
Blackwood, William, 111, 219, 220, 224, 227, 240–1, 245, 246–7
Blair, Mrs, 225, 227
Blake, Robert, Canadian politician, 181
Bleichröder, Gerson, Bismarck's banker, 226
Bligh, L.O.'s servant, 83, 85, 93
Blowitz, Henri de, 165–6, 173, 175
Bluestone, Joseph, a Lover of Zion, 242
Blunt, Wilfrid, 232
Borthwick, Algernon, newspaper proprietor, 110
Bowring, Sir John, Governor of Hong Kong, 47
Bright, Charles, engineer, 178
Bright, John, Radical M.P., 127, 129, 135–6, 144
Broadlands, Romsey, Hants., Palmerston's family seat, 17, 74, 90, 130, 143, 164, 205, 235, 236–7, 238
Brocton, N.Y. State, 'Salem-on-Erie', 134, 140–2, 146–7, 171, 174, 176–7, 183–4, 203, 213
Brotherhood of the New Life, the, 116, 122, 127, 132, 134, 148
  at Wassaic, 123
  at Amenia, 124, 138
  its members, 124–5, 145
  'breathing together', 123, 136
  at Fountain Grove, 183, 187–8
Broughton, Lord, 97

Browning, Robert, 168, 169, 170
Bruce, Lady Augusta (later Stanley), Elgin's sister, 29, 71, 169
Bruce, Frederick, Minister to Peking, Elgin's brother, 53, 63
Bruce, Robert, Governor of the Prince of Wales, Elgin's brother, 32, 34, 92
Buckner, Pitt, 'Earnest', Harrisite, 124, 141, 203, 227, 232, 254
Buckner, the Rev., Harrisite, 124, 203, 218, 253
Buller, Sir Arthur, of Newera Elliya, 13
Burgoyne, General Sir John, commander in the Crimea, 26, 38
'burned over districts' the, 116, 117
Burton, Isabel (Lady),
  on L.O., 111
  on Speke/Burton affair, 66, 69, 253
  on *Masollam*, 227
  her literary executor, 253
Burton, Captain (later Sir Richard), 68, 222
  mission to Schamyl, 39, 66
  letter to *The Times*, 39
  L.O.'s alleged dislike of, 39, 66
  at Aden (1859), 65
  quarrel with Speke, 66–69, 78, 111, 253
Bury, Madame Blaze de, 92
Bury, Viscount, 33, 178
Butterfield, William, ecclesiastical architect, 169

Calonne, Vicomte de, *Times* correspondent, 165
Cambridge House, Palmerston's London home, 74, 97, 114
Campbell, Colonel, L.O.'s grandfather, 1–2
Canning, Viscount, Governor General of India, 48, 49, 50
Canrobert, Madame la Maréchale, 'Madame C', 234
Carlyle, Thomas, 121
Carnarvon, Earl of, Secretary of State for the Colonies, 181

INDEX

Cavanagh, Orfeur, Indian political officer, 12, 18
Cavour, Count, 73, 75, 77, 81, 99
Chablais (Savoy), 73
Chateaubriand, François-René de, 169
Chauvin, Heinrich von, London Manager of Direct US Cable company, 178
Chenery, Thomas, Editor of *The Times*, 232
Chirol, Valentine, journalist, 164, 197, 223–4
Christ the Bridegroom, doctrine of, 220, 233–4
Christian IX, King of Denmark, 103, 104
Christian, Prince, of Schleswig-Holstein-Sonderburg-Augustenburg, husband of Princess Helena, 104
Christian, Princess, see Helena, The Princess
Churchill, Clementine, 151
Circassia, 35, 38–40
Civil War, the US, 29, 116, 123, 127, 134, 164
Clanricarde, Marquess of, 77
Clarendon, Earl of, Foreign Secretary, 28, 36, 37, 39, 129
Clark, Constance, Harrisite, 139, 183
Clark, Sir James, Queen Victoria's doctor, 70–1
Clark, Tom, Maria Oliphant's doctor, 15
Clifford, Edward, protégé of the Cowpers, 133
Cloete family, L.O.'s cousins, 2, 7
Cluseret, Gustave-Paul, Communard leader, 150
Cole, Sir Lowry, Governor of the Cape of Good Hope, 2
Coming Campaign, The, 35
Conder, Lieutenant Claude, Palestine Exploration Fund, 194, 200
Cooke, Wingrove, *Times* correspondent in China, 53, 71
Cooper, Fenimore, 33
Coote, William, Secretary, National Vigilance Association, 253

Corti, Count, Italian Ambassador to Turkey, 212
Cosmopolitan Club, the, 92
Costelloe, B. F. C., Executive member of the National Vigilance Association, 249
Couza, Prince, ruler of the Danubian Principalities, 102, 103
Cowley, Lord, Ambassador in Paris, 110
Cowper, Earl, 17
Cowper, Hon. Mrs Georgiana, (later, Cowper-Temple, then Lady Mount Temple), 142, 143, 144, 164, 173, 174, 203
  meets L.O., 131
  interest in spiritualism, 131
  friendship with Ruskin, 133, 137
  character, upbringing, 133–4
  'Use' name, 135, 183
  helps Alice, 172, 205
  receives 'Sympneuma', 233
  Alice's letters from Palestine, 214, 219, 220, 223, 224
  and Hannah Pearsall Smith, 235, 237
  and Rosamond Dale Owen, 253
Cowper, Hon. William (later Cowper-Temple, then Baron Mount Temple), 135, 137, 140, 164, 172, 173, 183, 203, 209
  friendship with L.O. and Harris, 130–4
  ecumenicalism, 131
  career, 130, 131–2
  on the Brotherhood of the New Life, 132
  refuses invitation to Brocton, 143
  helps Japanese, 143
  inherits Broadlands, 130, 236
  Harris's letter to, 204
  gives Harris money, 183
  and the Pearsall Smiths, 235, 237
  illness and death, 245
Crawfurd, John, Fellow of Royal Geographical Society, 68
Criminal Law Amendment Act, the (1885), 250, 252
Cromwell, Thomas, 103

INDEX

Cuthbert, Arthur, Harrisite, 124, 144, 147, 203–4, 213
Cuthbert, Violet, née Fawcett, Harrisite, 84, 124, 187, 203, 213, 218, 253
Czas, Polish newspaper, 98

Daily News, the, 25, 144, 159, 175
Daily Telegraph, the, 165
Dalieh, 222–3, 229–30, 232
Dana, Charles A., Editor, *New York Sun*, 216
Davies, Rev. Llewellyn, Christian Socialist, 132
Davis, Andrew Jackson, 'the Poughkeepsie seer', 118
de Grey and Ripon, Marquis of, Under Secretary for War, 74
Delane, John, Editor of *The Times*, 71, 151, 160, 232
  offers L.O. job as correspondent in Turkey, 27–8
  with L.O. to United States, 41
  L.O.'s letter from China, 51
  Maria's appeal, 135
  offers job in France (1870), 149
  L.O.'s resignation from *The Times*, 175, 258
de Norman, diplomatist, 82
de Ros, Lord, Army commander in the Crimea, 27
Deshima, the island of, in Nagasaki Bay, 55, 56–7
Direct United States Cable Company, the, 178–9, 184, 186, 252
Disraeli, Benjamin, Earl of Beaconsfield, 71, 128, 193
  interest in Palestine plan, 190–1, 192, 197
  L.O. reports progress to, 195–6
Dollie and the Two Smiths, 146
Doria, Princess Pamphili, 7
Druses, the, 222, 229–30, 235, 238, 254, 256
Duff, Lady, 246–7
Duff, Sir Mountstuart Grant, M.P., 246–7, 248
Dufferin, Lady, 180–1, 212

Dufferin, Earl of, Governor General of Canada, Ambassador to Turkey, 180–1
Dunraven, Earl of, (Lord Adare), spiritualist, war correspondent, 157, 226

Eber, General, *Times* correspondent, 80
Edo (Tokyo), 58–60, 84
Eggar, Georg, German engineer, 226
Elcho, Lady, 144
Elcho, Lord, 144
Elgin and Kincardine, eighth Earl of, 50, 60, 172
  friendship with Oliphant family, 28–9, 113
  invites L.O. to Washington, 29
  career in Canada, 29, 34
  appearance, 30
  relations with L.O., 31, 32, 53
  China mission (1857–9) 46 et seq.
  friendship with Canning, 48
  at Hong Kong, 51
  at Peiho River, 53–5
  and Treaty of Tientsin, 54, 63
  quarrel with Seymour, 52, 72
  in Japan, 56–62
Elgin's Mission to China and Japan, 49, 58, 72, 79
Emerson, Ralph Waldo, 41, 119, 121
Episodes in a Life of Adventure, 102, 103
Eugénie, Empress of the French, 111, 149, 157, 234

Fane, Julian, Secretary of Embassy at Vienna, 96
Faraday, the, 178, 184
Faucigny (Savoy), 73
Favre, Jules, 158
Fawcett, Violet, see Cuthbert
Fawcett, Millicent, 249
Fellowship of the New Life, the, 244
Feodore, Princess, Queen Victoria's half sister, 104
Ferdinand II, of the Two Sicilies 'King Bomba', 8, 80–1
Field, Cyrus, American entrepreneur, 178, 181

INDEX

Figaro, Le, 159
Footfalls on the boundary of another World, 243
Forbes, Alistair, war correspondent, 159
Foster, Dr, American spiritualist, 236–7
Fourier, Charles, utopian socialist, 78, 120
Fowler, Mrs, Harrisite, 164, 183, 218
Fowler, James, Harrisite, 164, 204
Fox sisters, the, 117, 118, 120
Franklin, Sir John, Arctic explorer, 53
Franz Joseph, Emperor of Austria, 96
Frederick William, Crown Prince of Prussia, 104, 107, 152, 153, 154, 157, 206
Frederick William, Crown Princess of Prussia, Princess Royal of England, the Empress Frederick, 109–10, 153, 206–7, 247
Fredonia Censor, the, 164, 165
Fujiyama, 59, 144
Fukusawa Yukichi, Japanese teacher, 143
Furious, H.M.S., 52, 53, 55, 56, 58, 63, 65, 67
Furley, James, *Times* employee, 162

Gallenga, Antonio, *Times* correspondent, 107, 232
Galton, Francis, Fellow of Royal Geographical Society, 68
Gambetta, Léon, 149
Garibaldi, Giuseppe, 17, 75–8, 80–1, 93
Gaster, Moses, Romanian doctor, 211
Galdstone, William Ewart, 113, 128, 191, 201, 214
Glover, Thomas, Scottish merchant at Nagasaki, 130, 143
Godai Tomoatsu, Satsuma delegate to England, 129, 136
Goldfaden, Abraham, New York Lover of Zion, 242
Goncourt, Edmond de, 165, 166
Gordon, Miss Augusta, 221, 222

Gordon, General Charles, 38, 221–2
Gordon, David, Editor of *Ha Magid*, 207–8
Gould, Jay, American entrepreneur, 182
Grant, James, African explorer, 98, 111, 247
Granville, Earl, Foreign Secretary, 149, 201
Greeley, Horace, Editor of *New York Tribune*, 41, 119, 120, 139
Gregory, Sir William, M.P. 185
Gregory, Lady, 198–9
Grosvenor, Lord, 14
Gurney, Emilia, 233, 250

Ham House, 133
Ha Magid, 207
Hamidiye railway, 225, 226
Hammond, Edmund, Permanent Under Secretary at the Foreign Office, 83, 84
Hankin, Mrs, of Malvern, 221, 233, 238, 241, 245
Hanover, the King of, 165
Hansard, 128, 134
Hardman, Frederick, *Times* correspondent, 160
Harris, Thomas Lake, 'Father Faithful', 115, 135, 144, 147, 163, 167, 248
  first mention, 81
  in England (1859), 115, 122–3, 134
  doctrine, 115–18, 119, 121, 123, 126, 177, 258
  birth and upbringing, 117
  Universalist minister, 117
  at Mountain Cove, 118
  marries Emily Waters, 119
  and *Arcana of Christianity*, 119
  founds Brotherhood, 123–4
  as 'Mr Masollam', 125, 227
  at Broadlands, 130, 235
  at Brocton, 138–9, 141, 144
  in Paris (1871), 164–5
  attitude to Alice, 171, 187–8, 238
  to California, 183, 187
  Breaks with L.O., 203, 223
  letter to William Mount Temple, 204

INDEX

Harris, Thomas Lake (*cont.*):
   and Hannah Pearsall Smith, 237–8
   marries Jane Waring, 252
   W. T. Stead on, 252–3
   abuses L.O., 256–7
   death, 257
Harris, Townsend, US Minister to Japan, 55, 57, 58, 59, 83, 145
Ha Shahar, 207
Haskett Smith, the Rev., 238, 247, 256
Ha Tikvah, the, Jewish hymn, 213
Hayward, Abraham, Lady Palmerston's 'chief of staff', 74, 80
Helena, The Princess (Princess Christian), Queen Victoria's third daughter, 71, 104, 192, 197, 232, 247, 253
Herald of Light, the, 122, 123
Herbert, Auberon, attaché at Athens, 80
Herzl, Theodor, 190, 217
Heusken, Henry, Townsend Harris's secretary, 55, 58, 59, 61, 83
Higo no Kami, Japanese Commissioner of Foreign Relations, 58, 60, 85
Hisanobu Sameshima, Harrisite, Japanese Minister in Paris, 143
Hobart Pasha, 196
Holland, Lady, 132
Home, Daniel Dunglass, 'Mr Sludge the medium', 131, 157, 243
Hope, Admiral, commander British naval forces in Far East, 88, 89, 90
Hopkins, Ellice, 249
Hozier, Captain Henry, assistant military attaché (1870), 151, 156
Hudson, Sir James, Minister to Turin, 75, 91, 95
Hyderabad, the State of, 184–6, 192
Hyderabad, the Nizam of, 184

Illustrated London News, the, 128, 132
Imber, Naphtali Herz, L.O.'s Hebrew Secretary, 213, 219, 234, 247

Invasion of the Crimea, The, 25, 26
Israelson, Swedish hired man at Brocton, 125, 177
Irving, Edward, Scottish divine, 3, 28, 122

James, Henry, Senior, 41, 119, 121
Jewish Chronicle, the, 199, 200, 208, 210, 211
Jews, the, 101, 200, 211, 217
   and flight from Russia, 205–6, 208
Johnson, J. Henry, 173
Jordan, Mrs, mistress of William IV, 94
Journey to Katmandu, 14, 18
Jung Bahadur Rana, Prime Minister of Nepal, 11, 13–14
Jung, Sir Salah, Chief Minister of Hyderabad, 184–6, 187

Kanagawa (Yokohama), 58, 86
Kanaye Nagasawa, Harrisite, 130, 183, 257
Khaireddin Pasha, Grand Vizier of Turkey, 195, 196, 197, 199
Kinglake, Alexander, 21, 25, 74, 92, 109, 137, 169, 182, 246
   on L.O.'s Russian book, 26
   on Alice, 170, 183, 189
   on *Sympneumata*, 220
   at the Athenaeum, 232
Kingsley, Charles, 181
Kingsford, Mrs Anna, medium, 224
Kitchener, Lieutenant Horatio Herbert, 194
Kossuth, Hungarian leader, 43
Kuroda Kiyotaka, Japanese Commissioner of Foreign Affairs, 144

Labouchère, Henry, Director, Direct US Cable Company, 178, 252
Lake Regions of Central Africa, The, 78
La Marmora, General, Sardinian army commander, 91, 94–5
Land of Gilead, The, 200, 217
Land of Khemi, The, 202
Landseer, Sir Edwin, 81
Langiewicz, Polish patriot, 98

INDEX

La Touche, Rose, 133
Lawless, Hon. Emily, 256–7
Lawrence, Sir Henry, 13
Lay, Horace, member of Elgin's China mission, 62
Layard, Austen Henry, Under Secretary at the Foreign Office, Minister to Madrid, Ambassador to Turkey, 91–2, 93, 98, 129, 174, 196
Layard, Lady, 198
Lazarus, Emma, poetess, 217–8
Leopold, King of the Belgians, 95–6
Le Strange, Alice, see Oliphant, Alice
Le Strange, Charles, Alice's brother, 174
Le Strange, Guy, Alice's youngest brother, 169, 179, 189
Le Strange, Hamon, Alice's eldest brother, 169, 172, 184, 201, 228, 247, 253
Le Strange, Henry, Alice's father, 168–9
Lever, Charles, contributor to 'Maga', 110
Levine, Swedish hired man at Brocton, 140, 177, 184
Levontin, Y. Y., 208
Liesching, Louis, civil servant in Ceylon, 11, 122
  on Antony Oliphant, 5
  on L.O., 9, 12
Lilienblum, Moses, 190
Lily Queen, the, 120, 122, 139, 144, 188
Lindau, Rudolf von, 152
Livingstone, Dr, 113
Lloyd, Colonel, agent in Circassia, 28, 35
Lloyd, Mr, naval chaplain, 130
Locker, Lady Charlotte, Elgin's sister, 28–9
Locker, Frederick, Elgin's brother-in-law, 172
London Review, the, 78, 79
Longworth, John, Consul General at Belgrade, 35, 36, 38, 80
Lovers of Zion, the, 217, 242

Lushington, E.T. Director, Direct US Cable Company, 178
Lyons, Lord, Ambassador to Paris (1870), 149
Lytton, Earl of, Viceroy of India, 184–6, 187, 197

Macdonald, John, Manager of *The Times*, 175
Mackenzie, Alexander, Canadian Prime Minister, 180, 181
Mackintosh, Colonel, Army Intelligence, 26
Mahdi, the, 221
Malakoff Tower, the, 26, 38
Manitoulin Island, 32
Markham, Sir Clements, Joint Secretary, Royal Geographical Society, 113
Marshall, Frederic, contributor to 'Maga', 165–6, 176
Martin, Robert, lapsed Harrisite, 141, 142, 223
Martin, Dr, Harrisite, 124, 139, 187, 203, 214, 229
Martin, Mrs, Harrisite, 124, 187, 203, 223
Marx, Karl, 161
Masollam, 125, 227
Matsuki Koan (later Terashima Munenori), Satsuma delegate, 129, 136, 143
Maurice, Rev. F. D., Christian Socialist, 132
Maximilian, Emperor of Mexico, 44, 93, 111
Mayville Sentinel, the, 164, 165
Mecklenburg Schwerin, Grand Duke of, Prussian army commander, 153, 154, 156
Mehemet Ali, 191, 195
Melbourne, Viscount, 31, 130, 143
Michael, Prince, of Serbia, 80
Midhat Pasha, Turkish Governor General at Damascus, 195, 197, 199
Mikado, the, Emperor of Japan, 60, 83, 87, 88
Milnes, Monckton, writer, politician, bibliophile, 96

Milnes, Mrs, 96
Minnesota and the Far West, 33, 39
Mitford, Algernon, later Lord Redesdale, 96, 97
Mito, the Prince of, 87
Mocha, the Sherif of, 6
Mohilever, Rabbi Samuel, of Bialystock, 209, 216–17
Mohl, Mary, 169
Mohl, Julius, Orientalist, 169
Monck, Lord, former Governor General of Canada, 181
Montagu, Samuel, 208
Montefiore, Sir Moses, 199, 205
Montez, Lola, 123
Moore, Lionel, 'the Irish Arab', 37
Morell, Lady Ottoline, 133
Mori Arinori, Harrisite, later Japanese Minister of Education, 143
Morier, Robert, diplomatist, 109, 152
Mormons, the, 28, 116
Morris, Mowbray, Manager of *The Times*, 151, 152, 154, 156, 158, 159, 160, 162, 163, 175
Morris, William, 132
Morrison, George, Consul at Nagasaki, 85
Mount Temple, see Cowper
Mosquito, Kingdom of, 42–3
Murchison, Sir Roderick, President, Royal Geographical Society, 68
Murray, John, 18
My Perilous Life in Palestine, 243

Nagasaki, Vice-Governor of, 57
Naib, the, Schamyl's lieutenant, 35, 39
Napoleon III, Emperor of the French, 25, 40, 73, 79, 97–8, 102, 111, 149, 151, 169, 234
National Vigilance Association, the, 234, 249, 250–2, 253–4
Nepal, the King of, 14
Newcastle, Duke of, 74
New Church, the, 119
Newera Elliya, 9–10
New York Sun, the, 216, 225

New York Tribune, the, 41, 119, 120, 121
Nicholas I, Tsar of Russia, 19, 24, 25, 36
Nightingale, Florence, 169
Nile, the, 65, 98, 111, 201, 212
Norton, Mrs Caroline, 79

Oliphant, Lord, L.O.'s ancestor, 4
Oliphant, Alice, L.O.'s first wife, 134, 167, 204, 210
  appearance, 168
  birth, upbringing, 169
  meets L.O., 170
  submits to Harris, 172, 176
  marriage, 172
  at Brocton, 176–7, 183
  in Canada, 180
  in California, 187–9
  and Lily Queen, 188
  health, 189, 228, 235
  influence on L.O., 192, 215
  in Egypt, 201–2
  at Therapia, 212–3
  at Prinkipo, 213–4
  at Haifa, 215–16, 218–19, 256
  at Dalieh, 222–4
  dictates *Sympneumata*, 219–20
  Chirol on, 223–4
  journey to Tiberias, 228–9
  fever and death, 229–30
  Hannah's accusations, 234–5
Oliphant, Sir Antony, L.O.'s father, 203, 258
  Attorney-General at the Cape, 1–2
  family, 2
  Evangelicalism, 2, 3, 258
  and Irving, 3, 122
  Chief Justice of Ceylon, 4, 10
  character, 5, 6, 9
  tours Continent (1848), 7–9
  L.O.'s letters to, 16, 26, 32
  retirement, 34–35
  in Crimea (1855), 36, 37, 38
  death, 63, 115
Oliphant, Arthur, L.O.'s cousin, 186, 247, 251
Oliphant James, L.O.'s uncle, 2, 5, 48

OLIPHANT, LAURENCE,
  birth, upbringing, 1
  in Scotland, 4
  at school, 4
  in Ceylon, 6
  crams law, 6, 18
  on Continent (1848), 7–9
  linguistic ability, 7
  relationship with mother, 1, 6, 30, 47, 67, 82
  hunts big game, 10
  in Nepal (1850), 12–13
  examines conscience, 2, 14, 39
  at Lincoln's Inn, 16
  friends in high places, 16
  Russian journey (1852), 18–23
  debut, in *Maga*, 24
  called to bar, 25
  briefs army on Sebastopol, 26
  in Washington (1854), 30
  Superintendent General of Indian Affairs, 32–3
  elected to Athenaeum, 34
  on Crimean War, 35
  meets Speke, 36
  with Stratford de Redcliffe, 37–8
  at Kamiesch Bay, 37, 38
  in Circassia, 38–40
  fits of depression, 8, 34, 40, 46, 55, 126, 257
  animosity towards Napoleon III, 40, 75, 78
  possible marriage, 41, 45–6, 70, 82
  US visit (1856), 41
  in Central America, 42–5
  Parliamentary ambition, 41, 46, 112
  serious illness, 46, 106, 126, 127, 257–8
  mission to China (1857–9), 46 et seq
  and spiritualism, 48, 81, 157
  approach to religion, 36, 40, 51, 86, 114–15
  in Japan (1858), 56–62
  on Japanese character, 61
  on comparative religion, 36, 63, 209, 239–40
  and Speke/Burton affair, 65–9, 78, 111–12
  homosexuality charge, 66–7, 252
  and Nice and Savoy (1860), 73–8
  at Gotha (1860), 79
  Secretary of Legation in Japan (1861), 82–90
  assassination attempt, 85–6
  at Tshushima, 89–90
  in Italy (1862), 91–4
  mission to Vienna, 95–6
  in Poland, 97–101
  and Schleswig-Holstein affair, 103–9
  elected to Parliament (1865), 113
  relations with Harris, 115, 123, 125, 134, 142, 203–4
  and Satsuma delegates, 129–30, 135–6, 143–4, 165
  as M.P., 128, 134, 137
  at Amenia, 127, 137–8
  at Brocton, 139–41, 144
  applies for Chiltern Hundreds, 142
  reports Franco-Prussian war, 151–8
  in Paris (1871), 159–67
  flight to Brocton, 163
  Engagement, marriage, 167, 168, 170–1, 172, 177
  Spanish journey (1873), 173–4
  resigns from *The Times*, 175
  and Direct US Cable Company, 177–182
  and Hyderabad (1876), 184–6
  at Fountain Grove, 189
  and Palestine scheme, 190–4
  at Constantinople (1879–80), 196–9
  in Egypt (1881), 201–2
  on Mansion House Committee (1882), 206–7
  at Brody and Jassy, 208–10
  failure at Constantinople, 211–12
  at Haifa (1882), 215–18, (1886–7), 238–41
  at Dalieh, 222–4
  railway speculation, 225
  and Alice's death, 229–30
  in England (1886), 232
  and the Sympneuma, 219, 221, 231–2, 233

Oliphant, Laurence (*cont.*):
  and *Scientific Religion*, 240–1
  Hannah's accusations, 233–4
  marriage to Rosamond, 242, 244–5
  death, 247
  obituaries, 248
  alleged prosecution, 249–50
  'Respiro' on, 251
  Rosamond's defence of his reputation, 254
Oliphant, Mrs Margaret (no relation to L.O.)
  Her biography of L.O., 2, 75, 135, 147, 255, 257
  access to lost letters, 2, 5, 171, 255–6
  on L.O. and his father, 9, 63–4
  on L.O. and his mother, 12, 15, 31, 163
  on his religion, 51
  on T. L. Harris, 122, 137, 256
  L.O.'s promiscuity, 126
  with L.O. in Paris (1872), 167
  on Alice, 170, 173, 202
  on the Palestine scheme, 193
  at Windsor, 203, 247
  on the Sympneuma, 220
  on *Masollam*, 227–8
  with L.O. (1886), 233
  on *Scientific Religion*, 239–40
  on L.O.'s second marriage, 245
  at Haifa and Dalieh, 256
Oliphant, Maria (Lady), L.O.'s mother, 6, 11, 25, 28, 35, 36, 82, 112
  parents, 1–2
  marriage, 1
  bad health, 3, 15, 258
  in Scotland, 4
  in Ceylon (1846), 5
  on Continent (1848), 7–9
  at Newera Elliya, 9
  with L.O. to England (1851), 15
  L.O.'s letters to, 12–13, 14–15, 30, 34, 40, 70
  influenced by preachers, 31, 115
  widowed, 63, 67
  and spiritualism, 81, 122
  character, 1, 127–8
  at Amenia, 127, 134

  at Brocton (1866), 138, 163
  in Paris (1871), 164, 167, 170, 173
  at Brocton (1873–), 174–5, 187
  with L.O. to Fountain Grove, 203
  death, 203
Oliphant, Robert, L.O.'s relation, 18
Oliphant, Thomas, L.O.'s uncle, 18
Omar Pasha, Turkish army commander, 17, 35, 37–8, 39
Oneida community, the, 116
Osborn, Captain Sherard, 53, 65, 70, 71
Owen, David Dale, 243
Owen, Robert, 121, 242–3, 244, 255
Owen, Robert Dale, US Congressman, 121, 243
Owen, Rosamond Dale, L.O.'s second wife, 177, 188, 202, 253
  knew Murray Templeton, 242
  birth, upbringing, 243–4
  appearance, 245–6
  character, 243, 245–6
  autobiography, 243, 255
  marriage to L.O., 244–5
  nurses L.O., 246
  and Jennie Tuttle, 251–2, 253–4
  defends L.O., 254
  marries Templeton, 254
  at Haifa and Dalieh, 254–5
  adopts Ronzevalle, 255
  at Worthing, 255
  death, 255
  proposes biography of L.O., 255
Owl, the, 110, 112

Paget, Sir Augustus, Minister to Denmark, 104
Palestine Exploration Fund, the, 194
Pall Mall Gazette, the, 249
Palmerston, Viscount (Henry John Temple), 17, 40, 44, 71, 90, 94, 97, 102, 113, 130, 131, 132
  out of office (1852), 17
  and Sebastopol, 26
  and Mosquito, 42, 44
  calls general election (1857), 46–7
  on Nice and Savoy, 73
  on L.O.'s mission to Vienna, 95
  and Poland, 98–100
  and Schleswig-Holstein, 104, 108

criticized by L.O., 108
and Georgiana Cowper, 133
and Palestine, 190
Palmerston, Lady, 17, 74, 96, 97, 114, 130, 236
Parkes, Sir Harry, Consul at Canton, Minister to Japan, 90, 129
Parr, Mr, L.O.'s schoolmaster, 4
Patriots and Filibusters, 43, 44
Pearsall Smith, see Smith
Pender, John, entrepreneur, 178, 184
Perry, Commander, US Navy, 55, 58
Petherick, John, African explorer, 70
Phibbs, Captain, L.O.'s companion in Palestine, 193
Piccadilly, 113–16, 123, 126, 135, 146, 227
Pius IX, 'Pio Nono', 8
Pollock, Walter, Chief Remembrancer, 28
Possadnik, Russian warship, 89–90
Potocka, Countess Augusta, 101
Potocki, Count Adam, Polish patriot, 99
Primkenau, Augustenburg family seat in Silesia, 103, 104, 111
Prince Imperial, the, 157
Pringle family, the, American plantation owners, 30, 41
'Progress and Policy of Russia in Central Asia, the', 27
Prowse, Judge, Newfoundland historian, 179–80
Pyat, Félix, Communard leader, 160, 162

Raglan, Lord, Army commander in the Crimea, 26, 27
Récamier, Madame, 169
Rechberg, Count, Austrian Foreign Minister, 92, 96
Religious Fanaticism, 234, 236, 249, 250
Requa, James, 'Steadfast', Harrisite, 124, 134, 135, 139
Requa, Mrs, 'Golden Rose', Harrisite, 135, 139, 164, 183, 188, 203

Rifle and Hound in Ceylon, The, 24
Ringdove, H.M.S., 86, 89
Ripley, George, founder of Brook Farm, 119
Roggenbach, Franz von, Minister of the Duke of Coburg, 152
Rokeah, Eliezer, Jewish reformer, protozionist, 199–200
Ronzevalle, Carlos, Rosamond's protégé, 255
Rosenberg, Adam, New York Lover of Zion, 242
Rosh Pina, Jewish settlement in Palestine, 216
Rossetti, Dante Gabriel, 132
Rothschild, Baron Edmond de, 216–17
Royal Albert, the, 38
Royal Geographical Society, the, 53, 65, 66, 68–9, 96, 111, 113, 135, 137
Ruskin, John, 130, 133, 137, 143
Russell, Arthur, 169
Russell, Bertrand, 81, 83
Russell, G. W. E., M.P., 249
Russell, Lord John (later Earl Russell), Foreign Secretary, 81, 87, 113
on Seymour–Elgin quarrel, 72
and Nice and Savoy, 73, 75, 77
and L.O. in China, 82
and L.O.'s Japanese post, 83, 84
sends L.O. to Italy (1862), 91–2, 93, 95
and his Viennese mission, 95–6
and Poland, 98, 100
and Schleswig-Holstein, 104, 108
policy condemned by L.O., 108
as Prime Minister, 128
Russell, Odo (later Lord Ampthill), 169
at Therapia (1855), 37
at Versailles (1870), 152, 153, 157, 158
L.O.'s letter to, on his marriage, 172
and his Palestine scheme, 198
at Berlin (1882), 206–7
Russell, Lady William, 169

INDEX

Russell, William Howard, *Times* correspondent, 28
  at Versailles (1870), 151, 153, 154, 156-7, 158
  in Paris (1871), 160-1, 162
  on L.O.'s flight to Brocton, 163
  and Hyderabad, 185-6
Russian Shores of the Black Sea, The, 18, 20, 22, 24, 26, 37, 38, 68
Ruxton family, the, lapsed Harrisites, 141-2, 147, 164

Salisbury, Lady, 192
Salisbury, Marquis of, Secretary of State for India (1876), Foreign Secretary (1879), 184-6, 190, 192, 193, 197
Samarin, Jewish settlement in Palestine, 216
San Francisco Chronicle, the, 157
Satsuma, the Prince of, 57, 129
Saxe-Coburg-Gotha, Alexandrine, Duchess of, 105
Saxe-Coburg-Gotha, Ernest, Duke of, 79, 104-5, 109, 152, 156
Schamyl, Emir and Imam, 21, 28, 35, 37, 39
Schmidt, Dr, of the Temple colony, 229
Schneider, Professor Herbert, Columbia University, New York, 249
Schumacher, Gottlieb, engineer, head of the Temple colony, 215, 226
Scientific Religion, 240, 241, 248, 254
Scott, James, early Harrisite, 118
Sebastopol, 19, 26, 37, 38
  appearance in 1852, 22
  undefended to the south, 23
Senior, Nassau, 169
Seward, Olive Risley, William Seward's adopted daughter, 187
Seymour, Sir Hamilton, Ambassador to Russia, 19, 26
Seymour, Admiral Sir Michael, naval commander in China, 52, 53, 72
Shaftesbury Countess of, 17
Shaftesbury, seventh Earl of (Anthony Ashley Cooper), 16, 17, 46, 71, 115, 131, 132, 191, 206

Shakers, the, 116, 124
Shand, Alexander Innes, *Times* correspondent, 155, 157, 160, 240, 246, 253
Shannon H.M.S., 49
Shimonoseki, Lord of, 143
Shogun, the (or Tycoon), 55, 56, 57, 60, 61, 86, 88, 90, 129
Sieh, a Chinese provincial judge, 62
Siemens Brothers, 178
Sitwell, Edith, 235
Smith, Alys Pearsall, 236
Smith, George, 110
Smith, Hannah Pearsall, 241
  invited to experience the Sympneuma, 233
  and *Religious Fanaticism*, 234-5
  birth and upbringing, 235
  and *The Christian's Secret*, 236
  and Dr Foster, 236
  visits Harris, 237-8
  and Mrs Tuttle, 250-1
  on Mrs Oliphant's biography of L.O., 256
Smith, Logan Pearsall, 133, 236
Smith, Mary Pearsall (Mrs Frank Costelloe, then Mrs Bernhard Berenson), 234, 236, 249, 250
Smith, Oswald, 26
  first meeting with L.O., 17
  on Russian journey, 18-23
  memoir in *Time*, 17, 19
Smith, Robert Pearsall, Evangelist, 233-4, 235-6, 236-8
Smolenskin, Peretz, protozionist, Editor of *Ha Shahar*, 207
Smythe, Percy (Lord Strangford), 37
Sodogora, Rabbi of, 210
Sokolov, Nahum, Jewish historian, 217
Solms, Prince Georg, 165
Somerset, Duchess of, 79, 84, 149, 153
Soulé, Pierre, Louisiana lawyer and filibuster, 42
Soyer, M. Alexis, chef, 38
Spectator, the, 248
Speke, Benjamin, 144
Speke, John Hanning, 98
  meets L.O. at Marseilles, 36

at Aden (1859), 65
and Royal Geographical Society, 68–9
introduced to Blackwood, 69
quarrel with Burton, 39, 66–9, 78, 111, 253
'the tail', 111
with L.O. in Paris (1864), 110–11
L.O. on his death, 111–12
Stanley, Dean, 169
Stanley, Henry, African explorer, 247
Stanley, Kate, 71, 81, 82
Stanley, Lyulph, 82
Stanley, Maude, 71, 82–3
Stanley, Rosalind, 71
Stead, W. T., Editor, *Pall Mall Gazette*, 249, 252–3
Stirling burghs, parliamentary constituency of, 45, 113
St Maur, Lord Edward, 79, 80
Strachey, Mrs Ray, 236, 250
Strangford, Lady, 213
Stratford de Redcliffe, Lord, 'the Great Eltchi', 28, 38
correspondence with Clarendon, 36, 37, 39
sends Longworth to Circassia, 35
character, career, 36
invites L.O. to be his private secretary, 37, 40, 41
Sursocks, Messrs, Syrian bankers, 225
Sutherland, third Duke of, 185, 193, 195, 197, 225
Swedenborg, Emmanuel, Swedish mystic, 115, 118, 119, 130
Swinburne, Algernon, 97
'Sympneuma', the, 219–20, 221, 231, 233, 234, 238, 248, 250
Sympneumata, 219–20, 221, 224, 227

Tann, General von der, Prussian army commander, 154
Temple colony, the, at Haifa, 215–16, 235
Templeton, Mr, Glasgow manufacturer, 242
Templeton, James Murray, Rosamond's second husband, 242, 249, 250, 254

Tent Work in Palestine, 194
Tewfik, Khedive of Egypt, the, 201
Thiers, Adolphe, President of Third Republic, 161, 163, 166, 167
Thimbleby, Miss, 93–4
Time, 17
Times, The, 25, 27, 39, 53, 80, 135
L.O.'s articles on Trans-Caucasus campaign, 39
on Seymour/Elgin quarrel, 72
on L.O.'s appointment to Japan, 82
L.O.'s articles on Franco-Prussian War, 149–54, 159, 160
on the Commune, 160–2
L.O.'s resignation, 175
letter on Jewish emigration, 206
obituary, 248
Todleben, General von, Russian siege engineer, 38
Tokkaido, the, Japanese Imperial highway, 84, 85, 87
Tollemache family, 133
Tosa, the Prince of, 143
Tozenji, temple of, English legation at Edo, 84, 85
Troubridge, Laura (Lady), 16, 115
Tsushima, island of, 89–90
Tsushima, the Prince of, 87, 89
'Turtle Dovery' the, 9
Tuttle, Mrs Jennie, 251–2, 253–4

Vanderbilt, Cornelius, 42, 43
Victor Emmanuel, King of Sardinia, 81, 91, 93, 94, 95, 106, 173
Victoria, Queen, 14, 55, 70, 82, 95, 121, 134, 241
L.O. presented to, 16
on his China mission, 71
his audience with, 109
receives at Balmoral (1859), 71, (1886), 232–3
and Schleswig-Holstein, 104, 105, 108, 109
and Hyderabad, 184–6
Vivian, General, commander, Turkish Contingent in the Crimea, 35
Vizetelly, Henri, 250

INDEX

Wade, Sir Thomas, 62, 246
Waddington, William, French Foreign Minister, 192
Waghorn, Lieutenant, 6
Wales, the Prince of, 110, 148, 192, 195, 201, 249
  invites L.O. to Corfu, 92
  L.O.'s opinion of, 92–3
  'sugar doodling the ladies', 147
  and Spain, 174
  and Hyderabad, 184–6
  at Abergeldie, 232
  sends telegram to funeral, 247
Wales, the Princess of, 104, 105, 148
Walewski, Count, 157
Walker, Mrs, 189, 204, 226, 246
Walker, James, San Francisco businessman, 189, 203, 246
Walker, William, American filibuster, 41–2, 43, 44, 45
Wallace, Lewis, US Minister to Turkey (1882), 212
Waller, Adolphus, Vicar of Hunstanton, 228, 229
Waller, Jamesina, Alice's sister, 169, 228, 229–30, 235, 255
Wang, Chinese provincial governor, 62
Waring, Jane Lee, Harris's third wife, 163, 258
  character, appearance, 125, 147
  in England (1865), 134
  'Use' name, 135
  on L.O., 139
  in Paris (1871), 164, 165
  on Alice, 171, 177
  exiled from Fountain Grove, 189
  marries Harris, 252, 257
Warren, Captain Charles, Palestine Exploration Fund, 194

Warsaw, Archbishop of, 100
Waters, Emily Isabella, Harris's second wife, 119, 120, 134, 140, 257
Weinberg, Joseph, Bucharest Jewish emigrant, 199
Whitaker, Edgar, Editor of *Levant Herald*, 196
Wielopolski, Marquis, Governor of Poland, 99
Wilde, Oscar, 252
Wilkes, John, M.P., 12
Wilkinson, Garth, Swedenborgian doctor, 121, 122, 123, 143
William I, King of Prussia, 151, 161
William IV, King of England, 94
Wolff, Henry Drummond, 110
Wright, Frances, 243
Wynne Finch, Ada, Alice's sister, 169
Wynne Finch, Charles, M.P. Alice's stepfather, 169, 174
Wynne Finch, Jamesina, Alice's mother
  character, appearance, 169
  attitude to L.O., 172, 174, 241, 245, 253
  Alice's letters to, 213, 218, 224
  Jamesina to, on Alice's death, 229
  relations with Rosamond, 255
  on Mrs Oliphant's biography, 256

Xavier, St Francis, 63

Yeh, Chinese Commissioner at Canton, 47, 48, 51, 52, 99
York House, Twickenham, 246
Young, Brigham, Mormon leader, 118, 141